JUST ABOUT *everything* A MANAGER NEEDS TO KNOW IN SOUTH AFRICA

By the same authors

Neil Flanagan and Jarvis Finger
Management in a Minute
The Manager's 100

Neil Flanagan
Creative Debt Collecting
Responsiveness: Double Your Profits in Half the Time with Brian Thomas

Jarvis Finger
Managing Your School: Vol. 1
Managing Your School: Vol. 2
Managing Your School: Vol. 3
The Educator's Book of Enlightening Lists
True Tales from the Classroom
More True Tales from the Classroom
Did I Really Say That?
The St Helena Island Prison
True Tales of Old St Helena
More True Tales of Old St Helena
The Wild Men of St Helena
The Escapes from St Helena

JUST ABOUT *everything* A MANAGER NEEDS TO KNOW IN SOUTH AFRICA

Neil Flanagan
&
Jarvis Finger

ZEBRA

ZEBRA

Published by Zebra Press
(a member of the New Holland Struik Publishing Group (Pty) Ltd)
PO Box 3103, Halfway House, 1685
Tel: (011) 315 3633
Fax: (011) 315 3810
E-mail: zebrastaff@icelogic.co.za

First South African edition September 1998
First published by Plum Press, Australia, 1998

Reproduction by Remata, Halfway House
Printed and bound by National Book Printers, Drukkery Street, Goodwood, 7460

ISBN 1-86872-239-2

Foreword

Managing any business today, particularly in Africa, is extremely challenging and requires a broad knowledge and understanding of a great number of issues, including economic, social and political matters. It is also widely acknowledged that managers in Africa are often overstretched, and face constant change. Throughout it all, managers must strive to achieve the best business results, motivate staff and maintain high levels of morale and be professional at all times. *Just about Everything a Manager Needs to Know in South Africa* is an invaluable source of advice, which will make the increasingly complex task of managing much easier.

It is a practical, pragmatic, user-friendly, hands-on book, which belongs on every manager's desk – accessible and ready to use. It is structured in three disctint and logical sections: Managing Yourself, Managing Others and Managing the Organisation. It covers a comprehensive range of subjects and presents a universal range of principles and practices in a readable, easy-to-understand, well-indexed and cross-referenced format. The matters dealt with show how to successfully manage many of the problems encountered daily by busy managers.

Just about Everything a Manager Needs to Know in South Africa is an important management tool for all levels of management. I recommend it to all those who aspire to manage effectively, whatever their level, field of endeavour or experience.

Stuart Morris
Chairman
KMPG

Contents

Managing Others

Managing the Organisation

Why every manager will treasure this book

Every so often something really useful comes along. And, for managers, this book is it. By distilling just about everything relating to successful management practice into practical and immediately accessible 'how-tos', this book provides answers to your management problems and questions in straightforward language with the minimum of fuss. If you, as a manager, needed to own just one book – this is it! And if after flicking through the pages, you're still not convinced, then consider these points…

1 This book is a short-cut to management expertise.

Management knowledge and experience are usually gained over many years in various ways:

- Management courses and workshops are valuable sources of information although they require a considerable commitment of time, and often it is left up to you to distil their theory into usable, workplace nuts-and-bolts.
- In-house support, often focusing only on administrative procedures, new technology, and flavour-of-the-month-topics, usually provides just enough information to help you 'get by'.
- Friends and colleagues in the network, too, are often eager to help – but your needs will be a competing priority forcing them to limit any time they spend with you.
- The library shelves and non-book sources are laden with information – if only you could locate, retrieve, and use it *when you really needed it*.
- On-the-job experience, of course, is the great teacher – but it takes a long time and can be very costly as well.

Whatever you do, sooner or later you're going to be on your own to manage as best you can. And that's where this book can help. We've assembled just about all the essential management expertise, advice, and solutions you'll require into one succinct, handy volume – that's why we've called it *Just about Everything a Manager Needs to Know*.

2 This book will help you climb the ladder.

The section *Managing Yourself* contains more than seventy chunks of essential know-how dealing with *you* – from the beginning to the peak of your career, and beyond. You are shown how to prepare yourself for a brilliant career, ready yourself for an interview, start successfully in your new position, improve your chances of promotion, become a leader, and attract the headhunter. As well, there are dozens of vital personal skills highlighted – how to make decisions, take the initiative, gain power, make speeches, play politics, save time, and chair meetings. If it's essential information you need about managing yourself and your career, you'll find it here.

3 This book will help you manage other people.

The section *Managing Others* is

chock-full of information about managing *other people* – from getting the right person for the job, to getting the person right for the job, to moving out those who aren't right for the job. You'll find just about everything you'll need to know about delegation, improving staff performance, motivating others, negotiating, handling angry people, comforting grieving employees, tackling absenteeism, mediating in staff disputes, and much, much more. If it's essential information you need about managing other people, you'll find it here.

4 This book will help you run your organisation.

The section *Managing the Organisation* provides essential advice that will help you manage your *organisation* more effectively – from articulating a vision for your company, to managing projects and implementing change. You'll be shown how to write a mission statement, develop policy, boost flagging morale, provide quality customer service, get the image you want for your company, crime-proof your workplace, and lots more. As well, you'll soon understand the basics of enterprise bargaining, reengineering, quality management, empowerment, and benchmarking. If it's essential information you need about managing your organisation, you'll find it here.

5 This book is so easy to use.

Each of the two hundred-plus topics is presented as a double-page spread, designed to deliver what you want – simply. There's no need for you to separate the practical ideas from the entangling theory and jargon – we've already done that, and presented the material as step-by-step solutions to management problems and issues. Each topic is cross-referenced to others to guide your reading even further. In addition, each topic is accompanied by its own short management memo adding an extra snippet of distilled wisdom. The page layout, the index, and the table of contents are all designed to allow you to access information you want to use – now.

Management Memo

It was Albert Einstein who advocated storing information in a way that it could be accessed, retrieved, and used when required, rather than taking up valuable brain space. Professor Einstein would have been impressed with the way *Just about Everything a Manager Needs to Know* respects his time-honoured advice.

6 This book is essential for new *and* experienced managers.

Most of us become managers quite suddenly, usually with no previous experience. As a rule, most people get promoted into a manager's job because they were good at some *other* job. What's more, they don't get much instruction in the skills and nuances of management. Where do they turn for help? What better starting place than this book! It has not been written to be read from cover to cover – though you could do that if you wanted a crash course in management. Ideally, however, the book should be kept near at hand to refer to when you're looking for advice and ideas about a problem that's currently worrying you.

– Neil Flanagan & Jarvis Finger

Here's what people are saying about this book...

In writing this book, the authors attempted to provide a *usable* tool for practising managers, a publication that would focus on the day-to-day nuts-and-bolts of management and be free from the distraction of theories, concepts and research (they have their place in management, say the authors, but not on the practising manager's desk). The extent to which the authors were successful in their quest is reflected in the comments of the following practitioners...

During our 110-year history, Hall Chadwick has found that we must continuously change our management emphasis and train our people in management methods in order to stay at the forefront of our profession. We take seriously the view that our staff are our most valuable resource and, in particular, those bright and ambitious younger staff who will be our leaders of the future. *Just about Everything a Manager Needs to Know* provides a wealth of information for these staff, as well as for our colleagues in the profession, and our clients.

Ian Donaldson
Chairman, Hall Chadwick Queensland
Chairman, Institute of Chartered Accountants (Queensland Division)

Managing a highly rated mortgage banking business demands that you're ready to tackle any 'emergency' with confidence. Those emergencies may be management as well as finance- or policy-related. Access to management know-how is essential – sometimes as a client service. First Mortgage Corporation has established many benchmarks for successful mortgage banking. *Just about Everything a Manager Needs to Know* is one tool that I've learnt to rely on.

Rob Mason
Managing Director
First Mortgage Corporation
Brisbane Australia

Although most lawyers and accountants pursue their professions for reasons other than management, increasingly they find a need to access and retrieve a broad and varied range of management information – usually at a moment's notice. *Just about Everything a Manager Needs to Know* complements the authors' previous publication, *Management in a Minute*, as my regular reference source of management information. An indication of its popularity is the numerous times colleagues borrow it. This is a valuable management tool for all professional managers.

Ken Adamson
General Manager
Phillips Fox Lawyers Australia

This book is an excellent starting point for the journey into management and its literature. It makes sense of the corpus that awaits the keen student of management. It provides the maps, compass and essential food pack to get new managers started, and they will find that they will come back time and time again to get their bearings before heading off once more into the rich world available. It will also help more experienced managers to keep on the right path...

Dr Michael Macklin
Business strategist, academic, and former Senator

Management Memo

We judge ourselves by what we feel capable of doing while others judge us by what we have already done.

– Henry Longfellow

Finding the very best solutions to your day-to-day management problems is easy. Just read *Just about Everything a Manager Needs to Know*. It's my constant companion – at work, travelling to and from meetings, and when training my key management staff.

Dr Warsowiwoho
General Manager
HRD & Organisation
PT Satelindo Indonesia

It's not an easy transition, graduating from university to the workforce and a business environment. As an international business graduate, I have found that *Just about Everything a Manager Needs to Know* helps bridge the gap between theory and practice. It has given me insight into what I may expect to face, and has also helped me deal with issues that I have come across previously. A must-read!

Nerida Marks
Graduate cadet trainee manager
Elders Ltd

Right Training prides itself in providing the RIGHT information and advice to its clients. *Just about Everything a Manager Needs to Know* provides us with all the right information. This book is to management what the All Blacks are to rugby – simply awesome!

Bill Cunliffe
Managing Director
Right Training New Zealand

Meetings are a fact of life in the corporate world. What you get out of those meetings depends on many things – especially your level of preparation and contribution. I don't know of a better quick reference containing that information than *Just about Everything a Manager Needs to Know*. I have been a long-time supporter of the authors' previous book, *Management in a Minute*. This book is even better.

Sir Llewellyn Edwards
Chancellor, University of Queensland

Today sport is big business and it demands effective management. From the local sports carnival to the Olympic Games, the focus is on efficiency, effectiveness, and profits. Our national think-tank of leading sports administrators rely on *Just about Everything a Manager Needs to Know* to help us make winning decisions.

Neil Douglas
Managing Director
Chandler Aquatics, Brisbane

The strength of *Just about Everything a Manager Needs to Know* is not necessarily the wise counsel but the ease in which this information is available through the format of the book. The structure enables the content to be accessed with ease and the instruction is clearly and concisely presented. This reference guide will be a great benefit to both those who are on the way and those who have arrived.

John Cox
Managing Director
Stanbroke Pastoral Company Pty Ltd

Original. Interesting. Succinct. A wonderful tool for any business.

Cheryl C. Macnaught
Joint Managing Director
Whittaker Macnaught Pty Ltd

Because *Just about Everything a Manager Needs to Know* contains just that, it's my constant travelling companion. And I recommend it as an essential reference tool to those serious about improving their presentation skills.

Sergio Carlo Maresca
International keynote and conference speaker, best-selling author, and corporate trainer

Small Business success depends on many factors – including capable management. I'm not only a regular user of *Just about Everything a Manager Needs to Know*, I also acted as a sounding board for some of its content regarding essential financial management. *Just about Everything a Manager Needs to Know* is partnering our business success.

Lionel Larman
Managing Director
Templeton's Financial Planning

Many women hold positions of leadership both within and beyond church structures. Our academic qualifications as well as our life experience with its spiritual dimension usually equip us well for these roles. But what of our skill as managers? We know there are things we don't know – but where can we find out in a way that saves time, money and effort? *Just about Everything a Manager Needs to Know* offers a host of simple, effective tips. And to think that, until we saw page 88, we thought the Monday Morning Blues could only be beaten by prayer and penance!

Vivienne Goldstein sm
Executive Director
Marist Mission Centre

There are two types of impactful management books – the practical, highly useful one that you keep close by on an accessible shelf because you use it constantly, and the one that leaves a strong impact because of the message in it. *Just about Everything a Manager Needs to Know* is definitely one of the first type and will be a constant and useful reference for busy managers interested in staying effective. I also believe that this constant usage will reveal as well that here is a book of the second type, which will make an impact because it is full of practical advice based on good sense.

Professor Michael Hough
Department of Management
University of Wollongong
President, Australian Council for Educational Administration

If you could choose one management book only for your bookshelf, this would have to be it! Indeed, the material is so comprehensive in nature that you'd be hard pressed to find a management issue NOT covered in the book. I personally like the well-organised approach to the book, as it has made the information it contains very easy to access.

Lorraine Marshall
State Marketing Manager
Jones Lang Wootton and
Friendly Marketing Manager
Carindale Shopping Centre

Business entrepreneurs are calculated risk-takers. Some years ago, we recognised the potential for *Crocodile Dundee*, took the risk, and saw it become an international box-office success. Being a party to the establishment of the Brisbane Broncos football team involved plenty of calculated risk-taking, too. Several years ago I was quick to recognise *Management in a Minute* as a business best-seller. I was right, again. Now I am confident that *Just about Everything a Manager Needs to Know* will be even more successful. I note that it even includes information on how to improve your risk-taking skills. There's something in it for everyone.

Paul E. Morgan
Business Entrepreneur and Executive Chairman
Paul Morgan Securities Pty Ltd

Management is all about knowing what ought to be done and what can be done. Here is a book that shows us *how* it can be done – just what school leaders need in an age of site-based management.

Dr Lester Mason
Principal
Boronia Heights Primary School

The best management books are those that crystallise common sense and transform it into a simple, structured process. This book does just that.

Dr Ron Swindells
Chief Executive
Mackay Sugar Co-operative Association Ltd

About the authors

Neil Flanagan

Neil Flanagan, B.A., B.Ed.St., M.Ed.Admin., Ph.D., is a highly regarded management strategist, a sought-after keynote, conference, and motivational speaker, and a best-selling author.

Neil's approach to strategy draws on the wisdom of the ancient sages, recognised strategists, and his own management experience to help individuals and organisations achieve their highest potential.

His previous books – *Management in a Minute*, *Creative Debt Collecting*, and *Responsiveness: Double Your Profits in Half the Time* – have all achieved international best-seller status.

Neil's management experience includes education and educational administration, corporate training, human resources management, management strategy, and company directorships. From that experience, and by working closely with managers in those fields, he has developed a clear understanding not only of managers' needs, but also of the way busy managers want information presented.

Jarvis Finger

Jarvis Finger, B.A., B.Ed., M.Ed. Admin., FACEA, FQIEA, AAIM, is a well-known author and editor of a range of management books and magazines.

A former executive manager in one of Australia's largest public organisations, he is the award-winning founder and editor of Australia's best-known management magazine for school administrators, *The Practising Administrator*, and author of several best-selling books on school management – the *Managing Your School* series.

Jarvis was awarded the Gold Medal of the Australian Council for Educational Administration for 'his services to the professional literature of educational administration in Australia'. He has also authored a series of books on Queensland's early colonial prison on St Helena Island, and several entertaining paperbacks in education.

Co-author with Neil Flanagan of *Management in a Minute*, he brings the same writing, presentation and editing skills to this book as he brought to his earlier best-sellers.

Managing Yourself

In reading the lives of great people,
I found that the first victory they won
was over themselves.

Harry S. Truman

 See also: 110, 116, 204

How to cultivate a better professional image for yourself

Like it or not, you do have an image: if you do not develop it by intent, then it will develop by default. So the answer is to make sure that the image you project is an asset rather than a liability. But knowing what image you present and how to go about improving it is more difficult than it would seem at first glance. The suggestions which follow are listed to help you enhance your personal image and to influence more positively the way others see you...

1 Know what image you want to project.

What kind of personal image do you want to project? Do you want to impress as a creative, energetic, innovative, and enthusiastic leader? Or a laid-back, let-it-all-happen, efficient manager? Or a sensitive, caring, people person? Other people read the signals you project, so analyse the image you would like to create and set about communicating the right signals to project that image.

2 Attend to your personal appearance.

Dress appropriately and well, as if you have already arrived at the top of your success pyramid. Wear what you consider will meet other people's expectations of you as a successful manager.

Compile and analyse your own personal dress and grooming checklist – ties, shoes, hair, accessories, pen, briefcase, glasses, fingernails, cosmetics, jewellery... How do you and others rate your appearance?

3 Be a positive communicator.

What you say and how you say it are important factors in image-building. Have you ever taped yourself in natural conversation, or in reading aloud to consider the loudness, pitch, tone, articulation, and speed of your voice? Audiotapes can reveal a lot: boring monotone, nasality, stridency, gotta's, dropped g's, over-use of um's and ah's, and y'knows... All can contribute to a negative personal image.

Be a good listener while at the same time keeping your employees and colleagues informed about what is going on in your department or organisation. Spend as much time listening as talking and make oral and written communication as positive as you can.

4 Check your non-verbal messages.

Your body signals could be impeding your chances of success as a manager. If you feel strong and confident you should stand tall and walk with assurance. If you sit with stooped shoulders or walk with a slow, hesitating gait, you will project one who is overwhelmed by life and is low on self-esteem. Posture and bearing disclose a lot – as any body language book will tell you.

Management Memo

The first impression is usually lasting, largely because people's perceptions are not easily changed, but also because you are likely to keep projecting the same image.

The way you look and what that conveys are part of your performance. Recognise that the way you look affects the way you work and the way other people perceive your work. Cultivating your image means defining and focusing more sharply on who you really are. But it is of the utmost importance that you be authentic and genuine and that you not seek artificially to blot out aspects of who you are and the way you act. [1]

5 Develop those essential interactive qualities.

Here are important aspects to remember in your dealings with others:

- Always be first to say hello. Offer a firm but not crushing handshake.
- Never be casual with your greeting. Be sincere and meaningful.
- A friendly smile projects an image of trust.
- Use the other person's name in your conversation.
- Do your homework when meeting with someone. Work your knowledge of them into the conversation.
- Show that you are interested in what the other person is saying.
- Observe the basic rules of politeness and etiquette.

6 Think about your work environment.

The appearance of your office or workplace says a lot about you. A cluttered desk, for example, can give others the idea that you are untidy and disorganised. Visitors are most impressed with an 'organised stacks' setting.

7 Always project a professional attitude.

Make certain your name is always associated with honest, ethical behaviour. Strive to develop good personal relationships. Demonstrate integrity, understanding, sensitivity, trust, respect and competence. Let colleagues know that you are tastefully ambitious, keen to get ahead, but avoid the impression that you are prepared to walk over others to get there. Tactfully make your skills and accomplishments known. Admit mistakes and never publicly criticise a superior or colleague. Seize every opportunity to prove that you are a good team player.

8 Be constantly aware of your image.

The key to image-building is to start early. You see, it's easier to build up a positive image before one has been formed in the eyes of others, than to change one that is already established. Unfortunately, few of us can begin with a clean slate.

But if you suspect that your present image is not helping you to advance your career, then you will need to change it – and this could take some time, since well established behaviours are hard to alter. Be aware always that the way you present yourself to others is one of the most important facets of any leader's makeup. Work at it daily.

In a nutshell, act like a professional and always look the part.

 See also: 20, 70, 82-84, 108, 132

How to prepare yourself for a brilliant career

Climbing the management ladder to success is not something to be left to chance. Unfortunately, there is no magic formula. In fact, no two management consultants would be in complete agreement on any certain recipe for reaching the top job. They would agree, however, that, if you have ambitions of reaching the top, then the best person to help you get there is you. So, here are a few guidelines to help you on your way…

1 Be prepared.

There are no better candidates for advancement than those who, while handling their own job in exemplary fashion, have also prepared themselves for the job above. Keep close to the people whose job you may want, for they often have a lot to say about their successors.

2 Attend seminars and courses regularly.

The sharpening of management skills through continuing education is an essential task for effective managers. Additionally, exposure to other managers at seminars and conferences is a stimulating exercise.

3 Build your own management library.

Exposure to the literature of management is vital to one who would manage. Management is a profession that can be taught, read about, and learned. Build up a personal management library – and use it.

4 Subscribe to at least one top management journal.

A good management journal is the primary source for new ideas and information and is an essential tool for managers who need to be up-to-date with the latest in the field.

5 Join at least one professional association.

Such associations provide the opportunity to 'get a fix' on the job; to mix with others facing similar problems and seeking similar answers; to break the daily routine; to hear professionals present topics of managerial interest.

6 Be seen.

Become visible and known by name – through networking, attending conferences and seminars, writing for professional journals and newsletters, joining committees and taskforces, being active in professional associations, attending company social get-togethers.

7 Develop a questioning mind.

A questioning mind is alert to change, is constantly in search of facts, relates facts to situations and projects them into future possibilities, views interruptions as opportunities, and seeks relationships between facts, situations and people.

8 Lead from the front.

Support the efforts of your subordinates. By helping their careers, you ensure strong loyalty. Build a strong team around you to complement your skills and undertake team tasks crucial to your organisation's success. Publicise the results.

9 Dedicate yourself to the organisation.

Show your interest and dedication to the organisation. Take on new assignments. Tackle existing tasks in different ways. Talk shop with your colleagues.

10 Build a reputation as a forward-looking manager.

Broad-mindedness, appreciation of innovation, creativity – all have a place in the portfolio of a modern manager. Experiment in the

> **Management Memo**
>
> People used to have a career master plan: get a degree, get a job, get a gold watch when you retire... To survive today, you have to learn to manage your career and your life in a changing workplace. [2]

application of new approaches to executive problems and routine tasks.

11 Be aware of the company culture.

If you seek to climb the company ladder, then be aware of the company culture. If others wear white shirts and tie, don't wear turtlenecks; if others work a twelve-hour day, don't arrive at 9.00 a.m. and leave at 4.30 p.m.; if others work as a team, don't hog the spotlight. If you want to be non-conformist, start by outperforming the others.

12 See yourself as a winner.

Understand the politics of your organisation. Understand the values of each level within your organisation and match your achievements to them. Be ready to make firm, sometimes unpopular decisions. Be loyal but don't jeopardise your career. Use talented people to cover your weaknesses. Be realistic about your strengths, weaknesses, and ambitions.

How to prepare a résumé that promotes you to best advantage

A résumé is a vital first step in achieving your next promotion. It is essentially your personal advertisement, a short document encapsulating your qualifications and experience, a door-opener to that all important next step, the job interview. The following checklist is designed to help you to prepare and present a winning résumé...

1 Format

Résumés can be prepared in various formats, the most common being:

- *Chronological*: your experience/ information is listed in reverse chronological order, present job being cited first. This format clearly shows your growth and development.
- *Functional*: organises work experience by function categories such as project management, leadership, personnel administration, stock control, community relations, finance, etc.

Burdette Bostwick (*Résumé Writing*, John Wiley, NY, 1990. 296 pp) details ten varieties; Richard Beatty (*The Résumé Kit*, John Wiley, NY, 1991. 335 pp) focuses on three. Serious résumé writers should consult such books which are rich in sample résumés and covering letters.

2 Process

The résumé writing process involves the following steps:

1. Gather the information on yourself.
2. Select that information which is relevant to the position(s) advertised.
3. Decide on résumé section headings.
4. Prepare a first draft.
5. Allow an 'incubation' period.
6. Revise your draft.
7. Review it with others – then rework it.
8. Use a quality secretarial service.

3 Content

Remember that *résumé* is from the French word meaning *summary* – so your text and headings must be concise and to the point. The document must infer your potential by *briefly* telling what you have already accomplished.

- ☐ Reveal your abilities, potential and what you can offer the employer by citing past experience as proof.
- ☐ Link your experiences and skills to the relevant job objectives.
- ☐ Emphasise your achievements rather than simply describe your responsibilities. They are not the same.
- ☐ Use section headings, such as Personal Directory (name, address, contact), Qualifications, Work History, Achievements, Honours, Professional Affiliations, References, etc.
- ☐ Your résumé should clearly indicate how well you are capable of performing rather than leave this to conjecture.

4 Style

Style relates to the way you express your content. A sloppy, dull style could cost you that all important interview.

- ☐ Use bullets to set off responsibilities or achievements.
- ☐ Use action verbs to describe your achievements or responsibilities – *led, initiated, prepared, reviewed, headed*, e.g.
  - *Addressed delays in mail-sorting procedures by introducing a programme which…'*
- ☐ Eliminate the use of such personal pronouns as *I, me, my, myself.*
- ☐ Avoid long paragraphs. They're too difficult to read.
- ☐ Avoid narrative descriptions.
- ☐ Check, and double-check, for typos, misspelling, and poor grammar.

5 Presentation

Your résumé *must* be visually inviting:

- ☐ Pay particular attention to the components of appearance – typing, layout, margins, typefaces, headlines, bullets, centering, spacing. Poorly done, they can wreck a good résumé; well done, they can enhance a poor one. When in doubt, use a reputable secretarial service.
- ☐ Use no borders, artwork or decoration on a résumé and never attempt to be cute or gimmicky.
- ☐ Do not cram the pages. Clutter distracts the reader. Leave plenty of white space.
- ☐ Keep at least a 2 cm margin on every side of your paper.
- ☐ Space between each paragraph.
- ☐ Consistency counts: ensure all headings, indents, margins, typesize, use of capitals, italics, etc. are uniform.
- ☐ Type/print your résumé on one side of good quality A4 white, cream or light grey paper, preferably via a quality laser printer or top-of-the-line photocopier.

Management Memo

The employment process is designed to be a 'negative' screening process. The employer establishes certain candidate selection criteria against which the candidate's qualifications are to be measured. A candidate who is poorly qualified or lacks some of the basic qualifications to fill the position is 'screened out' of the process. If you have a poorly prepared résumé, you will be screened out before you have a chance to get started.[3]

6 Other

Check out these points also:

- ☐ Limit your résumé to 2–3 pages, plus a one-page covering letter.
- ☐ The laws relating to equal opportunity employment make it illegal for an employer to discriminate by reason of age, race, disability, health, weight, religion, marital status, and sex. Judge for yourself whether to include such data in your résumé.
- ☐ Do not date your résumé. Your covering letter indicates its currency.
- ☐ File a copy of your résumé in a safe place. Update the document regularly.
- ☐ Know your résumé backwards before attending an interview.
- ☐ Take a couple of copies to your interview – just in case they're needed.
- ☐ Make sure your referees have a copy.
- ☐ Be aware of résumé readers' major criticisms of these documents: 'too long, too short, too condensed, too wordy, too smart, too amateurish, misspellings and poor grammar, poorly presented, dishonest, information lacking, poorly expressed'.
- ☐ If you do not value yourself highly, others will not value you highly. The way you feel about yourself will show through your résumé.
- ☐ If you post it, don't fold it.

How to prepare a professional portfolio

In today's competitive environment, you need to develop a range of effective and eye-catching strategies that can give you the edge over your colleagues when it comes to promotional opportunities. A well-presented résumé, letter of application, and a successful interview are of course very important, but a carefully prepared professional portfolio can also help you showcase your skills, experience and accomplishments. Gain that extra advantage by considering these helpful ideas...

1 Understand the purpose of a portfolio.

Basically, a portfolio is a tool that allows you to 'prove' your experience, skills, and achievement in the tough competition for management positions – as architects, designers, and similar professionals have found over the years. But as well, the very act of compiling your professional portfolio:

- allows you to evaluate your work and reflect on what you have accomplished, how others have responded, what you have learned, and what gaps there are in your professional experience
- demonstrates an approach to problem-solving and decision-making that research suggests are essential assets of a highly effective administrator
- encourages you to survey the big picture of your personal professional development over a long period of time
- permits you to gain a fairly accurate representation of yourself as a manager. Do you like what you see? If not, how can you change for the better?

In turn, an interview panel should find clear evidence to support your application for promotion, including:

- examples and illustrations of your accomplishments in abbreviated form
- breadth and depth of experience
- proof of your ability to perform as a manager
- a high level of organisation and presentation
- evidence that you know how to select the appropriate materials for a particular purpose.

2 Devise a suitable structure for content.

Consider how you can give structure to your content and logically present your documentation. For example, you may decide to divide your portfolio into, say, five sections:

a. Personal development
b. Knowledge and competence in management
c. Professional development
d. Community service
e. Notes and thank yous.

The search for content can then begin.

3 Collect your content materials.

Begin by including everything you can think of in each section, e.g.

Personal Development: Résumé; a short autobiography revealing how your professional life has developed to the point where pursuit of a career in management is a logical step; a list of short- and long-term goals; a statement that describes your values and beliefs; a statement of leadership style…

Knowledge and competence: Documents that provide evidence of experience in management tasks and initiatives such as committee leadership or membership; participation in interviews; samples of professional letters, newsletters or reports; system/regional level involvement; projects initiated; proof of having collected data and made decisions based on analysis of data…

Professional development: Samples of writing for journals, newspapers, newsletters, reports, submissions; a conference presentation; abstract of research or study completed; evidence of attendance at conferences, workshops, or study groups…

Community service: Evidence of awards and honours; memos requesting your services; news clippings; descriptions of voluntary actions; certificates of appreciation from agencies or community groups; proof of professional involvement in activities beyond the company for religious, service, or community groups…

From this weighty collection, delete that material which distracts from the overall picture you wish to present. On the other hand, if your collection is a little thin, it's vital to begin the process *now*, and to add to the portfolio over time. A quality portfolio is not compiled overnight.

4 Attend to its presentation.

A portfolio is not a scrapbook filled with thank-you letters, memos and newsletters. It should reflect a successful career. It should be a well-organised, attractively presented collection of professional material of which the author is proud. One suggestion is to present the portfolio as a solid white ring-binder, with transparent sleeves for insertion of your material. These page protectors keep the material clean, eliminate the need to punch holes in precious documents, and allow for easy additions and deletions.

Management Memo

Artists, designers and architects have long used portfolios to provide concrete evidence of their work. Such collections offer a job applicant a way to demonstrate competence beyond the typical letter of application, résumé and interview. Professional portfolios can help applicants showcase their experience and help employers make wise selection decisions. [4]

5 Know when to use it.

Consider this manager's approach :

"I carried the portfolio with me to the interview and placed it on the table next to me. I did not refer to it until the end of the session, when I was asked if I had any questions or additional comments to make. Explaining that I had brought along my portfolio and would like to leave it for a few days, I said, 'If you have any questions, or want more information regarding me, it is all in the portfolio.' This strategy also gave me the chance to return to the office in a few days to claim the portfolio and touch base once again."

It's important to be subtle, and to be strategic. And remember, the same collection of material may not always be appropriate for every interview. Include only those parts that best represent your qualifications for the position for which you are applying at the time.

6 Update the content regularly.

The challenge now is to maintain and update your portfolio. But you'll find it's easier once you have the foundation in place.

How to face your next job interview with confidence

In applying for a new job, you may indeed be experienced and well-qualified, and you may have submitted a wonderful letter of application and a perfect résumé – but today, more than ever, it's that face-to-face interview that really counts. To gain the advantage, you'll need to project a confident image, as the following strategies suggest...

1 Do your homework.

If you've done your research and preparation, it will come across confidently and naturally in the interview. In this regard:

- *Know your résumé thoroughly.* Be able to elaborate on each item and to discuss strengths and weaknesses confidently, positively, and honestly.
- *Assemble your résumé, other documentation, and examples of previous work* as support material for use when appropriate during the interview.
- *Familiarise yourself with the company and position you have applied for.* You needn't be an expert, but take note of a few important facts and try to make some global observations based on the information from materials you examine (company publications, local newspapers, annual reports) or the people you speak with beforehand. Be able to talk about the organisation's successes and emphasise what strengths you are now able to bring to the company or the specific position.
- *Prepare your responses – but don't overdo it.* By all means prepare thoroughly for the questions you expect to get at the interview, but don't be so thorough as to be unprepared for those you don't expect. And don't be so intent on giving your prepared responses that you answer questions you were never asked.
- *Be ready to ask some intelligent questions of your own.* Interviewers often give you that opportunity.

2 Rehearse.

The best way to build confidence and manage uncertainty is to practise beforehand. So, rehearse questions related to each of the selection criteria and other fundamental questions such as: Why did you apply for this position? Why are you the best person for the job? How will it fit in with your career plans?

Practise your responses out loud (running it through your mind is not the same). Engage in mental imaging: actually see yourself performing well; hear the certainty in your voice. Visualise the introductions, your final statement to the panel, and your exit. Remember Don Clayton's advice in *Up the Ladder without Snakes*:

> 'Most of us tend to make rehearsal a half-hearted affair and we are rewarded (or punished) for this when we walk into the room and feel our minds melt into mush.'

3 Pay attention to first impressions.

First impressions count a great deal:

- Look the part. Dress appropriately.
- Make sure you arrive ten minutes early – ample time to psych yourself up. Never arrive late. Ensure you don't feel rushed. Breathe in deeply, exhale slowly.
- Walk in confidently, be sure to smile, make direct eye contact, and introduce yourself. Carry your materials in your left hand, so that you are ready to return a handshake firmly without fumbling.
- Relax. Try to give the impression that you are approaching the interview confidently and calmly.

4 Use these proven interview tactics.

Be familiar with and enlist the following techniques during the interview itself:

- Support your answers with examples.
- Think before you open your mouth. Take a few seconds before responding.
- Make your answers long enough to cover the topic, short enough to hold interest.
- Gauge how the panel is reacting – tired, alert, interested, bored? Respond accordingly.
- Remember: most people only hear about 10 per cent of what you say. The rest is *how* you say it – your body language, facial expressions, the tone of your voice.
- A winning vocabulary is essential. Judiciously use buzzwords that emphasise your commitment, awareness, effectiveness, and knowledge – empower, excellence, mission, participate, initiate, collaborate, accountable, cooperative learning, lead, performance-based, etc.
- Speak positively of past experience. Emphasise the positive aspects of your previous positions. Acknowledge the contributions of colleagues to show you're a team player.
- Listen attentively during the session.
- Don't try to answer questions you don't understand. Seek clarification first.
- If you are interview number three or more for the day, the panel could well be in a daze by the time it's your turn. You'll need to revive interest – a non-routine answer, some appropriate humour, a novel solution – nothing out of character, just enthusiasm and pizzazz to set you apart from the pack.
- Watch your body language: don't deliver your lines from behind a tangle of crossed legs, folded arms, or slumped shoulders. Sit erect and try to mirror the body language of the interviewer.
- Answer questions truthfully. Misrepresentations could return to haunt you.

Management Memo

Interviewers say it repeatedly: All other things being equal, they offer the job to the person who projects the greatest confidence during the interview. The total image you project, of course, will be dictated by your own personality and style... But it's critical to remember that being well-prepared, being well-dressed, and following a carefully thought-out strategy will greatly enhance your confidence and give you a decided advantage in the interview. [5]

5 Leave a good impression.

Interviewers forget 85 per cent of what you have said an hour after you've gone. You need to make a positive impact in the final phases of the interview. The panel should remember you as confident, enthusiastic, energetic, and dependable. End, as you began, with a smile, direct eye contact, firm handshake, and a few positive words.

How to prepare yourself before taking up that new position

So you have been appointed to a new management position. Congratulations! Obviously, you will want to get off to the best possible start – that's important for your own self-confidence and for the impression you make on your colleagues. Often, however, some people feel inadequate in those first few weeks. So, to assist you to overcome any initial uncertainty and to help you feel secure when you take over your new job, here is some useful advice...

1 Take time to plan and prepare for the move.

Time spent in planning and preparing in advance for your new job will pay dividends. Usually you will have several weeks at least between the date of appointment and taking up your new position. Get yourself organised immediately and start thinking about your new role.

2 Brief yourself as fully as possible.

Make contact with your new boss and obtain as much printed material relating to your new organisation or position as you can. This will include mission statements, strategic plans, annual reports, organisational diagrams, projects in progress, productivity statements, policy handbooks, and the like.

Examine the material to become generally acquainted with the company, in particular that part for which you will be responsible. Check out the qualifications and responsibilities of staff. Sort through the information provided, listing questions for which you might need additional information.

3 Visit the organisation.

If possible, take time out to visit the premises of your new organisation, preferably when no one else is there. Walk around the buildings and environs. Visit empty offices or workrooms, read the bulletin boards. Browse and observe, not to be critical but to familiarise yourself with the surroundings. First impressions can be important later on, so take notes. In time, these can be very revealing.

4 Spend time with your predecessor.

If possible, try to have a long discussion with your predecessor. You will not, of course, be committed to continuing his/her policies but you want as much inside information about the position and the organisation as possible, so the present incumbent is the best source.

Ask for any information not previously forwarded to you, to help determine current practices, and details about staff, products, policies, and procedures. Be a good listener but don't press on issues which appear to be sensitive.

5 Meet your staff.

It is much easier to begin at your new job if the rest of your team are not complete strangers. Explore the possibility of meeting with them informally for a brief chat over coffee or lunch. It may not be possible to meet with all staff at this early stage, but at least target the key players in your team.

6 Clarify your role.

If you are a head of a department or work group, it is a useful strategy to talk over with your new boss your responsibilities in the organisation. You won't want to discover anything unexpected on your first day!

7 Plan your priorities.

Having now assembled a great deal of information about your new position and its environment, and having gained some preliminary impressions of the organisation's strengths and weaknesses, you can now begin to list some preliminary thoughts relating to short- and longer-term priorities for action in your new management position.

In determining your plans for the future, these points should be considered:

- Make no attempt to be master of all aspects of your new position.
- You do not have to do everything on your first day, or even your first week, or even your first month.
- Make a habit of consulting with your colleagues before doing anything drastic.
- Avoid making snap judgements. Keep an open mind early on and make your final judgements later.
- Your first staff meeting will be an important one, when you will establish your level of leadership and lay the foundation for your tenure in the position. Therefore, think long and hard about making it a success.
- You shouldn't have to establish your authority aggressively.
- Think about how you intend to establish two-way channels of communication.
- Consider how you intend in those early days to become more familiar with the people and the operations.
- Don't adopt a policy of wait-and-see. Show some initiative. What you do in those first few weeks will be setting the pattern for your leadership.

Management Memo

You will have your own personal aims and needs as a manager. But remember that those who work with you have also entered into a contract with the organisation. They will give a lot if handled correctly. They will want something in return. They, too, seek meaning in what they do. They must be nurtured *by* the organisation *through* you. [6]

How to position yourself in your new job

When you take up a new management position, and actually sit in the manager's chair, it is natural to feel some pangs of uncertainty in the new environment. The following guidelines will help you overcome the initial insecurity of those early days in the job...

1 Avoid becoming too visible too soon.

In the early days many people will be anxious to see what your approach will be, particularly in terms of changes to 'the way things are done around here'. Let there be a touch of mystery about your presence in these early stages. Just as you will go out to meet your staff, let some of them come to you. Don't show your hand until you are ready. Use this as a period of gathering information and planning.

2 Focus on the important things first.

Don't try to become the master of all aspects of your new position. Ask your superior to list the three or four most important responsibilities of your job and make every effort in these early days to master them first.

3 Avoid making snap judgements.

Don't fall into the trap of making snap judgements about who's important, who's going to be your ally, who's the most impressive operator, and so on. It's smart not to form a set opinion about anyone until you know them well and have seen them interacting with others. Similarly, be wary of those negative stories about who's out to get whom, who's about to get fired, who's cheating, and so on. Keep an open mind and make your own judgements much later.

4 Peruse the files.

Company files will provide you with essential background information about the organisation and help you find out what's important to the organisation, how things have been handled in the past, and what the current issues are.

5 Become familiar with the way the organisation works.

Familiarise yourself with the regular routine of the organisation, its communication networks, and the mechanics of daily life in the workplace. If necessary, fill your briefcase each night with reading matter which will help you, through home study, become acquainted with the organisation and, in particular, with that part of the business for which you are now responsible. Such documents would include annual reports, handbooks, newsletters, procedures manuals, and company prospectuses and brochures.

Management Memo

Concentrate and focus all your attention on getting the basics done quickly. The important thing is to come to grips with your new job quickly and be effective in your output. [7]

6 Get to know your staff.

If you're not provided with an organisational chart when you take up duty, you should put one together, showing people their positions and their responsibilities. Over the following weeks, as you purposefully seek out the missing information, the chart will become more detailed and your knowledge of the organisation will grow. Get to know your people by name and be able to talk to them about their areas of interest both inside and outside the workplace. You'll need to work on this, but it will pay off in terms of team building.

7 Endear yourself to your boss's secretary.

Entrepreneur and manager Mark McCormack offers the following counsel to all new managers, advising them to be aware of the importance of communicating upstairs: 'Most people either fail to appreciate the power of the boss's secretary as gatekeeper to the executive suite or neglect to turn that, through a warm personal comment, to their advantage. I'm convinced that my secretary could persuade me to see anyone – or, conversely, prevent me from hearing their name – depending on the impression that person has made.' The boss's personal assistant can become a valuable ally in getting your future ideas through the system. Cultivate the relationship.

8 Avoid the whingers.

Gripe sessions about other people are common practices in most organisations. There'll be those who will want to ingratiate themselves to you in the early days by downgrading the worth of others. Their remarks are often misleading, so try to stay clear of these encounters. Remember, if you are too receptive to such people, you may acquire the kind of reputation you don't want.

9 If necessary, restrict your social life.

For the first few weeks at least, you should try to keep your outside social life to a minimum. After at least nine hours of intense concentration learning the ins and outs of your new position, you should be exhausted anyway, and will need time to recover overnight. Besides, the new job should be the focus of your attention in these early days.

See also: 12-14

How to build on the successful start in your new job

A manager who has succeeded in making a successful start to a new job needs to consolidate the benefits gained in those first few weeks. To maintain this momentum, here are some further suggestions...

1 Seek out a mentor.

Ask for or identify a superior or colleague who can 'show you the ropes' and assist you through the first few months and beyond. Stay in contact with this mentor and take the opportunity to learn. Your mentor will acknowledge your enthusiasm, recognise your ability, and be eager for you to continue this working relationship.

2 Listen to what others have to say.

It's been said that listening is 50 per cent of our education – so do a lot of listening and much less talking. Use speech to post winners, not to attract attention. Accumulate information and use it to your advantage. Your aim should be to ask smart questions to find out what you want rather than let everyone know how much you think you know.

3 Adapt to the working style of those around you.

Without compromising your personal and professional standards, it is important for you to fit in with your new colleagues and staff, at least in the early days in your new position. If, after observing your new organisation during the first few months, you find a change of style is necessary, you can bring about the change in an appropriate fashion.

4 Specialise.

Stay out of other people's patches; let your staff members get on with their jobs without unnecessary involvement from you. Being a manager does not mean that you must neglect to focus on your own talents. Create winning ideas in your area of expertise. Use your own talents to become recognised as an expert in your field of specific interest.

5 Respect the efforts of your support staff.

Get on the good side of your secretarial and support staff right from the start. If you treat them with consideration and friendliness, they will always be eager to help you.

Never make unrealistic demands on them, don't harp on clerical errors, and don't demand impossible deadlines. Remember, the receptionist may one day be able to give you the most important piece of information of your life and that new junior clerk in the back office may one day be your boss.

6 Pick the brains of your peers.

Your fellow managers may hold many of the missing parts to a full understanding of your new position. Get to know them on an easy, informal, social basis. Assume an attitude of seeking their help to learn how the company works. If you make your peers understand that you need their assistance, that you know less about the company than they do, but need to know more in order to become a good team member, you'll find that they will help you and won't mind you, as the new guy, asking for information.

7 Take your time – be patient.

Unless you've been instructed to bring about change overnight, you should demonstrate your capabilities over time rather than trying to hit full pace on the first day or during the first week. Tread lightly, take one step at a time, and maintain a good sense of humour. Take all the time you need to get all the knowledge you need – about the business, your employees, your work, and the jobs you have to delegate. Only then can you give your people the time and attention they need to work well.

Management Memo

Remember the seven secrets of being a number one boss:

1. Develop professional expertise.
2. Sharpen your communication skills.
3. Cultivate enthusiasm.
4. Keep an open mind.
5. Pay attention to accomplishment.
6. Be accessible.
7. Respect your staff – treat your staff as you treat your clients.[8]

8 Focus on developing your management skills.

Developing, honing and deploying the essential skills of management should remain foremost in your mind as you settle into your new position. The key areas would include:

- *Communicating:* expressing yourself concisely, clearly, regularly and persuasively.
- *Decision-making:* developing the confidence and analytical skills to enable you to make timely, incisive judgements.
- *Motivating:* knowing what your staff can do, making it clear what you expect from them, enthusing them to maximum effort, and rewarding them according to their contribution.
- *Listening:* listening to ideas, acting on them, hearing what others say, showing an interest, letting people feel important for the contributions they make.
- *Problem-solving:* adopting a logical and creative approach to grappling with the problems which will confront you on a daily basis.
- *Self-managing:* achieving control over your day in terms of managing time, handling paper, simplifying the workload, and coping with the stress that shadows the managerial role.

 See also: 8, 86, 90

How to prepare for your own performance appraisal

It's hard to like performance appraisals, whether they're the traditional type or the 360^0 version. At one extreme, they're an annual ritual at which bosses or their nominees list a litany of your flaws, then send you away to take the necessary actions to reduce or eliminate them. At the other, however, they're a wonderful opportunity to discuss openly your job performance with your boss. If *you* show some initiative, you'll get a great deal from an appraisal interview, as the following points reveal...

1 Become a participant rather than a target.

Resolve to take an active part in any appraisal. Preparation is the key to that. Begin by accumulating evidence of your own performance throughout the year. For example, you might decide to:

- Keep 'hard' copies of your contributions, accomplishments, awards, and so on. File cards can be completed daily or weekly, thereby helping you to maintain an up-to-date record.
- Make regular updates on a computer file set up specifically for that purpose. A scanner will eliminate the need to accumulate hard copy samples of your work.
- The advantages of compiling a professional portfolio (see page 8) and a personal achievement list (see page 86) are obvious.
- Use a copy of the appraisal form to help structure your preparation, including an agenda and support materials. The quality of your preparation will also convey the right message to the person conducting the appraisal.

2 Talk to others about their interviews.

Colleagues and workmates will prove to be valuable sources of information to help in your preparation. You might ask them about:

- their impressions of their appraisal interviews – procedures, outcomes, questions
- the boss's level of preparedness and specific agenda items
- issues discussed
- follow-up items
- suggested improvements for future interviews.

3 Be prepared to assert your position.

To participate successfully as an equal partner in the discussion will require that you assert yourself rather than act submissively. Your assertion skills will be helped if you give some thought to the type of questions you will be asked and practise your responses out loud. You can disagree if you think the boss is wrong, but make certain you take issue with the facts, not the boss's judgement. Be prepared to look on any criticisms as opportunities for improvement.

4 Get your documentation right.

Documentation to support your case is important. It should contain a variety of data, supported by examples wherever possible, that will help you to lead the discussion and to respond to any queries. If salary increases are linked to performance appraisal, your prepared argument and supporting evidence should lead to acknowledgement of your worth. The effort that goes into your preparation may help make your job secure and the accumulated data will serve as a valuable addition to your résumé and portfolio in interviews for further promotions. Offer to leave any relevant material with the boss.

5 Rehearse.

The boss may not know the details of your job, and probably has no desire to – that's what *you* are paid for. The one key quality you need to convey, however, is confidence. All your actions and words must reinforce your boss's confidence in you. Practise your entry and exit. Give some thought to the layout of the room where the interview will be conducted and plan accordingly. Remember, most meaning is communicated nonverbally. For example, your bearing and the tempo (rhythm) of your voice are important factors so prepare by reaffirming: 'When I'm at the interview I'll be calm, confident, and relaxed.' You'll be impressed by the result.

Management Memo

Staff appraisal should not be a once-a-year ritual. Good managers do it all the year round. [9]

6 Confirm the interview.

The interview is about you and your future, so you want to make sure it goes ahead as planned. Confirm the time, place and duration. If you've followed the above suggestions you may decide to provide in advance a copy of your agenda and any documentation you have prepared. That will not only help the boss's preparation but also demonstrate the importance you place on the meeting.

7 And finally…

- Listen carefully.
- Ask questions if you need clarification.
- Focus on outcomes.
- Emphasise the future, not the past.
- Thank your boss and make a commitment to follow-up.
- Review the goals you reviewed with your boss and take steps to implement them. If professional development was an issue, sign up for a seminar. If you're supposed to make more decisions, make them…
- Prepare for the future now. Don't wait for the appraisal process to discuss your performance with your boss. Arrange for regularly scheduled progress reports. Short, focused sessions ensure that you're well prepared for the next appraisal session.

See also: 2-4, 24, 108, 112, 114, 260

How to improve your chances of getting promoted

To get promoted, you must build what management consultant Daniel Johnson has called 'career equity', thereby establishing your 'professional net worth'. This is done by developing, improving and strengthening each of eight specific assets which will enhance your professional value in the management marketplace...

1 Improve your knowledge and skills.

To progress in your career, you need to assess your knowledge and skills to uncover any deficiencies. Work purposefully on correcting these weaknesses. Continue to learn. Participate in training and updating programs. Attend seminars and conferences to build your knowledge, to inform yourself of new trends, and to meet influential people in your field. Read regularly the books and journals of your profession. Creative ideas can only be nurtured by broad up-to-date knowledge.

2 Strengthen your credentials.

Most employers still place a very high value on credentials earned through formal post-school education. This asset can also be strengthened through active membership of professional associations and committees, and involvement in community service organisations and clubs. Distinctions and honours gained through formal education, and through service to the profession and the community, will also gain important credit points for you.

3 Enhance your reputation.

Your reputation focuses on your overall image within the organisation and beyond. It is based on what people think of you and your accomplishments. The development of your credibility in terms of honesty, integrity, hard work, and consideration for others, will strengthen this asset immensely.

4 Build up your relationships.

It's been said before: 'It's not what you know, it's who you know. 'That's where the concepts of mentoring and networking come in. A mentor can provide career information and opportunities for you. Likewise, developing a network of professional contacts is also a positive career-strengthening strategy. Talk with senior people in your field; ask how they started and progressed. Try to develop a relationship with your superior, allowing you to discuss career options with him or her. Become visible and known by name. Get to know strategic people in the system by participating on relevant committees, and making worthwhile suggestions for consideration at higher levels. Working actively with others in professional associations can later lead to career advantages as well.

Remember also, it's important to get along with people at *all* levels: if you can't get on with others, you won't get on promotion-wise.

5 Nurture your track record.

To build up this asset, you need to be a proven performer at each stage of your career, for a listing of your achievements over time will provide the evidence of your track record. By developing expertise in a particular area you also embellish your routine accomplishments and make a name for yourself in the wider business community.

Finally, don't hide your light under a bushel – make sure others know of your successes, but be subtle about it.

6 Consider your tenure.

How tenure affects career equity varies greatly from profession to profession. In some organisations, however, it's still a case of the longer an employee's tenure, the greater the respect accorded. Increasingly, however, in an age of rapid change, effectiveness on the job is often far more important than tenure.

Management Memo

The benefits of career planning can be measured by your pay and status level. But of more lasting value will be your feelings of satisfaction, achievement, personal growth and increased self-tolerance – in other words, being more in charge of your destiny and less dependent on the opinions and actions of others. Career planning is worth undertaking unless by nature you have a preference for high-risk gambling. Once your career plans are formulated you will need to review and audit them regularly to reflect changing job conditions, career opportunities or dangers.[10]

7 Weigh up your life balance.

Your career will be greatly enhanced if your life as a whole is in balance. Work towards establishing harmony between your job and the following important life areas: health, spiritual-mental well-being, finances, social recreation, and family lifestyle.

8 Focus on your effectiveness.

In your quest for building career equity, this asset is dependent on all of the other assets. As well, it also encompasses a wide range of components of your job including, for example, self management, interpersonal communication skills, leadership style, motivating others, time management, public speaking, chairing meetings, and so on.

Take the time to analyse your assets in each of the eight categories listed, and then search for ways to improve in each one. In a year's time, you will see that, not only will your effectiveness have been increased, but your career equity and promotional prospects will have been boosted as well.

 See also: 74, 82-84

How to model yourself on successful people

Successful people have three things in common – they know where they are now, they know where they want to be, and they move along that path daily. Their actions become the key determinants of their success. The accumulated messages of their biographies and autobiographies provide added insights into their personal qualities, offering a model for you to emulate as you set and chart your own path. Here are those qualities and the actions required...

1 Know where you're going.

Knowing where you're going is part of the success story. Although your vision will encounter setbacks (we're told envisioned futures usually have less than a 70 per cent chance of being achieved), visions help to transform possibilities into realities. As the saying goes, 'If you don't know where you're going, you'll finish up somewhere else.'

2 Believe in yourself.

Successful people believe in themselves, confident in the knowledge that they can achieve. Their actions broadcast that belief and provide freedom and power. They let nothing limit their potential. Positive affirmations can be effective means of reinforcing that belief.

3 Be open to opportunities.

Your openness to opportunities will ensure a continuing flow of them. Guard against negative thoughts and inaction limiting your potential to achieve. Some success stories indicate such an abundance of opportunities that choosing which ones to pursue is made very difficult. Spreading yourself and your resources too thinly must be avoided.

4 Set goals that challenge.

Successful people know that what they focus on grows, and goals help to provide the necessary focus and direction. Challenging goals bring out the best in people.

5 Accept responsibility.

Successful people don't blame others when things don't go as planned. The responsibility for the fulfilment of your dreams lies with you. The power to succeed – or to fail – is yours. And no one can take that away.

6 Build desire.

You have to want something badly enough to let nothing stand in your way of achieving it. But that does not suggest any recourse to aggression; many success stories depict quiet achievers. Desire helps to overcome seemingly insurmountable odds. Successful people, we're told, help to make things happen.

7 Demonstrate courage.

Courage is a special personal quality that helps you distinguish between what ought to be feared and what need not be feared. Though history's successful people have never backed away from any encounter that threatened their progress, they made certain they were around to 'fight another day'.

8 Learn from failure.

The law of failure is one of the most powerful of all the success laws because you only really fail when you stop trying – that's why successful people never fail. Setbacks simply provide them with essential feedback to help them chart their course.

9 Make honesty the best policy.

Cheats may prosper – but not for long. You will be called on daily to choose between honesty and dishonesty, and those choices contribute to your reputation. With honesty, there is no middle-ground; you can't be 'a little honest' or 'slightly dishonest'. You're either honest or dishonest.

10 Strive for excellence.

Achieving excellence is the pinnacle, and it's attained by few. Make sure you go beyond the call of duty, doing more than others expect. Excellence comes from striving higher, maintaining the highest standards, looking after the smallest detail, and going that extra mile. Successful people never compromise their standards.

Management Memo

A traveller in ancient Greece met an old man on the road and asked him how to get to Mt Olympus. The old man, who happened to be Socrates, replied, 'If you really want to get to Mt Olympus, just make sure that every step you take is in that direction.' [11]

11 Be persistent – and flexible.

The power to hold on in the face of adversity and the power to endure – these are the qualities of a winner. Persistence is the ability to face setbacks without losing sight of your destination. Persistence is the skill of doing everything necessary to reach your goals, including making adjustments based on the feedback received.

12 Take action.

Action combines all of your insights, experiences and talents into physical performance. If you've set your vision, selected opportunities, rallied your courage, determination and desire, it's time to act. Outlaw procrastination. Successful people know that without action nothing happens.

13 Love what you do.

Love is the most important ingredient of success. Successful people rarely make distinctions between work and many of their other activities: they do what they do because they love it. Sharing that passion with a select few makes all the effort worthwhile.

How to get the most out of networking

Networking is the process which exposes you to new people, new ideas, new ways of looking at things and, importantly, can increase your visibility and advance your career prospects. But the creation of this structure of valuable personal interrelationships won't just happen. You have to develop this network of organisational contacts for yourself – and here's how you can do just that...

1 Be aware of the benefits of networking.

Although networking can be a very time-consuming activity, its benefits can be very rewarding to you professionally. It can:

- help you learn from an increasing range of contacts with whom you can share ideas, advice, and strategies.
- provide you with referrals for a variety of needs. A good network will always know somebody who can help you.
- supply you with a sounding board to test your ideas, let off steam, provide feedback, or discuss problems.
- promote your career as you become known, aware, and involved.
- lessen your professional isolation, particularly if your organisation is located in a remote area.
- be enjoyable by giving you the chance to meet new colleagues, socialise, and expand your professional horizons.

2 Work to develop areas of personal expertise.

Networking presumes that members have competence and expertise, so develop your own skills and knowledge. Become a recognised authority on something, someone worth getting to know, so that you can become a vital member of the network.

3 Analyse your current network of contacts.

Examine your current network's viability. Check your address book, business cards, correspondence files, professional association contacts and phone index. Create an up-to-date flexible card index or computer data base on which to build.

4 Establish your own networking goals.

Aim to revitalise your network file over the next year. Set yourself such achievable goals as these:

- Meet at least two new professional contacts each month.
- Attend two major conferences this year.
- Join an organisation comprising local business and community leaders.
- Submit two articles to a professional journal over the coming year.
- Contact at least four colleagues on the network file every month...

5 Get out there, promote yourself, make contact.

The key to networking is to raise your visibility. Attend meetings, serve on committees, write for journals, speak to gatherings, become a spokesperson. Meet as many people as you can. Whenever you meet a potential network contact, widen the conversation and find out all you can about the person. The longest journey always begins with a first step, so find out and file all you can about people you meet.

6 Sell networking to others.

Encourage colleagues to network. Talk it over with them. Your own network will get stronger if all those in it develop active networks of their own.

7 Make sure networking benefits all parties.

As John Naisbitt wrote in *Megatrends*, 'In the network environment, rewards come by empowering others, not by climbing over them.' Networking is a two-way street. Self-centredness becomes quite transparent to network contacts. The more you can help your contacts, the more they will want to help you. Networking is 'giving without hooks', as Robyn Henderson says in *Networking for Success*.

8 Be an advocate of others.

Talk regularly to members in your network and, if someone has a need you cannot fulfil, offer to share a contact. You'll be doing both a favour, fulfilling the needs of one while providing an opportunity of another contact for the other. And you'll be strengthening the network itself.

Management Memo

Nothing can move your career further and faster than having a base of associates positioned to support you in your goals. Conversely, few things feel better than using your talents to help others achieve their goals. Once considered informal, unstructured and random, networking is now viewed as an essential way of developing professional relationships. It keeps you in touch by connecting you to new people and information. It is one of the highest forms of collaboration. [12]

9 Consider these important points also…

- *Touch base regularly with your contacts* – through phonecalls, letters, swapping articles of interest, socialising, meetings, and so on – doing so often enough to maintain the relationship.
- *Don't expect instant miracles.* Positive outcomes are often not immediately apparent. Rewarding professional relationships, formed through networking, develop over a period of time.
- *The key word is ASK.* If someone can't help you, ask if she/he can refer you to someone who might be able to help.
- *Swap business cards at every opportunity.* Jot down useful information about your new contact on the back of his/her card.
- *Thank everyone who helps you.* A written note of thanks will strengthen links and encourage others to think of you in future.

 See also: 28, 34, 36, 92, 172, 358

How to get yourself organised – and save time

Time is a constant. There are twenty-four hours in a day, no more, no less. The challenge is to maximise their use – and it's possible, provided you approach the issue methodically. All accomplishment in life, other than that which results by accident, passes through three stages – the goal, the plan, the action. By focusing on this sequence, you will be able to get yourself better organised to squeeze more out of those twenty-four hours each day...

1 Identify what is strategic – to you.

Know exactly why you're doing what you're doing. Identify strategic issues – the essentials of your job or the main reasons why you are employed in your current position and isolate them from those that are non-strategic. An excessive number, more than six, say, indicates you need to clarify your role description with the appropriate person. Free yourself of the non-strategic issues: eliminate or reduce them significantly – usually by delegating.

2 Set goals and detail actions.

Having identified the issues that are strategic to your personal operation, you need to be quite clear about the goals associated with each issue. If you want to achieve these goals you will need to determine specific actions to be undertaken with realistic timelines. Activities which block progress towards the completion of these goals should be reduced or eliminated. You'll find many 'urgent' jobs now assume a different priority in your life.

3 Plan your year, month, week and day.

Planning how to make the best use of your time is a form of project management. And, of course, the parts of your project over which you'll have most control are those relating to today and the next twenty-four hours. So, while being aware of the overall picture, it's your diary for the next two days which will be your immediate focus; it will be far more detailed than next month's diary. Though effective time management is more than diaries and to-do lists, both play a vital function in staying focused on the key issues, being aware of the value of time – and being organised.

4 Practise key management techniques.

If you are to be an organised operator, you must become an effective time manager by making such strategies as these part of your daily operating psyche:

- Prioritise your tasks and plan your time to deal with top priority items when you are at your best.
- Learn to say 'No'.

- Establish and stick to deadlines.
- Delegate non-strategic tasks.
- Avoid over-commitment by being realistic about what can be done in the time available to you.
- Make a habit of biting the bullet instead of procrastinating.
- Avoid butterfly behaviour, flitting from one job to the next, often finishing up where you started.
- Educate people that a closed door means 'no interruptions'.
- Keep an index card or notebook and pencil on hand at all times.
- Take a speed reading course.
- Find a hide-away area at home or at work where you can get important jobs finished without interruption.

Management Memo

In order to improve permanently your current level of productivity and, even more important, to provide a continuous acceleration of productivity, you must make the self-discipline necessary to make *getting more done* the most important thing in your business life for at least a year. True, one-shot or short-term improvement can be made merely by utilising some gimmick or putting to work one single idea, but this is like a ripple compared with a tide. [13]

5 Use time-saving devices.

Keep yourself organised by keeping up with the technological and office management advances on offer. Telecommunications devices such as faxes, pagers, laptops, e-mail, mobile phones, and computer software, commercial time management diaries, even courier services, for example, provide opportunities for you to achieve more in less time. You can't afford not to be up-to-date on innovative management technology.

6 Be prepared when travelling – and waiting.

Although new technologies such as laptops and audio cassettes help to maximise the time available to you when travelling and waiting, the reading of books, articles and reports is still one of the most reliable means of getting information. Your time is too valuable to flip through the 'old' news and irrelevant literature on planes and in reception areas. Organise yourself now – how will you use those idle moments while driving, travelling or waiting? What reading matter will you put in your briefcase or glovebox – just in case.

7 Organise your work space.

Time management researcher Merrill Douglass confessed that he logged two-and-a-half hours daily looking for information on the top of his desk! If you want to save time, a key is to keep your work place organised. Pay attention to its location (e.g. away from interruptions) comfort and space; have your work tools readily accessible; fight that cluttered desk; establish a workable filing system; stick to one project at a time and clear your desk of the rest; and get a large wastepaper basket.

8 Don't worry.

Most of the things we worry about are unfounded and we have no control over much of the rest. So focus your efforts on the few things you *can* do something about. Live a happier, more productive life by disciplining yourself to change the few things you can and accept the many that you can't. Think of the time you'll save!

See also: 26

How to tackle your priorities

Setting priorities is a decision-making process in which you rank in order of importance the tasks you or your staff members must do. By completing the tasks on your list in order, you will achieve your goals. It sounds easy – but it's not. In fact, priority setting and sticking to the agreement you make with yourself will be one of your major challenges as a manager. Here are ten important suggestions to help you draw up a priority list – and make it work...

1 Address management problems first.

Give top priority to any problem on your list that is making you ineffective as a manager. If, for example, you have a personal conflict with your superior or your personal assistant, your effectiveness in dealing with other priorities could be seriously hampered. Face such problems immediately, get them out in the open and devise a solution quickly.

2 Group your priorities meaningfully.

It is sometimes possible to put your daily goals into a priority pattern that saves time and effort. For example, by postponing an inspection of new equipment in the factory block across the parking lot until after lunch, you might find that you're able to do this following a scheduled mid-afternoon meeting with the factory supervisor. You may even be able to accomplish a couple more of your goals for the day during that one trip. Forward planning brings its rewards.

3 Do it – or remove it.

Don't let an item become an irritation to you. If a task has been on your priority list for a long time, handle it immediately or drop it from the list. If it has to be done, do it. If not, get rid of it and make room for something more important.

4 Resist chopping and changing.

Jumping back and forth from one priority to another will get you nowhere. If you start something and keep switching to something else, you will lose motivation. If a task is near the top of your list, it's worth completing. Management consultant Ivy Lee's often repeated advice to US industrialist Charles Schwab is relevant here: 'Dig right in on priority job number one and stick to it until it's done. Tackle job number two in the same way; then number three and so on. Don't worry if you only finish one or two by the end of the day – you'll be concentrating on the most urgent ones.'

5 Balance your priorities.

However, by focusing on a major, very time-consuming task which you have listed at or near the top of your list, you can sometimes neglect the others, resulting in further problems in the long run. Keep *all* your priorities in mind to stop this happening.

Ivy Lee's advice – to stick at priority number one until it's completed – may well be wise counsel for some managers, but it pays to be flexible in focusing on your top priorities.

6 Reassign the priorities when necessary.

When a task proves to be so difficult that an immediate solution is not possible, you may be compelled to take more time to consider the facts and options. Drop it down the list where you can watch it but not forget it.

7 Follow up on your priorities.

Check on a daily basis to see that your priority tasks were actually completed and assess their achievement. Only when you're satisfied can you then confidently remove them from your list.

8 Confront those difficult tasks head-on.

Don't lower a high priority task just because you're afraid to face it. Playing for time doesn't solve problems. Your priority list will not serve you well unless you are honest with yourself and put the important though difficult things first. Once more, remind yourself of Ivy Lee's advice.

Management Memo

Do the important things first. Give the greatest and most immediate attention to the most important jobs. If you've got to take the heat because something isn't done, at least make sure it's minor. You want to be known as someone who always comes through on the big ones. That's where you make your reputation – not by accomplishing lots of little things that don't matter much. [14]

9 Communicate all vital information.

If one of the tasks on your priority list requires communication throughout the workplace or office, for example, then it should receive special treatment. Delaying such action could result in even more problems being added to your list.

10 Accept that you will always have a priority list.

Whenever you complete a task, another will appear to take its place. As a manager, that's what your job is all about. If your list gets too short, then you're simply not sufficiently involved in the life of your organisation.

How to keep paperwork from accumulating

Does your desk sometimes look like a cluttered mailroom? Do you then go on a neatness spree – only to watch the untidy stacks of paper mount up once again so that, in the following week or two, you have to clean up all over again? Some managers have a constant swirl of paper on their desks and assume that somehow the most important documents will float to the top. If you are being smothered in the paper avalanche, then here are some useful ideas which may prove to be your salvation…

1 Adopt a system to process your paperwork.

The key to managing the paper war is to develop an effective processing strategy. It is essential to find a structured system that will work for you – and to stick with it.

For example, the DRAFT system could be considered. Here, all incoming papers are sorted into one of the following five categories:

Delegation pile. Use routing or action slips to refer these items to staff members better equipped than you to respond.
Reading pile. Put the journals, articles and updates into a pile ready to grab when heading off to a dental appointment or the bus or for the weekend.
Action pile. These items will require a personal response from you in the form of a written reply, an analysis, a draft report, a decision. Sub-divide this pile into 'top priority' and 'lower priority' tasks.
Filing pile. Into a 'filing box' place all papers that need to be assigned to the office files for future reference.
Toss pile. Junk mail and throw-away items are destined for the wastepaper basket. If you are unsure of what to dump, ask: what's the worst thing that would happen if I tossed it? Will someone be calling me later about this? Is there a duplicate elsewhere? If you feel it is impossible to decide on dumping immediately, keep the flyers and catalogues in a separate file to be browsed in one quick sitting each week before discarding, filing or delegating.

2 Never handle a piece of paper twice.

The important thing is to sort all incoming papers in your in-basket as part of a regular daily routine by handling each item once – moving each from your desk to a delegation folder, to a read-later stack, to an action tray, to a file-later box, or to the wastepaper basket. (In reality, the goal should be to try to handle a document a maximum of only twice – once on sorting it into the relevant pile, and, in some instances, once when resolving it.)

3 Enlist your assistant's help if possible.

Your secretary or clerk can save you

much time by sorting your incoming paperwork for you, by having them handle the less significant items as a matter of routine, by filing routine papers before they reach you, by highlighting the essential elements of the documents, and by routing the material appropriately after sorting.

4 Develop skimming skills.

Move those papers across your desk promptly. Learn to skim background information so that you get an overall understanding of material without loitering. Consider a speed reading course. Take time to read in detail only priority documents.

5 Allocate a set time each day for paperwork.

Form the habit of processing paperwork at the same time every day if possible. Such discipline combats procrastination and prevents the choking of your in-basket. For example, 30 minutes of quiet time at the beginning of a day or after hours will send you home with a feeling of having accomplished much.

6 Screen unnecessary paper.

Have your name removed from mailing lists that provide you continually with junk mail. Cancel subscriptions to newsletters, magazines and catalogues that no longer serve a useful purpose. Cut down on photocopier use. Train your secretary to handle paper that does not require your personal attention. Work hard to stop the flow. Do you really need all those 'for your information' copies from staff?

Management Memo

Paper mismanagement can cripple your ability to function effectively... The real cause of a paperwork crisis is a problem with decision-making: picking up the same piece of paper five times and putting it down again because you can't decide what to do with it. It is curious but true that many executives who are experienced in making major decisions feel stymied by individual pieces of paper. [15]

7 Focus on your action file.

Developing a workable paperflow system, like DRAFT, is essential but, in personal terms, it's your action file that counts in the long run. How can you ensure that you keep it to a manageable size? Here are a few suggestions:

- Use a priority list.
- Explore time-saving options: form letters, form paragraphs, compliments slips, handwritten replies directly on to incoming correspondence, tickler files…
- Use the telephone or e-mail. It's faster and cheaper than mail.
- Make margin notes on incoming mail and have your assistant draft your reply.
- Ask that every report over three pages in length carry a cover page summary.
- Periodically check on the reports or bulletins you prepare – Who reads them? Are they of any use? Should you persist?
- Spotlight your tardiness. Mark a document with a red dot each time you handle it but fail to take action. Allow three dots – but no more.

How to use the telephone effectively – and save time

The telephone is an essential part of management life. The phone means business. Even though it is one of the most effective time-saving tools, it is potentially one of the biggest time-wasters as well. So, to derive maximum benefit from the telephone, without becoming a time slave to it, you'll need to gain control over it – and here's how you can…

1 Explore all available technologies.

Review regularly the technological advances made within the telecommunications industry. Such advances provide opportunities to save you time while improving efficiencies. Voicemail, message bank, fax, call redirection, conference calls, call waiting, e-mail, and the Internet are just a few examples worth exploring. And the good news is that the competition among providers not only guarantees expanded technologies but also increasingly competitive rates for users.

2 Adopt screening procedures.

Many incoming calls can be dealt with more effectively by others – your personal assistant, secretary, associate, or clerical assistant. Appropriately trained personnel should follow procedures that

- ascertain the purpose of the call,
- decide the person best situated to deal with it,
- redirect the call where necessary and, when the required information is not immediately available,
- commit to a specific turn-round time for a response.

Screening calls should not only save you time but also provide services more responsive to customers' needs.

3 Discipline yourself to keep calls brief.

Limit the length of your calls by considering the following techniques:

- Use an egg timer to remind you of a three- or six-minute maximum limit.
- Stand up when you make a call, and sit down only after you hang up.
- Use a stop watch to help you measure time taken for individual calls – you'll soon identify those people who take most of your time. Having done that, consider communicating with such people via a brief memo or e-mail – you could save lots of time.
- Make your calls when people are less likely to chat, such as just before lunch or near closing time.

4 Plan your outgoing calls.

The following system puts you in control:

- List calls to be made during the day.
- Place the calls in priority order – at

> **Management Memo**
>
> The telephone has been described by a sociologist as the greatest nuisance among conveniences and the greatest convenience among nuisances. [16]

least you'll have completed the important ones if you run out of time.

- Write a brief outline for each call, including what you want to say or the information you are seeking.
- Have any essential reference material close at hand.
- Set aside a specific period of the day for making the calls.
- Get to the point quickly, introducing yourself and the purpose for the call in the first sentence.
- Conclude the conversation promptly and courteously.

5 Develop techniques to keep all calls to the point.

Business calls are not the place for unnecessary chitchat.

- Your basic rule should be: don't contribute to a conversation that's not going anywhere; the caller will soon get to the point. Make your business calls, business calls.
- For incoming calls: 'Good morning, Sandy, how can I help you?' or 'Good afternoon, Sandy. I have three minutes before a scheduled meeting with my key staff. Go for it…'. In other words, make the caller get to the point quickly.
- For outgoing calls: 'Good morning, Sandy, if you have the time, I need two quick answers…' or 'Can we make a telephone date, Sandy. I have a break at 2.30 for ten minutes. I want to talk about… Can I call you then?'
- Adopt courteous strategies for terminating long-winded callers. For example, interrupt to say you have people waiting at the door for a scheduled meeting starting in two minutes. Or, when you're desperate, hang up in mid-sentence while *you* are talking.

6 Use your head when returning calls.

Your assistant, voicemail, or other message bank will have calls that must be answered. Allowing calls to bunch for several hours before returning them is an efficient approach. Knowing the technologies adopted by the person whose call you are returning allows even greater flexibility. You may, for example, return a call to that person's voicemail after business hours. When you don't want people to call you back, leave complete messages. When you want your calls returned, leave messages that will encourage them to do so.

7 Don't play games on the phone.

Refuse to play ping-pong or tag over the phone. If you are unable to reach the person, find out *when* she/he will be in – even make a telephone date, to avoid further futile attempts. Or if you return a client's call and she/he's out, let the secretary know when you'll be available to take a call.

8 Check that you're not causing calls.

Do your letters, brochures, and so on. lack sufficient information – and thus prompt phone calls? People who are uncertain of whom to ring usually start at the top – so are the titles of your staff members available and do they reflect clearly their functions?

9 Organise a phone-free hour for yourself.

Organise your day so that you have an hour to work free from all interruptions – including the phone!

How to put an end to procrastination

Procrastination is one of the main reasons why we don't perform to our full potential. It is a comfortable human habit and, as such, is not easy to break. However, if you allow procrastination to become a deeply entrenched behaviour pattern, it can wreck your personal effectiveness and, in turn, the effectiveness of your organisation. Here are a dozen simple techniques which have been successfully used by people over the years to beat procrastination. Through application, you can discover which will work best for you...

1 The priorities plan

If you are forced into procrastination beyond your control – because there are just too many tasks and so little time – do the important things first. Prioritise and give greatest and immediate attention to the most pressing jobs.

2 The divide-and-conquer strategy

If you are procrastinating because of the sheer awesomeness of the task, the key is to break it up into smaller, manageable components. Once you start accumulating small victories, you'll be well on your way. This is the approach advocated by management experts Edwin Bliss – the 'Salami Technique', because you slice up the task like a salami, and Alan Lakein – the 'Swiss Cheese Method', because you punch small holes in the big job.

3 The killer-punch plan

The divide-and-conquer strategy won't work if your problem is that you keep putting off a one-shot task like returning a phone call, firing a worker or writing a thank-you note. The killer punch is needed for that specific task which can only be accomplished in one hit. There *is* only one solution. Get it off your plate immediately. Act now.

4 The ten-minute treatment

Take the task you've been procrastinating over and resolve to spend ten minutes a day on it. After your first ten whole-hearted minutes, reconsider. If you put it aside until tomorrow, okay. Chances are, however, you'll realise that the job isn't all that dreadful and you'll have gained enough momentum to go beyond the planned ten minutes.

5 The bribe-yourself technique

Promise yourself a reward for getting the job done by a certain deadline. Bribe yourself with new clothes, a night out, a walk along the beach. But don't cheat yourself by accepting your bribe *before* you've finished, for that will only reinforce your procrastination.

6 The post-a-sign strategy

Display a small or large sign at work or home with a message to remind you of the job to be done (preferably where it will annoy your colleague or spouse so that she/he can pressure you as well). Such a reminder will make it harder for the 'out of sight, out of mind' principle to operate.

> **Management Memo**
>
> The key to overcoming procrastination is to just get started. In fact, within a few minutes of working on a project, you generally get your second wind. Runners, for instance, know that the first mile is always harder than the second. Getting past the barrier to your second wind is what overcoming procrastination is all about, because that's when you're warmed up, you've found your rhythm and you're working at peak efficiency.[17]

7 The do-nothing method

Do nothing for 15 minutes, nothing but stare at and think about the job at hand. According to Alan Lakein, 'you should become very uneasy – and after 10 minutes, you'll fire and be off and running'.

8 The see-it-all-done approach

We procrastinate when we cannot anticipate achievement. Calano and Salzman recommend this exercise if you're having trouble getting started:

> Close your eyes and relax… Imagine that you have just finished your project, done a terrific job, and are basking in the good feeling of having achieved another goal. In your vision, focus on every process you went through to complete the task: the details, the hang-ups, the breakthroughs. Concentrate particularly on the elation of realising your reward.

Such visualisation, they say, makes any task seem less intimidating.

9 The lock-away technique

Perhaps as a busy manager your problem is simply that you'll need to isolate yourself from interruption for a couple of hours to get a difficult job done. If that's the case, tell people about your problem and lock yourself away from others for the required period.

10 The monitoring manoeuvre

For those lengthy and seemingly overwhelming tasks, take a colleague into your confidence, not to do the job for you but to have a trusted friend to talk over the task with, to provide support, to check on progress, and to nudge you gently, and often, towards the deadline.

11 The go-public tactic

Motivate yourself negatively by committing yourself publicly to a deadline – to avoid embarrassment, you'll get the job done, or lose face. And if you want both an incentive for reaching your goal or a penalty for falling short, make a R50 bet with a colleague.

12 The peak performance time routine

Do your toughest jobs at that time of day when you are most alert, rested and energised. Or at an unusual time for you, e.g. set the alarm for 4.30 a.m. to work for an hour drafting that difficult letter you keep putting off.

How to use diaries and calendars effectively

Every manager should use a time planner... diary, day book, appointment calendar, daily organiser – call it what you will. Although effective time management is primarily a matter of personal discipline and willpower, time planners can help you make that daily battle with time less onerous. Here are a few guidelines to get you thinking about how to make best use of those essential management tools – diaries and calendars...

1 Know what a diary should be.

Pocket or desk diaries and calendars are the traditional 'appointment books' – but they are tools which ought to be used for more than recording appointments. They require enough space to list one day's appointments and, on the same page opening, enough room for extensive comments on the planning or recording of the day's work: telephone calls, reminders, meeting notes, goals, ideas, lists, happenings. Your diary should become a written record of events, thoughts and plans, a book you will want to keep dipping into, a basic tool you will not want to be without.

2 Be aware of how a diary can help you.

If you have any doubts as to a diary's value to you as a busy manager, then consider how it can:

- reduce your stress by minimising the incidence of forgotten appointments, overlooked telephone messages, broken promises and procrastination.
- enable you to summon incidents and ideas without resorting to memory.
- increase self-confidence and control because all the key aspects of your work are recorded in the one handy location.
- remind you that time has both an economic *and* a spiritual value.

If you intend to become an effective time manager, then you'll need a workable diary or calendar for daily use.

3 Choose your diary thoughtfully.

A survey by the US magazine *Business Week* found that effective managers look for certain qualities in their diaries and calendars. They prefer:

- a 'planner' format rather than a simple diary. For them, a diary is more than an appointment book; it's a planning tool.
- a diary that lies flat. It should lie open on a desk, without the help of hands.
- a diary with a time management section. They believe that a 'proper' planner can help them manage time.
- a diary with aesthetic appeal. It's a personal tool. It says something about the user, and they want to look good in front of others.
- a range of features, including a double-ribbon bookmark, to keep the

place in two locations; quarter-hour time subdivisions; simple uncluttered layout; and usable forward planning components.

What features do you require in a diary/planner?

4 Investigate the purchase of a commercial time management system.

For the ultimate in diaries, consider a commercial time planner. These are essentially diaries with enhancements. They literally organise your work life – if used correctly. In essence, you buy into a refined system of planning paraphernalia. Pages in the six-ring binders can be added or deleted and there is often a wide range of models from pocket to desk-top versions. You can, in effect, customise your organiser using a variety of page formats – daily schedules, to-do lists, appointments, delegations, new ideas, project planners, meeting agendas, expense sheets, blank and lined pages, directories, forward planners, and so on. Various systems are available, each with its own advantages.

Quality organisers are not cheap, however. But, as Robert McGarvey, writes in *As Time Goes By*:

> 'Sift through the rigmarole associated with any organiser, and ultimately the indispensable key is to use it. Write down all appointments, phone calls that must be made, and chores – half of what any organiser provides is the freeing of your mind from the job of remembering little details that are better committed to paper and forgotten until needed. Do all this and, say users, the systems will shortly pay for themselves.'

Management Memo

A well maintained diary, given the nature of life and time, is anything but systematic or neat: it is full of tentative plans, plans replanned, crossings-out, scribbled ideas and items suddenly remembered. The only diary system worth having has simplicity and flexibility; even then, it will be no more than a tool of time management. More important by far is a realistic attitude to planning... [18]

5 Make your diary work for you.

Your diary/planner/calendar can become a most powerful time management tool if you remember these points:

- At the beginning of the year, enter the important dates, e.g. staff meetings, product launches, conferences, vacations.
- Always break activities into time blocks, with a beginning – *and* an end. Time management problems are often caused by those fuzzy end-times.
- Don't allow the entire day to be booked out. Leave some spare time to accommodate unexpected interruptions and this will reduce messy reschedulings or cancellations.
- Avoid scheduling yourself too tightly. The pressure to finish one task or meeting in time to begin another cuts down on your effectiveness.
- Be sure to schedule time for rest, lunch and relaxation. Error rates and stress increase with lack of rest.
- Block in time to complete important projects. Schedule enough time to build up momentum.
- Always allocate important tasks to the beginning of a day.
- Schedule long-winded callers at strategic times – just before lunch or quitting time.
- Ensure that the diary/planner you use can be carried with you at all times.

How to become a better decision-maker

Decision-making is an inescapable task for managers. In the eyes of staff members, it is the managers who must take the final responsibility for decisions and, each year, they are required to make literally thousands of them, large and small. In the end, it is the quality of those decisions that determines the success of a manager's efforts. If you want to become a quality decision-maker, particularly when the 'big' decisions count, then these guidelines will help...

1 Adopt a systematic approach.

Decision-making is actually part of problem-solving: there would be no decision to make if there were no problem to solve. Decision-making is that component of the problem-solving process that follows analysis of the problem and is followed in turn by action to carry out the decision. The problem-solving process outlined on page 354 could well be used in arriving at major decisions.

2 Focus on important decisions.

Try not to spend too much time on small matters. It's the important decisions that must receive your full attention. Deciding who should fill the hot water urn each morning is of less importance than a decision about the focus of the new marketing strategy. Importance is determined by asking such questions as: How close is the deadline? What are the consequences of a poor decision? Who is affected by the decision? Is the decision reversible?

3 Avoid making snap decisions.

Spur-of-the-moment decisions are often merely guesses. Quantity can be no substitute for quality. Impetuous decisions could lead to a serious logjam of niggling problems. On the other hand...

4 Don't become a victim of analysis paralysis.

Limitations of time and resources do not allow for a thorough analysis of all issues, so don't drag your feet. By putting off a decision, you only add to an already overflowing agenda of unfinished business.

5 Base your decision on facts.

A decision is no better than the data upon which it is based. Have all the facts at your disposal. Improve your information search by asking yourself such questions as: What facts do I have? What else do I need to know? Whom should I ask? What should I ask? What printed material is available?

6 Don't be afraid of making the wrong decision.

There is a risk involved in every decision. No one is blessed with infinite wisdom. Ask yourself, what is the worst thing that can happen if I have made the wrong choice? Rarely is a disaster the consequence! A readiness to risk failure is a quality that characterises all good decision-makers.

7 Learn from your mistakes.

If your decision is later shown to be the wrong one, find out where you went wrong. Seek advice from others. Did you neglect or under-emphasise any problem-solving steps listed on page 354?

8 Use your imagination.

A logical decision is not always the best answer in all situations. Be prepared to use brainstorming techniques, analogies, and lateral thinking in your search for a new approach to the problem at hand. Use the technique that best fits the problem.

9 Resist making decisions under stress.

When you have to make a decision under crisis conditions, stand back from the problem and consider the situation. For example, you may not have to make an immediate decision. Use all the time available to ensure the best response. Avoid impulse decisions. If you are angry or upset, delay your response. Decisions made under stress can be faulty.

Management Memo

A decision is a judgement. It is a choice between alternatives. It is rarely a choice between right and wrong. It is at best a choice between almost right and probably wrong – but much more often a choice between two courses of action neither of which is probably more nearly right than the other... The best decisions emerge from a clash of conflicting points of view. One does not make a decision without disagreements... Decisions are made by men (sic). Men are fallible; at their best their works do not last long. Even the best decision has a high probability of being wrong. Even the most effective one eventually becomes obsolete.[19]

10 Make your decision, then move on.

Banish past decisions from your mind or you'll lose the capacity to give your full and undivided attention to the more pressing and important needs of the present.

11 And don't forget as well...

- View decision-making as a valuable opportunity for your professional growth.
- Ask: What would someone else do in my circumstances? Seek help from others, journals, or reference books.
- Refer to existing policies whenever possible: decisions can often be straightforward and immediate.
- Periodically review the results of your decisions to check that they worked.
- Discuss with your colleagues decisions that will affect other people – but assume the responsibility yourself for the final decision.

See also: 42-46, 236-238, 362-364

How to prepare for a meeting

It was Hendrik van Loon who once said that a meeting will only be successful if it has three participants – one of whom is off sick and another who is absent. Organisational life is never that generous to managers, however. Meetings have become an unavoidable aspect of a manager's role. Fortunately, it is possible to eliminate unnecessary meetings and to make the remaining ones more effective. An important ingredient is planning and preparation, as the following points reveal...

1 Make sure you've called the meeting for a reason.

Meetings should never become a ritual. They cost time and money so it's important to call a meeting *only* when one is warranted – to solve a problem, to coordinate activities, to disseminate and discuss urgent information, to reach a consensus or decision, to build morale, to reconcile conflicts. So don't ask people to attend a listening session only – send a memo or newsletter instead.

2 Prepare a benchmark of productivity.

Be clear on the purposes of the meeting and your hoped-for outcomes. And how will you know when you have achieved them? By preparing a 'benchmark of productivity' for the meeting – a checklist of what you want to accomplish, to refer to during the meeting and for use later to compare the hoped-for outcomes with the actual achievements.

3 Select the participants wisely.

Only those who need to attend should be invited to do so. Each non-essential attendee is wasting his/her time and costing your organisation money. As well, the more people attending, the more difficult it is to achieve a consensus. Consider inviting participants to be present at a particular time, that is, for the agenda item for which their personal contribution is required.

4 Select the right time and place for the meeting.

Call a meeting only when you have the information required for decision-making and you can be assured that the appropriate people will be in attendance. Ensure the venue is accessible to all participants, yet sufficiently remote to avoid interruptions. Check out and book the location – seating, lighting, ventilation, whiteboards, electrical requirements and other essentials.

5 Prepare and distribute an agenda that will work.

The more care you take with an agenda, the more productive the meeting will be. The agenda should be more than just a list of items handed out at the meeting. Key elements would include:

- date, time, place and duration of meeting
- list of items to be discussed in sequence, detailing for each item who will lead the discussion, time allocated and, importantly, the objective (information-sharing/ discussion only/decision required/ problem to be solved, etc.).

6 Despatch agenda and background papers.

By giving adequate advance notice and distributing the agenda and support documents for all items, you will demonstrate your thoroughness and instil confidence in your leadership. (Remember, people being what people are, to allow time at the beginning of your meeting for 'review' of documents you realise may not have been read in advance.)

7 Do your homework on the participants.

If emotional or controversial issues, for example, are to be discussed during the meeting, it is sometimes a good idea to talk through these items with some of the key participants beforehand. Consider their reactions and how you might handle them during the meeting to achieve the desired outcomes.

8 Gather appropriate tools for the meeting.

Make sure you have considered the following items frequently required during a meeting: notepaper, pens, flip chart, whiteboard, refreshments, overhead projector, telephone, tape recorder, and so on.

> **Management Memo**
>
> Conducting a meeting without a plan is much like trying to build a house without blueprints. It can be done, of course, but the end result is likely to be less than desirable and the process can be expensive and nerve-wracking.[20]

9 Be prepared – psychologically.

Mental preparation is also a vital consideration and, in this regard, the following suggestions are offered:

- *Know the meeting process and your role as the chairperson.* Understand the rules of the game before you play – whether these be formal rules of order involving motions, voting, adjournments, etc., or unofficial rules developed by your own organisation for meeting procedures.
- *Do your homework.* Be prepared and knowledgeable about the topics under discussion.
- *Believe you can lead.* If you have been called upon to lead, someone believes you can do it. So be confident yourself that you can.
- *Seize the opportunity.* Responsibility requires extra effort. Give it – and grow in the position.
- *Aim high.* Strive for excellence, set the example, and others will follow.

How to conduct a successful meeting

Every manager needs to be able to master the skills of chairing a meeting. A meeting chaired effectively will have the participants leaving with a sense of accomplishment and a clear understanding of future direction and tasks. If you want to conduct successful meetings as chairperson, here are the important steps in the process you should follow…

1 Start on time.

When you wait for latecomers, you penalise those who have arrived on time – and you inadvertently reward those who come late. Before long, everyone will arrive late. So, how do you get people to your meetings on time? By starting on time! Always.

2 Get the meeting off to a business-like start.

Welcome and introduce yourself and the other participants and, if necessary, explain their roles. Clarify the objectives of the meeting, ensuring that each member understands the task at hand and is aware of the expertise available in the group. Be brisk and business-like.

3 Preview and confirm the agenda.

Check that each member publicly agrees with the stated objective of each listed agenda item, thereby ensuring that all irrelevant and hidden agendas become redundant. Indicate the criteria for a successful meeting and, in particular, how the group will decide or know when the outcomes are achieved. Other items might be suggested and, after listing these in 'Other Business', close off the agenda.

4 Focus continually on your objectives.

A meeting is held for a purpose – so keep its main objectives and desired outcomes clearly in mind at all times. Consider the following process:

- *Initiate discussion on each item* by setting the scene briefly and asking for responses. You may refer the matter first to a member who can make the best initial contribution.
- *Reinforce each item.* When moving on to a new agenda item, reiterate and clarify its purpose and objective.
- *Clarify issues.* If debate leads to confusion, it's your task to unravel the strands so that a decision can be reached.
- *Summarise regularly.* Particularly during the lengthy discussion of an item, summarise progress

periodically to maintain a sense of direction.

- *Clarify the decision-making process beforehand.* If people aren't sure about whether a decision has been made or, if it has, by what means, then conflict and poor productivity will result.
- *Conclude discussion* of an item by summarising. When you sense consensus on major points, these should be tested with the group, voted upon if necessary, and recorded. Resist the temptation to try to force people into agreement in order to tidy up discussions.
- *When a decision has been made*, be clear on what the decision is and how it will be implemented. Assign responsibilities and set deadlines for action.
- *If an issue can't be resolved*, find out why, and appoint a task group or individual to investigate and report back to the next meeting.

5 End on a positive note – and on time.

Try to end on a positive note, even when there has been substantial disagreement during the meeting – perhaps save for last an agenda item on which everyone can agree. Respect the plans of those who assumed the meeting would end on time. This will mean bringing discussion to a halt about five minutes before the scheduled finishing time. Sum up the entire meeting, restate the outcomes, confirm allotted tasks and deadlines, and thank participants. Arrange the next meeting time with members.

Management Memo

Basically, there are three types of Chair: (1) the authoritarian, who conducts meetings like military drills and wonders why nothing very original is ever said or achieved in them; (2) the permissive, who lets the members run the meetings, and wonders why so many of them end in chaos; and (3) the majority, who are a little of both and who wonder why other people's meetings seem more effective than their own. This is because being an effective Chair does not come naturally. It requires certain skills, but the good news is that these skills can be learnt and they can be improved with practise. [21]

6 Review and analyse the success of your meeting.

While the meeting is still fresh in your mind, it is important to assess the meeting's effectiveness and your own leadership style. Use that information to make your next meeting better.

7 Follow-up promptly.

Concise minutes, including a listing of decisions made, the tasks assigned, and the deadlines for action and follow-up, should be completed and distributed promptly. Where necessary, inform other interested parties of outcomes as soon as possible after the meeting.

In the period following the meeting, monitor the progress of assignments if possible. At the next meeting, uncompleted assignments should be considered first and unmet deadlines discussed. Such accountability helps ensure that the agreed outcomes of your meeting have some meaning next time.

How to get the most out of meetings you chair

Good meetings have leadership; bad meetings do not. The success of a meeting will depend largely on your ability as chairperson to get things done efficiently and to reach group decisions in minimum time. The following strategies will help you conduct a successful meeting. Directly or indirectly, they all point to the one goal – ensuring that the meeting achieves its purpose...

1 Create a member-centred meeting.

A dominant chairperson will stifle a meeting. As chairperson, your primary job is to release the expertise of the group. This means you should refrain from voicing your opinions until everyone has had a chance to be heard – good ideas are lost when meeting members are reluctant to contradict or disagree with a manager who has already stated a position. Know your own biases and be prepared to handle contributions that may violate them. Be persuasive but not overly partisan. Be seen by all to have a balanced approach.

2 Encourage participation by all.

Make sure everyone has an equal chance to express a view. Allow no single member to monopolise, and avoid calling on the same speakers, even though they may be the most experienced, knowledgeable and eloquent. Encourage different points of view. Defend the weak against the strong. Tactfully draw out the reticent members by asking them for their opinions or comments.

3 Stimulate discussion and ideas.

A good meeting should be an exchange of ideas and information, and it is the chairperson's role to foster this exchange through probing and the use of open-ended questions:

- to clarify issues: 'Are you saying you can provide this material by the end of the week?'
- to restate certain points: 'So let's confirm this point...'
- to confront issues: 'Are we really prepared to...?'
- to question critically: 'What exactly do you mean by...?'
- to seek solutions: 'What should we do?', 'What do you think?', 'Why?'.

4 Ban those killer comments.

Crushing comments can kill enthusiasm and the flow of ideas. Treating a group member or a comment as uninformed, naive, or inferior, will suppress discussion. Monitor and disallow such put-downs as 'That won't work', 'You're joking', and 'You'll learn in time'. Instead, supportive comments should be encouraged: 'Let's follow that notion through a little…', 'Would anyone care to build on or refine that suggestion?', or 'I'd like to expand on that idea by looking at it from another angle…'.

5 Keep the meeting on course.

Many meetings lose themselves through side-tracking or by getting bogged down on one issue. Some wandering may be useful but it is frequently necessary to call the group back to the main topic at hand. Keep rambling speakers in check.

As well, be on the lookout for potential trouble. Deal with conflict, hostility and tension when it begins to appear. Create harmony by mediating differences. Use humour or call for a break at the right time to ease tension.

Keep an eye on the clock. Keep the meeting on the move. Respect the participants' personal schedules: aim to finish on time.

6 Vary your style.

The key to chairing a meeting is flexibility. You will be a good chairperson if you assess the kind of leadership that the meeting requires, then adjust your style accordingly. Be sensitive to the mood of the meeting – when to be relaxed, when to be firm, when to use humour, when to break. Each style exhibits effective leadership if it is right for the occasion.

7 Focus on the process.

Control the meeting by sticking to the agenda. Keep discussion to time limits, but allow adequate time to treat complex issues. Stop and clarify issues if they become obscure. Summarise from time to time to demonstrate progress. Monitor loss of attention. Watch for signs that an item has been discussed enough, finalise it, and move to the next item. Break up into small groups if this assists in reaching your desired outcomes more efficiently.

Management Memo

Good meeting planning is essential for having consistently good meetings. The other half of the meeting leader's responsibility consists of successfully managing the 'human energy' *during* the meeting.

The style of leadership the leader chooses is always an influencing factor. One may run meetings in the traditional fashion, like a captain running a ship, giving orders and taking full command. Another may prefer to view the leadership role as a subtle facilitator who is at the service of the group.

The concept of leadership has been changing rapidly in recent decades. It was once recommended that the leader be the master and controller of the group. Now it is more common for the meeting leader to be a manager and facilitator whose primary function is to foster a democratic and cooperative group process among participants. [22]

8 And finally…

- Take steps to ensure the meeting is not interrupted unless in an emergency.
- Be the first in the room and use this time to establish rapport with members.
- Start and finish on time.
- Remember to thank members after they make a contribution, and at the conclusion of the meeting.
- Always set the example. Be firm, polite, calm, business-like, supportive, even-handed and confident.

How to make a valuable contribution to a meeting

As a member of a committee or working party, or as a participant in a one-off meeting, you will have an excellent opportunity to influence decision-making and to make your talents known and available to the organisation. You can attend a meeting – or you can be a participant. Whether solving problems or pooling ideas, a meeting in which you are involved can be productive for you and the organisation, depending on how you act and what real contribution you make...

1 Understand why you have been asked to participate.

Ask yourself the following questions:

- Have I been brought in simply to fill a gap?
- Am I representing a department or section or specialist group?
- Have I been brought in to provide expertise or competence in a particular area?
- Am I here as the organisation's 'bright young person' with ideas?
- Am I here as the voice of experience, the steadying influence?

When you can answer such questions, you can channel your efforts appropriately.

2 Know the other participants.

Find out all you can about the other participants – their likes and dislikes, strong and weak points, the power brokers, the way they operate, and how they react to new ideas and proposals. Knowing this, you can adopt effective tactics for dealing with them.

3 Arrive prepared.

Prepare yourself by studying the agenda and all working papers in advance. Focus on items for your particular attention and anticipate any needs the group will have for data you can bring. Prepare for your involvement by compiling handouts or charts, working up suggestions or recommendations, and making notes from which to speak if required. You may choose to canvass the views of influential participants beforehand. The amount of preparation you do will determine how others view you – as a passenger or valued participant. Plan in advance to make at least one specific contribution.

4 Arrive early and use the time wisely.

Arrive early and take the opportunity if necessary to introduce yourself to other participants. Use the waiting time profitably, perhaps learning their position on certain agenda items. If possible, get a seat close to the chairperson – you'll get more involved and you'll be noticed.

5 Talk up, get involved.

Don't hesitate to get into the act. A

well-chosen question can often help to break the ice. Then you can enter into the discussion and speak freely. Research has shown that talkative participants usually contribute the most useful remarks, have the best ideas, and impress other members. The only drawback is that, in becoming influential, you also run the risk of becoming unpopular, since productivity can be seen by some as a kind of control mechanism and therefore resented.

6 Make your presence felt.

Make your points clearly, succinctly and positively. Remain silent when you have nothing useful to say. Listen, observe, and save your arguments until you can make a really telling point. Resist the urge to dominate the discussion.

The chairperson (and others) will recognise and appreciate your value to the group when you build on the ideas of others, pose 'what if?' questions, seek clarification of relevant issues, be supportive with constructive comments, and be open-minded, willing to compromise, and respectful of others' contributions.

7 Be an active listener.

Practise the skill of listening in meetings because it will lead to understanding and good questions. Often too many people try to talk at once and as a result there are too many interruptions. At other times, people are too busy thinking of what to say and fail to hear what others are saying. As well, animosity between participants often causes

Management Memo

Improving participation in a meeting is a learned skill. Practice and observation train the mind and, in a short while, a manager interested in being a better participant, becomes one... Good participation is, fortunately, contagious, as is, unfortunately, poor participation. Set an example as a participant, and others will follow. [23]

some not to listen or to prejudice what's been said. Whatever the reason, failing to listen actively can cause meetings to fail.

8 Be willing to learn.

Go into meetings with the attitude of being prepared to learn. Effective participation in meetings doesn't always mean getting your own way. Rather, it means learning from others, accepting criticism, incorporating the ideas of others into your proposal to make it better.

9 Volunteer to wrap up the meeting.

Impress the chairperson, who is usually pleased to find someone willing to bring things together in a final summary, report or action plan.

10 Adhere to the rules of meeting etiquette.

Consider the following:

- Avoid interrupting.
- Refrain from distracting behaviour, such as pencil-tapping.
- Avoid side comments to your neighbour. If you have something to say, say it to the group.
- Always be pleasant, courteous and tactful. If you must discredit another's proposal, expose its defects, not the person.

See also: 50-62

How to prepare your next speech – the right way

Managers are frequently called upon to speak at professional meetings, service clubs, and community groups, and to present briefings or reports within their organisation. If a speech has been well-prepared, with a definite purpose in mind, and well-rehearsed, then it will be successful. The most effective public speakers faithfully observe several important steps when preparing for a speaking engagement. As you prepare for your next speech, you might also wish to adhere to these proven guidelines...

1 Understand clearly why you have been invited.

If you have accepted an invitation to speak, be sure you know why you were invited and what the audience wants to hear. You shouldn't accept if you have little to contribute.

2 Sketch out a brief plan of attack.

Three preliminary considerations must be addressed before beginning:

First, clarify the purpose of your speech – to persuade, inform, amuse? What do you want your audience to feel, think or learn?

Second, what do you know about the audience that will affect the way you approach the speech? What are their concerns, training, background, attitude, knowledge, and feelings towards you?

Third, focus on the subject. You know the general theme, so now you can focus on a specific topic. Select a working title and identify the thrust of your message.

3 Research your topic.

Collect your facts and arguments:

- Brainstorm a list of random ideas relating to your central message.
- Look for natural clusters of ideas which gravitate around your main points.
- Isolate the main concepts you will present and collect further relevant data to support these key points.
- Check your facts.
- Roughly sequence your information.

4 Structure your speech.

A good structure is essential. It provides continuity and balance, makes your argument easy to follow, and enables you to drive your message home logically.

Your presentation will consist of three parts:

The *introduction* must arouse your audience's interest immediately. Within 60 seconds you must have answered their question: 'Why should we listen to you?'

The *body* will present your main points logically, simply and interestingly.

The *conclusion* should include a restatement of your objective, a reinforcement of what you presented, and a challenge for the audience. The conclusion is your big chance to leave a lasting impression – don't bomb it!

5 Prepare your notes.

Even if you believe you are word-perfect, never speak without notes. Try to avoid a fully-scripted speech – the audience usually does not like being read to. Instead, use card-size hand-held notes that won't blow away.

On each card write a lead-in sentence to the point to be made, perhaps a few key words or phrases to jog your memory, as well as a brief reminder of an anecdote or quotation to be used while making the point.

Your introduction and conclusion should be on separate cards. Know them off pat, ensuring a confident start and a positive end to your speech.

What are the images you want your audience to remember most? These become your visual aids – flip charts, OHTs, slides. Don't overdo them and keep them simple.

6 Always remember the fundamentals.

If it 'reads' well, it doesn't necessarily 'listen' well. So focus on simplicity, brightness, concrete words and declarative sentences. Avoid jargon and gobbledygook. Feed in your ideas little by little. Use anecdotes, real dialogue, personal stories and humour to reinforce your message. Keep it clean – there's always someone you'll offend. Don't geth bogged down in detail. And keep it short! Few speakers can hold attention for much longer than 20–30 minutes.

Management Memo

The classic way of structuring a talk is to 'tell them what you are going to say – say it – tell them what you have said'. Your audience will probably only listen to one-third of what you say. If you say it three times in three different ways they will at least hear you once... To keep their attention throughout, give interim summaries which reinforce what you are saying and, above all, hammer home your key points at intervals throughout your talk... You should build your argument progressively until you come to a positive and overwhelming conclusion. Provide signposts, interim summaries and bridging sections which lead your audience naturally from one point to the next. [24]

7 Rehearse.

Several practise runs will leave you more confident and at ease. Try this:

> Imagine, in your mind's eye, every detail of the event. Actually see the room, the platform, the chairs. Visualise the room filling up with people and the chairperson rising to introduce you as speaker. See yourself rising, walking confidently to the lectern, and looking at the assembled listeners. Control your nerves. Imagine yourself beginning to speak. Work your way aloud through the speech. Don't try to be word-perfect.

8 Check the final arrangements.

Provide the chairperson with a brief introductory statement about yourself and a list of resources you will require on the day. Check the visibility of your visuals at the venue. Ensure your notes and visuals are in correct sequence.

How to deliver a speech that will be remembered

From time to time, you may be required to make presentations to audiences of various sizes to inform, inspire, persuade, affect decisions or stimulate action. Internally, you may find yourself speaking to a group of employees or colleagues and, externally, to a community group, the press or a service organisation. Of course, preparation is vital but a poorly delivered speech can ruin weeks of careful groundwork. If you want to deliver an effective speech, then consider these key elements...

1 Try to control your nervousness.

Top speakers are never free of nervous tension before their presentations – studies have shown that even pros like Bob Hope and Johnny Carson had incredibly fast heart rates just before they started their monologues, but these rates quickly returned to normal once they were into their deliveries. Nerves are all part of a good performance. Accept them. As well, learn to defuse the tension through the process of auto-suggestion – the technique of imagining yourself in the speaking situation *prior* to the event. Having actually felt the natural anxiety beforehand, you are well on the way to controlling the ever-present jitters on the occasion.

2 Display confidence from the start.

When a speaker moves to the lectern, the audience will look, notice and listen. So start with energy and enthusiasm; smile, look pleased to be there; take your time, don't get flustered; make introductory comments without referring to your notes; project your voice to the back of the room. Look relaxed, confident and in command.

3 Establish rapport with the audience immediately.

Show that you're glad to be upfront, that you like the audience and appreciate the opportunity to speak to them. Establish and maintain good eye contact with as many people as possible. You can't go wrong if you begin by complimenting those present – for their professionalism, or for their success in a project being undertaken, or for being present, and so on. Make them feel pleased that you're there.

4 Get your delivery right.

Vitality, enthusiasm, style, fluency, and tempo all count. Consider these important points as well:

- Imagine you are talking to people you know well. Be conversational. Try not to read your speech.
- Stand naturally and upright, project your voice to the last row, vary pitch and change tempo to keep your audience alert.
- Look at individuals in turn as you talk.

- Use a variety of gestures but not to distraction.
- Be light of touch and good-humoured. Use jokes only if relevant (and funny).
- Don't preach or pontificate to your audience. Show sincerity and conviction, belief in your message and enthusiasm in putting it across.
- Signpost important points – pause before making a key point, to highlight it, and again afterwards to allow it to sink in.
- Pace your delivery. Start in low gear and gradually build up in intensity.

5 Avoid the common traps.

There are some things you should never do:

- Never read your talk or bury your head in your notes, the chalkboard or your audiovisual aids. Talk to faces.
- Never pace up and down, fidget or use other irritating mannerisms such as jingling keys or swaying.
- Never compete with distractions.
- Never compete with yourself. If you distribute an item to be looked at, stop talking until it has been examined by all.
- Never uncover your audiovisual aids until you need them. And put them away as soon as you've used them.
- Never 'um' or 'ah'. A moment's silence is preferable.
- Never overrun your time. As Mark Twain advised: 'Few sinners are saved after the first 20 minutes of a sermon.'

6 Drive home your key points.

It's important that you don't lose your audience. Summarise the main points regularly to help your listeners organise and assimilate the ideas presented. Repetition and restatement are vital for effective communication.

Management Memo

Become interested enough in your audience that your prime concern is how to get your message from you to them. When you think more about how you are going to put your message across and less about what people will think of you, you will end up a better communicator. So allow yourself to release your energy in a positive way. [25]

7 Keep a grip on your audience.

Watch your listeners. Be aware of how they're reacting to your speech. Are they getting your message – or are they yawning, doodling, reading, or cleaning fingernails? Watch for the nonverbal clues which provide valuable feedback. Adjust your style and modify your content or delivery accordingly. Use various strategies – questions, demonstrations and illustrations.

8 Finish conclusively.

Make sure you stop while your listeners are still with you. It's good to let them know when the end is in sight. Recap the key points. To strengthen the ideas presented, give your audience something specific to do or think about in the days that follow – further reading, practice, follow-up, observations, or a challenge. Leave them with more than just a warm glow – leave them with a memorable idea or thought, a dynamic closing sentence that you have rehearsed until it is part of you. The last impression is the lasting impression.

How to add sparkle to your speech-making

It's easy to spot a dull speaker – just count the number of nodding heads in the audience. You can avoid this dilemma by adding a little sizzle to your presentations, by learning to deliver a palatable blend of facts, figures, philosophy, humour, and the unexpected. The result can be rewarding – happy audiences, rapt attention and more support for your cause. Pep up your next presentation by considering this advice...

1 Use attention-grabbers wherever appropriate.

Handouts, audiovisual aids, props, yarns, facts and figures, questions, show-of-hands, anecdotes, humour and demonstrations – all are capable of complementing your speech and of demanding audience attention. And all are essential if you adhere to this basic principle of holding an audience: show them, don't tell them. If you illustrate your points with examples, demonstrations or analogies that are visual or oral, you'll hold their attention.

2 Get the audience into the act.

Involvement keeps people from nodding off. Try asking questions and seeking a show of hands. Work in some role-play. Keep their brains active. Remember, you're up there to speak, they're out there to listen. If they finish before you do, you're in trouble.

3 Use props to emphasise points.

Anything your audience can *see* makes you and your message more memorable. Try using props – a football jersey (when talking about teamwork), an account book (about spending), even a high school marching band. Be realistic, however, and use props only if you feel comfortable in doing so, if they are compatible with your speaking style, and only if they are appropriate to your topic.

4 Do something unexpected.

The element of surprise can lift your performance. Why not break down that physical barrier the audience expects between you and them? Desert the lectern and move out into the audience. Or at an appropriate moment and to illustrate a point, pull out an inflated balloon from beneath the lectern and explode it; or tear up and scatter a page from your speech.

5 Use technology.

Videos, computer graphics, audio, transparencies, slides, multimedia, and similar devices are all attention-grabbers. They divert attention from your talking head, clarify your content, generate interest in the topic, increase retention, and help to reduce your stage fright. Make sure you know how to use each. But remember, *you're* still the most important audio-visual device in the room.

6 Spin a yarn.

The best way to hold an audience's attention is to tell a story. Scatter anecdotes, real dialogue, and personal experiences throughout your speech to reinforce your message. Start a file of your favourite anecdotes and quotations. Rummage through joke and quotation books and magazines in your spare time – there are thousands of gems which can illustrate a range of themes.

7 Use humour, selectively.

Humour, used well, can reinforce your argument and keep your listeners wanting more, but don't forget these important points:

- *Make sure it's a funny story.* If you don't laugh when you first hear it, chances are nobody else will either. So, don't tell it if it's not all that funny.
- *Avoid puns.* They almost always cause listeners to groan, rather than laugh.
- *Make it sound like the truth.* People are more active listeners if they think it's *your* story, about you or your acquaintances. Adapt stories to suit.
- *Make sure it's clean.* Never tell a story that can offend in any way. There's always someone who'll get upset.
- *Make sure it's relevant to your argument or the occasion.* Lead into it smoothly, making sure it fits into the logical sequence of your speech.
- *Use a dual-purpose funny historical anecdote.* If the joke fails, at least the story still gets the point across.

Management Memo

If you don't give an interesting and lively speech, then you're not going to get your message across... Whether people yawn or sit up to attention depends to some extent on your speech-writing skills – and the techniques and tricks you use to present your facts in an interesting way. [26]

8 Use humour, skilfully.

Every speaker would love to be the life of the lectern, but humour can be hazardous if you ignore these warnings:

- *Make sure you learn the story.* Know it inside out. Memorise the punchline. A fumble can cost you the game.
- *Speak distinctly and with poise.* Every word must be heard. If the joke isn't heard, it won't raise a laugh.
- *Leave enough time for the laugh before proceeding.* Sometimes audiences react slowly, especially if the humour was unexpected.
- *Act out the story.* You're putting on a short show, so make it a good one gesticulate, whisper, shout. Use appropriate facial expressions.
- *Keep it short.* Limit the extraneous matter; include only the details that relate directly to the punchline.
- *Enjoy it.* Spread good cheer. You're happy to be telling the story and you're enjoying yourself. If you look like you are, the audience will join in.
- *Talk to individuals out there in turn,* not to the audience in general, and in doing so, smile with your mouth and with your voice.
- *Carry on smoothly if the audience doesn't laugh.* People soon forget that you laid an egg if you remain confident and calm. Don't try to salvage the situation with an explanation or apology.
- *Avoid humour when speaking out of doors.* The laugh tends to get lost, leaving people with the feeling that the point wasn't funny at all.

How to handle the question-and-answer session after your next speech

Often your speech may be followed by a Q&A session. People may ask for more information, seek clarification, or question the validity of your comments. Indeed, on those occasions when you seek to persuade or to stimulate action, questioners might even challenge your assumptions, offer opposing views, or attempt to undermine your credibility. The Q&A session can be a trying ordeal for the inexperienced speaker, so it is important to become skilled in fielding audience questions by following these guidelines...

1 Display confidence from the start.

You can't afford to relax when your formal presentation is over: be prepared for a lively series of questions from your audience. Give the impression that you are looking forward to this session and, with self-assurance, ask: 'Now, who has the first question?'

2 Start the ball rolling yourself if necessary.

If you have a reluctant or reticent audience, the first question is sometimes slow in coming. You may need to 'prime the pump' using such strategies as:

- Pose your own question: 'A question I'm usually asked is...' or 'Before the meeting, the chairperson posed an interesting question...'
- Before your speech, pass out index cards so listeners can jot down questions that arise during your speech. Ask for short questions, printed clearly, so that you can respond to them in turn from the lectern.
- Arrange with someone before the speech to ask the first question – you don't have to provide the actual question.

3 Always repeat the question.

For a large group, this allows everyone to hear the question. It also allows you to see if you really understand the question and provides you with a little time to frame your response.

4 Cover the entire room.

Try not to develop any blind spots as you look for questions. Let your eyes roam over the entire room. Keep eye contact with the speaker when the question is being asked; look at the entire group when answering; return your gaze to the questioner as you complete your response – particularly if you want to give that person another opportunity to comment.

5 Be brief with your reply.

Q&A sessions should not be tedious dialogues or debates but should provide a means for any listener to get quick clarification or additional information. So keep your answers short and to the point. Don't give another speech. If the question can't be answered in a minute or two, tell the person to see you after the session.

6 Remain in control at all times.

You hold the floor in this session, so you can control the situation:

- ***Answer only those questions you understand.*** If you didn't hear the question, ask the speaker to repeat it. If you didn't understand it, ask the speaker to explain it.
- ***Anticipate questions.*** Plan responses to questions you hope no one will ask. By considering common fears, assumptions, needs or problems that listeners will experience, you can identify likely questions.
- ***Keep your speech in focus.*** Don't allow questions to divert you from your main thrust. Don't hesitate to say: 'You make an interesting point, but it's beyond the scope of my presentation…'.
- ***Never dismiss a questioner.*** Even if the question is stupid, keep your feelings to yourself. If the person is interested enough to ask, be flattered and provide a direct response.
- ***Watch for several questions posing as one.*** Don't try to tackle them all with one response. Treat them separately.
- ***Discourage the long-winded questioner.*** Give all listeners a chance to ask questions. If one questioner makes a speech instead of arriving at a question, interrupt when the opportunity arises with, 'You've raised some interesting points, but in the interest of time, we should move on to some other questions...'.
- ***Avoid entering into debate.*** Sometimes a questioner is not satisfied with your answer and begins to engage in a debate. If this discussion is not fruitful, advise the questioner that you will be happy to continue the conversation after the session, and then move quickly on to the next question. Alternatively, have the debater rephrase his/her assertions as questions: never answer opinions – only questions.

Management Memo

Handling questions is the more difficult part of a presentation. You can never be as thoroughly prepared for this aspect of speaking as you can be for the planned remarks. There is always some element of the unexpected in question-and-answer sessions. Inevitably, you lose some of the control of the audience. On the positive side, if you can handle listeners' questions effectively, you have passed a major hurdle to the success of your presentation. [27]

- ***Remain composed and polite.*** Respond to challenges and objections with data, not emotion. Never lose control or show your frustration with a hot-headed questioner. Listeners will reject audience troublemakers and rally to your side; they appreciate good manners and fair play. Do not threaten, preach, blame, ridicule or argue. Do not become hostile or defensive. Remain confident and in charge of your emotions.

7 Be honest: some questions can't be answered.

It's always more credible to admit you don't have an answer than to try to bluff your way through it. Graceful sidestepping requires considerable skill. So, it's best to promise to follow up the question and to get back to the questioner at a later date – and do so.

8 Take charge at the end.

Whenever possible during a Q&A session, take the opportunity to repeat and reinforce the key elements of your speech. When you're ready, take control with a comment such as 'Before I make my concluding remarks, do we have one more question?' Then have your final say to end the session confidently.

How to handle a hostile audience

To be an effective manager, you need to be able to communicate in a variety of settings. Sooner or later you may be in the difficult position of having to address an angry or hostile group of employees, customers, stockholders, or community representatives. Even one hostile troublemaker in the audience can cause problems. The key is to neutralise the hostility using a range of strategies...

1 Stay relaxed and appear confident.

Prior to and during any introduction, sit confidently and in a relaxed manner before the audience. Act self-assuredly, but not arrogantly. Present a confident exterior by approaching the podium with assurance and composure and without any hint of cockiness. Be especially careful not to project any suggestion of animosity yourself.

2 Try to hose down the hostility at the very start.

If you're anticipating a hostile audience, or the nature of your subject is controversial and likely to arouse strong feelings, the secret is to address the disagreement before it addresses you. This can be accomplished in several ways:

- *Create rapport with your audience.* Do this as quickly as possible.
- *Express appreciation.* Thank the audience for being prepared to listen even though some of those present may hold ideas different from yours.
- *Advocate fair play.* Commend the spirit of sportsmanship and fair play that gives everyone the right to disagree without being disagreeable and to object without being objectionable.
- *Set aside time for audience comments and questions – later.* If you allocate time for comments and questions after you have finished, you should hopefully be able to keep interruptions during your delivery to a minimum.
- *Explore common ground.* In your opening remarks, review the shared goals and important points of agreement between you and your audience. Establish mutual interests and concerns as quickly as possible.
- *Burst your opponents' balloon upfront.* Take the wind out of your opponents' sails by summarising their point of view early, even concede a few points. If you are the one who brings it up, you can explain it in your own words and within the context of the view you are about to present. By stating their case for them, you'll take the sting out of their comments. And, in so doing, many in your audience will reflect on your evenhandedness and fairness.

3 Persuade people to your way of thinking.

The obvious strategy for coping with hostile elements in your audience is to persuade the majority of those present to your way of thinking, thereby minimising the damage that troublemakers can cause. Set the scene by prefacing your comments with the following: 'For the next 20 minutes, I'm going to present a new concept to you. All I ask is that we just keep an open mind and hold our comments and questions until I finish. Is that all right?' Who could object to that reasonable invitation? Then, if troublemakers react during the session, you'll find the audience is prepared to put them down for not having an open mind or for not biding their time as requested. In the meantime, it's your opportunity to sell your case.

4 Stay in control of yourself.

Avoid doing or saying anything to inflame your audience or to justify any abusive reaction. Keep your remarks strictly objective and impersonal. If possible ignore hecklers and never personalise your comments or insult an angry group. If the audience *is* noisy, deliberately lower your voice and resist the natural temptation to raise it. By raising your voice, you are encouraging a corresponding increase in noise by the audience, as well as suggesting that you are losing your composure.

5 Tackle the troublemakers with tact.

While remembering that negative comments or questions are not always hostile, you can defuse identified vocal troublemakers during or after your presentation, by considering such techniques as these:

- *Smother with facts.* You're the expert and you should have at your fingertips facts, figures, references and quotes to combat any objections. Logical, intelligent argument will win over reasonable people anyday.
- *Answer a hostile question with a question.* For example, 'If you feel that way about the situation, then what do *you* think should be done about it?' The response is likely to be rambling, emotional and illogical – a fact quickly picked up by the audience.
- *Seek clarification on emotionality.* Troublemakers often have hostile, emotional words embedded in their comments – like sneaky, stupid, hedging, rip-off, feeble… You can defuse such comments by asking for clarification of such words. Never answer a question by repeating hostile words.
- *Meet me out the back later.* If all else fails, say, 'It seems that we have different views on this subject. I'm happy to discuss it with you in more detail after the meeting.' Invariably they fail to turn up – they're usually more interested in posturing in front of an audience.
- *Pull the plug graciously.* If the hostility is excessive, you may find it necessary to announce that, because it is impossible to continue, you find it necessary to end your talk and promptly and quietly sit down.

Management Memo

Even among fair-minded people, not everyone will want to sing word for word out of our songbook. It's important for us to have a realistic attitude about our audience and our expectations. If we anticipate troublemakers, we are less likely to come unglued when someone says, 'It'll never work.'

The best way to anticipate the audience is to take the time to get background information on the audience. This will allow you to better understand the opinions, feelings, and biases of those who are likely to disagree with you. [28]

 See also: 48-52

How to make special speeches: -introducing a speaker -moving a vote of thanks

Managers usually get asked to make more short speeches than long speeches, and two short speeches which you may be called upon to give will be to introduce a speaker or to move a vote of thanks at the end of his/her presentation. For such occasions, here are a few guidelines worth remembering...

Introducing a speaker

1 Follow this format...

To introduce a guest speaker, you'll need to do a little homework and then structure your speech as follows:

- Welcome the speaker and announce the title of the talk.
- Elaborate briefly on the relevance of the topic.
- Outline the speaker's qualifications and experience. Indicate any link the speaker might have with your organisation or the audience. Briefly describe the speaker's other interests, if relevant.
- Conclude with the following statement: 'Ladies and gentlemen, please welcome...', and lead the applause.

2 Stay focused.

Your introduction must prepare the audience for the speaker by concentrating the listeners' attention on the new presentation. Keep your comments compatible with the focus and tone of the talk.

3 Be brief.

Keep your introduction to two minutes' duration and don't indulge in your own pet views on the subject. Do not commit the speaker to any particular line of approach.

4 Confirm if a Q&A session is warranted.

Check beforehand to determine if the speaker is prepared to take questions from the audience at the end of the talk, and advise the audience in advance so that appropriate questions are forthcoming after the speech.

5 And don't forget...

A good introduction must:

- provide a smooth transition, linking speaker to programme,
- whet the audience's appetite,
- throw out a welcome mat and mellow any audience resistance,
- express gratitude to the speaker for sharing both time and knowledge with those present.

Moving a vote of thanks

1 Be prepared to be spontaneous.

A vote of thanks is usually not the kind of speech you can prepare beforehand – unless you have a copy of your guest's talk in advance. So, as a rule, you'll need to be spontaneous.

2 Structure your response.

Listen carefully to the talk, and select and jot down two or three key points. Build your vote of thanks around these selected points. You might say: 'Madam Chair, ladies and gentlemen, our speaker tonight made two points which particularly appealed to me. First of all,... Secondly,... In conclusion, I found our speaker's presentation to be informative, incisive and entertaining, and so I am delighted to propose this vote of thanks. Please join with me in showing our appreciation...'

3 Remember these helpful suggestions...

- Be gracious, sincere – and brief. It is not the responsibility of the thanker to make another long speech.

> **Management Memo**
>
> The strength or weakness of an introduction will affect a speaker's task. A snappy, upbeat, interesting introduction clears the way for a quick takeoff. A dull, dreary introduction means that the guest speaker has to spend time on early damage control.
>
> Introductions – short and simple though they usually are – really *do* matter. A good introduction should set the tone for the featured speaker. It should help bring speaker and audience closer together, establish a congenial climate, and build bonds of common interest. [29]

- As a general rule, you should never voice your disagreement with the speaker, nor make corrections to the speech, nor use the occasion to push your views – no matter how much you might disagree with what was said.
- Stand in a position that gives you eye contact with the entire audience. Occasionally turn towards the speaker.
- And if it's been a woeful speech? Make as little reference to the content of the speech as possible: focus on the effort and preparation involved, thanking the speaker for making the time available in a busy schedule. Be courteous and brief.

How to make special speeches: –presenting an award –accepting an award

Speaking in public need no longer be something to be feared and avoided if you view such occasions as opportunities to be sought and prized. A public speech, no matter how brief, increases your visibility. So take advantage of the opportunity, for the podium can help pave your way to the executive suite once you learn the tricks of speech-making. Here are two more opportunities to help you make an impact...

Presenting an award

1 Give the background to the award.

Mention why people are gathered together for this presentation and provide, as appropriate, some background information relating to this particular award – its meaning, uses, history, previous winners, the selection process, and so on.

2 Elaborate on the person's achievements.

Provide details as to why this person has been selected to be honoured in this way. Support the selection with evidence of the person's accomplishments.

3 Punctuate your speech with appropriate attention-grabbers.

Do a little homework. Research a few books of 'quotable quotes' and drop one or two relevant quips into your presentation speech. For example, couple the accomplishments of your awardee with such statements as: 'It isn't how much you know, but what you get done that the world rewards and remembers', or 'The life of achievement is a life of hard work', or 'Footprints in the sands of time were not made by sitting down', or, as Helen Keller said, 'I long to accomplish a great and noble task, but it is my chief duty to accomplish *all* tasks as though they were great and noble. The world is moved along, not only by the mighty shoves of its heroes, but also by the aggregate of the tiny pushes of each honest worker.'

4 Make the formal presentation.

'On behalf of..., I'm delighted to present... with this well-deserved award. Our sincere congratulations!' Shake the recipient's hand, step back and allow the audience to hear the awardee's words of acceptance.

Accepting an award

1 Keep it short and simple.

Unless you are in a very formal gathering, an acceptance speech any longer than one or two minutes is usually too long. So do your audience and yourself a favour. Keep it genuine, simple, and as short as possible.

2 Express your sincere gratitude.

In one sentence, express your gratitude to and respect for the organisation presenting the award and for the kind wishes that accompany it.

3 Share the credit.

Acknowledge and voice your appreciation to others. Mention by name any colleagues or co-workers who helped you, and then thank them specifically for their contributions. Where appropriate, also thank your family members for their support.

4 Speak of the significance of the award.

Why is the award important to you and/or your organisation and what does it mean to win the honour?

5 Praise the competition.

The more highly you speak of those you outperformed, the more meaningful your award becomes, and the more you come across as a good sport.

> **Management Memo**
>
> A long-winded speaker was continuing to deliver his dry, lengthy and boring acceptance speech. He was running long over time. The master of ceremonies was trying to get him to stop, but he couldn't attract his attention. Finally, in desperation, he picked up the gavel, aimed and fired – but missed the speaker and hit a man in the first row.
>
> The man slumped to his knees, then groaned, 'Hit me again, I can still hear him!'[30]

6 Indicate what you will do with the award.

Show the award to those present and refer to its attractiveness, usefulness, and so on. Indicate what you will be doing with it, and where in your office or building it will be placed for all to see.

7 Conclude with a final thank-you.

Once more express your thanks: 'I/We shall cherish this award and what it stands for. Thank you.'

8 Remember: be humble.

By expressing your sense of humility, you add to the lustre of the honour while demonstrating your own modesty.

How to make special speeches: –an impromptu speech –a retirement speech

How strange it is that, while we may be able to manage human, financial and physical resources with complete confidence, we are so often transformed into a quivering mass of fear and trembling when called upon to 'say a few words'. Here are more suggestions to help you grapple with any anxieties in this area…

An impromptu speech

1 Acknowledge that an impromptu speech can be frightening.

You wouldn't be alone if you admitted that one of your greatest fears was to be asked to give an off-the-cuff speech at an important meeting. Impromptu presentations can be difficult to do as well. Speakers can easily ramble in a disjointed fashion, stumble – some literally go blank. But here is a helpful strategy to make the ordeal manageable…

2 Just remember the three-question trick.

The simplest way to handle the off-the-cuff speech is to compose, and then answer, three questions about the situation or topic you've been given.

For example, if you are invited at a meeting of associates to say a few words of farewell to a prominent colleague who is moving interstate, begin by asking three obvious questions, and then go back and provide an appropriate answer to each – 'What has been Diane's contribution to the organisation?', 'What incident will I remember most about Diane?' and 'How easy is it going to be for us to replace her as manager of personnel services?'

Remember the structure:

- state the topic
- pose your three questions
- go back and answer each one
- restate the topic.

So next time you're put on a spot and asked to make an impromptu presentation, you needn't be caught out.

After all, giving an excellent impromptu talk is no harder than asking and answering your own questions.

A retirement speech

1 Focus on the occasion.

Indicate that this is both a happy and a sad occasion – happy because everyone is here to congratulate your retiring colleague on his/her many years with the organisation, and sad because many people 'are sorry to lose you'.

2 Focus on length of service.

Mention the retiree's length of service, focusing in particular on his/her period with the organisation and the changes that have taken place during those years.

3 Outline the retiree's career.

Give a brief outline of the retiree's career in the service of your organisation – you'll need to do your homework.

4 Consider what made the retiree 'special'.

Highlight some of the retiree's outstanding achievements or contributions to the company. List also some of the personal things that have made him/her 'special'. One or two anecdotes to illustrate might also be appropriate.

5 Contemplate the future.

Give an indication of the retiree's intentions for retirement and how busy she/he will be in the years to come.

Management Memo

If you are in need of some humorous words for the farewell speech you are called upon to make to your parting colleague, then here are a few that you might consider using on the occasion:

- Retirement at fifty-five is ridiculous. When I was fifty-five, I still had pimples. – George Burns, US comedian (1898-1996)
- I am reminded of the professional football player who said when he retired from the game: 'Ninety per cent of me is very sad, but my knees are very, very happy.'
- Former US President Calvin Coolidge had to fill out a form confirming his membership of the National Press Club soon after he left the White House. In the space after 'Occupation' he wrote 'Retired!'. Next came the 'Remarks' column, where he wrote 'Glad of it!'.
- He is everything that (Robert) is not. He is young; he is handsome; he has lots of hair; he is fast; he is durable; he's worth millions; and his entire sex life is before him. – Columnist Si Burick, writing on the retirement of US racehorse legend, Secretariat.[31]

6 Conclude on a happy note.

Congratulate the retiree and make the presentation. Include, where appropriate in the speech, a couple of smart quips, e.g. 'Retirement takes all the fun out of Saturdays', 'Retirement is the time when there is too much of it or not enough of it'.

How to become a better writer

The ability to express oneself clearly on paper and to write effective reports, memos, letters and other business documents is one of a manager's most important skills. But some managers find it difficult to write clearly, concisely and convincingly. Others take far longer than necessary to complete a written assignment. No matter if your task is a letter, memo, report or novel, you can become a better writer if you follow this advice…

1 Prepare yourself.

Before you begin to write, consider these three key issues:

- ***Know precisely the purpose of your writing task.***

You must first be clear on the purpose of your task. Ask yourself: What do I want the reader to think, do or know? The more specific you can be with your answers, the easier it will be for you to plan your writing.

- ***Know your audience.***

Reading is a solo activity, so you must imagine you are writing to one reader at a time. Strike an appropriate balance between the formal and the casual approach. No matter how impressive your writing may seem to you, your reader is the final judge.

- ***Know the image you want to project personally.***

Are you trying to be helpful, formal, objective, appreciative, apologetic, caring, confident…? Try to be that.

2 Plan your approach.

Organise your thoughts, ideas and information before worrying about words and sentences because, if you spend time in planning and drafting an outline, particularly if you have to write something lengthy, you will save considerable time and energy in the long run. So it's essential first of all to programme your ideas into a logically sequenced structure before attempting to clothe your structure in words.

3 Write your first draft.

Having obtained a clear picture of your audience, your purpose, and the initial outline of your document, you can now begin to fill in the details of your first draft. It's important to get something written as soon as possible to 'prime the pump', even though you might scrap it later. So don't feel you must start at the beginning – if you find the beginning difficult, start somewhere else. The important thing at this stage is to get words on paper (or computer screen). Focus here on *what* is said, not on *how* it is being said. Most people are too critical of themselves at this stage and that becomes a major obstacle. Trust the writing process more: it does not have to start out right, only end that way – and the next step helps take care of that…

4 Polish your product.

Under no circumstances should you consider the first draft of your document to be the final version. Even the best of writers rework and revise their written material. The number of times you do this depends on your skill as a writer and the importance of the document. The more times you revisit your work, the tighter, more polished and more effective your product should become. Remember, good writing is really rewriting.

Here then are the strategies to help polish your draft to perfection:

- *Let the draft sit for a while* before revising it. Revisiting the material 'cold' will help you see it from a reader's perspective.
- *Underline the main points* to check that you actually said everything you intended to say. You may well change the order of things once you see how they appear to the reader.
- *Read it aloud.* Anything you find awkward or tedious to speak will be equally so for your readers to read.
- *Check the big words* – if they're not precise in meaning, replace them with shorter, clearer ones. Check every sentence: if it's possible for a reader to get lost in one, break it down into shorter sentences. Check spelling, grammar and punctuation.
- *Criticise the content severely.* Are the facts correct? Are they relevant? Do the conclusions follow logically? Can anything be cut out? Have you countered any likely objections?
- *Get comments from a colleague* if the task is important and if time permits.

Management Memo

The most important benefit of powerful writing is that it enables you to make yourself understood. That's no small feat. The professional world is plagued with all sorts of misread instructions, confused agreements, and crossed signals due to poor writing. By presenting your ideas clearly in writing and keeping track of important information, you minimise this kind of commotion in your professional life.

Another advantage of powerful writing is that when you present complex ideas in a way people can easily understand, you are regarded as being more intelligent, maybe even brilliant. Powerful writing impresses people, opens doors, and creates opportunities. That's as it should be. By forcing you to think through and organise what you have to say, good writing does make you 'cleverer'. [32]

5 Develop your own style.

Over time, you will refine your methods and create variations that make your style unique – as distinctive as your own personality. But you will do well to remember these basics:

- Be concise. Eliminate the unnecessary. Make every word count. Get to the point.
- Vary sentence length, structure and beginnings. As a rule, keep sentences short.
- Use familiar, concrete words. Write to express, not impress.
- Write naturally, using the words you typically use when speaking.
- Convert sentences from passive to active voice.
- Use transition words to link ideas and increase readability – 'In addition…', 'Thus…', 'Conversely…', 'Therefore'…
- Write for your reader, not for yourself.

How to write a better letter

Letter writing is an important managerial skill, and managers are often judged by the quality of the letters they write. The problem is that most of us usually become expert letter writers after years of trial and error. If you would like to short-cut those lengthy years of apprenticeship, here is a proven strategy and several important points to consider...

1 Take your time.

Letter writing is not something to do in a hurry. Routine business letters may require only a few minutes to think about phrasing and sequence, but more important letters can require many hours of planning and drafting, passing through several versions before completion.

2 Assemble all relevant data.

Gather all the data you will need to prepare the letter, including previous correspondence, company files, and policy handbooks. Extract those details necessary for drafting your response.

3 Group and sequence your material.

Know roughly what you want to say and collate all the relevant pieces of collected information under headings, arranging the material into a logical sequence. If your letter is being written in response to someone else's, know exactly what is wanted of you – information, opinion, clarification, instructions... and make sure your letter focuses on just that. It is often useful to underline the points to be answered. Make brief marginal notes against these items.

4 Prepare a first draft.

Convert your grouped and sequenced information into a first draft of continuous prose. Precision and polish need not be your concern at this stage. Refer to the originating correspondence in your first paragraph and provide the response sought. If yours is an originating letter, state your letter's aim upfront, provide an explanation, and close by stating what action you expect. The important thing at this stage is to get words on paper in a rough but logical sequence.

5 Revise your draft letter.

Rework your first effort, rephrasing unclear and ambiguous statements, removing unnecessary words and phrases, deleting unnecessary information, and simplifying and sharpening your argument.

6 Polish your revised version.

As you record your final document, make any improvements as you go. Your final version should be succinct, crisp and courteous. Attend to your letter's presentation and layout, paying particular attention to proofreading, good quality paper and envelope, generous margins, balanced blocks of type – all of which contribute to a favourable impression.

7 Remember these important points...

Here are some essential guidelines for good business letter writing:

- Put yourself in your reader's place. Adjust your language to what is most meaningful to your reader.
- Keep your writing simple, natural and concise.
- As a general rule, use short words, short sentences and short paragraphs.
- Avoid technical terms and jargon. You may end up confusing your reader.
- Letter reading research reveals that people look first at the salutation, then at the signature, then they scan the P.S. if there is one, and finally they return to the first paragraph. So, don't forget to use the P.S. to drive home the point of your letter, or to sell your message.
- Always be courteous and polite. How do *you* feel when you receive an abrupt, curt letter?

Management Memo

A significant part of your job revolves around expressing yourself on paper. But do your letters mean business? Or do they more often stand for fuzzy thinking, tough reading and fumbled opportunities? Here's a simple test to find out how your business writing rates.

During the last month,

- Did you have to write any additional letters or memos to explain what you meant in your initial communication?
- Did you receive any telephone calls or letters from puzzled recipients, asking for clarification of your message?
- Did you reread any of your own correspondence and wonder what on earth you were talking about?
- Did you start a letter more than once, only to find that you still weren't saying what you wanted to say?

If your answer to any of these questions is a sheepish yes, then you undoubtedly need to improve your present letter writing ability.[33]

- Don't forget that, to many people with whom you deal, your letters *are* you. They may never see you, nor shake your hand, nor speak to you. They must size you up by what you say in your written correspondence and how you say it.
- Take care with those special letters. In replying to letters of complaint, for example, explain why something happened and what you're going to do about it. Promote goodwill. Solve the problem, don't exacerbate it. Or, if writing a letter of refusal, do so without causing offence. Say 'no' plainly, giving reasons, and convey your appreciation of the writer's interest or concern.

How to write a good memo

Semantic sludge – that's how many of the memorandums that filter up, down and across our organisations can be described. Most people would prefer to receive clear memos – whether on paper or via e-mail – that say exactly what you mean and you, no doubt, would prefer to receive the same. Often, however, this is not the case, for an examination of these management communications reveal ill-conceived, poorly expressed, ineffective epistles. Memo writing is a skill which you can master by following this advice...

1 Know when to write a memo.

Memos should be written only if:

- it is essential that you avoid personal contact,
- it would take too long for the information to reach the audience by any other means,
- the material needs to be kept for future reference,
- you need proof that you have taken action.

2 Be brief and to the point.

If you have nothing to say, don't write a memo. If you have something to say, keep it short – short paragraphs, short sentences, short words. Keep your memo as short and as simple as you can. A one-paragraph memo is sometimes all that's required. Priority one is to express, not impress, so go for simplicity and clarity. Weigh every word against your readers' time and attention span. And get to the point early. If you're asking for a new computer, say so upfront, then provide the supporting argument.

3 Collect your thoughts.

For a memo longer than one paragraph, gather your main points in advance. When you begin the structuring process, you'll have a whole set of ideas to work from. A rambling style reflects a muddy thinker or a person too lazy to organise his/her thoughts.

4 'Talk' your ideas through to yourself.

Essentially a memo is a written conversation where the content is sequenced to the best advantage. So, having isolated your main points, talk your ideas through to yourself. This helps you decide the main point and the supporting arguments that hang off it. An outline then begins to take shape.

5 Focus on your audience.

Although you may be writing to a staff of 20 or 200, focus your written conversation on one person. By conversing with that individual, you'll end up answering everyone else's questions.

6 Structure your memo.

Consider adopting a standard structure for your longer proposals, writing under such headings as:

To:...
From:...
Date:...
Subject:...
Background:...
Proposal:...
Recommendation:...
If approved:...

Numbered paragraphs also make the memo easier to write, easier to read, and easier to refer to. You are forced to unravel your thoughts, to break your complicated idea down into its component parts and to develop your message sequentially. For larger memos, subheadings and bullets are also useful.

7 Be selective.

Rarely do readers want a blow-by-blow description of the issue – they normally want to get in and get out. So state your ideas early, clearly, directly and briefly. Include only information the reader needs to know. Avoid literary flourishes – in most memos, the main villain is pomposity. Stick to your main points and keep each idea simple.

8 Review and revise.

Reread what you've written. Ask yourself, 'Can I say this any more clearly?' Ensure that the final effect is one of clarity and crispness. Check that the memo is not too arrogant, demeaning, or abrupt. Polish to perfection – and remember, neatness counts. Sloppy managers send out sloppy memos. Set an example: you'll want perfect grammar, correct spelling and a neat presentation. Even if your proposals are rejected, you will at least gain credibility by displaying professionalism and courtesy to the reader.

Management Memo

I have a profound appreciation for short memos. My favourite memo is one sentence in length. My second favourite is two sentences. And so on. My executives know this. If they want to win me over, they better do it quickly. Lengthy memos don't impress me; they worry me. [34]

9 Check your subject heading carefully.

By glancing at the title of the memo, the reader should be able to focus immediately on the topic. Avoid murky, vague headings. For example, instead of writing, 'Subject: Computer', write: 'Subject: Proposal to purchase additional computer for personnel department'.

10 Compliment good memo writers.

Praise reinforces good writing skills in your staff members. Set the example by gaining the reputation as a good memo writer yourself. Only then can you wage war on muddied memos. Express appreciation to good memo writers. When murky, mumbling memos no longer are seen as the model for people to follow, all of your office memos or e-mail messages will begin to improve.

 See also: 256

How to make the most of your professional reading

To remain fully effective, managers can usually turn to a variety of sources for personal and professional growth – courses, conferences, networking, discussions, professional associations, workshops, and so on. But of all these avenues, research shows that independent reading of professional books and journals continues to be the most efficient, reliable, accessible, and indispensable source of growth. Leaders simply must be readers...

1 Acknowledge this fact: If you're not reading, you shouldn't be leading.

The American Association of School Administrators supports this message:

> 'Reading is *the* most fundamental, reliable and efficient resource for leaders. It is the purpose of professional reading to equip the leader for independent creative thinking. It is through the literature that executives live, learn and think about their swiftly moving and complex profession.'

2 Set aside time to read.

The problem for busy executives is not finding something to read – it's finding the time! The key is to discipline yourself: set aside a specific part of each day for concentrated reading – say 10 or 20 minutes. In this way you're saying: 'I value reading. There's a time and place for everything. This time belongs to reading.' Alternatively, develop the productive habit of reading in snatches – on the train, between meetings, before breakfast. Use precious time wisely by becoming a more efficient reader...

3 Become more selective in what you read.

The secret to professional reading is to do less better, rather than to do more or to do it faster. If you can't find enough time to read, then you must trim from your reading all unwanted and unnecessary reading matter. Reduce your reading load by determining those areas in which you *must* keep up to date and only select those books and journals which currently serve you best.

4 Adopt reading strategies that work for you.

To get value from your reading time, consider the following strategies:

- *Always scan a book before spending time on it* – the jacket, table of contents, preface, index, author's credentials, content and structure. Size up these aspects, know what you want from the book and only then decide whether it's worth spending valuable time on it.
- *Always read with a purpose.* Go in and find the meaning. Search for answers and key ideas. Feel free to skip

irrelevant sentences, paragraphs and chapters.

- *Resist the temptation to flick through the pages of a journal* if time is of the essence; you'll inevitably be distracted by the advertisements and peripheral material. Work from the contents page.
- *Learn to skim* – Peruse the first one or two sentences of a paragraph to see if the information in the paragraph is pertinent to your immediate quest; if not, pass on.
- *Pause to reflect after each reading session.* After each session, sit back for a few minutes to reflect on, criticise or summarise the author's message. By doing this, you substantially increase your comprehension and retention.
- *Make use of what you have read.* The reason for reading is to recall a useful idea later, when you need it. Underline, make notes in the margin, jot usable ideas on index cards, start a clip file of valuable points or articles. Impress your colleagues: be able to cite one or two key points from each item you've read.
- *Develop a sound working relationship with a good professional library.* Enquire at your local university about their Faculty of Management library, and/or join a professional association like the Institute for Marketing Management to get access to their library.
- *Consider speed-reading courses.* These can make a significant improvement in the reading effectiveness of some people.
- *Set yourself an achievable goal for the year.* Try beginning with a modest one book and two journals per month – that alone becomes an impressive 12 books and 24 journals annually!

5 Don't allow your reading to accumulate.

Professional literature can very quickly choke your in-basket. Resolve to read material by a certain date – or discard it. As Michael LeBoeuf advises in *Working Smart*:

> Think of professional reading material much as you would think of a movie playing at a local theatre. After a certain date it's gone, but if it's truly spectacular it will be around again.

Management Memo

Good readers aren't primarily readers at all. They are detectives, explorers, scientists, critics and editors – all active, seeking roles. The effective reader wants informationz – and uses reading as a searching technique to get what is wanted. Reading is a kind of treasure hunt. The trick is to find one's way to the gold nuggets in the most direct fashion, and in the shortest possible time. [35]

6 Delegate reading when appropriate.

Reading can be delegated to your staff if you don't have enough time to read yourself. They in turn can underline key points or summarise or make brief presentations to staff meetings, thus keeping you and themselves informed.

7 Don't feel guilty about reading.

Many managers feel guilty if they spend ten minutes at their desk reading a professional journal because they erroneously feel they are not 'doing something', and fear others may think they are not being productive. This is short-term thinking. As J.J. McCarthy reminds us in *Why Managers Fail*:

> Managers must realise that their organisation's continued progress will be based, in part, upon their ability, and that of their colleagues, to increase their knowledge and skills and to keep pace with progress and change – through the professional literature!

Be assertive. Promote the importance of reading of professional literature at staff meetings and by example.

See also: 74, 116, 222

How to make a good impression on the telephone

Often the only impression a customer or client gains about your organisation is the one generated by the people they talk to on the telephone. Research has shown that bad telephone etiquette can result in poor public relations and millions of rands in lost revenue. Having invested large sums of money in equipment to improve communications with customers, some organisations simply forget to invest in the human skills. As a starter, consider the following advice at least...

1 Know what really frustrates your callers.

Organisations have suffered in recent years through staff failure to use the telephone appropriately. Recent research reveals that the main frustrations customers or clients experience today in dealing with organisations by telephone are:

- taking too long to answer the ring
- being put 'on hold' and forgotten
- being transferred and having to repeat the inquiry
- being answered by voicemail and other 'machines'
- not having calls returned
- music on hold, rudeness, perceived indifference, not getting to the point...

If you can do something about these frustrations, then you'll restore the phone to a position as your organisation's most valuable communications tool.

2 Be familiar with the new technology.

Make sure you and your staff become expert in dealing with the equipment first of all. If you have the technology, it's foolish not to be fully familiar with the advantages it can provide. Do you know how to...

- transfer a call
- park a call
- discern a distinctive ring tone
- redirect calls in your absence
- place calls on hold
- set up 'automatic callback'
- operate the PABX
- use the conference phone facility?

Don't test your caller's patience while you bumble your way through the basics of the technology at your end.

3 Pick up the handset – consciously.

Remember the saying: 'You never get a second chance to make a first impression.' Always be conscious of that advice whenever you pick up the phone. Consider these pointers:

- Answer promptly. If possible, pick up the handset before the third ring ends.
- Quickly finish off any office conversation before lifting the handset so that the caller doesn't hear any irrelevant discussion.
- Put a smile in your voice. It may sound silly, but your voice actually has a more pleasant tone when you're smiling. So, answer the phone with a smile.
- When answering, say 'Good morning/ afternoon', then identify your organisation and yourself.

4 Be organised.

By being organised you will keep caller frustration to a minimum:

- No caller likes to wait for you to 'find a scrap of paper to write on'. Always have message pads and pens on hand.
- Minimise screening questions. It may be justifiable for staff to screen your calls but make sure they don't turn the call into an interrogation.
- Listen carefully for how callers pronounce their names – phonetically spell tricky names on any message slip.
- Make sure your assistant has a copy of your schedule in case a caller requests an appointment or wishes to call back.
- Keep your internal telephone directory up-to-date for accurate call transfers.
- Ensure your phones are never left unattended during lunch breaks, holiday periods and staff sickness. A continuously ringing phone advertises a slack organisation.

5 Take pride in the quality of your conversation.

Train your employees (and yourself) to be concerned, interested and efficient on the phone. In particular:

- Sound confident, knowledgeable and unrushed.
- Take sufficient time to clearly establish the caller's needs.
- Try to eliminate verbal pauses, abrupt or garbled speech habits, 'ums', 'ahs', 'you knows', and other sloppy talk.
- Speak slowly and distinctly. The information being sought may be routine to you but it's not to most callers. Make the caller feel important. Repeat the information if necessary. Leave the caller happy.
- Don't smoke, chew, slouch, shout or whisper when on the phone.
- Cover the mouthpiece if you must talk to another staff member – be warned, however, the caller can probably still hear what you are saying.

Management Memo

The telephone may have progressed considerably since its invention in 1876, but plenty of people would argue that telephone etiquette hasn't progressed much beyond 'Mr Watson, come here – I want you'. At least Alexander Graham Bell had an excuse: he had just spilled acid on himself, and he didn't know he was speaking over the phone.

The first contact that most people have with your organisation is usually via the telephone. That's why it's important for people to be trained in how to use it... [36]

6 Put yourself in the place of the caller.

Empathise with the person on the other end of the phone. Treat callers as you'd like to be treated – so be courteous and helpful:

- Don't keep your caller on hold for any inordinate length of time.
- Give callers the option of holding, or of speaking to someone else, or of leaving a message, or having their call returned.
- Avoid terse, unfriendly phrases such as 'Hold on ...'.
- Never answer a question with 'I don't know'. Instead, say: 'I'm not sure – but I'll find out and get back to you before close of business.'
- If you promise to return a call, do so – promptly – even to say you're still working on the caller's request.
- Be prompt in your response. If the caller wanted an answer next week, she/he would have written a letter!

7 And finally...

- Check that your message distribution procedures are efficient.
- Make sure your staff know how to handle complaints and irate callers, and how to terminate long-winded calls courteously.
- Don't forget: The telephone hides your face but not your attitude.

 See also: 208, 220-222

How to get the most out of a conversation with an employee

Face-to-face communication remains the most important form of communicating whether it occurs formally, as in a scheduled interview or disciplinary situation, or informally, as in a chance meeting in the car park or corridor. Cordial, cooperative discussions with employees ensure that their opinions are heard and provide a very effective means of obtaining information that will make your job much easier. The following approaches are worth considering…

1 Build trust and confidence.

Your initial aim must be to establish rapport by making employees feel comfortable in your presence and converse freely with you. Although there is no magic formula for creating that situation, authenticity and empathy are essential qualities – it's OK to be yourself (apart from the fact that people are very quick to recognise incongruence, where physical and verbal messages contradict each other). A good starting point for any conversation is to get people talking about the most important person in their lives – themselves.

2 Listen and be listened to.

Listening actively is hard work and is more than just not talking. Not only must you hear what the other person is saying but you must also convey understanding and interest through clarifying, summarising, paraphrasing and reflecting feelings. Consider tailoring your conversations according to your employees' preferences – are they listeners or readers? 'Listeners' won't read long written reports – they prefer to hear about them and the details, with a brief note to remind them if necessary. On the other hand, 'readers' have difficulty following a great deal of oral detail – they prefer to see it in black-and-white – so tell them the bare facts and leave your detailed message written out for digestion later.

3 Follow a successful formula.

The key to conducting a fruitful conversation involves the following:

- Get to the point.
- Get all the facts before reaching any conclusion.
- Avoid using too much direct questioning; don't cross-examine.
- Don't use verbal or facial cues that alert the listener to what is coming.
- Keep your conversation factual and objective.
- Confront issues, not people.
- Slow down and instil confidence.
- Lighten up. You can find humour in day-to-day events without being a comedian.

4 Practise conversation skills.

If you're alert, you learn something new from every conversation if you practise these skills:

- Call people by their name – it's the word they most like to hear.
- Ask questions, show interest, listen attentively.
- Develop techniques for bringing conversations to a close: 'Thanks again, Joan. I've enjoyed our chat. I'll see you on Friday at 3.30.'
- Maintain eye contact but don't stare. Research indicates that in a conversation the less assertive person often disengages eye contact first, usually after only a few seconds.
- Use non-verbal invitations to encourage talking – head nods, eye contact, leaning forward, narrowing physical distance. It isn't only *what* you say that registers but *how* you say it.

5 Use clear, straightforward communication.

Clear, effective oral communication is more than not talking down to people. It's also about:

- eliminating space fillers like 'um' and 'er' and catchphrases like 'you know', 'basically', 'in actual fact', and 'sort of thing'.
- slowing down, watching for signs of uncertainty and checking for understanding.
- not talking too much. Even when you're giving information, the other person needs at least 20 per cent of the air time. In other conversations do less than 50 per cent of the talking.

Management Memo

You must realise that a conversation only takes place when each person understands and is understood by the other. That means the listener has to put in as much effort as the speaker. When you speak, you concentrate on speaking in a way the listener can understand. When you listen, you concentrate on understanding all that the other person is telling you. That dimension alone – to focus on understanding, not reacting or preparing to speak – will start the conversation ball bouncing between you. [37]

6 Keep the conversation rolling along.

Use motivational phrases like 'We're here to solve this problem together', 'I'm concerned. I care about what happens to you', 'I'm finding this chat to be very helpful', to keep the conversation moving. Phrases like 'Can you add anything else?', 'I'd like to hear more about that', 'Do you see any problems with any of that?', help to steer the conversation. Remaining silent is another way of keeping the conversation flowing.

7 Organise your thoughts.

Abraham Lincoln once said of an acquaintance: 'He can compress the most words into the smallest ideas of any man I ever met.' So know what you want to say and say it. Keep a small notebook with you at all times, indexed with key persons' names. Jot down in the notebook subjects you want to discuss with any of these people. Those jottings will act as memory joggers and others will be impressed by your knowledge and attention to detail. Make a note of the outcome of any discussion to remind you of any necessary follow-up.

How to remember people's names

A good memory for people's names is not only an important social asset – it's a basic requirement for successful managers. Remember people's names and what they're interested in, and you'll flatter them and get them on your side immediately. But forget their names, and the things important to them, and you're telling them you don't consider them to be important. If you want to avoid the embarrassment of forgetting the names of people you meet, then here are some suggestions for you to consider…

1 Get the name clearly.

The most common problem in remembering the names of people we meet is that during the introduction we really don't pay attention. Whether we're self-conscious about meeting a new person or we feel out of place – whatever the reason, we tend to focus instead on the *How do you do*'s and the *Nice to meet you*'s.

What's more important, as the person is being introduced to you, is to listen for the name. Pay more attention to it than to anything else being said. If you don't pick it up, ask for it to be repeated. Be in no doubt as to the correct pronunciation or spelling. This all shows that the name – and the person – mean something to you.

2 Repeat the name to the person.

Take a second to repeat the name when you are introduced. Indeed, find an excuse for the name to be repeated (and reinforced): 'Hello, Mike. I'm sorry, I missed your last name…' Thereupon, follow up with: 'Mike Buckman! It's nice to meet you, Mike.' The process of retention has begun. During subsequent conversation, try to repeat the name – 'Mike' or 'Mr Buckman', thereby not only strengthening the goodwill but getting your memory processes into gear as well.

3 If possible, focus on the name's derivation.

A useful suggestion, especially if it is an unusual name, is to inquire about its origins. Many people enjoy talking about the derivation and history of their name – particularly if it's unusual, and what they have to say may help make them more memorable for you.

4 Look for a memory hook.

To remember names, the literature usually recommends we establish 'mental filing systems' or 'memory hooks' which will instantly attach a name to a familiar face. Such hooks may, or may not, work for you.

This tactic of linking names to images needs to make sense to no one but yourself, and at first the process may seem cumbersome – but anything is probably better than trying to remember names by just repeating them. Five options may be considered:

- ***Try to put a name to the face.*** Perhaps Mr Baldwin is bald, Mr Bigge has a large body, and Ms Sharpe has a sharp nose.
- ***Check whether the name has a meaning in itself.*** Meaningful names are valuable footholds for memory – like animals such as Wolff, cities such as York or Washington, identities such as Monroe or Kennedy, or adjectives such as Strong or Little. Create a vivid mental image – Mr Strong as a weightlifter.
- ***Find a word substitute.*** If the name has no meaning, substitute a meaningful word that comes close in sound to the name in question, e.g. Buckman – bucket or buckle, and create a mental picture…but be warned, there is a hazard with such associations: don't go calling Mr Buckman Mr Bucket!
- ***Link the mental picture with the location.*** To remember where you first met the person, create your image at the location – picture Mr Strong waltzing through the Hyatt Regency ballroom with a bar-bell held high over his head.
- ***Link the mental picture to the person's interests.*** To remember Mr Buckman's interest in sailing, imagine him bailing out his sinking yacht with a bucket!

We're told that, the sillier the image, the better we retain the information.

5 Repeat the name to yourself.

Following the initial encounter, look back at the person a few times to reinforce the episode. Repetition is the essence of good memory. The more often you say the name to yourself, in association with the memory hook you may have devised, the more entrenched your mental image becomes, and the harder it will be to forget that person's name.

> **Management Memo**
>
> There are courses and books on the topic of remembering names. One problem is that the skill is similar to speed reading. When you come out of the course, or put down the book, you're impressive enough to appear on the Tonight Show – but if you don't practise, the skill fades. Still, it's a great, and imperative, ability for managers.[38]

6 Use pen and paper.

By writing information down, you increase the chance of information being committed to memory. Exchange business cards if possible. As soon as the opportunity arises, jot down the name along with a line or two of description about the person you've just met. Include when and where you met, any memory hooks you have created, and what common interests you found. Later you might transfer this data to index cards for regular review, taking time to recall the person's appearance. If you adopt this strategy, you'll soon earn a reputation for having a terrific memory for names.

7 Work on it.

The best way to remember a name is to tell yourself firmly to do so. It requires discipline and hard work for most people but, to be an effective manager of others, you have to get to know them by name. The effort will be worth it, however, for you will be rewarded – by winning friends instead of just nodding acquaintances.

See also: 146, 160, 270, 272

How to improve your interviewing skills

Interviews have been defined as 'conversations with a purpose' and are essential fact-finding management tools. Job interviews, discipline interviews, appraisal interviews, exit interviews... For managers, it is simply a matter of good sense to learn how to interview other people well because, in the hands of an expert, an interview can be a short straight road to the right answers. You can head down that road by adopting the following proven practices...

1 Do your homework.

If you are unprepared for an interview, you'll make inefficient use of time, present a poor image, and struggle to obtain pertinent details. Don't try to muddle through or start an interview cold. Know exactly the purpose of the session, read and familiarise yourself with all relevant documentation, and prepare a set of questions or topics in advance.

2 Put the interviewee at ease.

Interviews can be stressful affairs. A relaxed setting, a warm welcome, and a few introductory pleasantries are enough to establish a friendly atmosphere. If you do all you can to reduce the intimidating aspects of the occasion and show genuine interest in the person, the more likely it is that you will get honest and thorough information – and, after all, that's the purpose of the exercise.

3 Remain focused on your objective.

Know in advance what facts and information you wish to obtain during the interview and frame your questions to get that data. Don't focus the session on yourself nor allow the interview to be sidetracked by irrelevancies.

4 Keep the initiative.

You are conducting the interview, so stay in control of the situation. You must keep things moving by directing the flow of conversation along specific lines towards your desired goal and to cover your key topics. Your aim should be to maintain a pleasant atmosphere in which the interviewee is encouraged to talk freely while you maintain an objective and impartial stance.

5 Ask the right questions.

Your questions should be framed in such a way that they get complete and detailed answers. Limit those questions which elicit yes/no responses. Avoid multiple questions: by asking two or three at once, you'll not get satisfactory answers to any. Use follow-up questions to probe areas of uncertainty.

6 Keep the interviewee talking.

Your job is to encourage the interviewee to talk. Remember, she/he is a captive audience and probably has no option but to sit and listen if *you* choose to do all the talking. So, always listen objectively and attentively. Don't worry about conversational gaps. If the interviewee stops talking, and you want to hear more on the same topic, just remain silent. Your silence will indicate you expect him/her to continue. The more the interviewee talks, the more will be revealed.

7 Be aware of legal issues.

These days it's illegal to ask questions that aren't related to a person's capacity to do a job. It's best to avoid questions relating to marital status, child-care arrangements, religious practices, age, plans for having children, racial background, or physical disability.

8 Take notes.

As unobtrusively as possible, make notes during the interview, for important points are soon forgotten. Where appropriate make use of checklists. For example, use a list of qualities you want to find in a job applicant, or a list of topics you want to cover in an exit interview. Such lists help you focus the interview on pertinent matters and provide written data for analysis later.

9 Analyse and act on your information.

Immediately after the interview, take some time to elaborate on your notes, summarise answers, record factual information, and review the data. If you conduct several interviews in succession, e.g. job interviews, this process is essential, for you'll find it difficult to associate information with particular candidates without the aid of detailed, objective notes on each person. As well, the time spent on this task will prove invaluable if you need to share your findings later with others.

Management Memo

Skill as an interviewer depends on two factors: an ability to ask the right questions in the right words and a talent for listening and understanding what is said. Although many managers do not realise it, an interviewer is in the spotlight much more than the person being interviewed... Yet, strangely, too many executives and supervisors are amateur interviewers, and they make little effort to improve themselves. [39]

10 Remember also...

- Ensure the interview session is free from interruption.
- Keep the interview going at an apparently unhurried pace. Don't keep looking at your watch – or you will unnecessarily make the interviewee feel unwanted or upset, on the edge of the chair ready for a hasty departure.
- Watch as well as listen.
- Don't let your feelings interfere with your judgement.
- Don't waste time repeating what is already known.
- Don't criticise or indicate disapproval.
- At the finish, invite questions about any issues not covered during the session and explain what the next step will be.
- Always end on a positive, friendly note.

How to handle a media interview

The press and broadcasting media can offer enormous opportunities to highlight a positive side of your organisation. They can also cause problems and create embarrassment when they find that something has gone wrong. These are the two sides of the media coin – and you must be prepared for both. You could find yourself talking to journalists when you send out a press release and the media respond to it, or when the media itself has nosed out a story about your company. Are you prepared to cope with such interviews? Perhaps the following suggestions will help…

1 Know the medium.

When providing an interview for a newspaper, radio or television, it's important to know the peculiarities of each medium. Newspapers cover stories in greater depth, need more backgound material and seek human interest items with local angles. Television newsrooms rarely send crews on good news stories without first making an appointment; but they can disconcertingly arrive unannounced when something more sensational breaks. Television is an immediate, visual medium. Radio news does not have the visual impact of television but commands a large audience. Radio interviews take various forms – a notebook interview (information sought for a story to be read on air), tape-recorded (for replay later), or talkback (live to air).

2 Be clear as to the purpose of the interview.

When invited to be interviewed, ask about the context – what is the issue? why ask me?; and about the format – will it be live or recorded? for news or a magazine feature or programme? studio-based or on the run? If time permits, study the style of the interviewer. Is it likely to be a relaxed, entertaining or difficult session? What will be its duration? Know what you are letting yourself in for so you can prepare adequately.

3 Do your homework.

Preparation is the key to performing well. Never go into an interview without having had time to think about what you might say. If necessary, tell a radio interviewer that you'll ring back in ten minutes or ask the TV journalist for a few moments to think the issue through before the camera rolls. Focus on three or four main points and how you intend to get them across simply and clearly. Check your facts and figures – it's too late after the event.

4 Get your message across.

Most encounters with the media should be pleasant, even exhilarating. The important thing is to come across in a confident, positive, friendly and interesting way, whether you are promoting a success story or dealing with controversy. Consider these points:

- Be helpful and informative, never dismissive or patronising, if dealing with a reporter whose knowledge of the issue seems less than adequate.
- Keep it simple. Stick to the three or four points you want to make and, if the interviewer is not asking the right questions, lead him/her back to your points.
- For radio or TV, find out the first question in advance so that you can prepare a crisp initial response.
- Remember, radio and TV programmes don't have time for lengthy statements. Keep your answers short, relevant and to the point. Practise giving a 30-second grab; get your points across in that time.
- Don't be hoodwinked into accepting views that you do not hold. Don't be bluffed, intimidated or bullied – but remain polite, firm and cool.
- Be prepared for the curly question. If you are concerned that the interview might stray into delicate areas, make the interview conditional on the reporter keeping within agreed parameters.

5 Look and act the part.

Expect to be a little nervous in radio or television interview situations. Breathe slowly and deeply to help you relax. Speak clearly, confidently but naturally. Avoid the 'ums' and 'ahs' and other aggravating vocal gestures. Check your appearance for television – neat, tidy, conservatively dressed. Focus on the interviewer and forget the microphone, camera and lights – they're someone else's problem. But remember, microphones can pick up anything – rustling papers, moving chair, dropped pencil, a whispered aside.

Management Memo

The media are among the most important publics an organisation has, for through the media other publics can be reached... The relationship between a journalist and an interviewee should be a position of mutual trust. The reporter trusts you to tell the facts and the full story; you trust the reporter to present the story in an even-handed and fair manner.[40]

6 Beware of the traps of defamation and litigation.

Take the utmost care when making statements that relate to other people or organisations. If you utter a defamatory statement, and it appears in any form, you, as well as the media outlet, can be sued. If there is any chance of an official enquiry or pending litigation, be careful what you say in public. Seek advice beforehand if necessary.

7 And if something goes wrong...?

Often your story will not run in the media the way you expected – you were misinterpreted, misquoted, taken out of context. Try not to nitpick. On the other hand, if it's a serious mistake, damaging to you or to the company, contact the editor of the publication or the station involved. Consider your options: apology, a printed retraction, a follow-up story to remedy the first. Seek an harmonious solution.

8 Foster sound relations with the media.

Work to cultivate cordial and co-operative relations with the media. They can do much to enhance the public image of you and your organisation.

 See also: 22, 84, 90, 94

How to develop a positive mental attitude

We've all met people who seem to have everything going for them – ideal upbringing, seemingly unlimited talents, useful contacts, and so on. But why is it they never seem to get to first base, careerwise? The answer: attitude. It is often their attitude that limits their achievements. Although changing attitudes is not easy, it can be done and here's an eight-step process that can lead to the development of a positive mental attitude, a will to win, and career success...

1 Practise visualisation.

Visualisation is one of the most powerful techniques of self-image modification because your visual image can become your reality. Management guru Brian Tracy tells us that there are four elements of visualisation and an increase in any one of them will accelerate the rate at which we create the physical equivalent of that mental picture of our life. These four elements are:

- *Frequency*. People who accomplish extraordinary things continually visualise their desired results.
- *Vividness*. This is literally seeing things clearly.
- *Intensity*. When you intensely desire something it occurs much faster.
- *Duration*. The longer you imagine a desired future event, the more likely it is to appear.

2 Make affirmations.

Affirmations are strong statements or commands from our conscious mind to our subconscious mind. They override old information and reinforce new, positive habits of thought and behaviour. Affirmations need to be based on the 3Ps – they must be positive, present tense and personal. For example, if you're trying to improve your health and general well-being, then positive self-talk such as this will help: 'I'm feeling better now', 'I feel young and vital', 'I'm reaching my best weight' and 'I can really feel the difference my exercise programme and change in eating habits are having'.

3 Affirm aloud.

Begin and end each day verbalising your affirmations. You'll be amazed how more confidently you will behave and feel when you're feeding yourself the right messages. So, in the days leading up to a job interview, for example, tell yourself – aloud, whenever you get the chance: 'During my interview I will be calm, confident and in control!' Don't forget: what you 'see' is what you get; what you 'feel' is what you are.

4 Act the part.

Walk, talk and act exactly as if you are the person you want to be. St Thomas Aquinas referred to this philosophy as 'as if', while others call it 'fake it till you make it'. The first step in becoming more confident then is to act 'as if' you already are.

5 Expose yourself to high-quality information only.

The more you read, listen, watch and learn about your subject area, the more confident and capable you'll feel. But we need to be discerning about the quality of information we expose ourselves to. Look on information as food – we should be careful to feed ourselves only the best food.

In this regard the famous T-Cell study of the 1980s is worth remembering, 'T-Cell' being a measure of the blood's healthfulness. The T-Cell of a group actually changed after exposure to varying amounts of positive and negative information. One outcome of the study was that regular exposure to negative information was a health hazard!

6 Associate with positive people.

Fly with the eagles instead of scratching with the chooks. Our parents taught us that 'we are judged by the company we keep'. They were right. To meet new, positive people, you have to stop associating with the loser-brigade, those dull excuse-makers who end up dragging you down to their level of complacency and incompetence.

Management Memo

After decades of quest, we now know that high achievers have a high degree of self-motivation. The enduring power that moves them to action comes from inside themselves. Success is not reserved for the talented. It is not in the high I.Q.. Not in the gifted birth. Not in the best equipment. Not even in ability. Success is almost totally dependent upon drive, focus and persistence. The extra energy required to make an extra effort – try another approach – concentrate on the desired outcome – is the secret of winning. Out of desire – the energy and will to win. Get that urge to win! There's no time to lose. [41]

7 Imitate positive people.

The qualities we admire and envy in others usually reflect our own under-developed capacities. Imitation is essential to learning. Identify those around you with a positive mental attitude and watch what they do. How do they work, what do they say, how do they carry themselves? Select one small behaviour at a time and emulate it.

8 Teach others.

When you attempt to articulate and explain a concept to others, you will understand it and internalise it better yourself. Seize every opportunity to share with others as a way of helping you to become even more familiar with it.

 See also: 82, 90, 94

How to boost your self-confidence

Personal confidence is something most of us would like more of. And where do we turn to get it? Basically, to ourselves, by bolstering and developing those low-confidence areas which need attention. Increasing self-confidence is primarily a matter of finding out what makes us feel good about ourselves and then practising the relevant behaviour patterns. To grow in confidence yourself, here are strategies which you might consider…

1 Set realistic targets for yourself.

Self-confidence will not turn you into Superman or Wonderwoman – only allow you to make the best of what you are personally capable of doing. So set reasonable and realistic expectations for yourself, rather than comparing yourself with others. Keep upgrading your own standards in lifestyle, behaviour, relationships, and professional achievements.

2 Know what you do best.

If you stop and think about even the small things you do each day, you may be surprised to find some abilities and positive features that you haven't given yourself ample credit for in the past. Try to emphasise the positive at all times – and you'll gain confidence to work on those less positive aspects.

3 Monitor negative thoughts and feelings.

How negative are you about yourself? Do you spend large amounts of time worrying about your inadequacies? Do you hold back because you think your report or response is not good enough? Do you compare yourself with another person and always come out second best? Such thinking will get you nowhere. When you find yourself thinking negatively, clench your fist, say 'Stop!' to yourself, and replace negative thoughts with positive ones. Consider your blessings… what and whom you are thankful for, your accomplishments… what you have done that you are proud of so far, and your goals… what your ambitions and dreams are.

4 Look for small victories.

All is not lost if that big achievement eludes you. If everything seems to be falling apart in one area of your life or work, consider your accomplishments in another area. Give yourself a pat on the back for what you have already achieved.

5 Learn from your mistakes.

Don't let your mistakes drag you down. Look on each stumble as a learning experience. Ask what went wrong and what will I do next time?

6 Look and sound confident.

Learn to walk more erectly and authoritatively in public. No matter how you feel, always act, walk and dress as though you're feeling on top of the world and master of the task. Others will respond to your positive vibes and, that, in turn, will boost *your* confidence. Try to delete negative or uncertain words from your conversation – 'maybe', 'I'm not sure', 'but'. Use positive terms such as 'I will' and 'I can'.

7 Adopt a confident approach to your day.

Consider the following confidence-boosters:

- Plan a positive experience for the day and look forward to it.
- As you travel to work, at every stop light, get yourself into a positive frame of mind: 'I *can* finish the Gordon report today!'
- At work, get your tasks into priority order and work positively to your plan.
- Participate actively in meetings.
- Show a colleague how well your day is going.
- At day's end, review your plan and celebrate the crossing off of tasks completed.
- Reward yourself for a good day's work.

Management Memo

Winners have a deep-down feeling of their own worth. Recognising their own uniqueness they develop and maintain their own high standards... Accept yourself as you are right now – an imperfect, changing, growing and worthwhile person. Realise that liking yourself and feeling that you're a super individual in your own special way is not necessarily egotistical. In addition to taking pride in what you are accomplishing – and even more importantly – enjoy the unique person that you are just in being alive right now. Understand the truth that although we as individuals are not born with equal physical and mental attributes, we are born with equal rights to feel the excitement and joy in believing that we deserve the very best in life. Most successful people believe in their own worth, even when they have nothing but a dream to hold on to. Perhaps more than any other quality, healthy self-esteem is the door to high achievement and happiness. [42]

8 Please yourself.

Extending yourself just to impress other people runs counter to what self-confidence is all about. You need to spend more time doing things simply because you want to do them, because these are the things you can succeed in. Use them to bolster your confidence when they go well.

9 Reward yourself.

Enjoy your successes, however small, and celebrate them by yourself or with others. In this way you will be taking the focus off your inadequacies.

How to accomplish more through the use of a personal achievement list

Too often managers modestly, and often unjustly, even unwittingly, hide their successes from others – and indeed from themselves. They fail to appreciate that the simple strategy of recording personal successes can motivate, increase self-productivity and support career advancement. The compilation of a personal achievement list can have a considerable impact on a manager's professional life…

1 Acknowledge your achievements to date.

The majority of managers see themselves as 'modest achievers'. They're so accustomed to doing what they do and what is expected of them that they rarely, if ever, class any of their accomplishments as 'achievements'. Indeed, when someone is impressed with something they've done, something that perhaps seems rather ordinary to them, they're surprised.

As a manager, you can use your past achievements more positively to motivate you to greater heights. To shrug them off modestly, as most professionals are prone to do, or to forget about them, will just make it harder to add further successes to your repertoire. By acknowledging your achievements, you'll be able to build on them (with a little planning and persistence), and motivate yourself to strive towards greater successes.

2 Appreciate how achievement-motivated you really are.

If you are achievement-motivated, then you'll be able to answer these questions in the positive…

- Do you want to accomplish something significant?
- Do you like to set your own goals?
- Do you like doing your own thing, rather than being told what to do?
- Are you self-motivated?
- Do you prefer to select moderate, practical, achievable goals for yourself?
- Do you like immediate feedback on how you are progressing towards your goals?
- Do you want full responsibility for attaining your goals?

If you are very low or completely bereft in achievement motivation, then you may find your work and your life empty of vitality and vigour.

3 Start a Personal Achievement List.

You'll be surprised how much you achieve as a manager in a year, and systematically writing it down is the only way to keep track. So, keep a list of your successes in chronological order, divided by month, over the span of a year – initiatives, milestones, articles, talks, interviews, books read, awards and the like that signify that you've accomplished something.

4 Use your Personal Achievement List.

The benefits of keeping and reviewing your list soon become obvious, e.g.

- *for gauging progress.* Seeing your achievements all in one place, in chronological order, helps you determine if you're making the kind of professional and personal progress you have in mind for yourself. Do the successes support your goals? Or do they simply consume time and energy?
- *for getting the attention of others.* You can promote yourself well at interviews and meetings only when you know yourself well.
- *for supporting your documentation.* The process of putting together your résumé is streamlined when you have already isolated your successes over time via the list.
- *for motivating yourself.* Use the stimulation of success to accomplish even more.

5 Begin a Projected Personal Achievement List.

Once you have mastered the process of putting your achievements in writing, it makes sense to project achievements into the future to guide your progress.The achievements that go into this list are the ones you can realistically accomplish, again chronologically by month, in support of your overall goals. American management authority Jeffrey

Management Memo

I long to accomplish a great and noble task, but it is my chief duty to accomplish all tasks as though they were great and noble. The world is moved along, not only by the mighty shoves of its heroes, but also by the aggregate of the tiny pushes of each honest worker. [43]

Davidson says:

> This projected list is a 'living' document that requires continual revision as achievement occurs. It is important to revise along the lines of goals and steps to achieve them, rather than just along the lines of what you know for sure will happen. In this way, you will be in charge of a logical pattern of accomplishments, and it will be more likely that they will bear a concrete relationship to your own goals.

6 Follow this advice to reach your full potential...

Finally, if your Projected Personal Achievement List is to make a significant impact on your own productivity as a manager and achiever, then bear in mind these thoughts from the motivational literature:

- It's lucky for people who aim high that most people have no aim at all.
- If what you did yesterday still looks significant to you, then you haven't done much today.
- Unless you undertake more than you possibly can do, you will never do all that you can.
- It isn't how much you know, but what you get done that the world rewards and remembers.

How to beat the Monday morning blues

A productive, happy and effective day is usually achieved by starting out fast and peppy in the morning. Unfortunately, the day is often lost to many of us even before we get out of bed – we self-destruct as soon as we wake up, dreading the thought of having to go to work. For most people, Monday mornings in particular can be the most difficult time of all. If you have trouble getting started each week, then here is some timely advice on beating those Monday morning blues...

1 Finish as many jobs as possible on Friday.

If you finish as many tasks as you can before the weekend, you will feel much better knowing that these matters are not hanging over for Monday morning.

2 Tidy up your office before leaving on Friday evening.

Never arrive on Monday morning to find the cluttered remnants of the previous week's work.

3 Get Monday off to a flying start on Friday.

Try not to start a project from scratch on Monday. Begin a task on Friday so that you can pick it up first thing Monday morning, thus giving yourself momentum and an immediate sense of accomplishment.

4 Set a new goal for Monday.

On Friday afternoon, write down a simple goal to be tackled first thing Monday morning. It won't hurt to think about Monday's goal while pruning the roses on Sunday.

5 Leave weekend matters to the weekend.

Never carry non-business issues and tasks from your weekend over to Monday morning. Get them out of the way before Monday morning or postpone them until later in the week.

6 Take it easy on Sunday night.

Schedule your weekend activities for Saturday and for Sunday morning and afternoon. Reserve Sunday night for relaxation, winding down weekend activities in preparation for a new working week.

7 Exercise on Monday morning.

Before heading off to work on Monday morning, jog around the block or try some exercises. Bring some zest back into your life. Keep your body fit so that your emotions and your body don't become a drag on your mind.

8 Get up early on Mondays.

If you sleep in on Monday mornings, you will only be adding to your misery. Rise early, exercise, have breakfast, read the paper, and snap yourself into the routine of the coming week.

9 Schedule interesting meetings for Monday mornings.

Good company and stimulating conversation can lift your spirits. If you want to get a good start to the week, schedule a meeting with interesting colleagues.

10 Avoid big jobs on Monday morning.

Spread major jobs throughout the week. This will make the thought of going back to work after the weekend less oppressive.

11 Plan to vary your activities.

Schedule something enjoyable for Wednesday. On Monday morning, this mid-week reprieve won't seem as far away as Saturday. And it could work wonders to improve your depressed outlook.

12 Set an example for staff.

Chances are, you're not the only one with Monday morning blues. But if the boss suffers from the Monday morning blues as well, those on staff who *are* enthusiastic may well decide to follow the boss's example. You see, the blues are contagious!

Management Memo

For inalienable biological reasons, Monday tends to be the least productive for most people. It's simply natural to feel stress when making the transition from pleasurable engagement back into work. [44]

Managers need to set the example. See work as an enjoyable experience, and demonstrate this to staff – particularly on Monday mornings.

And don't forget: there's nothing worse for worker motivation than to have them turn up to find a stuffy office first thing on Monday morning – so make sure the air conditioning has been switched on well in advance of their arrival.

13 And finally...

For a fast and enthusiastic start to any new day, heed the advice of internationally-known motivational speaker Tom Hopkins. He suggests:

- Listen to lively, exciting, zingy and upbeat music. It will do wonders for your morning mood.
- Listen to motivational tapes which you can alternate with the music tapes. In fact, make your own tapes.
- Psyche yourself up with your own words: 'OK. Today is the most beautiful day I've ever had. Today I must really perform for my staff...'
- Push positive thinking all the way. Either enthusiasm must take over or negativism will.
- Start your day the night before.

 See also: 82-84, 212

How to stand up for yourself

If you express your beliefs, feelings and opinions honestly and directly in a socially acceptable manner, you are being assertive. Assertiveness means standing up for yourself but respecting the rights of others in the process. To be an effective manager, there will be times when you need to act assertively - when negotiating, giving or receiving feedback, dealing with staff or customers, or defending your position. Here's how you can become a more effective manager by becoming more assertive...

1 Understand what assertiveness means.

Assertiveness falls midway between aggression and submission.

- Aggressive people are brutally direct, inconsiderate, and domineering when dealing with others.
- Submissive people are the other extreme – submissive people are indirect, subtle, vague, even shy.
- Assertive people are honest, communicate feelings, are direct but tactful, and leave people feeling comfortable and positive.

2 Adopt a clear stance and restate your position regularly.

In situations that call for resoluteness, make your stance known from the start and make it obvious that you intend to stand firm. Calmly repeat your position whenever the need arises. Being clear and resolute, refusing to be side-tracked, you avoid unnecessary argument.

3 Know when you need to be assertive.

Some situations will require that you take a stance and stick to it. For example:

- *Saying no.*
  Can you turn down other people's requests assertively? Learn to say no directly and calmly without hesitation and without lengthy excuses or apologies. Don't fall into the trap of being made to feel guilty, manipulated, or coaxed into giving in.
- *Making requests.*
  When you want something, ask for it specifically and directly, rather than hinting, manipulating or demanding. To make a request assertively, state your need, ask for action, and give a reason for your request.
- *Giving criticism.*
  The ability to be fair and firm when criticising another person is the hallmark of an assertive manager. Be firm, direct, clear, tactful and compassionate.

- *Receiving criticism.* An assertive person is able to listen to criticism without becoming aggressive or defensive, to examine that feedback objectively, and to use the information constructively.

In each of these situations, keep your outcome in mind. Do not engage in a verbal slinging match. Instead, respond positively – either as a gracious loser or as a generous winner.

4 Learn to communicate assertively.

To be assertive, you need to look assertive, sound assertive and use assertive language.

Maintain direct and steady eye contact, check that your posture is businesslike, make sure your expression is serious but relaxed, and get rid of those nervous giggles and angry frowns.

Don't shout or mumble, speak steadily and calmly, be sincere, and keep anger, excitement, nervousness, and sarcasm in check. Keep your statements concise, clear and direct, avoid name-calling and emotive labels such as 'lazy' and 'stupid', and don't use such indecisive phrases as 'kind of' and 'that's just my view anyway'.

5 Leave the other person feeling positive.

Where the situation demands, offer and reach agreement on a workable compromise so that there is no confusion by you or the other party about any follow-up action to be adopted, and so that the other party can save face.

Management Memo

When dealing with other people in trying to accomplish certain tasks, you will undoubtedly find that the assertive approach is the most effective. You will find that you are more likely to get the cooperation of others in getting things done, since they respect you and feel respected by you. [45]

6 And finally...

Gael Lindenfield, author of *Assert Yourself*, advises that, if you want to be assertive, then you must:

- decide what you want
- decide if it's fair
- ask clearly for it
- not be afraid of taking risks
- be calm and relaxed
- express your feelings openly
- give and take compliments easily
- give and take criticism.

You must not:

- beat about the bush
- go behind people's backs
- bully
- call people names
- bottle up your feelings.

How to say no

In difficult times, managers are often called upon to exercise their powers of veto. Saying 'yes' is so much easier – it's certainly so much less confrontationalist and unpleasant. But managers often have to say 'no' – to proposed expenditures, to the call for extra staff, and to new ideas and other proposals from staff. There is a right way to say 'no' and to minimise the rejection or disappointment that may result…

1 Be courteous in considering the request.

If you want to maintain your dignity and to prevent the discussion from degenerating into a shouting match, remember to be polite, pleasant and courteous throughout the conversation. As a rule, if you are courteous and polite, then most people are courteous and polite in return.

2 Listen to the proposal.

People expect their views to be heard and considered. If you refuse to listen, even if you are familiar with the arguments, then you'll be asking for trouble. If you ignore what people are saying to you, and off-handedly dismiss their request, you will only create animosity.

3 Do not procrastinate.

A delayed decision can only increase the chances of disappointment and resentment. You should try to make a quick decision. By delaying, people will begin to anticipate that you may say yes. So, if you know what your response will be, then answers such as 'I'm not sure yet' and 'Let me think about it' only get people's hopes up – and then it's even more devastating when you finally say no.

4 Say no, then explain.

There's nothing wrong with saying no – but say it politely, having based the decision upon a just consideration of the facts. Explain why you decided the way you did. Outline the supporting information which went into the decision, and make it very clear that all the options were carefully taken into account.

5 Never argue.

The disappointment or rejection can sometimes lead into a heated debate about your decision, allowing people to force their views upon you again, rather than accept your decision. You should firmly tell people that your decision is correct, having weighed up all the facts and given justifiable reasons – and there the matter should rest.

By all means allow people to rationally discuss your decision with you, perhaps exploring alternatives, but limit their speaking time. Be fair, but always be firm because ultimately your decision is still going to be no.

6 Don't apologise.

Easier said than done, but try. You have done nothing that warrants an apology so, having made your decision after considering all aspects, you can confidently run with the outcome. Be sympathetic but point out that ultimately your decision was for the good of the organisation.

7 Offer a counter-proposal.

If you think it's appropriate and the request is a valid one, you may consider offering a counter-proposal. For example: 'I have a lot of work on my plate, Gordon, so I can't sit in for you at this afternoon's meeting. However, I'll be happy to answer your telephone while you're out.' Such an approach can soften your refusal.

8 Follow-up.

When your no is accepted, don't assume that the episode is over as far as you are concerned. Depending on the degree of disappointment, you must rebuild the bridges between you and your staff member. This helps to relieve any lingering tensions and to strengthen your hand on the next occasion.

Management Memo

No is a powerful word. Here's when you can use it...

- ☐ *Say NO to allow you to define your priorities.* Consider international speaker Dr James Dobson. He had to say no to hundreds of speaking invitations that were taking him away from his family.
- ☐ *Say NO to take control of your time.* Control this precious resource by saying a selective, definite no to those meetings and invitations which consume your valuable time but produce little.
- ☐ *Say NO to maintain integrity.* Men and women of integrity have to say no to temptations which threaten their personal or professional beliefs or code of ethics.
- ☐ *Say NO if the cost or risk is too high.* You might need courage to say no in meetings where ideas are presented which involve unacceptable risks or impose too high a price.
- ☐ *Say NO to allow you to say YES.* By having the courage to say no to some things, you allow yourself the benefits of saying yes to finer, more productive, more lasting activities and experiences.
- ☐ *Say NO to provide breathing space.* Saying no to an idea or proposal can provide a constructive 'waiting period' for conditions or timing to be more opportune.

NO can be a gloriously positive word, as well as a negative retort. And don't forget that there are many circumstances when it's important to remember that *NO isn't forever!* [46]

9 And, don't forget...

Expect to say no several times a day. This is your right as a manager. Then, when it happens, you shouldn't be too upset or tinged with guilt because you've already come to terms with this responsibility.

See also: 34, 96, 130, 132

How to take the initiative and make things happen

What is it that separates the achievers and the go-getters from those managers who sit there, spinning their wheels, or worse still, just waiting for something to happen? The real achievers are those who take the initiative and make things happen. Do you want to stand around and wait for something to happen – or do you want to make it happen? The following guidelines are provided for the latter…

1 Adopt a positive approach at all times.

If you want to be a successful initiator, you must begin by having the right attitude. You must speak and act with confidence, even being a little pushy in your approach. If you assume that your ideas will be listened to and respected, then you immediately increase the chances of that being the case. If you see the initiative as a possible disaster, it is likely a disaster will occur.

Your attitude will be contagious. If you exude confidence about the outcome of your initiative, your enthusiasm will be transferred on to your staff.

2 Challenge the routine way of doing things.

It is very comfortable to stop thinking critically about our routine tasks, to go through the motions, to retreat to the familiar. It can be habit-forming.

When did you last look critically at everything you do with the eye of an initiator? Try it for a week. You'll find that some of the best initiatives are small improvements to old routines – the way you run meetings, how you organise your day, when you meet with clients, and so on.

Remember too: success is usually a result of being one per cent better at 1 000 things, rather than 100 per cent better at one thing. Besides, small initiatives are not as risky, so it is easier to get support from your staff for the changes.

3 Look for opportunities.

Look for ways of improving things in your workplace. Force yourself to stop for a minute every hour, to step outside of yourself, to look at what you're doing and what's going on around you.

Ask yourself: 'What's not working?', 'What could be done better?'. By opening your eyes, you'll see opportunities for initiative everywhere. The trick is to discipline yourself to set aside that minute every hour.

4 Be action-oriented.

Don't wait to be asked, trained or told. Whenever you see an opportunity to improve the operation of your organisation, pursue it. As Peters and Waterman in *In Search of Excellence* write: 'do it, fix it, try it'. Initiators are thinkers and doers, planners and workers. They get involved using a 'hands-on' approach.

5 Look beyond your own world.

Winners learn from winners, so be on the lookout for other organisations' successful ideas. Who's trying what? What's working and what isn't? Proactively seek out 'initiatable ideas' from elsewhere.

Develop your own formal and informal networks through professional organisations, clubs, and so on. The professional journals are goldmines for action-oriented leaders – and they usually come with the whys, wheres, hows and valuable contacts. Don't limit your horizons. Look beyond the confines of your own organisation.

6 Accept the challenges and the risks.

Many of the best opportunities for initiative reside in those activities that others are reluctant to handle. Make a name for yourself: take on the challenge that nobody else wants. That's how successful leaders are made. Remember that every new initiative involves a risk – theory doesn't always work in practice. But a mistake doesn't mean failure. Mistakes are inevitable; they're also invaluable, apparently, for superachievers in life usually have a long string of failures behind them.

> **Management Memo**
>
> Achievers have one crucial characteristic in common: they are constantly looking for new ways to impact their environment. The initiator knows that there are dozens of opportunities to initiate in every organisation. It's a way of looking at the world that spawns not only major breakthroughs, but a steady stream of small gains (which in retrospect often look like breakthroughs).
>
> When you decide to initiate, you become a player instead of a spectator. And though taking initiative certainly has its material rewards, the good feelings of accomplishment and control over your life are even better.[47]

7 Foster initiative in others.

As a manager, you must not only take the initiative – you must inspire others of your staff to do so as well.

One simple way of doing this is to require your employees to come to you, not only with a problem, but with some options and a recommended solution. An added bonus is that you may end up with a better solution than if you were the sole problem-solver. As well, it creates a wonderful opportunity for staff development.

8 And don't forget...

- Some people fight change. Initiators embrace it. They know that change is the one constant of today's world.
- Develop the ability to visualise the steps from idea to fulfilment.
- Be assertive rather than aggressive. Do not alienate your staff members by flaunting your innovative nature.
- A successful initiator relies on imagination, strength of purpose, intelligence – and a little luck.

 See also: 100, 106

How to take risks

If you're keen to display the qualities of true leadership, then risk-taking must become part of your executive weaponry. Leaders must be disrupters of the *status quo*, something that often requires them to take risks. Calculated risk-taking helps 'creative edge' organisations to thrive and earns an enviable reputation for individuals who deliver the positive results. But risk-taking requires courage, and an awareness of the following advice...

1 Be aware of the pros and cons of risk-taking.

Risk-taking means moving from a situation of some security to another less secure position. But, in order to advance, there'll be times when you must place yourself, or even your organisation, at risk. Courage is a basic requirement for risk-taking, sometimes at great professional and personal cost. The alternative – choosing *not* to show leadership – will no doubt result in fewer risks and greater security, but it will also mean the loss of opportunity to bring about needed improvement in your organisation.

2 Confront fear first – then bite the bullet.

Fear is a demotivating factor in any situation. People don't do things because they fear the consequences of doing them (and vice versa). People who do not learn to confront their fears may go through life in the company of embarrassment, failure, rejection, disapproval, uncertainty, and a myriad of other doubts. Confronting fear is a precursor to taking risks. So, if you find yourself hesitating about taking a risk, ask: 'What am I *really* scared of?' By isolating and facing up to that fear, by weighing the disadvantages and the advantages, you can decide whether or not the risk – the calculated risk – is worth taking.

3 Ensure the risk is justified.

Remember that risk-taking can be something of a gamble and that one of the rules of gambling is never to risk more than you can afford to lose. Size up the odds, the rewards, and the risks. Don't risk a lot for a little – particularly useful advice when you're sticking your neck out only to take revenge, save face, or on a matter of principle.

4 Forget the rules.

The thing about risk-taking is that there *are* no rules. In fact, risk-taking often involves breaking or stretching any existing rules to breaking point. It's all about change. And to bring about change, you can best assess the risks by becoming an observer of human and organisational behaviour. If you understand the way your superiors, peers or subordinates work and think, then you can venture a guess as to how they will react to any breathtaking initiative you undertake or propose.

5 Determine in advance just how far you can go.

Risk-taking often involves threatening certain existing values, resources and vested interests, and many people dislike change when it upsets their way of thinking, work style or life pattern. It's important to gauge upfront just how far you can push these boundaries. History is punctuated with stories of risk-takers who stepped where angels feared to tread. The difficulty for risk- takers, and for you, however, is to know when *not* to step over the line.

6 Know your limitations.

A long-shot is one thing – a no-win situation is quite another. So, if you figure you'll be outclassed, outfoxed, outranked, underresourced, or undermined, then don't be rash. Step back and rethink your strategy.

7 Prepare a contingency plan – just in case.

Suppose your risk doesn't pay off – how can you save face, cut your losses, or cash in your chips? Be prepared, by having a range of alternatives and contingencies in place which will allow you to reach a compromise by negotiating a mutually agreeable outcome.

Management Memo

To get ahead, you must put yourself on the line. That's how individuals succeed, and that's how companies succeed. With the increasing rate of change, 'the *status quo*' is almost nonexistent – you are constantly at risk. [48]

8 Jump in and maximise the impact.

Once you've decided to take the risk, use whatever techniques are necessary to instil confidence in those around you and to keep your momentum going. It's not only what you say, it's how you say it – so be dramatic, stylish and enthusiastic. The 'as if' philosophy is appropriate here – if you want to succeed, begin by acting 'as if' you have.

9 Gain and remain in control.

You're taking the risk so seek to control as many variables as possible. Use power and influence – your own and that of your boss, and by your actions, earn the authority of other key players.

10 Learn to live to fight another day.

Fights are rarely won in the first round; the winner is the one still there at the end. Unless it's a winner-take-all situation, don't be discouraged if your venture doesn't come off. The important thing is where you stand over the long haul, but to remember the turtle always – it will get nowhere if it doesn't stick its neck out!

How to sell your new idea to other people

As a manager, you'll often have to persuade people to believe in your views and to accept your ideas. If you're good at selling your ideas to employees and colleagues, you'll go further faster in your career. Unfortunately, good ideas must first be sold to staff and, if you can't get your proposals across in the way you envisaged, they may well go the way of many other good ideas – into oblivion. Here are some simple rules that will help you sell your ideas more effectively in the future…

1 Know what you want – exactly.

Don't settle for a vague fuzzy shadow of an idea, only to grow angry when you fail to get it across to others. Pretest your idea for clarity: put it on paper. If it can't be written down – goal, numbers, key players, deadlines, budgets – then it isn't a completely developed idea. The very act of finding the appropriate words with which to express an idea compels you to think it through.

2 Double-check everything.

Make sure that all the necessary research and validation has been done to support your idea, and that you have all the facts and figures readily available. You'll need these down the track.

3 Consider current circumstances.

Ensure that the idea sits well in the current climate of your organisation. For example, you wouldn't want to suggest a costly idea if little money were available in your organisation's coffers.

4 Highlight the benefits.

The key to persuasion is to see your proposition from other people's points of view. Their questions (to themselves usually) will be: 'How does this affect me?' and 'What do I stand to gain or lose?' Make sure you can clearly demonstrate the specific benefits to be gained by others if adopting your idea – and keep these foremost in your mind, *and theirs*, during your presentations and subsequent discussions.

5 Be prepared for the objections.

People are always suspicious of new ideas; most prefer the *status quo*. Anticipate their objections beforehand by consciously and diligently examining your idea for flaws. List potential objections and prepare yourself to tackle them with data, not emotion. Of course, the surest way to squash an objection is to incorporate both the objection and its solution into your presentation. Another useful strategy is to overcome people's objections, not by showing them the error of their logic, but by reiterating what's in it for them.

6 Make your idea their idea.

A great way of gaining support is to give away the credit for an idea. By skilfully making suggestions, you can often get people to adopt and commit themselves to your ideas as their own. It's amazing how much you can achieve if you don't mind who gets the credit! As well, it's important for you to sow the seeds of ownership by getting them to contribute in some way to the idea themselves.

7 Get some kind of 'yes' early on in the process.

Good salespeople know that it always pays to start their sales pitch on a point – however minor, even irrelevant – with which your audience can agree. In other words, find some common ground quickly in order to start off with agreement of any kind early on.

8 Solicit the support of colleagues.

Discuss the idea in advance with your close colleagues and opinion leaders in your organisation. Their support and agreement can then be called upon at the meeting at which you present your idea for consideration.

9 Prepare for a simple and effective presentation.

Your presentation should take two forms: written and oral. Writing adds weight to an idea by indicating that the ideas are less likely to be half-baked or lacking in commitment. Keep your written proposal to a graphic, simply expressed, concise page or two.

Management Memo

Nothing turns off enthusiasm faster than consistently watching ideas get shot down, either by active objectors and/or passive resisters. The main reason that ideas aren't accepted – assuming they're practical to start with – is that little thought is given to the selling effort involved.[49]

Your oral presentation should simply get across the main points of your proposal, its benefits and costs. Avoid being drawn into too much detail. You cannot be accused of hiding or concealing something if you also bring out the disadvantages – before shooting them down yourself. Be convincing and enthusiastic in your summing up.

The effectiveness of your presentation will also depend largely on how well you prepared for it, having your facts and figures straight, deciding what you are going to say in what order, and how you are going to say it. It's wise to rehearse your presentation.

10 Check timing and sequence.

Determine precisely when you should present your idea. Make sure your timing is appropriate, thereby giving your idea a greater chance of being accepted.

11 Check your fallback position.

If your proposal is not acceptable to your audience in its entirety, make sure you have a fallback position with which you're comfortable, ensuring that if your first idea is defeated, you are not left with nothing. Don't let your planning inhibit flexibility.

See also: 82-84, 96, 104

How to overcome the fear of failure

How often have you avoided tackling a job because you were afraid of not doing it well, or backed off a new initiative because you feared it might not succeed, or not accepted a speaking engagement because you were afraid of embarrassing yourself. Fear of failure is surprisingly common. But it is a fear that can be conquered, especially when you realise that it isn't failure that counts in life; it's what you can learn from the experience that matters. Heed this advice to help overcome your fear of failure...

1 Try not to be hard on yourself.

If your company's aim was to make an annual profit of R100 000 and you managed a profit of only R78 000 – is that *really* failure? Failure is a relative term, depending on who is doing the measuring.

2 Set your own standards of success or failure.

Success, or failure, is in many instances only a matter of opinion. If your spouse has always wanted you to become managing director of the company, just remember that you don't have to be if you don't want to. In the long run, it's your choice. Don't allow your life's goals to be set by anyone else. It's better to succeed in doing your best than to fail in doing nothing.

3 Don't confuse 'success' with 'excellence'.

Why do we always think we have to win or achieve excellence in everything we do to be successful? There's nothing wrong with a par round of golf, the same way as there's nothing wrong with an ordinary game of tennis – so long as we have fun doing it, and do it as best we can.

4 Stop seeing everything in black-and-white terms.

Why must everything we do be seen in terms of success – failure? In future, if you set yourself a goal, try judging your performance in terms of degrees of success.

5 Consider the worst case scenario.

Next time you're fearful about biting the bullet, ask yourself: 'What's the worst that can happen if I fail?' If your answer is something you can live with, why not give it a go? Remember, too, that fear of failure is the father of failure.

6 Accept that you're not alone.

If you analyse the performance of your work colleagues, you will quickly find that they are all composed of strengths, weaknesses, successes, and failures – unless you are working with fail-proof robots. This is the human condition. So, by acknowledging that others around you are also capable of failure – and do, then you may be better prepared to fail once or twice yourself.

7 Stop trying to be a perfectionist.

Being a perfectionist is laudable, if not essential, for such people as brain surgeons or aircraft maintenance personnel. But for the rest of us, the quest for perfectionism is demanding, frustrating, even futile. What's important is that we display a willingness to try and not be put off by failure. Remember the adage: 'Those who are not trying and many times failing are either stagnant or dead.'

8 View failure for what it is – a learning experience.

Failure is only an opportunity to begin again, more intelligently. If you perceive failure as part of the growing process, then failure becomes something positive, a contribution to future success, and not something to be feared. So, your recent speech to your trade association was disappointing? Never mind, you can always learn more from your failures than from your successes – a good thing to remember. As Josh Billings once said: 'It ain't no disgrace for a man to fall, but to lay there and grunt is.'

> **Management Memo**
>
> The worst possible outcome of trying a work task and then failing is probably transient embarrassment. You might be embarrassed for a while, but that will fade. The residue hopefully will be a valuable learning experience. Trial-and-error learning is a time-honoured process and one familiar to most successful people. [50]

9 Talk about your fears with others.

Discuss your campaign of courage with a close friend or colleague. Talking about your fear of fouling-up can be helpful if you have a friend who is understanding and supportive. Meet regularly to analyse the risks you have recently taken, their 'success' rate, and to set specific targets for the future.

10 Plunge right in!

The purpose of fear is to warn us of danger, not to make us afraid to face it. So, next time you fear trying something, throw caution to the wind and do it! If you're concerned about the danger involved, set a safety net in place first – but do it! Even if you achieve only partial success, you'll be doing what you really want to do, and that's a good feeling. And even if you do stumble, remember that a worm is about the only thing that doesn't fall down.

See also: 206, 270

How to use anger constructively

Anger is a destructive human emotion. Rarely do we profit in any way from a spontaneous outburst of temper. It accomplishes nothing, regardless of whether it is aimed at others, inanimate objects, or ourselves. But at times it can be a powerful management tool, provided it is used with precision and timing, and it is used to create energy rather than draining it. Here are some useful considerations to help you make constructive use of anger...

1 Realise *you* get angry; no one forces you to.

Each of us has our very own emotional buttons that don't just wait to be pushed – they reach out like antennae and actively pick up trouble. It's these buttons that hurt us. It's not what someone says or does that hurts – it's our *own* buttons that do it. The incident simply pushes our provocative, sensitive button and – *clunk!*

Anger is one such button. You're the only person who can be in control of your anger button, so don't relinquish that control to others by getting angered in situations of *their* making where *you*'ll be sorry afterwards.

2 Try hard to put the lid on spontaneous anger.

Keep your immediate anger in check by considering those time-honoured coping devices: count to ten, bite your tongue, walk away. The best coping strategy is to give your anger a raincheck. Provide yourself with a cooling-off period. If someone upsets you, tell yourself, 'I'll get mad about this tomorrow.' Postponing anger is the best way to minimise its damage. If you spontaneously unload this potentially destructive emotion onto an employee or colleague, then minor mishaps can escalate into major catastrophes. Postponing an angry outburst can reduce the odds of that happening. It also helps to take a minute or two to remind yourself of the offender's good points and value to your organisation – that too may prevent you from jumping in boots and all. Postponing anger is the first vital step to using it constructively.

3 Identify the cause and arrange a meeting.

Never resort to venting your anger on another person in public. To get the best results, tell the person concerned that a serious discussion is coming up. You might say, 'We have a problem and I'm going to talk to you about it later. When can we get together where we won't be interrupted for a while?' The news is unlikely to come as a shock to the other person, but your announcement will create a little healthy anxiety.

Management Memo

Ridding yourself of guilt, worry, fear of failure, and excessive anger can make you a new person. Suddenly you will find that you have time, energy, and abilities you never dreamed you had.[51]

4 Talk problems, not personalities.

People can normally justify behaving as they do, so try to understand why they behaved in the manner which resulted in your anger – this will help your discussions considerably. Separating the personality from the problem can be a challenge but this can, and must, be done if you are, in the end, to get people to help you rather than want to get even with you.

5 Be precise.

When people earn your rejection, tell them. Let them know that you are angry, what is making you feel that way, and exactly what has to be done to eliminate your anger. Express it in plain language, choosing words that will get the point across. Your choice of words must not only provide relief to your own frustrations but must influence the other person to change.

6 Seek immediate feedback.

Remember, *you* don't own the problem – the cause of your anger – so leave the monkey where it belongs – with its rightful owner. Find out what actions the other person is going to take to remove the monkey and agree on a timetable for those actions. Any decisions made must be owned by the other person or your efforts will go unrewarded.

7 Quit when you're in front.

You've relayed your concerns, communicated your feelings and hopes, and the other person has got the message. Quit. If you ramble on after you've covered the matter, the other person will decide that you're simply unloading your own problems rather than sincerely trying to achieve anything positive. Thank the person for contributing to a solution, offer help with any follow-up actions, and end the meeting. Make a note (mental or written) to touch base informally with the person over the next forty-eight hours. During that get-together you may decide to express your appreciation of their contributions.

8 Review your performance.

Evaluate the way you handled the situation. Did your postponed display of anger achieve its desired outcome? Would you use a similar approach again in a similar situation? Hopefully, you will conclude that responding through anger to people, rather than reacting angrily to them, is the preferred alternative.

How to make the most of your mistakes

If only we lived in a world where we never made mistakes... We don't, of course, and managers are not without fault in this regard. Since we do err, success will come to those who learn to turn their goofs into gold. The golden rule is to *never ignore your mistakes* – if you do, you are liable to repeat them. In short, it is no crime to err; the crime is not to learn from the mistake and not to improve as a result. Turn your goofs into gold by considering the following advice...

1 Admit your mistake.

Never ignore a mistake or try to cover it up. Confession can be good for the soul and, in management, it can sometimes be a very effective strategy. Unless the mistake is catastrophic, a manager has little to lose by admitting an error. In fact, you will gain the respect of your staff. By admitting your error, you lend credibility to those occasions when you are right; and your staff will be less likely to challenge your judgement if they know you are honest and as demanding of yourself as you are of them. As well, you demonstrate that you value truth above excuses, and truth is what you will get in turn from your staff. If they know that you know that everyone, including yourself, is human, they will do their best for you.

2 Do not try to shift the blame.

As the manager, you are ultimately responsible for the final decision and for the error. Your job now is to find ways to overcome the blunder, not to find someone to blame. If you side-step accountability by manufacturing excuses or by being defensive, you lose everyone's respect. Instead of the mistake becoming a learning opportunity, it will simply become another exploding problem.

3 Assess the damage.

You cannot deal with a mistake intelligently unless you know how bad it is. Consider first its *importance* – there is a great deal of difference between miscalculating product sales in one district and re-tooling a factory to produce a new product line with no customer appeal; then its *cost* – there's a great difference between a R500 goof and a R50 000 blunder; and finally its *implications* for you, your unit or the organisation. The significance of the damage will determine the extent to which you must move into damage control.

4 Determine the cause of the problem.

To learn from your mistake you must find out why it happened. Only then can you take appropriate steps to prevent the mistake from recurring.

Seek answers to such questions as:

How good was my planning? Did I allow enough time, enough money? Did I allocate the right equipment, material and people? Were bottlenecks anticipated?

How good was my information? Was it incomplete, unreliable, out-of-date? Were my sources appropriate?

How good was my timing? Did I launch the plan or initiative on the wrong day, in the wrong week, month, or season?

How well was the plan supervised? Did I rely too much on others? Were they as committed as I? Did I check progress adequately and often enough?

Was anyone else at fault? We're not always personally to blame. Was a supplier late? Did a supervisor take an unauthorised shortcut? Did someone miss a deadline? You're not looking for a scapegoat, just a cause.

Did we run into unexpected problems? Did equipment break down? Did we encounter a maritime strike?

Were communications poor? ...and so on.

In answering such questions, you should be able to pinpoint the cause of your mistake. You should now be in a position to cash in on what you have learned.

5 Prepare a plan of action to remedy the situation.

Any remedial action is usually dictated by the identified causes. Often, simple mistakes have simple remedies. If, for example, you underestimated costs, you must provide better budget estimates next time. For more complex resolutions, follow these steps:

- *Salvage what you can.* Isolate those components of your original plan that worked well. They're reusable. Now attend to those parts which did not work...
- *Explore new approaches.* Investigate new ideas and solutions through reading, consultation and discussion, and get these new methods down on paper.
- *Look for flaws in the new plan* – don't replace your original mistake with one of a different kind.
- *Assign tasks and implement the new plan.*

Ask yourself: 'How much smarter am I for this experience?'

Management Memo

The best thing about mistakes is that they are gifts of opportunity. Mistakes are opportunities to learn, change, grow and improve. The key is not to see the mistake as the end result. It is a beginning. Accept that the mistake is an opportunity, even if at the outset this acceptance is in the form of an act of faith. If we learn from mistakes, we will never become chronic mistake-makers. [52]

6 Encourage all staff to be on the alert for mistakes.

If you ensure your staff understand that mistakes are opportunities for growth and that they can learn from everybody's blunders, then you and your employees should be prepared to disclose errors as soon as they appear. Indeed, if a member of your staff tells you that you have made a mistake, applaud him or her for it – for three reasons:

- They are probably right and, if so, you'd better know about it.
- It helps staff get used to telling you unpleasant things quickly, so you can put them right before they really go wrong.
- This way you can learn from your own mistakes and show staff how to learn from the mistakes of others at the same time.

How to show entrepreneurial flair

An entrepreneur is someone who sees an opportunity and creates the organisational structures to pursue it. The entrepreneurial process involves all the functions, activities, and actions associated with pursuing that opportunity. If you decide to establish your own business, or remain where you are, entrepreneurial behaviour can be learned and used to strengthen your existing management skills – even open new doors for you. Here's how to sharpen your entrepreneurial skills...

1 Develop appropriate personal attributes.

Though entrepreneurs come from a wide variety of backgrounds, the literature can provide an accurate picture of these innovative types.

Wayne Bygraves in *Portable MBA in Entrepreneurship* refers to the *10 Ds* that characterise entrepreneurs – they *d*ream or envision what the future could be like, they're *d*ecisive and *d*oers, showing *d*edication, *d*etermination, *d*evotion and attention to *d*etail, are in charge of their *d*estiny, expect *d*ollars (i.e. money) as a sign of their success, and *d*istribute ownership of their business with key employees.

John Miner in *The Four Roots to Entrepreneurial Success* sees entrepreneurs as having high personal achievement, characterised by a need to succeed, with a strong belief in themselves – that they *can* make a difference, an energetic personal commitment to their organisation (existing or new), a desire for feedback, a desire to plan and set goals, and a preparedness to take the initiative.

How do you measure up?

2 Learn to work with people.

Entrepreneurs are in some respects loners, preferring their own company best of all, but they realise the impact others can have if they are to achieve their goals. They can expect to spend a great deal of their time selling their ideas to others, so it's important to adopt an encouraging style, a high human-interest focus and a desire to help others, as well as to be empathetic, to develop strong positive relationships, and to be prepared to influence others to their way of thinking. Entrepreneurs, being the type of people they are, often rapidly advance in the system but then, when frustrated by the constraints of the organisation, reject the system to form their own.

3 Seek innovation and change.

Connecting ideas to opportunities is a form of constant engagement for entrepreneurs (some call it innovating). Associated with this desire to innovate, entrepreneurs search out new ideas, and encourage new product development. Though entrepreneurs may like to give the impression of being risk-takers, their desire to maintain control ensures that detailed preparation eliminates, or significantly reduces, any risk. They always like to check things out before engaging. So, the message for you is to aspire to innovate, but make sure you always do your homework first.

Management Memo

Entrepreneurship is not a personality trait. Entrepreneurs see change as the norm and as healthy. Usually they do not bring about change themselves. The entrepreneur always searches for change, responds to it, and exploits it as an opportunity.[53]

4 Look for role models.

Environmental factors (external influences, if you like) have a significant impact on the development of entrepreneurs. Knowing successful entrepreneurs makes the act of becoming one yourself seem much more credible. Some workplaces – Silicon Valley, for example – tend to attract people with entrepreneurial flair. Though your role model may be working in the industry, don't discount the influence your family and friends can have as well.

5 Gain industry experience and management know-how.

Industry experience and management know-how – preferably with accountability for profit and loss – are indispensable qualities of successful entrepreneurs. In excess of 80 per cent of all new businesses are founded in industries the same as, or closely related to, the ones which the entrepreneur has previously experienced. Additional skills are always a bonus, but make sure you focus your energies in familiar areas where they will get the best results.

6 Exploit timing.

Timing is more than recognising and responding to windows of opportunity. In fact, successful entrepreneurs resist the temptation to rush into new enterprises before they have had a chance to gather all of the resources they will need. For the entrepreneur, timing is not about speed but selecting the moment of engagement. Be prepared for when your moment arrives.

7 Make entrepreneurship a lifetime focus.

Leopards don't change their spots, nor entrepreneurs their dreams, desires, ambitions and decisiveness. If you believe entrepreneurship is your destiny, go for it!

How to survive and thrive in the politics of your organisation

In every organisation, people will play politics for personal gain or sectional interests. On the darker side, more organisations are diseased by internal politics than their bosses dare to admit. But internal politics need not be characterised by dirty tricks, back-stabbing, manoeuvering and skulduggery. Indeed, it is possible to survive and thrive by legitimate and acceptable means. The following suggestions will help you to become a politically astute manager...

1 Assume that political undercurrents run through your organisation.

Political behaviour exists in all organisations because of the presence of hierarchical structures, power, influence, and human beings. Indeed, whenever we do something to affect other people's perceptions of us and our work, to gain power and credibility in the organisation, that is a political act. Politics is all-pervasive, and works constantly below the surface. Learn to play the game, or you'll be left behind.

2 Know what it means to play politics.

You become politically astute when you become skilled at working your way up the promotional ladder and gaining power within the organisation. You display your political ingenuity when you hold influence, have many loyal followers, and are able to get your ideas, views, actions and yourself recognised and accepted. This can be accomplished in two ways – one manipulative and devious, the other legitimate and acceptable to the majority.

- *The dirty face of organisational politics* is the scheming and self-seeking that advances one's career or sectional interests regardless of what's best for the organisation. It is characterised by back-biting, white-anting, self-interest, lip-service, cheating, misinformation, lying, crawling, point-scoring, treachery and back-stabbing. Such corrupt behaviours occur with unprincipled people, and in a corroded organisational culture and an overall climate of mistrust.
- *The acceptable face of internal politics* is the struggle between individuals and groups who all have the best interests of the organisation at heart, but disagree as to what these interests are and how they might be best achieved.

Organisational politics has become equated with self-serving actions that can hurt others and the company. But it can operate both ethically and appropriately. It is a personal choice.

3 Listen, observe, and learn how to play the game.

Develop political awareness by seeing and hearing what happens in your organisation. Reflect upon:

- what gets people promoted?
- who's in the 'in' crowd and who's 'out'?
- who's got the *real* power?

- who are the opinion leaders?
- who supports whom, and why?
- who are the fence-sitters?
- who is the competition – age? experience? background? attitudes? abilities? prospects?
- who are the ideas people, the cautious, the risk-takers, the blockers?
- who makes the decisions?…

By being observant and patient, you can learn to recognise and employ behaviour that is politically advantageous in your workplace.

4 Be subtle.

If you blatantly try to gain power or to influence others, you will meet with resistance. It's subtlety that makes political behaviour successful. For example, you'll have more success with promoting a pet project by lobbying in the corridors and exchanging positive comments about it over coffee, than by trying to bludgeon it through a staff meeting. Subtle persuasion is always more convincing than blatant use of power.

5 Lay the foundation by working hard.

If you can't justify your claim to power, no amount of politicking will help. You earn your spurs by showing that you can work hard, assist others, and accept unpleasant tasks, and also are tolerant, principled, trustworthy, courteous and caring. People who lack these qualities usually resort to character assassination, skulduggery, nepotism and treachery – and sooner or later it catches up with them. Until then, they're forever looking over their shoulder. Competence alone won't guarantee advancement, but it's essential in the long run.

Management Memo

In the internal politics of organisations, when people sell out to someone else, they also sell out themselves.

> Still as of old
> Men by themselves are priced –
> For thirty pieces Judas sold
> Himself, not Christ. [54]

6 Build relationships.

Politically astute managers build alliances according to the principle of reciprocal favours. Maxims such as 'one good turn deserves another' illustrate the ethic of political reciprocity. Build healthy relationships with supervisors and colleagues, and treat subordinates with respect and fairness to foster a group of loyal supporters.

7 Learn to negotiate.

Knowing when to make concessions, when to compromise, and when to hold out, are all part of the political process, because negotiation involves subtle attempts to influence others to achieve a goal or to gain power.

8 Keep the power brokers on side.

It is political suicide to alienate those in power. Never disagree with them in public; find ways to make them look good; follow the chain of command; be a team player; don't create problems that make them look bad. This does not mean you must say yes to everything they say, for that would damage your credibility; but it does require that you must support and remain loyal to those who can help you most.

How to gain a reputation for honesty and integrity

Integrity has been defined as 'honesty, soundness, uprightness, true to self or stated values, beliefs or ethics'. Success will come when employees and customers respect an organisation for its integrity – and that integrity will be reflected in its leadership and management. Image is what people think we are; integrity is what we really are. Indecision concerning matters of ethics can be fatal for individuals and organisations – the following considerations will help clarify your thinking in this regard...

1 Develop moral courage.

With moral courage, you will be capable of standing up for what you know to be right, to do the right thing regardless of the consequences, and to accept the blame when you are in the wrong. You will be respected by all if you have strong moral courage. Indeed, it is the very foundation on which integrity rests.

2 Practise truthfulness and honesty at all times.

Unless you are honest, you cannot be relied upon at all. If you get caught out misrepresenting the facts or covering up a problem, you will lose credibility instantly. Guard against white lies, too – they often are the crack in the dam wall. Of course, this doesn't mean you should insult or hurt a person by telling the truth – if you can say nothing good about a person, it's best to say nothing at all.

3 Take a stand for what you believe is morally right.

Never compromise your high moral standards; never prostitute your principles. Have the courage of your convictions, for your stance in a situation where a tough decision is required can point the way for an entire group. General Norman Schwarzkopf talks about leadership and about 'Rule 14: Do what's right.'

4 Practise what you preach.

Make sure your behaviour mirrors your professional attitudes and the high standards laid down by others. This means that you must also follow the rules of your organisation. If you tell your staff to do as you tell them to do, they won't listen if your own actions are different to your words. They'll do as you do or they'll do as they want. Practise what you preach.

5 Don't abuse the privileges of your position.

If you divert any of the managerial resources at your disposal for personal gain, you're risking your reputation and your position. The simple act of having your office secretary type a letter to your brother to organise your family vacation reveals how easily company resources can be abused – people (you and your secretary, both paid by the company), materials (company stationery, envelope and stamp), facilities (use of office facilities), time (your's and your secretary's), and money (the company pays for salaries, facilities, and materials). Petty abuses can so easily lead to much more serious transgressions, such as nepotism, falsifying accounts, padding expense claims, cheating, back-stabbing, disloyalty, or theft of office supplies and equipment. Remember, our personal values become the navigating system that guides us through the seas of temptation.

6 Make no promise you cannot keep.

If you know you can't live up to your promises, don't make them. You must be as good as your word, and your word must be as good as your bond.

7 Accept the blame when you are wrong.

It's very hard to criticise a person when that person admits she/he's wrong and, when at fault, accepts the blame without question. When you foul-up, admit it. Don't try to look for scapegoats, rationalise away your mistakes, or sulk. And never lie – remember one lie always seems to lead to another, and to another, and to another…

8 Know why it's important.

It's essential to understand why integrity is so important for someone in a position of leadership:

It builds trust. When people know you are not using your position for personal gain or at their expense, you'll gain their trust, confidence, loyalty, and whole-hearted support.

It influences others. As Emerson said: 'Every great institution is the lengthened shadow of a single man. His character determines the character of the organisation.'

It builds for you a reputation, not just an image. Regrettably, some of us work harder on our outside than our inside – forgetting that 'image promises much but produces little, while integrity never disappoints', as Thomas Macauley wrote.

It creates high standards. Your own integrity in the workplace will set a positive example for all to follow. By your actions alone, you can inspire your staff to reach to your high standards. People do what people see.

It helps you live with yourself. You'll be able to sleep at night.

It doesn't have to be advertised. Integrity is visible in everything you do and soon becomes common knowledge to everyone.

Finally, if you're ever tempted to compromise – as no doubt you will be – then always place honour, a sense of duty and moral values above all else. If you do that, you cannot possibly fail yourself, your family, your colleagues, or your organisation.

Management Memo

In order to be a leader, a man must have followers. And to have followers, a man must have their confidence. Hence, the supreme quality for a leader is unquestionably integrity. Without it no real success is possible, no matter whether it is on a section gang, a football field, in the army or in the office. If he lacks forthright integrity, he will fail. His teachings and actions must square with each other. The first great need, therefore, is integrity and high purpose.[55]

See also: 108, 114

How to gain power and influence

Enthusiastic and committed managers strive to get things done. They do this by exerting influence, a process that involves the use of power. If you have power, you have the capacity to influence the behaviour of others, to get people to do what you want them to do. Normally it should come with the job, but it is possible to gain it by other means. Here are some of the ways by which you can accumulate power in your organisation…

1 Gain control by moving into a position of power.

Seek promotion. Power and influence are normally part and parcel of the formal authority which is vested in a senior managerial position. But remember, as well as your recognised title and role in the organisation, you may need to bolster this legitimate coercive power with other forces to increase your influence over others…

2 Gain control over resources.

You will gain additional power over others if you are in a position to approve their request for one or more of the following essential resources: money, equipment, space, staffing, transportation or facilities.

3 Gain control over the flow of information.

People rely on access to information to do their jobs, so the more you know about what's going on, the more you are in a position to decide how to use that information to influence others. Find out what is going on through formal channels, and through your own informal network. Get yourself on to the right committees and distribution lists. And if you know what's going on behind the scenes by accumulating privileged information, all the better – you can act far more effectively than those who are not in the know.

4 Gain power by possessing knowledge.

Expert power can be yours when others choose to act as you suggest because they acknowledge that you know more than they do in this area. So build your knowledge of matters technical or professional, or in terms of the running of the organisation, so that others rely on your expertise and defer to your judgement.

5 Gain power by establishing credibility.

You can build up the trust of your employees and colleagues and, in time, their dependence, by earning a reputation as a performer, one who delivers, and who backs up one's word once it's given.

6 Gain power by doing others a favour or two.

Get others to feel obligated to you in some way so that gratitude is a natural consequence. Good managers can do this without any sinister Mafia-type underpinnings – they do so because it's good business and it makes sense. Usually the organisation benefits from such favours, but it pays to remember that you can also gain influence over others by doing them a good turn or two.

7 Gain influence through the power of your personality.

If you have a powerful physique or a deep and resonant voice that unnerves or even intimidates others, you are well on the way to having others defer to your wishes. But nature has blessed few of us in that way. You can influence others, however, if you possess or develop some kind of charisma or self-confidence or sense of mission that persuades colleagues and employees to go along with you. Try to make yourself personally compatible with people at all levels in your organisation. And, if necessary, create the illusion of power by attending to the way you look, dress, and furbish your office. The company you keep is also important.

8 Develop strong links with other people with power.

One of the smart organisational strategies is to get to know the boss's secretary well – because she/he has the boss's ear and is, for that reason alone, in a position of power. Why? She/he is powerful because she/he has direct access to someone with power. Proximity or a direct line to the powerful obviously gives you more scope to exert influence, direct or perceived. So develop close links yourself by:

- identifying your organisation's opinion leaders and power brokers – and they're not all higher level people. What would these people welcome in terms of 'favours' (help with a project, more resources, respect, etc.)?
- providing such favours if you feel this is not disloyal to colleagues, or unethical.
- antagonising no one unless some greater purpose is at stake.

Management Memo

Power is clearly linked to position and rank. But to a certain degree it has to be earned. You can give orders to your subordinates but you are going to get more out of them if you obtain their willing cooperation rather than their grudging submission. Power is bestowed upon you as manager but you have to justify your use of it... As Mary Parker Follett wrote: 'Our task is to learn how to develop power. Genuine power can only be grown; it will slip from every arbitrary hand.' [56]

9 Do some thinking...

- List the sources of power in your organisation – and that means more than just perusing an organisation chart – and seek ways to tap into that reservoir.
- Think about using some of the power you already have to build up more.
- Consider joining unofficial networks (clubs, social groups) in your organisation so that, through involvement, you could build a personal support base.

How to use power appropriately

All managers have power. It comes with the position. Some use it well, some use it poorly, and some let it slip from their grasp. The challenge for managers is how to use power to enhance the organisation they serve, as well as their own reputation. If they abuse their power, the odds are that they and the organisation will suffer. Power used well, however, can lead to growth, better service, greater efficiency and quality – and more power...

1 Know how you feel personally about using power.

If you seek power, then you must know why you want it and what you're going to do with it. Determine your motives for wanting power, because only by analysing and understanding these motives can you develop a positive and clear picture of what it means to you and if you're prepared to use it appropriately.

2 Be aware of the darker side of power.

Sometimes power is perceived as something evil, and associated with self-seeking and scheming individuals. This dark side of the use of power is apparent when someone uses such tactics as:

- withholding information from others who need it
- empire-building
- pursuing personal vendettas
- blocking other people's legitimate work plans and proposals for one's own benefit
- inventing new rules and procedures to obstruct other people
- passing off other people's ideas as one's own
- blackmail, sabotage, slanderous gossip, even threats of violence
- forming cliques, and fostering a climate of 'us' and 'them'
- pursuing personal advancement unfairly or at the expense of the organisation and others.

3 Stay within acceptable limits of fair play.

Remember Watergate – driving ambition and the quest for power that ignores the greater good can be potentially self-destructive. Outfox and outmanoeuvre other people by all means, but avoid cheating, lying or breaking your word. In power struggles, chickens have an uncanny tendency to come home to roost.

4 Do not overuse power.

If you become blatant in your use of power, you're likely to create resistance in the ranks. So it is that managers who regularly make unilateral decisions and arbitrarily mandate new procedures and rules often get complaints, refusals, even sabotage, from employees. On the other hand, those who gradually and subtly influence staff members to see the value of a new procedure, will often gain ready acceptance and support for the same idea or procedure. An oppressive display of power is a sure way to lose it.

5 Vary the way you influence others.

Flexibility in your use of power will always be important – what works in one setting may be less successful in another. Your choice will vary from direct – face-to-face, confrontationist, collaborative – to indirect methods – controlling schedules, meeting agendas, and memos. Build up a selection of both methods and use those to achieve your outcomes.

6 Understand people in your organisation.

Employees will always want to protect their self-interests, so it's important to be able to define those interests and behaviour styles if you are to become skilled in dealing with and influencing them. You need to be aware of the different types of power to which others respond. Experts, for example, respect expertise. So, power will be afforded to you by experts if you are seen as a genuine expert in your field – and you live up to that image you have helped to build. As well, when you appeal to individuals' preferred power types, they get a feeling of satisfaction from their imagined influence over you.

7 Learn to use power openly and legitimately.

Gain a reputation for exerting your influence in a mature and self-controlled way. Resist the impulsive use of power or using it for your own aggrandisement. Create a healthy balance between your own personal goals and those of your organisation. Commitment to your organisation generates personal power, which leads to increased service, which in turn attracts more power, and so on.

Management Memo

For some people, power is perceived as something destructive, selfish and arrogant. But power, in itself, is neutral: It's the ability to get things done, to meet goals, to complete tasks. Without power, you cannot manage. Management is the practice of getting things done through others. Power simply is a set of skills you develop that enable you to get things done.

To have power, you must develop it, use it to sustain your influence, and continually draw on it. You'll find that power, like an electrical current, works for you when you put it to work.

Where power sometimes goes sour is in the motives behind its use. Why you want power and what you do with it determine whether it's good or bad. Using power is something like being able to drive – you can use your skill to transport a blind person to the doctor, or you can drive the getaway car in a bank robbery.[57]

8 Don't abuse power.

When *Fortune* magazine listed its 'Ten Toughest Bosses', their portraits were pretty unpleasant. They were variously described as 'ridiculing, aloof, strident, obnoxious, brutal, egocentric, autocratic'… even 'unpopular'. Not surprising, perhaps. They may have been very effective in their jobs, but the ways in which they were described suggest ways in which managers can abuse their power. The decision is yours.

How to use body language to improve your communication

According to researchers, it's possible to 'read' bodies – we all have a range of mannerisms that we're not even aware of, and these are capable of sending out messages to other people. Gestures, posture, head and eye movement, facial expressions and voice qualities all provide important cues – body language speaks volumes. Understanding body language signals in other people – and being aware of your own non-verbal cues – can make you a better communicator...

1 Face the facts.

Effective communication depends more on *how* we send and receive rather than the *what*. While words are of course important, we are told that they convey only about 7 per cent of the meaning of the messages we communicate. The rate and inflection of our speech accounts for about 38 per cent of the exchange, and our gestures and body signals, often unconsciously exhibited, account for about 55 per cent. These non-verbal messages serve to either reinforce or contradict the message we want to send, and for that reason deserve our attention.

2 Be aware of posture.

Posture can indicate boredom, interest, or even fear. If seated, sit up straight and don't cross your legs – crossed legs and arms could be interpreted as not being open to others' ideas; both feet should be flat on the floor. Slouching can indicate low self-esteem. If standing, try not to shift body weight from one foot to another. When listening, lean forward slightly. Though leaning back may be a sign that you're relaxed, it also may be interpreted as disrespectful and not giving the speaker your full attention. Leaning back with your hands behind your head can convey contemplation or scepticism.

3 Keep control of hands and arm movements.

Pay attention to your arms and hands. Arms folded across the chest can suggest that you are feeling defensive, rather than receptive. Clasping your hands in your lap gives the impression that you are in control and making critical evaluations. Don't fidget, or finger your jewellery, hair or clothing while someone else is speaking. It may come across as impatience, boredom or discomfort with the subject being discussed. Never point at your listener. This may indicate hostility and aggressiveness. And keep your hands off your hips or risk coming over as being arrogant. If you finger your watch, squirm in the chair or turn to face the exit, you're conveying a wish to terminate the discussion.

Management Memo

It is not so much what we hear as what we see. By understanding the basic gestures that accompany many of the everyday thought processes, a valuable insight into people around us can be gained. We must train ourselves to read the non-verbal signals of behaviour, custom and etiquette given out by others. [58]

4 Avoid using flamboyant gestures.

Using your hands to emphasise a point can be an effective tool, but generally hand movements should be confined to an area about the width of your body. Excessive gestures can be distracting or give the impression that you are out of control.

5 Make eye contact.

Eye contact suggests that you are paying attention and are at ease with the topic. Don't stare, however – this may be interpreted as being hostile or aggressive. If you nod your head from time to time, you acknowledge you are actively listening. Note, however, that men and women interpret this body cue differently. For women, nodding means 'I'm paying attention', while for men, it usually indicates agreement.

Aristotle Onassis once admitted that he normally wore dark glasses when negotiating so that his inner thoughts would not be revealed. Indeed, researchers tell us that eyes reveal a lot, such as:

- darting eyes can convey anxiousness or lack of confidence.
- a slow blink can communicate you don't enjoy being there.
- glancing to top right can indicate the person is imagining or making up information.

6 Face the listener directly.

Don't sit at an angle or face away from the other person – unless you want to appear indifferent or come across as rude. If you're wearing glasses, if you look at the listener over the top of the rim, then you could be interpreted as evaluative or sceptical. A smile, of course, will show your enjoyment and pleasure.

7 Keep your distance.

When speaking, don't get too close or the listener may feel threatened and become defensive. Of course, that's OK if your intention is to intimidate. Otherwise maintain a distance that allows you to observe the listener's body language.

8 Use voice volume, tone and tempo to effect.

Avoid monotone by changing the rate of speech throughout the conversation for emphasis. Also use inflection and moderate changes in pitch and volume to engage the listener's attention. An incident at the fish market, involving British writer G.K. Chesterton illustrates the power of voice qualities. In a low, endearing voice, he told a woman waiting on him, 'You are a noun, a verb, and a preposition.' The woman blushed. After buying the fish, Chesterton said in a lecherous tone, 'And you're an adjective, an adverb, and a conjunction as well!' The woman slapped him with a flounder.

How to kick those irritating supervisory habits that employees complain about

Like most people, managers are rarely perfect. They allow themselves to acquire a range of personal quirks and annoying habits that can become extremely irritating to their staff members. Over time, there is a danger that these mannerisms will ossify and become integral and unattractive parts of their personalities and managerial styles. You can guard against the most irritating and frustrating of these habits by heeding the following advice...

1 Do not skimp on praise.

"You rarely compliment me on a job I think I've done well." Everyone responds well to praise. One or two compliments won't take much of your time but it will do wonders for an employee's morale. Why not make a quick workroom or office visit or pen a short note to a staff member who deserves praise for a job well done?

2 Be decisive when decisions are required.

"You avoid making decisions." First, clarify the real problem: Is it your poor decision-making ability or simply procrastination? If the former, read up on the literature on decision-making; and also make sure that your staff have a clear definition of where your decision-making responsibility ends and theirs begins. If the latter, then there are certainly occasions when a problem is best attacked after you have spent sufficient time thinking about it; just as there are other instances when a lack of action will only inflame the issue. As a supervisor, you are expected to make timely decisions based on the available evidence and information.

3 Be available when needed.

"You're always too inaccessible." Schedule regular staff or department meetings. Make yourself available for urgent matters and at least be accessible by appointment for non-urgent issues. Don't go overboard, however – an open-door policy can become very time-consuming.

4 Listen.

"You never seem to be listening to what I say." To listen attentively and patiently is a skill which takes sincere effort. We don't always hear what others are saying to us: we fidget, look elsewhere, shuffle paper – all visual clues reflecting an attitude of less than full attention to the speaker. Working to improve this irritating habit is well worth the effort.

5 Stand by what you say.

"You say something – and then deny it later." Honesty and integrity are

crucial to a manager's reputation. To ensure that your statements are not misinterpreted, keep notes of meetings and ensure all participants get a copy of relevant minutes.

6 Hold those calls.

"You always take telephone calls during our meetings." Have all your calls held until after the meeting or hold your meetings away from the office. Accept inward calls only in dire emergencies. Show your colleague that you consider his/her discussion with you to be important.

7 Let them get on with the job.

"You won't let me do my job – you're always interfering." Encourage your staff to complain to you when they feel you're interfering, but use the occasion to discuss the reasons for your involvement. Implement and foster an understanding of a staff appraisal system to ensure you become an integral and valued part of an employee's life, rather than be seen as an 'interruption'.

8 Do not play favourites.

"You play favourites." There is no quicker path to sagging staff morale than to show favouritism in your daily relationships with staff. Of course, some employees are brighter, more dependable, and more personable than others, but you must guard against any display of personal bias. It is perfectly proper to assign a task to an employee who is better equipped than others to handle it; it is improper to overdo such delegation or to deny others the opportunity to develop their talents and skills.

> **Management Memo**
>
> If you suspect that any irritating habits are sabotaging your own image, take counter-measures immediately. Grow purposefully self-conscious. Police yourself by watching how you behave in front of others and note their reactions to you. Encourage your friends, family and trusted colleagues to point out any annoying mannerisms you may possess. Accept their criticisms gracefully, work on them and you will stamp out the 'executive gremlins' in your life. [59]

9 Keep in touch with what's going on.

"You're out of touch with what's going on in the workplace." With a heavy managerial load, managers often find it difficult to remain abreast of day to-day action in the workplace or office. Try to schedule at least a few periods a month at the workface – your credibility as a supervisor will be enhanced.

10 Be open to the ideas of employees.

"You always pooh-pooh our ideas." Do you kill a staff member's idea simply because it challenges the *status quo*? If an idea is clearly poor, do you enjoy shooting down the originator's kite – or do you haul it down with tact? Creativity is not the exclusive province of the talented few. Everyone has creative qualities that lie dormant and untapped, just waiting to be let out. By word and deed, it is your responsibility to encourage creativity to flourish in the workplace.

How to avoid causing conflict

Conflict is inevitable in any organisation. When handled properly, it can contribute significantly to personal and organisational health, better understanding, and innovative solutions to problems. When handled poorly, however, it leads to hurt feelings, damaged relationships and low staff morale. Managers must be able to minimise hostility between themselves and their staff members – the best way to manage such harmful conflict is to prevent it from ever arising. Here are some suggestions in this regard...

1 Learn to be an effective communicator.

Communication is the lifeblood of an organisation. Much conflict is caused through people not listening to or not understanding each other. Misunderstandings can result in accusations, blame and personal attacks. At times, there is no real conflict, simply misinterpretation.

Work at improving your communication skills for listening and speaking so that you minimise misunderstanding. Convey the need for clarity in all your discussions.

2 Keep your staff informed.

By withholding information from all those it affects, you can create tension amongst staff, often causing some of them to react adversely and, in doing so, generate conflict situations.

3 Be honest and open with your staff.

When people feel threatened, they become defensive. Thus, the best way to discourage any fear of intimidation is for you to behave in a nonthreatening manner. Be open and honest with staff at all times. The more you are perceived as honest and forthright, and receptive and open to the feelings and opinions of others, the less inclined employees will be to go on the defensive. A climate of openness and honesty will prevent minor issues from blowing up into major catastrophes.

4 Stay cool.

Don't let other people push your 'get angry' button. There are times when a show of anger may serve you well; there are times when it is smarter to keep your cool. Before over-reacting to anything, count to ten and check out the facts: perhaps you misunderstood, perhaps you misheard... Skirmishes can readily develop into battles.

5 Criticise with caution.

You will from time to time be required to point out mistakes or critique the work of your staff. This should be undertaken in a spirit of support: never criticise anyone's work unless you can make practical suggestions for improvement.

6 Avoid the use of threats, demands and put-downs.

When you denigrate, moralise, threaten or make demands of others, you are creating a conflict situation. Resist becoming involved in the conflict-generating games that people play.

Do not be hasty to judge others openly; never make personal attacks on people behind their backs or in public; never belittle others' achievements – rather, celebrate with them; and keep your pessimism to yourself.

7 For the sake of argument, don't.

Arguing is a needless waste of energy and time. A battle between two closed minds only results in both parties clinging more tenaciously to their positions. It is far wiser to listen to the other point of view, understand the stance being taken, and attempt to guide the other party towards your point of view through negotiation.

8 Try to be tolerant of others.

Be aware that rarely is anyone 'right', because all of us view situations through our own unique perceptual filters. Conflict arises when we refuse to respect or tolerate another person's values or opinions. Never condemn someone for failing to live up to your expectations, for such behaviour breeds hostility and frustration that is guaranteed to hurt your colleague – and you as well.

> **Management Memo**
>
> It is the hostility which is usually seen as the harmful aspect of conflict. The management of conflict thus becomes an effort to eliminate or minimise hostility, acknowledging that it is inevitable, if not healthy, for individuals or groups to strive to attain their own preferred outcomes or to satisfy their own particular interests.[60]

9 Never play favourites.

The teacher's pet is often the cause of much resentment in the classroom. So too in the management situation. Avoid the friction caused among staff when you intentionally or unintentionally show preference for one staff member over another.

10 Confront an emerging conflict head-on.

Finally, if a conflict situation between you and a member of staff seems inevitable, tackle it immediately by discussing it with those involved. Never leave the scene, sulk or withdraw support or cooperation when the going gets tough – such behaviour will not defuse the core issue. Ignoring conflict situations will only ensure greater problems later on.

Carl Rogers suggested that, to clear up misunderstanding promptly, each party should restate the other's position to the other's satisfaction, thereby forcing each to briefly adopt the other's frame of reference. The situation then becomes less emotional, with both parties doing more thinking and listening. The more rational people become, the greater the opportunity for conflict resolution.

How to learn to live with change

As a manager, you are in a position to influence others. Take change, for example – the way you personally relate to change and cope with it will have a lasting impact on your employees. But before you can help others, you must be able to help yourself. When they see how effectively you cope with change, your staff, too, will see change for what it really is – an opportunity to lead a much fuller and more productive life. Here's what you must do to survive in an age of ongoing change…

1 Accept that you must look to the future.

It's futile trying to cling to the past – or the present, for that matter. Their passing is inevitable. By trying to hold on to the past, you impair your ability to relate effectively to what is new and coming. And so you begin to feel anxious, fear the unknown, display ignorance, or desperately seek attachments. Moving forward is not a matter of giving up what you have, it's a matter of being free from what you have. By your behaviour, employees will see that moving forward is usually the only viable option.

2 See change as opportunity.

All changes, even those you'd rather not have, contain the seeds of opportunity. Those opportunities can be ideas, relationships, points of view and new career directions. You'll see difficulties and obstacles until you absorb their wisdom and gather from them the essentials for further growth. Change is the price we must pay for growth, improvement, achievement and, finally, satisfaction and happiness. The way you grasp opportunities from change will help to inspire others to do the same.

3 Develop a coping strategy for yourself.

You must be able to help yourself before you can hope to help others cope with change. Consider the following coping mechanisms. They may help you live through the next major change in your organisation…

Don't rush the change cycle. Be aware of the four phases through which you (and your staff) will pass, to varying degrees, in coping with sudden change:

Denial – the announcement is greeted with shock, and a refusal to accept that it's happening.

Resistance – acceptance is accompanied by personal distress, blame and complaining, even illness.

Exploration – after a period of struggle, you emerge from your negativity and move into a more positive, future-focused phase, attempting to find the 'best way' of coping.

Commitment – having weathered the storm and accepted the situation, you now focus on the new and pour your energies into it.

Think it through. Isolate yourself in a relaxed environment and jot down answers to such questions as these:

What changes can I expect? How reliable are my sources of information? Can I find better sources? What's the best thing that could happen as a result of the anticipated change? The worst? What tasks will be added to or removed from my current responsibilities? How will the changes affect my staff?

Come to terms with yourself. Now is the time to consider your future. Decide what you will be doing – staying, transferring, retraining, retiring, resigning… Your decision need not be permanent but, unless you are at peace with yourself, you'll enter the change process stressed and uncertain.

Shine in a time of uncertainty. A period of high change can be very good for your career. During this uncertain time, if you do your job very well, you will shine while others around you fall apart at the seams. So, plan ahead, organise yourself, set up new systems to cope with the changes, and motivate your staff to shine with you.

Talk it over with your family and friends. If the anticipated changes will mean extra work, stress, and anxiety for you, make sure your family members understand. They will feel more secure and better able to help you through a difficult time.

Take up stress-reducing activities. Eat right, organise regular physical activity, take vitamin supplements, find a few spare minutes to relax each day, and do the things you enjoy and which boost your energy.

Remember your staff members. What are the ramifications of the change for your employees? What information do you need and what must you do to help them cope with the changes?

Stay organised. Draw up contingency plans for everything you can think of. Allow time for anticipated problems, for the unexpected will happen – although it will be easier to handle if you expect it.

> **Management Memo**
>
> Periods of change are periods of opportunity for both you and your members of staff. Change, if you let it, gives you the excuse to examine your life. It is a time of high risk and high reward. Without it we could never grow or learn. If you can learn to use it to your advantage, you will have an asset to your upward mobility. If you are properly prepared, it can also be great fun. [61]

4 Accept that nothing is permanent.

Your career (and life) is dynamic and fluid. How you cope with the dynamic process will not only affect your growth but also your ability as a manager to influence others. You need to demonstrate to yourself and others that you understand and accept why things must change. When there is no permanence, stay-put behaviour serves no purpose. Giving up a lifetime of judgemental behaviour, negative thinking, aggressive self-protection, or ego-driven striving isn't easy but, in one sense, it is inevitable if you are going to mature and grow. Your transition will be slow, incremental even. But that will give others a chance to observe how you live with change and allow them to learn from you.

 See also: 100, 122, 126, 128

How to manage stress at work

Work stress is not necessarily a negative force. In fact, without a certain level of stress to challenge us, our jobs would be boring and unrewarding. Stress becomes a problem, however, when it builds to such an extreme that we are unable to cope with it. The solution to stress, therefore, is not to eliminate it altogether, but to maintain it at a level where it remains a positive motivating force. Here are ten of the best simple strategies for keeping stress in check. They're easy to remember – and they work...

1 Create a pleasant work environment for yourself.

If you spend a great deal of time in your office, make it pleasant, without being self-indulgent. Convert your tired office into a place for you to enjoy – art pieces, rug, greenery, bookcase, paintings, tapestries. Discipline yourself to keep that desk uncluttered.

2 Manage your time.

If you want to manage stress, you have to manage time. Of the stress faced by administrators, none is so pervasive as the stress of time. Forget about finding more hours in a day. Instead, use the existing hours more effectively. Set aside time for planning, contemplation, relaxation, and problem-solving. Tackle the problems of drop-in visitors, the open-door, telephone interruptions, and procrastination. Remember that time is the lit fuse of stress.

3 Avoid false guilt.

Be determined not to allow staff to make you feel guilty about something you or your organisation did. Be tolerant about your own mistakes: will anyone really care 100 years or 100 days from now? Try not to judge, criticise or devalue yourself and your sense of adequacy. Be prepared to lose a few battles without feeling you are losing face. Learn to ignore that 'inner voice' that tells you you 'should do' this or 'should have done' that. Becoming stressed about things beyond your control does little to resolve the problem.

4 Keep perfectionism in check.

Trying to be perfect in everything is not only self-defeating, it's also a major stress generator. Learn what you are good at doing and perfect those skills.

5 Drive your own bus.

You can't allow everyone's problems to become your problems. By all means provide a sympathetic ear – but remember that most people are capable of solving their own problems, and will grow from the experience.

Nor is there a rule that says you must be available to everyone, or that you must never say 'no' to any request. You simply can't satisfy all demands. So, since you're the person in the driving seat, take charge of the controls.

6 Be selective about what you take on.

Resist the urge to take on everything. Remember that you're judged on the work you complete, not on the amount you take on. Slow down. Be selective. Learn to delegate duties and responsibilities. Say 'no' a little more often. Winning every round of the contest may not be necessary to succeed in the long term. Learn to discern what is worth being competitive about and what isn't. Focus on the things that really matter.

7 Plan and prioritise.

Stress often results from loss of direction. So, by establishing clear, detailed objectives and formulating plans and priorities to meet them, you will eradicate many ambiguities, eliminate confusion, and remove the anxiety that accompanies unplanned activity. Help to neutralise stress by achieving the sense of accomplishment that is associated with projects completed, deadlines met, and goals achieved.

8 Develop a support system for yourself.

Create an informal support network which will enable you to let off steam, receive moral support, accept helpful advice, and share ideas and feelings in a leisure or social setting.

Management Memo

The simple fact is that the answers to combatting stress are within the grasp of each individual. Each of us, as a manager, has the power to break out of the lemming herd and turn away from the precipice that awaits the incompetent stress-handler. The tools are simple, the sacrifices few, and the rewards rich. [62]

The network might comprise mentors, professional colleagues, friends or relatives – but make sure they're positive, trustworthy and enthusiastic, and not prophets of doom and gloom.

9 Look after your body and soul.

You can go a long way towards managing personal stress at work by improving your own lifestyle. Consider these strategies:

- Take a short break every few hours.
- Practise relaxation techniques daily.
- Eat only nutritious food.
- Commit yourself to exercise.
- Get enough sleep.
- Have an annual medical check-up.
- Avoid harbouring resentments.
- Have fun. Enjoy life outside work.
- Think positively.
- Develop a network of social support.
- Protect your leisure time: make time for play and hobbies.

10 Accept stress as a natural part of life.

Remember that you are not life's target, so don't react to stressful situations with 'why me'? Instead, have confidence in your ability to work through the potentially stressful periods and recognise that 'this too shall pass'. Stress goes with the territory – it comes with the job. Learn to manage it.

How to stay healthy

Studies which analyse the attributes of an effective manager invariably list good health as an important contributing quality. Being healthy promotes a more satisfying and productive work experience for all of us. So, if you want to improve your fitness level and to enjoy a happier, more productive worklife, seriously consider the following suggestions...

1 Be aware of the benefits of good health.

By focusing on your personal health, you can take advantage of the following reported benefits:

- less sickness
- decrease in blood pressure
- reduction in cardiac risk factors
- improved oxygen uptake
- reduction in body weight
- improved diet
- improved disposition
- better self-image
- expansion of friendship circles.

Is this not a strong and convincing case for personal health and fitness?

2 Get a regular check-up and fitness assessment.

Pay attention to the warning messages your body sends you – migraines, palpitations, stomach upsets – and see your doctor immediately. In fact, a regular medical check-up should be seen as part of your managerial responsibility. Knowledge of health and fitness is expanding daily and a regular assessment means that you are ensuring you are at least physically prepared for your managerial role.

3 Exercise regularly.

Exercise several times a week. Undertake a programme which is enjoyable, convenient, and appropriate for your age and state of fitness – perhaps walking, jogging, golf, gym, swimming or cycling. Self-discipline can sometimes be a problem – which is why some people prefer a specifically designed programme with a fitness instructor; others pair up with a colleague and keep fit together.

The important thing is that exercise should be fun. The moment regular exercising becomes drudgery, it's time to vary your routine. Exercising is not only about staying alive – it's also about *being* alive. And it's an important component in your physical health and work performance.

4 Keep a check on your diet.

Most of your exercise time and effort can be negated by what you eat and drink. In fact, it is a good idea to work on your diet before you get serious about exercising. Eat well-balanced meals as regularly and unhurriedly as you can. Encourage your family to be health conscious by maintaining a nutritionally sound diet. Literature abounds on this topic.

5 Get plenty of sleep.

Sleep recharges our batteries. Many people worry about the amount of sleep they get – some think they sleep too much, others worry they are not sleeping enough. How much do you need? Research has shown that the average sleep period is 7 to 8 hours daily. In the washup, it seems to depend on the individual: make sure you get as much sleep as *you* need. What seems to be important is that you sleep soundly.

6 Try to cut back on the health no-nos.

The health and social consequences of excessive use of tobacco smoking, alcohol, drugs and medication in the form of tranquillisers, headache pills, and sleeping medication have been well-documented elsewhere. Overuse of these substances can affect personal health and, consequently, productivity in the workplace.

7 Take full advantage of your leisure time.

All work and no play make Jack and Jill dull people. Take the old adage to heart. Become involved in a hobby or other interests outside work time – something that distracts you and extends you psychologically, socially and intellectually. But don't get so competitive in your pastime, whether it be Scrabble or golf, that it becomes stressful too. The essential qualities of a leisure time activity are that it should be relaxing and enjoyable. And don't put off taking your holidays. Getting away from work for a few weeks can make you happier, healthier, and more productive on your return.

> **Management Memo**
>
> Employers who offer health facilities don't do it out of pure altruism. Fit employees mean fewer absences, possibly higher productivity, and a healthier bottom line. [63]

8 Maintain a balanced lifestyle.

The ancient Chinese sages stressed the importance of balance by keeping all things in perspective – friends, finances, fun, faith, family, formal and informal education, and fitness – often referred to as the '7Fs'. Overemphasising any one to the detriment of others can result in disharmony and imbalance.

9 Resolve to feel how you behave.

Most people have been brought up to *behave how they feel*; that's one reason why so many of us feel and act depressed on Monday mornings. Active, energetic, and enthusiastic people can't afford to have feelings dictate behaviour. A much better alternative is to decide to behave in a certain way and experience the corresponding feelings – that is, *feel how you behave*. Make the change and experience the difference.

How to fight fatigue

Despite your best efforts to plan your day, there are often additional demands on your time. To cope, you will frequently have to call on your energy reserves to boost your staying power. You can't afford to wilt when the pressure is on – so here are some tips to have you feeling more zip instead of feeling zapped...

1 Understand your rhythms.

It's okay to experience fatigue, because it's natural to get tired at the same time every day – it's part of a rhythm. That's why understanding that rhythm is so important. The best way to cope with your daily rhythm is to work it into your schedule – doing the things that demand the most energy when you're fresh and, conversely, keeping the less demanding tasks for when you're in a trough. The highs and lows can be different for each individual.

2 Watch what you eat.

You are what you eat, so select foods that keep you competitive. Consider these tips to fuel your brain and body:

- Carbohydrates are good fuel but a lunch of pasta can slow you down in the afternoon. Stay away from foods high in fat. Food that combines protein with carbohydrates – a chicken sandwich, for example – helps offset fatigue.
- Fresh fruit and vegetables are essential, for providing vitamins and minerals, preventing fatigue, and boosting mental recall and concentration.
- Maintain an even blood-sugar level that keeps fuel flowing to your brain and muscles by eating small, regular helpings. Avoid a large meal when you need to be alert.
- Go for complex carbohydrates – fruit or crackers – they will keep you going longer than lollies.
- Drink caffeine in moderation. It can improve mental performance, but excessive amounts don't increase mental alertness beyond the effects of the original dose.

3 Eat smart.

A well-balanced diet is one thing; but if you don't have good eating habits as well, sooner or later you will do yourself a lot of damage. So, don't skip breakfast, and make sure it's a healthy one. Don't miss lunch, or rush it, or eat it on the run – and eat light. And watch those during-the-day snacks – often they're loaded with fat, salt, caffeine and sugar.

4 Exercise regularly.

Get an energy boost by doing something you enjoy. How about 30 to 45 minutes of brisk walking four to five times a week before breakfast? Or 30 minutes of more vigorous activity, such as jogging or aerobics, three to four times a week? A short walk after lunch brushes away early afternoon cobwebs. Remember, too, a short exercise break, even a few stretching and breathing exercises in the office, will do more good for you than a caffeine break.

Management Memo

We don't usually think of mental work in terms of energy, but your mind works very much like your body. If you're uncoordinated in your muscular motions, moving in several directions at once, you don't get much work done, and you soon are exhausted. Mental activity appears to follow the same principles. If you permit your mental energies to spread out, you get little done and you tire quickly. If you focus on a primary objective, you get the most done with the least fatigue. If you can learn to husband your mental and emotional resources as you do your muscular resources, then you will function maximally. [64]

5 Get enough sleep.

Get the amount of sleep your body needs. Some people can do with less than others. Study yourself to learn how much sleep you require to feel rested and invigorated.

6 Identify and handle those spirit zappers.

Though fatigue seems physical, it can also be a sign of mental distress – even depression and anger. Excessive tiredness and that run-down feeling should be viewed as danger signs.

Be alert to what's bothering you, whether it's a change in your life, a new boss perhaps, anger over a domestic problem, or some other stressful situation. This does not mean that you should suppress your feelings – that consumes a lot of energy. A much better alternative is to change how you view and deal with such events.

7 Learn from those who rely on energy.

Athletes can't afford fatigue when they're engaged in competition. One of their favourite 'energy-grabbers' is deep breathing. By taking three long, slow, deep breaths, pausing for long enough to let the air circulate, then exhaling slowly, pulling in their abdomen as they do, they're refuelled and ready to proceed. The technique can be used just as well when the 'competition' you're facing is a boss waiting for a report, an irate customer, or drowsiness.

8 Choose your company wisely.

Energy is catching – so too is a feeling of fatigue. Associate with people whose energy you can feed off. Similarly, stay away from negative people. Life is too short to go around with your battery half-charged and being continually drained by depressing colleagues.

See also: 132

How to become a leader

Leadership is not an exclusive club for those who are 'born with it'. While leadership relies on some inherited characteristics, it also depends on training and experience, and indeed many of the traits and abilities that are the raw materials of leadership can be acquired. If you link these up with an essential desire to achieve, then nothing can keep you from becoming a leader – you may even become a great leader. This 10-point programme will get you started...

1 Believe that you *can* become a leader.

Leadership is a function; it is something that a person does, a set of skills – and any skill can be learned, strengthened and enhanced. Not all leaders are 'born leaders' – and leadership is certainly not just a group of personality traits. The leader lives within each of us. So acknowledge that leadership begins with your own belief in yourself.

2 Be sure you have a burning desire to lead.

Are you 'fired-up' and enthused enough to get something done? Leaders must have a desire to serve, to achieve a goal, and to leave things better than they were when they found them. Remember, leaders need causes and causes need leaders. So make sure you have a clear sense of mission, a focus, a bandwagon to leap onto – and a passion to achieve.

3 Study the qualities of recognised leaders.

What distinguishes them from the others in the group or organisation? Interview, observe, read about and study leaders you admire. Purchase or borrow biographies of leaders you respect and explore what makes them exemplars in the art of leadership.

4 Be clear as to what leadership entails.

Know what it means to lead. According to Kouzes & Posner you must be able to:

Challenge the **status quo***:* seek out challenging opportunities to change, grow, innovate, improve, experiment, take risks.

Inspire a shared vision: envision an uplifting and ennobling future; enlist others to share the vision by appealing to their values, interests, hopes and dreams.

Empower others to act: foster collaboration by promoting cooperative goals and building trust; strengthen people by giving power away, providing choice, developing competence, assigning critical tasks, and offering visible support.

Model the way: set the example by behaving in ways consistent with shared values; achieve small wins that promote consistent progress; build commitment.

Encourage the heart: recognise individual contributions; celebrate team accomplishments regularly.

5 Learn to lead by leading.

The more opportunities you have to serve in leadership roles, the more likely it is that you'll develop the skills to lead. Warren Bennis writes that 'effective leaders learn by leading' – and they learn from failures as well as from successes.

6 Volunteer for leadership roles.

Seek ways to broaden your base of leadership experience by looking beyond the workplace. Remember that there are many opportunities to develop, practise and sharpen your leadership skills and talents, e.g.

- Volunteer for leadership roles in community groups and professional associations. Such organisations are always in need of good people and they provide great avenues to learn leading skills.
- Seek tougher assignments. They usually involve greater risk, but have a greater payoff in terms of your leadership development (and promotional prospects).

7 Learn from your experiences.

Take the time to reflect on what you've learned from life's successes and failures. Think back over one of your leadership episodes and review the experience, by asking:

- Where and when did the episode take place? Who was involved? Who initiated it? Why did I get involved? How did I challenge myself and others?
- What did I aspire to achieve? How did I generate enthusiasm in others?
- How did I involve others? How did I encourage collaboration? How did I foster trust and respect?
- What principles and values guided me and others? How did I set the example? What strategies and structures did I apply? How did I progress from one milestone to the next?
- How did I acknowledge the work of others? How did we celebrate success?
- What lessons did I learn from this experience about myself and about leadership?

> **Management Memo**
>
> A manager can make a good team work well. A good manager can make an average team work well. A true leader can change the whole attitude, philosophy, and spirit of any group of people. [65]

8 Study yourself.

What are your strong and weak points? What should you be doing to strengthen the former and eliminate the latter? Ask for feedback from people you know. Make your own list of developmental needs – in public speaking, understanding the change process, handling people, motivating others, and so on.

9 Learn as much as you can about group action.

Make sure you understand the dynamics of your group. We no longer motivate our teams with a whip; we give them a dream and help them reach it – that's leadership.

10 Develop a plan of learning.

Effective leaders are constantly learning. Devise a plan to improve your leadership, including formal study, and work to your plan. Leadership is a capacity that doesn't just happen for most people. It needs to be worked at.

How to release the leader within you

There is nothing elusive about leadership. Although great leaders may be as rare as great runners, great painters, or great actors, everyone has leadership potential – just as everyone has some ability at running, painting and acting. Unfortunately, there is no simple formula, no foolproof handbook, that leads inexorably to successful leadership. But don't despair, for if you are able to release the following essential leadership qualities, you'll be well on the way to displaying the features of a great leader...

1 Display integrity.

Integrity is a quality you must develop. It helps to build trust, allows you to influence others, sets and maintains high standards, and builds your reputation as one who can be relied upon. Socrates told us that 'the first key to greatness is to be in reality what we appear to be'. In today's terminology it's known as congruence... followers are acutely aware of any difference between what you say and what you do.

2 Demonstrate extraordinary persistence.

Researchers have identified three major opportunities for learning to lead – trial and error, observation of others, and education. All three require 'stickability' – seeing tasks through despite the setbacks, and learning from your mistakes. Success is experienced only by those who are prepared to persist.

3 Show confidence.

Overwhelming confidence in your own ability is essential. If you don't believe in yourself, others can't be expected to. Confidence can be acquired through experience, skill, and positive affirmation. People will 'buy into' the leader before they 'buy into' his or her leadership.

4 Make a commitment to hard work.

Nothing of worth comes easily. Most great leaders thrived on hard work and their main motivator was their desire to satisfy their own high standards. You'll find that a combination of self-discipline and a desire to make a difference will provide the necessary commitment to succeed.

5 Focus on being responsive.

Responsiveness is giving customers or employees what they want, courteously, when they want it, at a price that matches their expectations. You will be remembered not for the number of tasks you take on but those that you complete successfully. Your level of responsiveness will be the quality you will be recognised for.

6 Bring out the best in others.

Leadership doesn't occur in a vacuum. Invariably it involves working with others – selling them your dream, instilling in them a desire to achieve, motivating, cajoling, even coercing. Your ability to influence is a key leadership factor. Be tolerant of those less competent than yourself, providing they are willing to make the effort to perform to the best of their ability.

7 Demonstrate a high degree of energy.

There are many times when actions speak louder than words. Be prepared to share the load, roll up your sleeves and mix it with the others, apply yourself longer, and give that little bit extra. To that end, maintain a level of fitness that ensures you are physically capable of leading by example.

8 Back your judgement.

Boldness and courage are two key leadership qualities. You need to demonstrate a willingness to take chances, to experiment, and display a level of optimism that rejects any prospect of failure. Any failure is viewed as an opportunity to begin again better prepared than before.

9 Develop humility.

Learn to recognise your place in the scheme of things. Demonstrate high ideals, a strong sense of personal morality, and keep out of the 'sand-pit behaviour' that is reminiscent of child's play.

Management Memo

Beyond the horizon of time is a changed world, very different from today's world. Some people see beyond that horizon and into the future. They believe that dreams can become reality. They open our eyes and lift our spirits. They build trust and strengthen our relationships. They stand firm against the winds of resistance and give us the courage to continue the quest. We call these people leaders.[66]

10 Get your timing right.

Seizing the moment is the key to any successful endeavour, so make sure you get your timing right. Timing is a combination of alertness, foresight, and imagination.

11 Develop a winning attitude.

It's not what happens to you, it's what you do about it that counts – and your attitude will determine your response. As John Maxwell explains: 'The pessimist complains about the wind. The optimist expects it to change. The leader adjusts the sails.' Resolve now to start thinking and acting like a leader.

12 And finally, focus on the 10 Cs of leadership...

Bear in mind Michael Pegg's 10 Cs – the characteristics of compelling leadership. You'll need to be...

1. Charismatic
2. Caring
3. Committed
4. Crystal-clear
5. Communicative
6. Consistent
7. Creative
8. Competent
9. Courageous
10. Crazy (well, just a little), to believe that you really *can* make a difference.

How to get the most out of a conference, seminar or workshop

To stay on top of your career and ahead of your competition, you have to make learning a lifelong, ongoing process. Conferences, seminars and workshops are acknowledged forms of training, information gathering and networking. They are usually short, practical and up-to-the-minute. But such events must be more than just a day away from the office. If you want to take full advantage of these opportunities to invest in yourself, you'll need to be aware of the following advice...

1 Prepare yourself beforehand.

Your attendance and participation is an investment in yourself, so don't leave preparation to the last minute or allow 'emergencies' to limit your pre-event preparation...

- Study the agenda, and focus on what you want to get out of the event.
- Talk to your boss about the programme and find out if there is information she/he would like you to concentrate on.
- Do any pre-reading, either recommended or otherwise, that will increase your knowledge and understanding of the topic. If the presenter or facilitator is the author of a particular book related to the event, read it. Take notes and list follow-up items and possible discussion points.
- Consider who else from your organisation is attending. Contact them and discuss thoughts and ideas triggered by your pre-work to date. You may consider others who should be going and recommend their attendance – either to them or to their bosses. You might consider contacting those from other organisations who may be interested. Your actions will be appreciated.
- Make a 'learning contract' with yourself by listing what *you* want from the event and will actively seek out.

2 Be determined to maximise outcomes.

Your attendance and participation deserve maximum results, so resolve to behave in ways that deliver those outcomes. Your list of resolutions might include:

- Be on time so that you don't miss parts of sessions.
- Avoid internal and external distractions.
- Take risks and try some new behaviours.
- Raise issues of concern to you.
- Disagree with an opinion you think is wrong.
- Be open to ideas or approaches you would normally reject.
- Ask the speaker the questions that are in your mind.
- Start conversations with strangers during the breaks.
- Stay attentive and avoid the temptation to daydream.
- Be optimistic that a problem you have can be solved at the conference.

3 Arrive early and network.

Look on your attendance as an opportunity to spread your network of contacts. Tom Peters in *In Search of*

Excellence says that 'meeting your colleagues and friends is the most important aspect of a convention'. After registering, select a position near the door or the coffee service area where you will get to see and acknowledge most others attending. A mix of familiar and new faces will add variety to your networking. Don't forget to include a presenter or facilitator on your list of networking contacts. Remember the one topic that most people enjoy discussing is 'themselves'. Exchange business cards and, if necessary, arrange follow-up meetings. Jot on the back of the cards points about the contact and where you met. Don't leave it too late to take a seat at or near the front of the room.

4 Participate, listen, learn.

Introduce yourself to those seated near you. Seize this opportunity to be proactive in the interests of your learning. Take notes, but be careful not to let your note-taking interfere with the act of learning. Remember too that people tend to record points with which they agree – as opposed to disagree. Why not try writing down what you're going to do with what the presenter is saying? Keep asking yourself: 'How can I use this information to improve my job or my life?' As well, jot down questions to ask at the end of the talk or at an informal gathering.

5 Share information on your return to the job.

Avoid post-conference paralysis. What can you implement in the workplace? What can you change for the better? Consider also ways to disseminate information about the event within forty-eight hours of your return to work. You may decide to include your summary as an agenda item at an appropriate meeting, assemble a group with an interest in the outcomes, send an e-mail or circulate a hard copy of your notes and/or report outcomes individually. Use this opportunity to show how committed you are to your own professional growth. Others will be interested to see how you apply the information you acquired, so don't disappoint them.

> **Management Memo**
>
> Nothing beats a day away from your desk for a close examination of your role in your company, the people with whom you work, and your personal goals and how well you're achieving them. You meet other people who are in the same boat as you. Ever wonder how other people do it? Ever need a little reassurance you're doing it the 'right' way? Making contacts is one of the best hidden benefits of seminars. [67]

6 Set specific requirements if you send an employee.

Before the event inform those you're sending that you will require a succinct written report within forty-eight hours of their return to work. The report could include responses to the following questions:

- How can the organisation directly benefit from your attendance?
- Will it be possible for the organisation to recoup the cost of your attendance?
- Would you recommend other staff attend the event if it is repeated?
- What immediate action should be taken to commit the organisation to an improvement process based on what you have learned?

How to attract the headhunter

Headhunters are specialised corporate recruiters who are employed by businesses to 'search out' top management talent for hire in new jobs. Many managers dream of being phoned by a headhunter seeking an appointment or luncheon meeting to canvass interest in a too-good-to-refuse offer to join another organisation. Seldom, however, do dreams come true without planning and preparation by you...

1 Know what you want.

Successful organisations rarely want generalists in charge, so you will need to identify what you want to gain a reputation for – setting up new companies, planning mergers, troubleshooting, strategic planning, cost-cutting, and so on. The best thing you can have going for you is to be acknowledged by your peers as being good at what you do.

2 Assess demand for your skills.

The familiar supply and demand concept applies to headhunting. If you can satisfy a demand or create a new one for your services, you are in the box seat and have progressed a long way toward attracting an offer.

3 Keep a check on your track record.

Results, not ego, will gain for you the reputation you want. Stay focused on what you want to achieve. Remember, success requires just three things – knowing where you are now, knowing where you want to be and, each day in some way, progressing along the path to where you want to be.

4 Maintain quality networks.

Whom you know, or more importantly who knows you, *does* make a difference. All decisions ultimately come down to subjective assessments... Do I like this person? Is she/he respected by her/his peers? Does she/he get on well with people? Could I rely on her/him in a crisis? Such issues as these are why the network is so essential. This does not mean that you should rush out and join every club or professional association, but it is important that you find rewarding ways to associate with individuals and groups who are positioned to assist you in satisfying your career aspirations. The word will soon get around the network.

5 Be prepared – always.

In front of every talented person there must be a vacancy somewhere – and there's sure to be a vacant position in front of you at some time. So, be ready for when that opening occurs. Remain up-to-date with developments in your field; keep your slate clean; keep your CV current. And don't despair: Pope John XXIII accepted the top position in the world's largest organisation at age 76 and made one of the greatest contributions in the history of the Papacy. So be ready for when your moment of glory arrives.

6 Make things happen.

You'll just grow old if you simply wait around, hoping for that call. It will be your actions that make the difference. Stay focused; don't expect anything of others; drive your own bus; and tell others only those things that you want made public.

More importantly, make yourself visible. You must attract the attention of the headhunter. Try these strategies…

- Publish in trade journals and the press.
- Work on your public speaking skills so that when you do a presentation you do it well.
- Deliver speeches at public meetings, service clubs and professional conferences.
- Make a good name for yourself by being newsworthy and active in professional, community and social affairs.
- Think, on behalf of your company, of public relations ideas that will indirectly have you quoted in newspapers or trade journals as the author of the ideas.
- Keep doing a good job.

> **Management Memo**
>
> On-line networking can do more in a few weeks than traditional job search methods can do in months… and try posting your electronic résumé on your own 'home page'…[68]

- Cultivate professional contacts. Headhunters always have an ear to the corporate grapevine.

7 Establish your own 'home page'.

The Internet offers a great opportunity to promote yourself to a much larger audience. Talk to your existing web site guru about designing a home page for you that will present you to the national and international business community. Be prepared to respond to requests for more information by having your self-promotional pack on-the-ready as e-mail or hard copy.

8 And, as a last resort…

Still no phonecall? As a last resort, introduce yourself to a headhunter – send a résumé, wait a week, then phone for an interview. If you are lucky enough to get an interview – and you just may if a vacancy exists in your area – follow up with a thank-you note and a short reiteration of your current situation. Do not follow up with a phonecall. Remember, headhunters work for client organisations, not for you.

Even if you miss out on your preferred position, the headhunter may be sufficiently impressed to come calling on you the next time a position becomes available.

 See also: 76-78, 82-84, 140

How to use your retrenchment to your advantage

Restructuring, downsizing, and other forms of cost-cutting inevitably mean that some jobs just won't exist any more. One unfortunate outcome of the remarkable change in today's workplace is redundancy – termination of a worker's employment because that worker is now excess to company requirements. But redundancy need not be bad news if you're the person directly affected – providing you're prepared to make the most of the opportunities…

1 Keep your ear to the ground.

Retrenchment should rarely come as a surprise. By keeping yourself informed about developments inside and outside of your organisation, you will have a pretty good idea about how the organisation is travelling and about your prospects. Current management literature, the media, even the office grapevine, are all sources of information. These days, you should be preparing yourself long before the news is broken.

2 See retrenchment in a positive light.

As one door closes, another invariably opens. Being retrenched can provide the encouragement for you to make a break – even pursue a new career path that you may not have considered previously. Remember, it is your choice whether you see any event positively or negatively – and career changes are no different. As the ancient sages taught us, our interpretation of 'good news' or 'bad news' often depends on the way we view it.

3 Pull yourself together.

It's not a nice feeling to lose your job, but you'll gain little by indulging your emotions. Self-pity will not get you another job or help pay the groceries bill. By the time of your exit interview you should have already begun to take positive action.

4 Be prepared for your exit interview.

In-house or contracted outplacement services is a growing field in today's workplace. Find out in advance about the outplacement services provided by your organisation. In addition to helping you finalise your payout, the services may also include assistance with your résumé, interview coaching, career advice, counselling, advice on superannuation and financial planning, and temporary work accommodation. As well, you'll need to agree with the organisation about any public statement that will be made about your career change. You can't afford to have mixed messages communicated – particularly at your expense.

5 Negotiate fair severance compensation.

You have a right to be fairly compensated and to negotiate for the best severance arrangement to suit your situation. Become fully-versed in your organisation's severance policies and be firm in any negotiations.

6 Adopt a positive position and stick to it.

This is an opportunity to show some of your real qualities. Avoid whingeing, complaining, or carrying on a 'poor me campaign' with others. Realise that 70 per cent don't care, and the other 30 per cent enjoy the entertainment. If you want to let off steam, save it for a select, trusted few; better still, belt a golf ball, go for a run, meditate, or find some other form of relaxation. People will think the better of you if you adopt a rational approach.

7 Resist moving immediately into a similar position.

A common and predictable response from people who fear change and crave security is to seek out a position similar to the one that they have just left. A better approach is to take time, to play it cool, to consider your options and to decide rationally what you *really* want to do. After all, you only get one chance at life so you want to make sure you get the best from it.

Management Memo

In preparing for the possibility of retrenchment, ask yourself, 'What makes me professionally unique at work?' Identify the things that make you attractive and employable. And if nothing special comes to mind, see what you can do to add to your professional portfolio of skills, starting today. [69]

8 Resist burning bridges.

Business is a series of relationships between people so, if possible, try to maintain existing relationships, because you never know what the future holds. Wish your former employer and colleagues every success and move on to the next chapter in your life. There is no other person out there quite like you, so move on with confidence.

9 Think and act strategically.

Again, panic will get you nowhere. Set about planning your next life transition, considering how you want to spend the next phase in your life, the names of others who may be able to help you, and how you are going to go about letting people know that you are on the market. Your outplacement support professional will be able to help in setting up winning strategies.

Being made redundant can be tough on the ego, but that's all the more reason to attack the job market with a vengeance. Develop your job search strategy and follow it through.

 See also: 94-96, 106, 286

How to go it alone and establish your own consultancy

More and more managers are abandoning the safety of company careers to become consultants in their chosen fields. They cite a number of reasons – a need to pursue one's vision, a desire for increased independence, the lack of a meaningful future in a large organisation, or the reality of redundancy. If you're contemplating such a move, here are some important actions to consider...

1 Identify existing demand.

Successful businesses provide services that people want and are prepared to pay for – supply and demand. Demand will result either from providing different services or from providing those services differently. Given that very few consultants have different products or services, they usually attempt to differentiate their services in other ways, such as targeting niche markets, being increasingly responsive, and so on. One indicator of demand will be that you have potential customers lined up before you start, so that, prior to making the jump, you are able to tell existing clients of your plans and secure their continuing support before going it alone.

2 Get your networks established.

Abraham Lincoln advised: 'Good things come to those who wait – but only that left by those who hustle.' Networking is an important means of hustling, so use your existing contacts to make new contacts. Hustle at business breakfasts and lunches, industry seminars and other events conducted by professional associations; have your work published in industry journals or in the local media. Then, when potential clients have a need for the type of services you provide, you want them to associate your name immediately with the need to be satisfied. Hustle also in directory listings and Yellow Pages. Try starting a newsletter. Even approach former employers. Hustle for work.

3 Get a mentor and a coach.

A mentor will be someone who has succeeded in your field or in another field and who is prepared to nurture your development by taking you under his or her wing, offering fatherly or motherly guidance and advice. Mentors are role models and a valuable source of advice in such areas as getting started, services, niche markets, and advertising. Coaching differs from mentoring in that its focus is on providing specific assistance with an identified problem. A coach, for example, may instruct and assist you to improve your public presentation skills so that you can increase demand for your services as a conference speaker.

4 Choose your business name wisely.

Time spent on choosing a company name and logo is time well spent. You'll want a name that helps to identify you and your services from the competition – and one that provides credibility. Stay away from adding 'and Associates'. In business, 'and Associates' often means 'small', usually a one-person operation trying to sound 'big' by inventing associates. Register your chosen name with the relevant authority.

5 Establish essential support.

Develop a sound working relationship with those whose support you will need – for example, an accountant, a banker, a solicitor. Initially, you may employ part-time accounting/bookkeeping support, seek income protection and other professional insurance, use a graphic designer to design your logo and present your reports and tenders professionally, an office supplier to provide everything from furniture to stationery, and a fashion consultant who keeps you looking the part.

6 Know what it takes.

Being a consultant and being outstanding are two different things. Top consultants possess:

a bedside manner or a capacity to get along with clients, an ability to diagnose problems and to find their solutions, technical expertise and knowledge, communication skills, self-marketing and selling skills, management skills, a willingness to work erratic hours…

Management Memo

A consultant is simply anyone who gives advice or performs other services of a professional or semi-professional nature, in return for compensation. This means that regardless of your area of interest or expertise, you can become a consultant. Everyone has a unique background, with special experiences and interests duplicated by few others, and in demand by certain individuals or companies at certain times.[70]

7 Ask: 'Do I really need that…?'

It can be tempting to want upfront all the 'trimmings' often associated with operating a successful business, for example:

- A fancy office – most consultants go to their clients, not the other way around. Use technology and save on rentals.
- A bank loan – some would even say that if you can't set up a consultancy without a loan, don't do it.
- Elaborate marketing and advertising – but you know your own business best. Keep these experts on tap, but never on top.
- Partners – by joining forces with other consultants you can offer a broader base of skills, target a wider range of market niches, and reduce overheads. Informal partnerships are often preferred.

8 Stay focused on the bottom line.

It is likely that, in the establishment phase of your business, expenses will exceed income. Don't panic. Just keep overheads low without skimping. You'll need the best equipment you can afford, but the Mercedes can wait until you're well established.

How to begin each month on a positive note

A lot of things are going to happen to you over the next month. You can wait for them to happen, you can just let them happen – or you can make them happen. If you want to change your professional or personal life for the better, you must start with resolve and determination, and the following resolutions are provided to help you improve the way you function as a manager. Refer to them at the start of each month, photocopy and decide which you will focus on. How determined are you to improve?

1 Upgrade your professionalism.

Take responsibility for your own learning and development:

- ☐ Read two journals this month.
- ☐ Read one book this month.
- ☐ Contribute in some way to my professional association.
- ☐ Attend a seminar/course, and make an input.
- ☐ Beef up my technology skills and know-how in some way.
- ☐ Write an item for a professional journal, newsletter or newspaper.
- ☐

2 Improve the way you work.

When you can't work any harder or longer, working smarter is the only other option. Streamline the way you work:

- ☐ At the start of each week, set goals to be achieved by week's end.
- ☐ Plan each day by completing a daily to-do list.
- ☐ Keep each telephone call to a minimum.
- ☐ Make a determined effort to handle each piece of paper no more than twice.
- ☐ Be aware of any act of procrastination – and bite the bullet!
- ☐ Be on time for every meeting and prepare myself beforehand to make a worthwhile contribution.
- ☐ Ask myself often – 'Is this the best use of my time and energy?'
- ☐ Become a better delegator – by doing it right.
- ☐ Be aware of every interruption. Can I do something about this?
- ☐ Focus on one thing each day that requires of me a special 110 per cent effort.
- ☐

3 Improve your relationships.

Do your best to get on well with other people, and your managerial task will be much simpler:

- ☐ Make the effort to remember the name of each new person I meet.
- ☐ Catch at least three employees a day doing something right, and praise them accordingly.

- ☐ Work at eliminating a personal mannerism or habit that annoys others or hampers my effectiveness.
- ☐ Show a special interest in the work and life of three colleagues during the coming month.
- ☐ Act consistently in ways I believe to be fair and ethical.
- ☐ Say thank you more often.
- ☐ Defuse any grudge or hostility I have with a colleague or worker.
- ☐ Do one special thing this month to make this environment a better place for others to work in.
- ☐

4 Look after your own personal wellbeing.

Life and work are not to be endured, but enjoyed. You work to live, not live to work:

- ☐ Think about the need for balance in my life – work, family, friends, church, community, self…
- ☐ Put aside the time to enjoy special activities with my family this month.
- ☐ Exercise daily – in what way?
- ☐ Make a few changes for the better in what I eat – in what way?
- ☐ Set aside time for myself each day – for reading, hobbies, or play.
- ☐ Give something back to the community this month – and enhance the company's image at the same time.
- ☐ What major task am I about to complete? Is there a task over which I have been procrastinating? Finish it this month – and my reward will be………
- ☐

Management Memo

Managers can benefit from a periodic opportunity to renew, to regroup, to recommit, and to reinvent themselves as leaders. That's where resolutions can help. Unfortunately, the rite of making resolutions has gotten a bad rap. Too many people make them and break them without a second thought. For many people, resolutions are nothing more than lipservice tributes or half-hearted efforts to make change. It doesn't have to be that way… It's a process that can change lives and rejuvenate careers. [71]

5 Make good use of your travelling/waiting time.

Travelling to and from work and waiting for meetings/appointments can be very time-consuming and inefficient. Do something about it:

- ☐ Do job-related reading of documents, books or journals.
- ☐ Reflect on three encouraging incidents that occur each day.
- ☐ List three tasks I felt most happy about accomplishing for the day.
- ☐ Listen to a management-related cassette tape.
- ☐ Do some fresh thinking about a work-related problem requiring a solution.
- ☐

6 Add your own monthly resolutions…

- ☐
- ☐
- ☐

Managing Others

I will pay more for the ability to deal with people than for any other ability under the sun.

John D. Rockefeller

See also: 78, 408

How to hire the right person for the job

Think back to the last time you recruited someone. Were you absolutely confident at the time that you had selected the right person for the job? And has that person turned out to be a real winner? Hiring staff is a huge responsibility, and can arouse feelings of anxiety and hesitancy. In today's competitive world, however, the search for top quality people is paramount and that's why your skills in hiring the right person must come to the fore. Here are some key considerations to help you with your selection process...

1 Get the job description right.

Examine the current job description thoroughly. Is it still appropriate? Consult with the position's immediate supervisor, even the present incumbent, and then revise the requirements in terms of title, purpose of job, key responsibilities and duties, skills, limits of authority, job relationships, special demands, and conditions of employment.

2 Create a picture of the ideal person.

Review and itemise the job description, personal attributes, and the specific expectations of the person sought to fill the position. The list, which could be over 30 items in length, would include educational and professional qualifications, experience, special attributes and skills, ability to communicate, interpersonal skills, organisational skills, motivation, and so on. This will create a picture of the ideal person – although rarely will such a person exist. Therefore, break the list of requirements into three levels: must-have, should-have, and like-to-have.

3 Devise a standard evaluation form.

A standard data collection form for interviewers should be prepared to collect for each candidate as much high quality information relating to credentials, experience, skills and behaviour as possible, together with the interviewer's interpretative comments. This will later assist in reviewing the relevant merits of candidates.

4 Generate a battery of relevant questions.

A range of searching questions should be drafted in preparation for interviews. These are designed to collect as much information as possible on the behavioural specifications and personal attributes you have already targeted.

5 Begin the search.

Attracting suitable candidates is rarely a problem if you use advertisements, employment agencies, selection and search consultants, people you know, the grapevine, and your network, to spread the word. Compile a list of five to ten interviewees on the basis of your screening of résumés received; send a thank-you letter to the remainder.

6 Conduct first-round interviews.

Interviews are used to assess a candidate's compatibility and suitability in relation to future job performance. They enable you to gather and interpret the facts, so that you can compare all candidates with your picture of the ideal person. Refer to page 78 for guidelines on conducting these initial interviews, structured as follows: establish rapport; set the agenda; gather information; describe the job, organisation and conditions of employment; answer questions; and terminate the interview.

7 Conduct interviews of short-listed candidates.

The first round of interviews identifies the most suitable candidates. Advise and thank unsuccessful interviewees. Follow-up interviews with a short-list of the three most promising people permit in-depth questioning about specifics. Do not accept a candidate's accomplishments at face value since probing questions can reveal a great deal more than a résumé or initial interview can disclose.

8 Consider replacing 'gut feel' with a screening test.

It's important to hire someone whose personality fits your work culture and environment, and complements the personality of others they'll be working with. 'Gut feel' has traditionally been the measuring tool, but these days, psychometric testing procedures can be used to do this scientifically. Tests are available to check most qualities. *Myers-Briggs Type Indicator, DISC* and *Gatekeeper* are popular examples.

> **Management Memo**
>
> It is far better to hire right than to hire fast and hope that training makes someone right for the job. Training is expensive. It takes time, years in some cases, to develop the person you want. Hiring the right person can take a matter of a few hours or days. A need exists for smart hiring... [72]

9 Review all data.

Analyse all the information collected on your short listed candidates and assess individual strengths and weaknesses. Conduct a thorough check of qualifications and references. Talk to former bosses, peers, subordinates, and customers or clients if possible.

10 Make a decision – and an offer.

After having followed the rigorous steps outlined above, you should be in a position to select the best person for the job. Confirm with the candidate the package on offer and follow up with official documentation within forty-eight hours and, where required, make arrangements for the signing of an employment contract. Write and thank the unsuccessful short-listed candidates, remembering that they may well be worth considering for positions elsewhere in your organisation. Prepare an induction programme for your new member of staff.

How to make new staff members feel part of the organisation

For new employees, those early days in your organisation can be more of a test of survival than a time of growth and development. Often new staff members are thrown into the workplace and expected to succeed with little support – it's no wonder many of them become disillusioned. How newcomers progress depends on many variables, but research shows that the help they receive in the early days from management and colleagues makes all the difference...

1 Begin the familiarisation process immediately.

Instigate procedures which will enable new staff members to become familiar with important features of the organisation and its administration. For example, newcomers should:

- *undertake a guided tour of the company*, particularly those areas with which they will have most contact, such as the office, staff facilities, reprographics room, storeroom.
- *meet formally and socially with staff colleagues*, especially those with whom they will be working closely.
- *read relevant documents*, such as staff handbook, policy guidelines, safety instructions, annual report, and the like.
- *be briefed on procedures*, including office or factory routine, record-keeping, assessment, channels of communication, committee structures and staff development.

Such activity best takes place before the newcomer officially takes up duty in the organisation.

2 Create a supportive atmosphere.

What is needed are managers and experienced staff members with a commitment to being available to help newcomers as needed. Those who unite to meet the needs of beginners develop in that process structures of collegiality and collaboration that will also serve the organisation in other ways. Foster a warm climate of support.

3 Explain the job.

Outline the exact work to be done and how the work fits into the overall activities of the workplace. Do not make it sound too difficult at first and don't overburden the new arrival with information and rules. Provide tasks that at first are readily accomplished to ease the recent arrival into the new job.

4 Appoint a mentor.

An experienced employee who is asked to serve as mentor or 'buddy' for the new arrival provides the newcomer with friendship and open access to a colleague's expertise. Consider the support the mentor can provide:

- *Teaching* the newcomer about the job through coaching, conversations and demonstrations.
- *Guiding* him/her through the unwritten rules of the organisation and in recognising group norms.
- *Advising* about the quality of expected work and the nuances of company policies and procedures.
- *Counselling* the newcomer if stressed, lonely or in conflict with others.
- *Sponsoring* or giving stature to the newcomer in negotiations with others.
- *Role modelling* by providing an image of the effective professional or worker to which the newcomer can aspire.
- *Validating* over time the newcomer's goals and aspirations.
- *Protecting* the new arrival by being a buffer to the hazards of the company.
- *Motivating* by providing feedback and encouragement.
- *Communicating* openly with the newcomer so that all the other behaviours can be effective.

5 Schedule visits to other areas of the workplace.

Once the employee has established reference points as to what it is like to be a worker in your organisation, then structured visits to other departments can be scheduled to enable the newcomer to observe how experienced employees handle specific issues and tasks.

6 Visit the newcomer's workplace regularly.

Practical advice from experienced colleagues during the early days is best based on the newcomer's own experience. Therefore, arrange for regular visits with the aim of helping and working alongside – rather than judging or inspecting – the new employee. Give genuine feedback.

> **Management Memo**
>
> First impressions are the lasting ones. The induction and orientation period is an emotionally charged time for the new employee and those early experiences imprint lasting memories. [73]

7 Provide assistance in identified areas of need.

Research reveals that beginning employees commonly face similar problems in a new work environment. Work with your newcomers to pinpoint and remediate their specific areas of need, whether they be personal or professional.

8 Make them feel important.

Most newcomers feel uneasy, nervous and out-of-place at first. Take time to greet them personally on their first day. Show an interest in them. Make them feel the company genuinely needs them. Ask questions and invite questions. Be sincere.

9 Provide opportunities for review and discussion.

Show interest in the employee's progress through, firstly, formal sessions to review progress and to address concerns and, secondly, through informal discussions in a relaxed setting. Be generous with your comments, supportive, honest and sensitive, and let newcomers know their efforts are appreciated.

How to take people under your wing

The term 'mentor' originated in Homer's classic, *The Iliad*. Before Odysseus, king of Ithaca, left his family to fight in the Trojan War, he asked an old and trusted friend, Mentor, to raise his son, Telemachus, to succeed him as a wise and good ruler. To do this, Mentor had to become a father figure, teacher, role model, trusted adviser, challenger, encourager, and counsellor. Individuals will need to be 'mentored' in your organisation, nurtured in growth and development. This advice will help...

1 Understand why mentoring is required.

Try to see mentoring not as a programme, but as a way of life. Mentors can play a variety of roles. They can:

- help new staff members to feel part of the organisation.
- provide information about the way the organisation 'really' works.
- help protégés set goals, plan careers, and develop the skills necessary for career advancement.
- listen to problems, calm fears, provide feedback, and boost the confidence of their protégés.
- provide a role model for protégés to observe and emulate.

Though you may act as the mentor, it does not mean you will not enlist the support of others (workmates or 'buddies', if you prefer) in helping to provide general support.

2 Allocate mentoring tasks.

Mentoring should be a consideration when a new employee is set to join your organisation although, remember, *you* can't possibly act in that role for every newcomer. Before the new employee arrives, you (or the designated mentor) should:

- Make contact with the employee, complete introductions, and generally make the employee feel welcome. Don't forget, one of the most common reasons for people leaving an organisation is that they feel they do not fit.
- Arrange a meeting to determine any particular needs the new employee may have, provide any preliminary reading that may be of assistance, and explain the mentoring function. If you're involved in these preliminaries but are not going to be the mentor, tell the employee who will be.
- During the first two weeks of the employee arriving, do everything you can to make him/her feel part of the organisation (Refer to page 148).
- On an ongoing basis, remain available for questions while encouraging independence, and take an active interest in the new employee's work, reading, etc.

3 Identify and encourage rising stars.

Though your open management style will encourage most employees, there will be those whose qualities and potential impress you more than others. You consider that those people have a great deal to offer the organisation if their talents are nurtured and developed. They will be the ones you are more likely to put under your wing.

> **Management Memo**
>
> Two are better than one; for if they fall, the one will lift up his fellow; but woe on him that is alone when he falleth, and hath not another to lift him up. [74]

4 Distinguish between buddies and mentors.

Mentors appoint buddies to provide on-the-job support. The buddy will most likely be a peer with similar academic and work backgrounds, have at least two years in the organisation, be a recognised good performer, and present the desired image of the organisation. Those qualities far outweigh considerations of race and gender when selecting buddies. Allocation of buddies, therefore, can be used to exemplify and reinforce important messages about day-to-day life in your organisation.

5 Promote individuality.

One of the potential downsides of mentoring can be the desire to 'make' protégés resemble the mentor. Such outcomes are counter-productive. Experienced mentors will work at building a relationship, but maintain the individuality of their protégés and themselves. Mentors' expectations can be explicit without dominating the behaviour of their protégés.

6 Realise how the process can benefit the mentor.

The practice of mentoring has stood the test of time because it is a win – win for the mentor and the protégé. Mentors experience a high degree of personal satisfaction as they see their protégé 'grow'. Protégés often bring to a position fresh insights that can provide challenges and motivation. In addition to being encouraged to consider different perspectives, protégés can help to keep you abreast of new developments and new skills. The protégé also becomes a walking advertisement for the mentor. Not only does the protégé speak highly of the mentor in discussions with others in the organisation, but the mentor also gets to bask in the glow of the protégé's success.

7 And, finally...

- Although there are those who mentor for the personal satisfaction of contributing to the organisation, some organisations formalise the process by providing perks, funding for pet projects, and recognition dinners for those who take on the mentor role.
- Organisations benefit from the process: socialisation occurs faster, protégés learn quicker, potential is realised faster, youthful talent is tapped, and mentors' skills and motivation are maintained.
- Relationships should not be forced but evolve naturally over time.
- Mentors should guard against discriminating, often unintentionally, against other people on their team.
- If the mentor/protégé is of the opposite sex, recognise that professionalism, discretion and decorum are paramount. People talk – so make sure they have nothing to talk about.

How to improve employee performance through coaching

Managers have a two-fold role. They must correct their employees' performance problems and also help them to grow professionally, so that they can contribute to the organisation while advancing their own careers. This means that, to be effective, managers must be coaches, employing face-to-face techniques for solving performance problems, and for helping staff develop to their fullest potential. Here's how you can improve performance through the coaching process...

1 Know when to coach.

Coaching is usually initiated by an employee who recognises the need for help, by you when you spot a need to intervene, or when you are delegating, giving instructions or encouraging an employee's growth and development. Normally, you'll be too busy to adopt a coaching stance every time an employee comes to you with a problem. You'll therefore need to be quite selective about when you use coaching. You may also decide to delegate the task to a colleague better qualified to help with that particular problem.

2 Decide if a formal remedial coaching session is warranted.

Before committing yourself to a remedial coaching initiative, confirm that such a session is necessary by asking the following questions:

- Is there really a problem where an employee is not meeting a performance standard? Or is that employee simply not performing quite as well as another?
- If a problem exists, is the problem correctable? Have previous attempts failed with this employee?
- Is the problem beyond the control of the employee – i.e. faulty materials, late deliveries, lack of information, equipment failures, unrealistic deadlines?

Coaching is not the solution to all performance problems.

3 Prepare for a coaching session.

Advance planning is essential for a remedial coaching session: collect data, materials and records, structure the message to suit the needs and experience of the employee, anticipate possible outcomes and reactions, and select a time and place for the session.

4 Agree on a need for change.

No matter if the session has been at your instigation or your employee's, you must first agree on the exact nature of the problem – taking into account all the facts, as the staff member's definition may be different to yours. Establish clearly the purpose and importance of the session.

5 Define and discuss the various options.

This step is at the heart of the coaching process. Together with your employee, develop a strategy by:

- anticipating potential problems
- identifying the best ways to handle the situation.

Encourage employee participation by:

- asking open-ended questions
- discussing the pros and cons of each idea and examining possible options
- anticipating potential pitfalls and roadblocks, and identify alternative strategies.

Acknowledge good suggestions but be prepared to tell the employee if you disagree with a proposed approach. Build on as many ideas as possible from the employee.

6 Agree on specific actions to be taken.

Now you are ready to decide on how the desired outcome will best be achieved. Both of you should agree on the best option(s), measurable goals by which progress can be gauged, and a timeline. Remember, the best approach is likely to be the one that the employee feels committed to achieving.

7 Set up a programme of review.

Establish and agree upon a schedule of review at the coaching session to ensure the plan of action is working.

8 Summarise actions.

Recap the actions you have agreed on and check for understanding. Acknowledge the employee's participation and contribution to the discussion. End on a positive note.

Management Memo

Coaching is a key step in building an effective team. But it can't be done offhandedly or haphazardly. Schedule periodic coaching sessions. If you don't, you risk letting your firefighting activity crowd the obligation out. You should certainly plan at least one coaching session with each employee during the year, perhaps two. Give them plenty of opportunity to discuss their interests, strengths and ambitions so that you can build on what is already there. [75]

9 Follow up and provide feedback.

Set a follow-up date to review progress and stress that you're willing to help if required. Follow up to make sure tasks are accomplished and remember to acknowledge achievement.

10 Avoid these common coaching traps.

- *Lecturing instead of coaching.* Coaching involves dialogue and shared decision-making.
- *Coaching only problem employees.* Coaching should not be seen as a short-term punitive measure for problem staff only. Remember to use long-term coaching to help all employees develop and grow.
- *Not being specific.* Avoid dealing in generalities. Provide examples, statistics, dates and documentation to support your attempts to change employee behaviour.
- *Assuming too much.* Don't assume an employee is aware of the performance problem, or what is required; or will perform appropriately when agreement is reached, or even know when a good job has been done. Explain every step clearly.
- *Confusing a coaching session with a disciplinary session.* Coaching is a positive, non-threatening process.

 See also: 150-152, 156, 160, 184, 192

How to maintain improved performance

Improving the performance of staff is hard enough; maintaining and building on that improvement present even greater challenges for managers. Most improvement processes consist of four broad stages: agreeing on the standards or expectations, monitoring progress, recognising achievement, and reviewing the performance displayed, with recognition and review featuring prominently in the maintenance plan. To foster ongoing improvement in your staff, consider the following...

1 Link behaviour to outcomes.

Employees have to know what their improved performance, and the maintenance of that improvement, means to the organisation for two main reasons. Firstly, employees need to realise that if the organisation prospers, so too do their opportunities for advancement and their job security is enhanced. Secondly, employees must understand that their actions impact on others, thereby increasing interdependence and a desire to continue to improve.

2 Demonstrate your commitment to continuing improvement.

Schedule regular meetings with individual employees to talk about the importance of improved work performance – for the organisation and for them. At those meetings you need to demonstrate your knowledge of the employee's accomplishments by describing in specific terms what you have observed. Be sure to compliment his/her achievements and offer further appropriate encouragement. Maintaining improved performance means that you have to be 'on the ball' at all times.

3 Reinforce desirable behaviours.

Recognition is a powerful motivating tool that helps to bring out the best in people by reinforcing observed improvements. A few well-chosen words at the right time can mean a lot to someone trying to do better. But that's only one example of how you can reinforce desirable behaviour. Positive reinforcement can also be traced to these four managerial behaviours:

- Create a work climate that is warm, supportive, trusting and encouraging.
- Provide learning opportunities that let employees know that it's okay to fail.
- Be available to listen, even when you know it's news you'd rather not hear.
- Show that you know *what* employees are doing so that you can tell them *how* they're doing.

4 Encourage staff to blow their own horn.

When people are proud of their accomplishments, they will want to tell you how they did it. However, the majority are likely to be reluctant starters in self-promotion. Provide opportunities for them to talk about their improvements and to bask in their moments of glory. Your actions will indicate that you consider their accomplishments to be important and, more particularly, that you value their extra efforts. When employees see that you understand and value their contributions, they will be inspired to give even more. And, of course, your active listening is helping to maintain improved performance.

5 Listen to what staff have to say.

If you've worked at building a positive and constructive climate, don't hesitate to ask employees for suggestions on how you can help them to maintain their improved performance. Together, you will come up with ideas to minimise or eliminate any problems that get in the way of continuing improvements. If you're able to grant a request or act on a suggestion, indicate what actions you are able to take, and when. If you're not sure, explain that you will have to look into the situation further and you will respond by a certain date. Your actions will encourage employees to be involved in future projects.

> **Management Memo**
>
> Employees today want bosses who act naturally rather than inspirationally, bosses who treat them as responsible adults. Unfortunately, there are still managers who feel they must constantly rekindle fires in their employees. Picture the manager who is always 'up', booming confidence that all is well and going to get better if we all perform even better. No one believes it. It is not a realistic, caring, person-to-person way of communicating.[76]

6 Show your appreciation.

Thanking employees for improved performance reinforces any praise given earlier. The effectiveness of a simple 'thank you' is increased when it is the last thing the employee hears at the end of a conversation with you. Realistically, employees cannot expect that you can solve all of their problems, but they have every right to expect courteous and reinforcing behaviour from you.

 See also: 152, 158, 166, 184

How to improve employee performance on the run

Staff performance problems can occur at any time and, when someone is under-producing or having problems meeting quality standards, immediate action is often required to remedy the situation. The effective manager must be quick to act to effect a turnaround. Here's one approach for improving employee performance on the run, without having to resort to the formality of a discipline or performance appraisal interview...

1 Outline the problem in a friendly manner.

Meet with the employee – a discussion that will usually take place away from your office. Describe any apparent problem as specifically as possible, bearing in mind that most people have days when they do not perform at their best. So make sure that this is not just one of those days.

Focus on the problem, not the employee. Refer to any available data that will help you show that there is a problem. Leave discussions about attitude to a more formal, regular appraisal or discipline interview, because such comments in the context of this meeting will put the employee on the defensive and make it difficult to have a productive discussion. Your intention should be to effect an immediate turnaround in performance.

2 Ask for the employee's help to solve the problem.

You need the employee on your side so that you can work together to get performance back to an acceptable level. For this reason, telling a staff member what to do is unlikely to stand much chance of success, particularly if the employee doesn't want to improve performance. You can get commitment by simply asking for help in deciding what to do about the performance problem. In this way you are signalling that you value the employee's ideas and your consultative approach will be appreciated in most cases, and help to gain employee cooperation and commitment.

3 Discuss possible causes of the problem.

Remember, the discussion is about the person's performance problem, not the person's attitude or personality. Gather all the information you can by asking open-ended questions beginning with words such as 'when', 'what', 'who' and 'how'. The employee will not be threatened by these kinds of questions and will be encouraged to answer them. Listen, respond with empathy, and take notes if necessary. This is another way of demonstrating to the employee that you are interested in what is being said.

Summarise the causes you have identified and make sure there is agreement about those.

4 Identify possible solutions.

Having identified the causes of the performance problem, you now want to correct them. Given that it is the employee's problem, ask for ideas and solutions. Discuss them. Perhaps write them down, listing as many ideas as you both can come up with. You will find that people are more committed to solving problems if they've had a say in the solution.

5 Decide on the specific action to be taken.

Now choose the best solution. At this point in the discussion, you should be ready to pinpoint exactly what must be done by whom and by when, to correct the performance problem. Assign responsibilities for specific action and write them down. Remember, support the employee's efforts to improve performance, but emphasise that the responsibility for improvement rests with the individual. Express confidence in the employee's ability to take the agreed actions.

Management Memo

Performance is a complex dimension that is more than 'doing things right' or 'doing the right things'. It is the responsibility of the manager to consider carefully who or what is performing, what performance is to be measured, how performance is to be measured, and when it is to be measured. [77]

6 Agree on a specific follow-up date.

By setting a date to meet again, you are sending a message that solving the performance problem is important to you and that you will be available to assist in making sure the problem is addressed satisfactorily. A follow-up meeting will encourage discussion of progress.

7 Record the details.

If the meeting is held away from your office, record the details of your discussion immediately on your return, using your notes as a guide and memory trigger. Enter any follow-up arrangements in your diary.

 See also: 154-156, 192-194, 200, 358

How to improve the performance of your secretary

Your secretary, perhaps known as your personal assistant, professional assistant or executive secretary, can be the key operative in the office of any manager. If highly trained in all aspects of office supervision, communications, human relations and organisation, as well as in the basic skills of paper management and keyboarding, the secretary can be a true professional and your most valuable management asset. To form a very effective 'team of two', consider the following...

1 Know what your secretary can and should do.

Today's top secretaries must be as familiar with the management of people as they once were with paper and keyboard. Of course, core skills are still required: keyboarding, filing, telephone, screening of calls, mail and visitors, appointments and paperwork. However, higher-level assistants are called upon to display more sophisticated skills: composing letters, summarising reports and articles, supervising others and the office, scheduling your day, standing in for you at meetings, managing your calendar, tracking your jobs and keeping you up to speed.

Personal assistants display essential qualities: helpful, hard-working, courteous, reliable, loyal, respectful, imaginative, creative, resourceful, efficient, level-headed.

Do you really know where your secretary's strengths lie and what you want from the partnership? Take the time to sit with your assistant, to clarify expectations based on shared needs and goals, and to determine what steps are required to forge a quality 'team of two'.

2 Meet daily to plan your day.

To minimise interruptions throughout the day, set aside time each morning to organise the day for you both: checking assignments, appointments and priorities, clarifying tasks, processing paper, discussing problems. A five-minute wrap-up session at the end of the day is also useful to assist planning for the next day.

3 Keep your secretary – and yourself – informed.

The more your assistant knows what you're doing, where you're going, when you'll be back, what's behind this memo, why this is important, and what your plans, goals and projects are, the more she/he will be able to help you and handle her own priorities. By demonstrating confidence in your secretary in this way, you'll be surprised at what you learn in return. Secretaries, being hooked into the office grapevine, often know more about what's going on than their bosses do. Use them as a sounding board, and their advice and information may prove invaluable.

4 Show you care about your secretary's welfare.

If you want to build trust and loyalty, cultivate a little sensitivity and thoughtfulness. Make her task easier by being organised yourself; when her routine tasks pile up, or when she is undertaking a time-consuming higher-level task, bring in a temp to help out; keep her advised of your whereabouts; ask for her suggestions on how you can help her become more effective. Do something special whenever you can – cards, awards, lunch, a surprise gift. Like all other key members of the team, secretaries appreciate recognition and acknowledgement when jobs are well done.

5 Share the blame and the credit.

Shoulder the responsibility for a mistake or share it with your assistant. If your secretary is responsible for the problem, discuss it privately and offer positive suggestions for improvement. Never complain about performance or criticise in public. Always focus on what is right, rather than who is right. Your tact and support in times of crisis will be reciprocated down the track. Give credit where credit is due. Let everyone know when your assistant has done a job well or come up with a great idea. Bask in the reflected glory.

6 Work as a team.

Foster the belief that you are both working as a team to make the office, and the organisation, a more effective and efficient enterprise. Let others know that your assistant has your complete confidence and that it's likely that they'll get a faster response by working directly with her on routine matters. This is one reason why your early morning session to coordinate appointments, meetings, reminders, paperwork and other matters is so important.

> **Management Memo**
>
> Of the many resources contributing to the manager's effectiveness, none is more critical than his secretary. Some managers act as though they want a secretary to mind her own business and simply do what she is told. The truth is that his business is also her business if he is to be as effective as he should. [78]

7 Help your secretary grow.

Managers are frequently guilty of over-management. Consider those jobs you currently handle which could just as effectively be undertaken by your assistant. Take time to train your secretary to do them – and then let go. Show an interest in your assistant's further education. Encourage the undertaking of further studies and courses, and involvement in professional associations. Provide moral and financial support where possible.

8 Practise job enlargement.

Over time, by selectively and patiently adding to your assistant's raft of responsibilities, you will add greatly to her job satisfaction, especially as the less skilful demands on her time are reduced. But remember, greater responsibility also requires greater compensation.

 See also: 154, 208, 220-222, 228

How to conduct a performance appraisal interview

Most employees want to know the answer to this basic question: 'How am I doing?' Regular staff performance appraisals should fulfil that need and more. In these sessions, staff member and manager sit down at least annually and review the employee's past and present performances and set future directions. The most effective sessions are simple and encourage open dialogue between manager and employee. Here are some steps to follow when conducting a basic performance appraisal interview...

1 Allocate interview times for all employees.

Employees need to know well in advance the date and time for their appraisal. The performance appraisal interview may occur, for example, during the month of their birthday, or at some other time mutually convenient to the employee and to you. Both you and the staff member then have adequate time to prepare for the meeting.

2 Encourage the employee to prepare for the session.

With adequate forewarning, the employee should be able to prepare for the session. The design of the interview form or an agenda can assist in this regard. Ask the employee to focus particularly on his/her performance since the last meeting, comparing against goals previously agreed to.

3 Prepare yourself for the session.

As part of your planning, assemble material relevant to achieving your outcomes. Review the records of the employee's past performance appraisal meetings and decide if there are any other issues you wish to raise or emphasise. Arrange for a location where you will not be interrupted and ensure you both allocate sufficient time for the meeting.

4 Establish a rapport.

Gaining the employee's trust and confidence is essential to successful outcomes. This process cannot be rushed and the interview should not proceed until you feel a rapport has been successfully established.

5 Reach agreement on past and present performance.

Give the employee an opportunity up front to describe how she/he feels the job is progressing generally. Examine together how well the previously set goals in key result areas were achieved: were the standards met adequately, were they met on time, what improvement is needed, any problem areas? If both parties have completed their pre-meeting preparation, agreement can be reached by each person walking through their respective lists. Remember, those lists will include positive items and others in need of attention.

6 Acknowledge employee successes.

Give full and generous acknowledgement for appropriate performance, and special emphasis on above average achievements. Indicate your intention to build upon these personal strengths.

Management Memo

Performance improvement is an area of responsibility for each manager. However, it does not just happen. An effective means of accomplishing improvement includes considering all factors influencing performance in a collaborative discussion with the employee. Through the discussion, you can establish improvement goals and develop a strategy and schedule for attaining them... You are an active part of the discussion, but *you* should not necessarily be directing the outcome. [79]

7 Identify and agree on areas needing improvement.

Gain the employee's commitment to addressing those areas in need of attention. Focus particularly on no more than two or three areas. Explain why improvement is necessary, express improvement in measurable terms if possible, and record actions to be taken. This process should not be rushed and should involve considerable employee input, as ownership of the issues is essential.

8 Stay focused.

If you are criticised or forced to defend your position at any stage, remain calm and focused on outcomes. Adopt the attitude that nothing can happen in the interview that you can't handle competently.

9 List future directions.

Avoid dwelling on the past – very little can be gained from that. Devote maximum time to discussing the employee's future. Reach agreement on the next stage and list the steps to be taken. Agree on new goals or standards together with an action plan to achieve them. Consider any staff training that may be appropriate. How can you assist? Update the job description if necessary. Document the outcome and include it on the employee's file. A review of that list will form the basis for the next performance appraisal interview.

10 Close on a positive note.

Conclude the meeting by summarising what you think the appraisal interview has achieved. Ensure that the employee leaves in a positive frame of mind, feeling prepared to tackle the next stage with confidence. Fix a date for a follow-up meeting if required.

11 Monitor outcomes.

You must continue to look critically at the real results of your staff appraisal interviews and make changes accordingly. Those changes may even involve moving to a 360^0 appraisal system.

See also: 150, 168

How to help an employee whose career has plateaued

Plateauing is a normal phase in many careers. Usually coinciding with mid-career, employees (and managers) can experience a levelling out of their progress as a result of downsizing, restructuring or plain old boredom. Previously high-achievers seem to lose their zest, sparkle and enthusiasm. They become disenchanted, frustrated and, over time, their morale and productivity decline. What can you do to revitalise the career of a stuck-in-a-rut employee?

1 Understand the reasons why individuals plateau.

Plateauing can occur for several reasons:

- There are too few jobs to satisfy the number of competitors for those jobs. Those who miss out feel 'dead-ended'.
- The employee's ability does not match the job: lack of skills, aptitude, inability to respond to changing job requirements.
- Men are faced with the so-called 'mid-life crisis'.
- Some women feel betrayed after having rejected traditional roles, like life partnerships and children, for their careers.
- The extension, or even abolition, of the mandatory retirement age results in some older workers becoming 'trapped' in upper-level positions.
- Increasing numbers of younger, highly-qualified employees progress too rapidly up the corporate ladder – a move followed by a frustrating period of career stagnation.

Employees, too, can contribute to their own plateauing by:

- being less active than others in adapting to change
- displaying an inflated opinion of their actual work performance
- showing little interest in understanding their boss's problem
- being unwilling to improve their work performance.

2 Be aware of the social and economic impact.

Lay-offs, mergers and other cutbacks in staff contribute to plateauing. High unemployment, too, has reduced outside options for plateaued employees and they stay put. The two-income family may also mean that the employee may not be able to afford to transfer to other employment. The removal of layers of management through restructuring and downsizing has also resulted in more plateauing.

The 'baby boomers', those born between 1946 and 1964, account for a major proportion of our working population, and the number of higher management positions and others will not be sufficient to accommodate them. As a result, 'baby boomers' will have to adjust their expectation – usually downwards. No longer will a university degree (or two) guarantee advancement or even a job.

3 Be pro-active in dealing with the phenomenon.

Although you may feel inadequate in dealing with this omnipresent phenomenon, ignoring it won't make it disappear. Alternatively, you can take a tough stance and demand greater productivity, an approach that will not work in most authentic cases. Or you can try to be understanding and offer assistance by considering one or more of the following options:

- ***Help individual employees recognise that plateauing is a normal occurrence.*** Honest feedback can send clear signals to employees that their activities are important and that you are prepared to provide support to assist them over this period.
- ***Reduce the focus on promotion as a major indicator of success.*** Where reduced promotional opportunities lie at the cause of employee plateauing, organisations can emphasise alternative ways by which success can be measured –
  - Provide opportunities for greater participation in setting goals and determining methods and procedures. Plateaued employees usually have a wealth of experience for the organisation to draw upon.
  - Assign the staffer to train new employees and bring others up to speed.
  - Devise a major project for the worker, with full autonomy, to show your trust and to provide new zest.
  - Since plateaued employees are often bored, ensure they are given useful activities; avoid particularly assigning them duties and responsibilities that are clearly beneath them, just to keep them occupied.

Management Memo

Plateauing exists in virtually all organisations and affects both good and bad performers. But if both employee and manager address the situation through counselling and training, career plateauing does not have to be the end of a person's career with an organisation. Rather, it can be the start of a productive and rejuvenated career. [80]

- ***Change the structure of the organisation.*** Make modifications to create a more horizontal structure and establish additional responsible positions.
- ***Consider lateral promotions.*** If demoralised workers have little chance of promotion in your area, their skills and talents may be valuable in another area.
- ***Seek the employee's input.*** Explore with him/her how the current job can be made more stimulating, without overstepping current parameters.
- ***Provide specialist, qualified counselling.*** Where necessary, this will help them overcome individual crises associated with career plateauing.

4 Don't pamper the employee.

Maintain your high standards. By all means be supportive of the plateaued worker, but resist the temptation of letting such employees coast for a while, hoping that they'll lift their game after the crisis passes. By ignoring the problem, you are sending the message that you don't care whether or not a good job is done – which may translate into 'You have no future around here any more!'
That only exacerbates the problem.

 See also: 162, 168, 240

How to help older employees stay valuable in your organisation

Older employees represent a valuable resource for they possess experience, know-how and seasoned judgement. Many, however, become less enthusiastic as their careers draw to a close and indeed often feel threatened in an age of youth, technology and redundancy. Age discrimination protection measures, however, are forcing many employers to focus on this ageing component of the workforce. A few pointers will help you cope with this issue...

1 Review your attitude towards the older employee.

It's so easy to regard our older employees negatively – we stereotype them as less productive, less likely to keep up with new developments and technologies, less flexible, more difficult to supervise and train, more resistant to change, more likely to miss work for health reasons, less enthusiastic... Often, we reinforce these attitudes by being indifferent towards them. But if you adopt this stance, you are in fact creating a liability your organisation cannot afford. Seniors are a valuable resource – if you treat them as such.

2 Explore a range of policies and practices to introduce.

Ensure your company policy includes statements to the effect that older employees are valued members of your organisation. Adopt such flexible working arrangements as job rotation, job sharing, flexitime, part-time work, or using older workers as independent consultants. Such options to the working day of older employees can save you money by reducing turnover, and replacement and retraining costs, and help to re-enthuse older workers and fully utilise their abilities.

3 Consider adding to the older worker's responsibilities.

Revitalise the motivation of older employees by dangling new challenges in front of them. Expand their work role. Provide them with new responsibilities and tasks.

4 Try changing the employee's job completely.

If given the choice of remaining in the same comfortable routine until retirement or of experiencing a completely new role, senior employees often prefer to go out in glory. A couple of years in a new position, or on a special project where their experience and knowledge can be better used, does wonders for their enthusiasm and self-esteem.

5 Use the employee's experience and knowledge of your operation.

Old timers can always draw on their long experience with your organisation to become valuable members of task forces or committees. The stimulation and pressure of working with younger colleagues in such groups often enable your organisation to tap into a dormant goldmine.

Management Memo

In 1953, Henry Baily Little celebrated fifty-five years as president of the U.S. Institution for Savings in Newburyport, Mass.

Respected by his board of directors, Little was asked to serve another term. Surprisingly, he declined, stating it was time for a younger man to assume the leadership.

'So what's the big deal?' you may ask. Well, Henry Baily Little was 102 years old and the 'younger man' chosen to take his place was William Black. And he was eighty-three [81]

6 Sit down and set goals with the employee.

A session with the older employee to set personal goals for the remaining few years can spur the senior to greater productivity. Ensure that the goals are practical and satisfy both the individual's and the company's needs; that they are specific within preset time limits; that they are challenging, so that the older worker does not feel 'pushed aside'; and that they are attainable.

7 Prevent obsolescence through training.

It is shortsighted to see training as the sole province of the younger worker. Training can enhance the older workers' productivity considerably, enabling the company to reap the benefits for several years to come.

8 Relieve anxiety: provide counselling geared to the future.

As employees approach career's end, if you are able to relieve their pre-retirement anxiety, you can only improve their productivity. Provide counselling on financial, health and recreational matters.

 See also: 152, 168, 184, 332

How to recognise unsatisfactory job performance

One of the most important and demanding responsibilities facing a manager is evaluating the performance of staff. It should be an ongoing day-to-day activity, for without such knowledge, a manager is unable to make sound decisions regarding promotion, transfer, training, counselling, even dismissal. The identification of poor employee performance is particularly important because it can foreshadow the need for remedial action. To assist in identifying unsatisfactory performance, consider the following…

1 Be alert for the signs.

When an employee's work performance diminishes to an unsatisfactory level, the cost to both employee and the organisation can be significant. From time to time, employees may exhibit one or more of the unsatisfactory indicators which are listed below and many of these can be addressed fairly quickly by the manager in consultation with the staff member.

However, in the case of some of the more serious indicators, or when several signs recur in the same employee, a session with the organisation's employee adviser or counsellor may be warranted.

2 Assess the obvious signs of diminishing performance.

There are numerous outward signs of a poorly performing employee:

- excessive time required to complete work tasks
- missed deadlines
- untidiness in the workplace
- high accident rate
- decline in the quality of work
- complaints received from other staff and customers
- wasted materials
- indications of tiredness, loss of enthusiasm and decline in concentration
- erratic performance
- lapses in fulfilling requests, tasks and responsibilities
- increasing failure to attend to detail
- poor decision-making and judgement
- overall decline in standards.

3 Examine attendance patterns.

The factors which reveal signs of unsatisfactory attendance would be:

- consistent lateness
- early departure
- absences after weekends and paydays
- extended lunch breaks
- increased absenteeism
- frequent time off
- decline in organisation-related social activities.

A poor attendance record could be a symptom of more serious problems.

4 Investigate reasons for sick leave.

Poor job performance could be the result of real or feigned illness, or of more serious physical/emotional problems. Signs in this area would include:

- frequent excuses made for minor illnesses
- more frequent sickness than other employees, e.g. colds and flu.
- illnesses tend to recur
- more serious physical illnesses.

5 Look for examples of deteriorating behaviour.

Behaviours which can result in unsatisfactory performance, and which require follow-up action, would include:

- mood changes
- trembling
- breath smelling of alcohol
- memory lapses
- increasingly dishevelled appearance
- speech difficulties
- increasing use of abusive language
- destruction of property
- hostile attitude towards others.

6 Consider changes in personality.

The underlying causes of the following personality changes must be treated if performance at work is to be improved:

- undue emotion or aggression
- increased irritability
- increased moodiness and unpredictability
- inability to sustain effort
- disputes with others
- violence
- avoidance of work colleagues
- over-reaction to real or imagined criticism
- general withdrawal.

Management Memo

Performance evaluation implies three major functions:

1. *Observation and identification* refers to the process of viewing or scrutinising certain job behaviours. It concerns the process of choosing what behaviours to observe, as well as how often to observe them.
2. *Measurement* occurs after managers choose what behaviours to examine. It relates to the comparison of this information about the behaviour against a set of organisational standards. The degree to which the observed behaviour meets or exceeds the standards determines the level of performance it reflects.
3. *Development* refers to performance improvement over time.

A performance evaluation system must be able to point out deficiencies and strengths in people's behaviour so that they can be motivated to improve future performance. [82]

7 Take appropriate action.

Knowledge of an employee's unsatisfactory performance and a pin-pointing of the outward signs of that diminished effort is one thing. What to do about it is another. A manager might consider a range of options: corrective action to bring the employee back to the required standard, re-training, coaching, counselling, mentoring, demotion, transfer, termination…

 See also: 152-154, 166, 184, 220

How to improve the performance of at-risk employees

If you have a staff member who is not performing to expectations, whose approach to the task is slipping, who is ineffective, even counterproductive, then you need to put into practice a process that can help that employee get back on the path to improved performance and increased productivity. The following process of rehabilitation will help to isolate the cause of, and generate a possible solution to the problem of this at-risk employee...

1 Ensure that action is necessary.

Everyone has an occasional off-day, but at-risk employees are those whose performance has been observed on several occasions as being in a state of decline. When you are certain you have identified at-risk performance, then it is time to gather accurate information from a wide variety of sources.

2 Gather the facts.

Your information search should involve colleagues, supervisors and others who have regular contact with the at-risk employee. The perceptions of such people can be compared with your own, thereby helping you to make an informed judgement. Determine the relationship of this information to job performance, enabling you to omit information not specifically related to the issues under investigation. These information-gathering meetings will clear the air, establish the facts, help decide on possible actions, and suggest the types of assistance that can be offered.

3 Decide on appropriate actions – beforehand.

You should now have accumulated quality information to assist you to develop a plan of action. Remember, all this is done *before* you meet with the employee. The plan will list 'who' is to do 'what' by 'when' and 'how', and should consider the following strategies:

- *Make goals and standards specific and clear* in terms of what you expect and how you expect it. Spell this out clearly, in writing if necessary, so that the employee can't claim later that your requirements were vague.
- *Investigate ways of providing more challenging work.* It's often the case that at-risk employees are simply bored. If you can generate more challenging tasks, you may create a complete turnaround in that employee's attitude to work.
- *Plan a procedure to monitor the at-risk employee's performance.* How will you be able to get immediate feedback if there is no improvement or a significant lapse in performance? If the set goals

haven't been met, why is this? A lack of immediate response from you will diminish your credibility and you'll lose whatever influence you might have.

4 Approach the staff member.

Raise the matter with the staff member, making your concerns quite clear and indicating that you both need to meet. The discussion is not whether a meeting will occur, but when. Make an appropriate time.

5 Hold a meeting and get right to the point.

Your meeting should cover the following points:

- *Express your disappointment* in your staff member's recent lacklustre performance. Play on the employee's pride by revealing that she/he has lost your esteem as a result.
- *State the facts* as you see them.
- *Encourage a response.* Be prepared to listen to any reasons for poor or declining performance.
- *Create peer pressure* by letting the employee know how much she/he is letting colleagues down, forcing them to work harder to carry her/his share of the workload.
- *Offer assistance and present your draft action plan.* Agree on the actions to be taken. You've done the necessary research, you've done all you can to put in place a set of procedures to help the at-risk employee improve, so it's now time to assert your position and insist on results in the future.
- *Ensure the employee is aware of the consequences of continued poor performance.*
- *End the meeting on an optimistic note.*

> **Management Memo**
>
> Some employees fall into behaviour patterns on the job that constitute management problems for you. Some of those behaviours get in the way of the employee's own effectiveness. At other times the behaviours interfere with smooth working with others. Often the people who exhibit such irritating behaviours know how to do the job adequately, but you suspect that they could do much better if you could neutralise their self-imposed impediments. Usually you can do just that, without having to go through a counselling procedure.
>
> The key is to take steps on a regular basis to discourage behaviour that you don't want and to encourage substitute behaviour... Most people, you will find, are less resistant to gradual attempts to get them to change their ways. [83]

6 Set follow-up procedures in place.

At-risk employees cannot be left too long without frequent reviews. Regular follow-up meetings should be a feature of the rescue package, thereby underscoring the priority you have placed on this matter. You may also decide to appoint a mentor or 'buddy' to provide additional support in the workplace.

 See also: 358

How to get others organised – and save time

Time management invariably focuses on self – how you organise your day, your papers, your workload. But how well do your staff members use *their* time to best advantage the organisation, you, and themselves? Do you really know if they, and you, are getting full value out of their day? Your staff can save your time and theirs if *you* take the initiative that encourages them to be time-conscious...

1 Watch for the indicators of a disorganised staff.

Be on the lookout for messages which indicate that the human component in your organisation is not being used, timewise, to best advantage:

- You are frequently interrupted by staff seeking assistance, instruction or direction.
- Your staff practises reverse delegation – refers tasks back to you.
- Deadlines are often missed/postponed.
- Staff assignments often need to be redone because they are of poor quality.
- Your action tray is choking and you seem to be taking more and more work home.
- Staff morale is low and work is no longer challenging.
- Employees seem to spend a lot of time chatting and socialising.

2 Find out how they spend their time.

Before staff can manage their time more effectively, it is important that they, and you, know how they are currently using their time. You might keep a time/task schedule, entering the employee's name, the task assigned, date assigned, your estimate of the completion date, and actual completion date, with a comments column for unexpected interruptions to the task. Or have them keep an accurate record in their diaries, or construct a simple matrix indicating times and tasks. All this is valuable information for future discussions with individual employees.

3 Help staff to organise their work areas.

By observing what staff do and how they do it, you can identify efficiencies that can be introduced. Consider office layout, for example. Proximity to essential equipment like photocopiers, computer printers and telephones is a key consideration. If employees have to walk the length of the office to use a copier, your observations will have detected a real time-waster. Office landscaping, too, improves productivity by not only enhancing the visual appeal, but by reducing distractions as well.

4 Compile a skills index for staff.

A skills index for staff can be easily

calculated using the many commercially available measurement tools, or you may prefer to construct your own. You may find, for example, that clerical staff use their word processing package to only 40 per cent of its capability. Training in that specific area will make a significant change to individuals' confidence and productivity. Employees possessing the skills necessary to complete their jobs will be less likely to interrupt others by asking for their help.

5 Provide the right mix of resources.

The right mix of people and other resources is essential if staff are to complete the jobs assigned to them. Allocating too few resources not only affects productivity and profitability but also means that idle people fill their spare time interrupting others.

6 Implement procedures and work instructions.

ISO 9000 certification will ensure that you have in place documented procedures relating to all work practices. Given that staff will be involved in the certification process, ISO 9000 and its associated training will help staff to become organised. Documented procedures and work instructions will serve as common sources of reference among all staff.

7 Teach staff time-saving techniques.

Never assume 'everyone knows that' when it comes to time-saving techniques. Teach staff about your time-savers. Those might include:

- allocating tasks for periods when you'll be the most productive
- setting daily priorities and sticking to them
- handling each piece of paper only once
- continuing to ask, 'What is the best use of my time, right now?'

Management Memo

Time management is really a misnomer – the challenge is not to manage time, but to manage ourselves. [84]

8 Make sure you're not part of the problem.

Compile a list of time-wasters identified by employees. If 'the boss' features on that list, find out what aspects of your behaviour need attention. It could be that you need to:

- communicate more clearly or more frequently
- avoid interrupting staff unnecessarily
- ensure staff are not kept waiting for an appointment with you
- stop being indecisive…

9 And don't forget to…

- *Set deadlines for staff.* Without them, projects tend to use up more time than is really necessary.
- *Keep their work challenging* – and employees will be enthusiastic and time-conscious.
- *Build interdependencies.* When employees rely on colleagues, they realise that their actions affect others. Time-wasters (the office gossip) and time-wasting habits (arriving late or leaving early) are soon brought under control by peers.
- *Keep communication lines open.* Blocked channels or slow-flowing information can waste valuable staff time.
- *Set the example.* By your actions, demonstrate that you disapprove of time-wasting.

How to handle drop-in visitors – and save time

As a manager, an open-door policy may well be a noble intention. Total accessibility, however, can be counter-productive in terms of your valuable time. Unless you are prepared to control the extent to which unexpected visitors consume your time, your efficiency as a manager will suffer. Limiting the time taken up by drop-in visitors demands courtesy, good judgment and tact. Here's some advice to help you minimise the debilitating impact of those often trivial and time-consuming drop-in visits...

1 Have your secretary intercept all visitors.

Your personal assistant, if you have one, should discreetly screen all visitors. Normally she/he can handle most routine problems. If not, three strategies are possible:

- Determine the purpose of the visit and make an appointment.
- 'The manager is busy now. Can I have her contact you later when she's free?'
- 'He's busy at the moment. Is the matter serious enough for me to interrupt him?'

2 Check out your office furniture.

Eye contact often invites passers-by to enter your office. Preferably position your desk so that it is not visible from the door. Or turn your desk so that your back is to the door: most corridor socialites will not interrupt you if they see you are busy.

As well, your office should not be too cosy – straight-back chairs, a bit hard not plush. Remove excess seating. In fact, chairs are for scheduled guests. Think twice about offering a chair to a drop-in visitor.

3 Set a time limit for each visit.

Be forthright with drop-ins. In response to 'Got a minute?' reply with 'I'm busy right now. Can you come back at 11.15?' Or, tell the visitor, 'I can only spare five minutes now. Is that enough?' If not, set up a time for later. Or ask, 'Is it a matter that can wait until tomorrow's staff meeting?'

4 Hold the meeting outside your office.

You can prevent drop-ins from planting themselves firmly in your office by:

- meeting the unexpected visitor in the outer office or corridor.
- suggesting the meeting be held in his/her office or workplace, where you would have control over the length of the visit.
- asking the drop-in to walk with you on your way to another meeting or location, thereby limiting the length of the meeting to the length of the journey.

5 Hold your meeting standing up.

When unwelcome drop-ins arrive,

get on your feet, get out from behind your desk, greet them and stay standing. You can then decide on the importance of the interruption and whether a chair should be offered. If not, work your way to the door. Stand-up meetings rarely last too long.

6 Be available at certain times only.

Being accessible is essential for managers, but it can sometimes be a blueprint for wasting time. Consider being available for drop-ins at certain times only – for an hour before work is scheduled to commence, from 9.00 to 11.00 a.m., and so on. For sanity, there must be a limit to the open-door policy.

7 Be creative in terminating the visit.

You can control the length of a drop-in's visit in several ways:

- Say little. Don't contribute to a needless conversation and there won't be one.
- 'I'm afraid I'm expecting a rather tricky phone call any minute so I won't ask you to sit down.'
- 'I'm sorry I don't have any more time but I'm rushed this morning.'
- 'You've caught me in the middle of getting ready for an important meeting later today. I can spare two minutes.'
- Your secretary can remind you after a few minutes that you have another matter (real or imagined) to attend to. You respond: 'That's okay. We'll be finished in two minutes.' Then stand.
- For a drifting conversation, *you* suggest what you believe is on the visitor's mind. If you're right, you've focused the discussion; if you're wrong, you've made the drop-in get to the point.

Management memo

One of the chief problems of the work world is drop-in visitors. It's quite common for many of us to spend one-half or more of our workday dealing with the unexpected interruptions of the visitor... Of course, visitors are necessary. Many of them keep us informed and provide us with ideas that enable us to be more effective. My recommendation is that you minimise the unnecessary ones and schedule necessary visits so that they don't cause random havoc on your workday. [85]

8 And consider these useful strategies...

- Let staff know that you require, before they drop in, a brief written summary of the problem for discussion plus at least two possible solutions. Often the need for a drop-in meeting dissipates.
- Keep a clock in full view of yourself and the visitor.
- Drop-in visits by staff can be largely eliminated if you hold regular staff meetings, department planning meetings or have your lunch with staff.
- Make it known that, whenever your door is closed, you do not want to be interrupted. Justify your unavailability on the grounds that you are 'at a meeting' (with yourself!).
- Simply learn to say 'no' or 'later' if you have something important to do.
- Keep a visitor log for a month. When you know who your main interrupters are, you will be better placed to devise a strategy for minimising their impact.
- Plan your day with time to accommodate those inevitable drop-in visitors.

See also: 176-186

How to delegate

Managers get things done through other people. They delegate primarily because it makes their job easier. If they try to do everything themselves, they become unnecessarily burdened, their performance (and health) deteriorates, they fail to develop their staff adequately and, in time, the organisation will suffer. Indeed, many writers believe that delegation is the central ingredient in distinguishing between good and bad managers. Knowing how to delegate is a crucial management and leadership skill...

1 Select a task to delegate from your prioritised jobs.

List in priority order those tasks you might consider delegating. To qualify for this list, a task should be taking too much of your time, be not strictly related to your key role, be rather routine, be appropriate and challenging for another staff member, or be better undertaken by someone with more appropriate skills or know-how than you. The purpose of delegating is not just to dodge work, or to unload tedious, unrewarding or difficult tasks; nor should you just keep the jobs you enjoy. Select the list on the basis that these are tasks that could, and should, be delegated.

2 Define clearly for yourself the task to be delegated.

Clarify in your own mind the task chosen to be delegated. Think through the task so that you can outline it clearly. For example, be able to provide details of:

- the expected results or product
- how the task might be approached
- sub-tasks within the overall task
- the limits of authority
- the necessary timelines
- how you will know the task is done
- what resources will be required
- what training might be necessary.

Understand the task fully yourself so that you will later be able to brief a staff member thoroughly.

3 Select the right person for the job.

As a good manager you should be aware of your staff's strengths and limitations and delegate accordingly. Ideally, the person you choose should have the ability, knowledge, skills, enthusiasm, talent and time needed to get the job done. Unfortunately, such qualities are not always found in the one person. Before selecting someone, ask yourself:

- Who has the necessary skills?
- Who would be most challenged?
- Who would learn most? Who wouldn't?
- Does the task require previous experience? Will the person need training?
- What particular personal qualities are needed? Who has them?
- Who can be trusted to do the job?
- What other work does this person have?
- Is more than one person needed? If so, can they work together successfully?
- Who would love to have a shot at a

job like this? How will others react? Delegation to the right person should improve skills, morale and esteem.

4 Conduct a thorough briefing.

In handing over the assignment, be prepared to set aside adequate time in private to communicate clearly:

- the scope of the task
- specific results to be achieved
- the time schedule and deadlines
- the available resources
- authority needed to carry out the job
- how performance can be measured
- sensitive or risky aspects of the task
- reporting procedures
- your confidence in the person.

Seek feedback and encourage questions to eliminate any confusion.

5 Delegate appropriate authority.

When you give people a job, make sure you tell them how much authority you are handing over. For example:

- 'Look into the problem, suggest three solutions, and I'll choose the best'; or
- 'Look into the problem, tell me how you plan to solve it, and do so unless I tell you otherwise'; or
- 'Look into the problem and tell me when you've solved it'.

Set parameters and establish controls to ensure this authority and the accompanying power will be properly used. If necessary, advise other relevant staff.

6 Keep lines of communication open.

When you delegate, you do not abdicate responsibility: you must maintain some control over the project. At the minimum, agree to have your delegate inform you only when things are *not* going according to plan. Be accessible but not meddlesome. The first approach should be from the delegate.

Management Memo

One definition of management is that it is 'achieving objectives through others'. You cannot hope to achieve all your objectives on your own – indeed you should not even try. Your job is to *manage* the operation in such a way that its objectives are achieved. If you cannot do it all yourself, you have to delegate. Successful delegation is the key to successful management. [86]

7 Monitor progress unobtrusively.

Keep an eye on your delegate's progress without intruding. If warranted, set up checkpoints in advance for reporting on progress. As the delegate gains confidence, tactfully withdraw, but remain alert for problems and help if needed.

8 Reward performance.

Be appreciative of a job well done by recognising good work privately and publicly. Sincere recognition will increase your effectiveness in working through others.

9 Delegate as part of a master plan.

Review the project upon completion to make sure your delegate has also gained from the task. See delegation as part of the process of planned growth for your staff. Through delegation, they grow in confidence, and they, and your organisation, will benefit in the long run.

How to keep the delegation ball rolling

Some managers still believe that the best way to get something done is to do it themselves. But, with this attitude, no matter how productive they think they are, at some point they will reach their limit. Beyond that point, their output decreases and their stress level increases. As well, the talent and potential of their staff are ignored. In a nutshell, to ignore delegation is to mismanage. If you want to embrace delegation as a most effective management tool, then consider these strategies...

1 Become delegation conscious.

Have you really thought about those of your tasks which you could rightly give to your subordinates to complete? Spend a day or two considering what you do. Are there things only you can do? Are there things others could do? Who could do these jobs? Would they need training? Sometimes your subordinates are better qualified than you to answer these questions. You might be surprised how much of your own work can be delegated.

2 Stop postponing projects.

We all have tasks that we continually postpone or ignore for whatever reason, yet they will not go away. At some stage they have to be done. If you are in this predicament, you must learn to delegate such tasks to other people to complete, freeing you to get on with other things.

3 Stop the habit of taking work home.

All occupations have their peak periods when additional work loads necessitate work being taken home to complete. But, if you find yourself taking work home regularly, you need to question the effectiveness of your delegating skills.

4 Make sure you get your share of free time.

Those managers who are successful can maintain a hectic pace while they are at work, but they allow themselves regular periods to sit back and enjoy some free time. If you find that you are missing out on this time, then it is probably an indication that you need to delegate some of your work load to others.

5 Stop comparing the performance of others with your own.

Perhaps you hold back assignments from staff because you have no faith in the quality of their work, or because you think you could do a better job. Or perhaps you feel insecure, fearing that your subordinate might do too well and outshine you as delegator. If so, then you have yet to grasp the value of delegation; or, as one writer has noted, 'if you are employed by the kind of company where you can delegate yourself out of a job, then it's the best thing that could happen to you!'

6 Attend to staff development.

Staff may be reluctant to offer to undertake some delegated tasks if they feel they lack the required skills. Perhaps this lies at the root of your hesitancy also. Where staff are not taking personal responsibility for developing these skills, take the lead and organise a programme for them.

7 Accept other ways of doing things.

There is a difference between telling a subordinate to carry out a task according to your instructions, and delegation. Until you understand that there is usually no one best way of tackling a task, you'll find delegation hard to embrace. Emphasise the result, not the process.

8 Develop healthy staff relationships.

Cooperation is the key to an effective organisation and, where this cooperation exists, staff members will be eagerly awaiting the chance to participate even further. Work towards creating this healthy staff climate, and you will find your employees keener to take on delegated responsibilities.

Management Memo

Aside from being an important part of your job you will also reap some perhaps unexpected benefits from delegating well. First, it is a part of investing in your staff. When a staff member has worked particularly hard on a project, you can provide a reward in the opportunity to learn something new. Secondly, effective delegation will help you to create a successful plan – bringing up managers who can replace you when it is time for you to move on. Thirdly, delegation can free some of your time to learn new skills and prepare yourself for new opportunities. All in all, how can you miss? [87]

9 Always be available for advice.

Employees feel secure if you make it clear that you are always there as a resource, ever ready to provide assistance and support if required. However, resist the urge to be too helpful; instead, train yourself to toss any problems back to the employee with some well-focused questions. Seldom should you take the task back or provide an easy answer, that takes the growth out of the experience for the staff member.

10 Be prepared to share your ideas.

Your experience took years to acquire and is your most valuable resource. Don't let all your accumulated wisdom and knowledge remain hidden from others. Be prepared to demonstrate to others that you are happy to share your particular skills when necessary.

How to overcome your reluctance to delegate

Even though there are very good reasons for delegating, there is sound evidence to suggest that delegation does not occur as often as it should. And why not? Managers talk themselves out of it. In fact, they are capable of citing a whole array of 'reasons' as to why they are reluctant to delegate but they can all be discredited. If you are to be an effective manager, then you simply must delegate. You must...

1 Find the time to delegate.
If you refuse to delegate because you 'are too busy to delegate' or 'the process takes too long', then not only do you have a delegation problem, you have a time management problem as well. Remember, skilful delegation is designed to save time.

2 Appreciate that others can do it as well as you.
If you think you can do the job better yourself, and therefore you do it yourself, then you'll find yourself doing *all* the work in future because nobody else has learned how to do it! In the long run, your ability and energy can hinder delegation and the development of your staff.

3 Accept that others might make mistakes.
So you think your subordinates might make a mess of the job? Everyone makes mistakes. Your staff must be allowed to do so and the cost must be invested as staff development. Through skills development training, counselling, detailed instructions and so on, you can avoid repeated mistakes without discouraging delegation.

4 Put your ego in second place.
To receive personal credit from superiors, do you try to do all the important tasks yourself? Do you fear that, by delegating the task to a subordinate, your promotional prospects may even lessen if she/he succeeds? Ask yourself: 'If I can't get my subordinates promoted, should I be promoted myself?'

5 Give up the tasks you enjoy doing yourself.
Managers are usually promoted from the shopfloor because they excel in, and enjoy, particular tasks. It's hard to hand over jobs you enjoy doing yourself, isn't it? But managers are paid to manage – and that includes delegation.

6 Let someone else do your former job.
Do you, as a promoted manager, like to continue making decisions associated with your former position? You must understand that

you will contribute better to the organisation by concentrating on current tasks and letting others perform your former tasks.

7 Learn to trust your subordinates' abilities.

Perhaps you lack confidence in your staff's ability to get the job done. This lack of trust is usually unwarranted. Familiarise yourself with each staff member's capabilities. You'll find that many people only need to be given a chance to prove themselves.

8 Become more receptive to the ideas of others.

You're not an obstruction in the system, or are you? Managers must not only be able to welcome eagerly the ideas of others, but also must be prepared to plant their own ideas in the minds of staff and to compliment them later on their ingenuity.

9 Allay all fears that you'll lose control.

Only insecure managers fear that they'll lose control of their empire, even their position, if subordinates are trained to perform more duties through delegation. Such fears have no basis. If you hold others back for this reason, you are preventing them and the organisation from realising their true potential.

10 Believe that delegation is not a sign of weakness.

If you fear you'll be criticised for 'passing-the-buck' whenever you delegate, then you have still to learn that managers face criticism of their style and reputation every day. That's part of a manager's baggage. You must overcome such fears if you are to delegate freely and effectively. Delegation is anything but a sign of weakness. In fact, not to delegate is to ignore one of management's most valuable assets.

Management Memo

Rarely can an organisation afford to risk its life by maintaining blockages. Sooner or later they must resort to surgery. Henry Ford is claimed to have said 'if anyone is indispensable, fire him'. A little extreme perhaps; but it does get the message across that people who do not delegate actually impede an organisation's progress. If they hog all the information to themselves and refuse to delegate, quite possibly they can't be replaced. But they can't be promoted either! [88]

11 Dispel any fear of being disliked because you hand out jobs.

The fear of being unpopular or resented by staff for passing too much work into the system looms large for some managers. US research has revealed that leaders who are rated good or excellent by their staff are those who make greatest use of delegation. Your staff expect you to delegate, so do so. Indeed, most people want to feel that they are valued by their organisation and, to make a contribution, they want be given something meaningful to do. By not delegating to them, you could be even more likely to get them offside.

See also: 174-178, 182-186

How to steer clear of those delegation traps

The good delegator and the good golfer are very much alike – they both know how to avoid the traps. Unfortunately for you, as manager, the delegation fairway is lined with hazards and, if you do not handle this essential management skill sensitively, then you will spend much of your time digging your way out of these traps. Here are some words of wisdom to help the manager-delegator avoid the pitfalls...

1 Do not delegate tasks at random.

The art of delegation involves handing out tasks to those who are likely to be able to guarantee successful completion. This will not be achieved by delegating tasks haphazardly.

2 Do not delegate only the unpleasant jobs.

Delegation is not simply another word for dumping. Resist the temptation to offload only your unpleasant tasks. Delegate the good and the bad. A motivated staff member will soon become disgruntled if only given the boring, routine or distasteful projects.

3 Do not delegate without providing adequate information.

Spell out exactly what you want so that your intentions are complete and understood. Too little information means that the delegate has to keep coming back to you or that the final product will be incomplete or inadequate. So, ensure that the person is given access to the right tools, resources, people and records.

4 Do not delegate too much for a person to handle.

Avoid falling into the trap of overloading the eager beaver. Staff members who are keen to please you may find that they have taken on more tasks than they can successfully complete.

5 Do not delegate responsibility without authority as well.

Delegation means giving another person the authority to act in your place. Clearly define the limits of that authority and, where appropriate, let other people know what you've delegated and to whom, and that you expect their assistance as required.

6 Do not delegate and then want things your own way.

When you delegate, you should only be interested in the final product. *How* your delegates do the job should be left to them as long as they understand the limits. If they have to check with you before every move, you not only undermine the trust that should accompany delegation, but you might as well do the job yourself. By all means offer help, but let them do it their way – and they may well discover new and better ways to solve old problems.

7 Do not delegate and then expect an overnight response.

In delegating a task you formerly handled yourself, it may take some time for the delegate to achieve your level of performance. Be patient and, in time, the task will be mastered. Do not expect error-free, independent performance overnight.

8 Do not delegate and then worry about foul-ups.

Assign tasks initially where success is probable, because success is what builds self-confidence. Resist the temptation to dive in to prevent mistakes happening. And when a staff member makes a mistake on a delegated job, don't make a big issue of it. Consider it all part of the learning process – for you and your employee. After all, it may not entirely be the employee's fault. Maybe you picked the wrong person for the job, or didn't inform, train, motivate or monitor that person sufficiently.

9 Do not delegate without a periodic review.

Monitor your staff member's progress but don't expel excessive quantities of hot breath on the delegate's neck. Your employee will need a reasonable amount of freedom, independence and trust to display real talent. Depending on the person's experience and ability, keep your ear to the ground without being overly obtrusive.

Management Memo

When it comes to delegation, stop focusing on the unknown – on what disasters *might* occur. Instead, form a clear idea of *what* has to be done and *how* you can facilitate success.

For any project you will have three known goals. You want the job done (1) well, (2) on time, and (3) under your control.

Your job is to direct, guide, and oversee your employees' efforts – not do their work. You can make sure the job is done well by giving them clear, explicit instructions, sufficient time and resources, and motivation. And you keep your team on schedule by setting up many short-term deadlines that you personally supervise. [89]

10 Do not delegate and then blame others for the outcome.

You're still the boss, irrespective of who performs a delegated task, so you must ultimately be prepared to carry the can for outcomes. If your staff know that you are likely to blame them for any unpopular decisions or outcome, then they will resist any future delegated responsibilities.

 See also: 174-180, 184-186

How to use delegation to develop your staff

In a nutshell, managers need to delegate to get things done. But if used wisely, delegation has other advantages as well. It can also enrich the work of your staff, develop their management skills, and instil in them a sense of commitment to the organisation's goals. It can also reveal to you their previously undisclosed talents through hands-on experience, and prepare staff for advancement. Delegation can indeed be a rewarding tool for staff development - provided you adhere to a number of important principles...

1 Try not to delegate to the most capable people only.

Resist the temptation to delegate continually to the most capable staff members. Certainly the strong will get stronger, but the weak will only get weaker. By distributing assignments across the board, you will be building a team of versatile performers, and a handy group to have when emergencies arise. When delegating to someone who has less than ideal experience, skills or knowledge, select at least an individual who has a willingness to learn how to do the job with some help. This is how people develop and staff development should be one of your major aims whenever you delegate.

2 Select assignments that will stretch your staff.

The purpose of developmental delegation is to build staff confidence in handling unfamiliar tasks, though the aim is ill-served if they fail on the first try. Delegate more than just 'jobs'. Motivate staff by delegating tasks that are interesting, and that challenge them, but not to breaking point.

3 Treat any foul-up as a learning experience.

An effective way to develop staff is to let them make mistakes on their own. If the consequences aren't too great, watch them do it wrong the first time so they'll appreciate the right way the next time. If they foul up on an assignment, don't make a big issue of it, for if you punish learning behaviour, you paralyse staff members and undermine their confidence. If they fear reprimands and criticism, they'll take fewer risks and ultimately perform poorly. To guard against foul-ups, remember to assign tasks only where success is probable, and always take the time up front to check that your delegated assignment is clearly understood.

4 Recognise those teaching moments.

When staff members come to you with insightful questions or opinions, they are extremely open to expanding their horizons and learning new skills. This is precisely when the teaching moment turns into the delegation moment. As Calano and

Salzman write: 'Training and delegation are two sides of the coin. By developing a sensitivity to teaching moments, you will become a far more effective delegator and leader.'

5 Be aware that you'll always be a role model.

Ensure that you function as an effective role model because your staff will normally follow your example. Research shows that staff initially learn how to organise, make decisions, manage time, deal with crises, run meetings, and handle problems by observing their managers.

6 Show confidence in your staff's ability to carry out the assignment.

You must believe in, support and help your subordinates succeed with their delegated assignments. If you trusted staff sufficiently to delegate projects in the first place, that trust must be carried through to a project's completion. Display your trust by word and deed: by not continually looking over their shoulders, or interfering with their methods, or jumping on them when they stumble. In time, their confidence, sense of responsibility and powers of judgement will grow, and you will be able to trust them with more demanding and responsible tasks.

7 Set the foundations for success.

If you want to use delegation to develop your staff's managerial skills, and to improve their performance and ability to carry out more responsible work, then there are certain key ground rules to which you must also adhere. Among these are the following:

- **Delegate the objective, not the procedure.** You are interested in the result, so let them do it their way, as long as they are clear on the required outcome. Offer to help – but don't push your methods on them.
- **Delegate authority, not just responsibility.** Authority is needed to get a job done, but set the limits up front – budget, deadlines, resources and the parameters of their authority.
- **Establish standards of performance.** The final result will reflect on you, so help yourself and the delegate by setting your standards beforehand.
- **Delegate but don't abdicate.** Remember that accountability rests with you. Monitor the task through periodic feedback. Offer help only if it is asked for or warranted.
- **Give credit for tasks well done.** You look good when a delegated task turns out well so, by letting your staff shine, both you and the organisation benefit.

Management Memo

Delegation is difficult. It is perhaps the hardest thing that managers have to do. The problem is getting the balance right between delegating too much or too little and between over- or under-supervision. When you give someone something to do you have to make sure that it gets done. And you have to do that without breathing down his (or her) neck, wasting your time and his, and getting in the way. There has to be trust as well as guidance and supervision. [90]

How to take those follow-up actions

Most interventions end with an agreement to follow up, making that concluding action an important part of a manager's role. Follow-up actions need to be more than ad hoc additions to daily routines. Effective follow-up discussions not only demonstrate to employees that you mean what you say, that you actually *do* follow up, but also show your interest in the employee's progress. Here's how to make the best use of this important, though often neglected, aspect of management practice...

1 Review previous discussions.

Having set aside a time for a follow-up meeting, make sure it happens. Begin the meeting by briefly recapping any previous discussions including any actions you had both agreed upon at that time. Be specific and highlight only important aspects of those discussions. Again, focus only on identified problems, not on the person.

2 Arrive at an assessment.

If progress since the initial meeting has been positive, encourage the employee to talk about the achievements made. Take time to outline to the employee your assessment of his/her contributions and accomplishments. Express your pleasure at obvious progress. If you are satisfied with the improvements, you should proceed to point 7.

If, however, you do not consider that the problem has been solved to your satisfaction, refer to specific data to show that the employee still has work to do, and continue to explore the issue...

3 Explore possible solutions.

In the case of insufficient improvement, suggest as many different options as possible to overcome the problem but avoid demanding specific actions. People will work harder to solve their problems when they themselves have a say in the strategy to be adopted. Let the employee decide on a suitable plan of action. You, of course, will need to agree on and be prepared to support or disagree with the proposed solution.

4 Clarify the consequences of continued lack of improvement.

This is a very sensitive part of the discussion because you want the employee to understand what will happen if the problem isn't corrected. You must not appear threatening or aggressive, nor do you want the employee to become defensive. Stress that you are on the employee's side and that the purpose of the discussion is to solve the problem. But you may need to broach the subject of consequences.

In doing so, be specific and keep discussions focused on the facts.

5 Agree on actions to be taken.

If the plan is going to work, it will need the employee's commitment and your support. It must be seen as a cooperative effort, the end product being improvement in the staff member's performance in the workplace. To gain that commitment, reach agreement on the specific actions to be taken, preferably using the employee's ideas and solutions. Support the plan that seems the best.

6 Set a date for another follow-up meeting.

Agree to meet again at a later date to review progress. This again reinforces the fact that you're serious about correcting the problem.

7 Confirm your confidence in the employee.

End on a positive note by acknowledging your confidence in the staff member. People are far more responsive when they know that you want them to succeed. Your demonstration of confidence and encouragement will contribute to a workable and lasting solution.

Management Memo

It's universally agreed that check-ups and follow-ups are most important things in the people management cycle... The follow-up period may be a matter of hours on very simple jobs or weeks and even longer periods for the more complex issues. But, since the supervisor should always be in contact with workers, in a sense the follow-up period perhaps never ends. [91]

8 Record outcomes.

Whatever the outcome of the follow-up meeting, record all information immediately following that meeting. This action not only signifies completion of another important management task, but also ensures that you have a permanent record of any further follow-up action required. You then also have detailed comments for reference at the next meeting if required.

9 Stay in touch.

Remain 'visible' by retaining regular contact with all employees. In that way you can't help but be there to ensure essential follow-up action is taken.

How to give orders

Not everyone can give orders that are clearly understood and carried out to the letter. If you've been frustrated by not having your orders (or 'requests' or 'suggestions') carried out, you may be overlooking the fact that in most cases the fault belongs not with your staff, but with you. Here are some suggestions that will ensure your orders are understood and followed...

1 Know exactly what you want.

Before delivering your instructions, know exactly what you want and how you are going to communicate this clearly. What precisely is the result you have in mind?

2 Select the right person for the job.

Orders will be more effectively carried out when you select a person with the ability and desire to carry out the task, so get to know the capabilities of your staff. Make sure that the person you select for a particular job is capable of carrying it through to completion.

3 Use your established chain of authority.

No matter how big or small the organisation, it should have in place a structured chain or line of authority through which orders, commands or instructions are transmitted. If employees expect orders to come from their supervisors, make sure you communicate your orders via those people.

4 Use clear, concise, simple language.

Sequence your instructions in a clear, logical order. Use simple, concrete and specific language, avoiding jargon if possible. Speak in the language of the receiver. Allow time for comprehension. Remember to be brief, accurate and to the point; use short words and short sentences; and use one sentence for each idea.

5 Give the reasons and explain the significance.

Only when the employee has all relevant information, including the reasons for the task, can intelligent decisions be made by that person, particularly if complications develop later when carrying out your orders. Try to anticipate the employee's feelings, needs and concerns. If you once held the job, remember what it felt like when you were given instructions and weren't sure why.

6 Check for understanding.

Be sure the employee remembers the essentials. If possible, show employees what you want, or what things should look like when your order has been carried out. By repeating the order and by giving the employee the opportunity to ask questions or, better still, by asking that your instructions be repeated back to you, you will identify any areas of doubt or misunderstanding.

Management Memo

No matter what your instructions, no matter what your 'students', you will be a more effective 'teacher' if you move from the simple to the complex. [92]

7 Avoid overwhelming your staff.

Learn to anticipate reactions to an instruction and time its presentation accordingly. You can't afford to overwhelm people with orders. Try to have each task completed before assigning additional tasks. Let employees know you'll remain accessible should problems or other questions arise.

8 Respect individual experience.

The nature of your order-giving will be conditional upon the experience of individual employees and the particular situation or context. Although you can't expect inexperienced employees to display the understanding of those who have worked with you for some time, you must be fair. If you invite feedback from experienced employees, afford that courtesy to others as well.

9 Make sure you're able to enforce your order.

Assuming that you're sure the employee knows how to carry out your order, insist that your instructions are followed through. Employees should be aware that you're prepared to take action against any refusals. Orders disguised as suggestions or requests, however, are preferable to any dictatorial approach.

10 Distribute tasks evenly among staff members.

Don't overwork some employees because they will accept orders with less fuss than others, nor give all the unpopular jobs to the same people all of the time.

11 Follow-up.

Check periodically to see that your directions are being carried out in the desired manner within the agreed time frame. Monitor progress and check on the final results to ensure they are in line with what was requested. If appropriate, praise or thank the employees for their efforts.

12 And remember...

- Always assume that the listener knows less than you do.
- Let people in on goals and priorities if you want them to use initiative.
- Always think of an order in terms of these headings: quality, quantity, time, why, how and safety.
- Encourage note taking.
- Don't be casual or off-handed, or your order might not be taken seriously.
- Anticipate problems and suggest ways of handling them should they occur.
- When issuing the order, show confidence in the person. It's contagious.

How to give feedback

Feedback is a powerful management process which, if used effectively, will maintain or improve your employees' output and, in turn, improve the overall performance of the organisation. Employees want feedback because it helps them learn about themselves and their performance. To provide effective feedback – either positive or negative – you need to consider these guidelines...

1 Provide feedback on a continuing basis.
Whether it takes the form of informal, on-the-run comments or formal performance reviews, feedback will be less traumatic and more effective if it is given on an ongoing basis. Continuity of reporting is essential.

2 Provide immediate feedback if possible.
Feedback will have maximum impact if it is given while the behaviour is fresh in the minds of both parties. The most powerful feedback is given when you actually catch someone doing the right or wrong thing. Delayed feedback should occur only if it would embarrass the employee or if you require further information.

3 Be specific.

The more specific you can be with examples, the more telling the feedback will be. For instance, it would be inadequate to advise an employee that, 'Your manners leave a lot to be desired'. However, if the person was told, 'I was disappointed at this morning's committee meeting because you kept talking while I was speaking', then the person would be able to take some purposeful action to address this behaviour.

4 Be descriptive, not evaluative.
Describe behaviour in observable terms, rather than using emotional, judgemental language. Refer to the observable fact that the employee 'missed four deadlines last month'; don't call him/her 'lazy, slack and irresponsible' (even though you might like to). Labelling and character attacks only add unnecessary fire to the situation. Such judgements are merely your opinion anyway – you may be wrong!

5 Focus only on things that can be changed.
There are some things about an employee that can't be changed – such as personality or physical features... intelligence, a speech impediment, shyness, left-

handedness, a poor complexion. So don't focus on such aspects unless they are somehow affecting the work environment. Concentrate instead on those areas where change can be brought about: output, writing style, appearance, untidy work desk or behaviour.

6 Adjust feedback to individual needs.

Individual employees differ in their approach to feedback. Most people appreciate positive feedback; high performers usually like a lot of it; some employees become scarred for life by negative feedback; others simply reject all feedback if it is negative. You must learn to match the content and timing of feedback to the individual and the situation.

7 Try not to mix positive and negative messages.

When you have negative feedback to impart, do not sandwich it between positive introductory comments and glowing statements of appreciation at the end. This only dilutes the importance of the negative message and sometimes sends a mixed and confusing signal to the employee.

8 Ensure feedback is always constructive.

When used as a weapon, rather than as a valuable tool for improving employee performance, feedback can be very destructive. Negative feedback should be seen by both parties as a critical component of performance improvement and the ongoing review process.

Management Memo

Research shows that effective feedback leads to increased employee performance. Feedback can help subordinates set and achieve goals. Adequate provision of feedback from a trusted superior also seems to be related to the level of communication satisfaction and workplace commitment felt by employees. [93]

9 And don't forget...

- Make sure the employee is actually listening. Feedback not heeded is feedback not heard.
- Make sure the feedback is understood. If necessary, probe for understanding.
- Guard against any hint of the 'I am better than you' syndrome where you communicate your superiority in knowledge, wisdom or power.
- Be alert for an employee asking for feedback. It's easier to feed a hungry person.
- Feedback calls for objectivity. Don't communicate if you're upset, angry or hurt.
- Give the employee the opportunity to discuss the issue and to explore how the behaviour might be further explored. After all, feedback should be part of the employee's learning experience.
- Use the giving process as an opportunity to seek feedback yourself. The process is helped if you demonstrate that *you* are open to feedback.

 See also: 74, 188, 222

How to encourage feedback from your staff

Feedback provides managers with the information they need for sound decision-making. Indeed, it's important for bosses to stay in touch with their employees – that's where many winning ideas come from. As well, feedback acts as a kind of early warning system about potential problems and grievances. Unfortunately, many managers don't realise that achieving this form of upward communication requires a good deal of intelligent activity on their part...

1 Tell people you want feedback and be prepared to seek it.

Publicise in various ways the fact that you value feedback from staff and, if necessary, identify those elements where information is required for the good of the organisation. Your task then is to make it easy for employees to gain access to you. An 'open door policy' is one approach. Visibility and accessibility are important considerations and, for that reason, some managers prefer management-by-walking-around (MBWA). The best way to understand what's happening in the workplace is to be part of it, they argue.

2 Install regular avenues for feedback.

More formal feedback strategies require structure, planning and effort. Some organisations set aside certain times when top executives are available for phone calls or visits from employees on any topic. Others train facilitators in the mechanics of information gathering and presentation, while elsewhere staff meetings are used for the receipt of regular oral or written status reports. Formal exit interviews with employees who resign or retire are also revealing, as are employee-opinion surveys and questionnaires. Many employees are sceptical as to the value of suggestion boxes.

3 Try informal get-togethers to encourage feedback.

From time to time, informal gatherings, such as staff breakfasts, morning coffee conferences, parties, barbecues, dinners and picnics, can be used effectively to stimulate the free flow of communication on work-related matters.

4 Show that you're serious.

Whatever the strategy you adopt, a positive and interested response from you will guarantee staff acceptance and determine the quality and frequency of future feedback. Accordingly, you should:

- *Listen*. Give the employee your undivided attention and the clear impression that you *are* interested in what your employee is saying.

- *Take notes.* Use a palm card or diary to take notes, there and then.
- *Promote understanding through questions.* If an issue requires clarification, ask such questions as 'What did you mean when you said…?' or 'Is this what you mean…?'
- *Encourage elaboration.* By using such leads as 'Tell me more about…', 'Tell me what you think about…' and following up with statements such as 'As I understand it, this is what you are saying…', you clarify important issues and show your interest.
- *Never react badly when you hear something amiss.* Try not to 'kill' the bearer of bad tidings. Get the message across that the only bad news is the news that is *not* communicated upwards. You want to hear the good news *and* the bad.
- *Thank people for their feedback.*

5 Seek as much specific information as possible.

People usually tend to be vague with their responses or comments. The more specific the information provided, the more useful it will be. If you intend to use the feedback to make changes to your organisation's performance or programme, then it will normally need to be detailed and specific.

Management Memo

Seeking feedback is a very important part of being a good manager. Like everyone else, you are dependent upon feedback to find out how you are performing. You should be seeking feedback actively, every day, from everyone in your working environment – your boss, your peers, your staff and your customers. If you don't, you run a terrible risk – the risk of coasting along and never fine-tuning your direction. [94]

6 Communicate results.

Employees don't expect that every one of their suggestions will be implemented, but they do expect that, at some stage, you will give reasonable consideration to their comments. If employees' suggestions *are* acted upon, let them know, and such feedback will be more effective if made publicly in the presence of colleagues. As well, commendation is a powerful motivator for encouraging feedback from others.

7 Stay clear of unprofessional issues.

At times, you will no doubt receive feedback through the company grapevine. When this feedback takes the form of malicious gossip, indicate that you have no desire to become involved in unprofessional issues and unproductive behaviour. Your assertive stance may encourage employees to reassess the quality of grapevine communications.

 See also: 154, 194-202, 334

How to motivate your employees

From the lounge-chair sports expert to the company CEO, most people have definite views on what motivates others – and they're probably right, in part at least. Valiant attempts to convert theory into practice, however, have not always succeeded in getting people to give that little bit extra, the outcome often being a reversion to manipulative and kick-in-the-backside approaches. From the plethora of information and advice about motivation, here are the essential principles...

1 Understand motivation.

There are only two types of motivation, love motivation or fear motivation. People do what they do either out of love or out of fear. Many go to work because they fear what will happen if they don't. Others go because they love it, the sense of achievement they get, the opportunity to meet with friends. Your challenge is to help employees be driven by love as opposed to fear.

2 Focus on job enrichment.

Frederick Herzberg advocated enriching people's jobs as a principal motivator. By making the job more enjoyable you will ensure that:

- the job will provide challenges commensurate with the employee's skills
- the employee with more ability will be able to stand out and win promotion to higher-level jobs
- there will be long-term gains in employee attitudes.

Though not all jobs can be enriched, nor do they need to be, it is through job enrichment that big gains can occur.

3 Learn to like people.

From your own experiences, you already know lots about motivation – so continue to:

- focus on individuals, showing a genuine interest in them
- get to know your employees, their families and their interests
- listen to what they have to say
- take time to talk with them
- recognise their contributions
- promote a relaxed and trusting relationship.

4 Encourage genuine participation.

Most people spend a significant part of their day at work, usually in the company of others. They are often looking for additional opportunities to make maximum use of their talents and to develop new ones. Wherever possible then, you should:

- involve employees in decisions whose outcomes require their commitment
- seek their views
- provide opportunities for achievement through interesting, varied, relatively short and challenging tasks or projects
- delegate tasks that help them to display particular talents
- build interdependencies among people that encourage cohesiveness.

5 Provide open communication.

Open, two-way communication is vital, and feedback is an essential part of that process. People like to know how you think they're doing and how they might improve even further. That's one reason why management-by-walking-around is so successful; employees receive first-hand feedback on performance and have a chance to present issues to you that are important to them.

6 Make work itself a motivator.

Work can be a motivator if you…

- give employees more scope to vary the methods, sequence and pace of their work
- give people the control information needed to monitor their own performance
- encourage employee participation in planning and evaluating new techniques
- increase individual responsibility for achieving defined targets or standards.

7 Lead the way by example.

Nothing turns people off faster than those who don't practise what they preach. Motivators must be motivated, energetic, animated, with loads of zest and sparkle, striving to achieve new heights. You also need to convey confidence in others – people who are expected to achieve usually will. It's all part of a 'self-fulfilling prophesy'.

8 Instil a desire to win.

If it works in sport, why not in business? Managers often fail to exploit the benefits that can be derived from competition and, as a result, employees don't bother extending themselves. Be aware, however, that the impact of this type of motivating decreases significantly immediately after the event.

> **Management Memo**
>
> Good managers don't motivate others. Motivation comes from within the individual. It is not something that one person does to another. What a manager must do is to find ways to enhance and reinforce the motivating forces within their employees. Employees who hear their bosses talking about motivating them may worry about being manipulated rather than motivated. [95]

9 Reward accomplishments.

People expect to be rewarded in some way. To make sure rewards match individual value systems, you should:

- spell out the relationship between effort and reward – payment by results, commissions or bonuses
- set stretch targets that require that little bit of extra effort
- tell people what they have to do to gain the rewards they seek
- place responsibility firmly with the individual
- give praise when praise is due.

Make sure your rewards unite rather than divide your team.

10 Provide opportunities.

Though the doors of opportunity are marked 'push', it's often managers who must show their employees those doors. Motivate your staff by revealing to them the doors of opportunity in your organisation: for rewards, for achievement, for taking on additional responsibilities, for resolving problems, for sharing, for recognition, for advancement…

See also: 192, 196, 200

How to make best use of praise to motivate your staff

The use of praise is a management skill which is simple, inexpensive and inexhaustible. Praise rewards when reward is due. It builds a feeling of goodwill. It provides positive encouragement to continue good practice and creative endeavour. It has a ripple effect. Not only does it provide deserved acknowledgement for the person who is performing well, it also broadcasts to an entire staff that good work will be recognised. But it is important that praise be the right kind, given in the right way, at the right time, and for the right reasons...

1 Find something to praise in every staff member.

If a compliment can boost the spirit, lack of one from important people can hurt for a long time. People need praise. If you look hard enough, you'll catch even your borderline employees doing something right. Compliment them on that action right there and then. If you continue to do this over time, you'll see their performance improve.

2 Use praise spontaneously and frequently, but only if warranted.

The sooner you praise someone, the more it means to them. Spontaneous compliments are usually sincere and reinforce the exhilaration the person may be experiencing in the first glow of accomplishment or success. But compliments can be short-lived. They tend to dissolve soon after they are received. That's why people need them often. A word of warning, however. Undeserved praise rarely produces positive results. Not only do you lose credibility through unjustified use of praise, but over time your staff will begin to ask themselves, 'If she keeps saying I'm doing so great, then why try any harder?'

3 Be specific with your praise.

Generalities are rarely as effective as specifics. Don't simply say, 'Well done!' Say instead, 'I'm really impressed with the way you led our discussions at today's staff meeting. You must have been putting a lot of thought into your suggestions on budgeting. A first rate job!' Tell people exactly what you liked about their work and, in that way, they're more likely to repeat the behaviours that pleased you.

4 Link your praise to skills requiring development.

You can help an employee develop a skill if you focus your compliments on the activity you want that person to master. If you praise in small increments, you'll be surprised at the cumulative effect it has on skill development.

5 Be sincere.

Nothing will backfire more quickly than phony flattery. As British essayist Richard Steele once advised: 'When you praise, add your reasons for doing so; it is this which distinguishes the approbation of a man of sense from the flattery of the sycophants and admiration of fools.'

6 Praise efforts not just achievements.

By showing heartfelt appreciation to a person who has attempted to reach a goal you provide an incentive for that person to work harder. Your praise for having genuinely tried will motivate that person to strive even further.

7 Praise initiative.

The typist who quietly takes on the unpleasant tasks, the clerk who goes the extra mile without being asked, the assistant who accepts the unpopular assignment without complaining; these are the people, far too few in number, who deserve praise, recognition and commendation ... and often fail to receive it.

8 Praise individually and in public.

Offering praise for a group effort is fine in its place, but every person craves individual recognition. Praise has a more lasting impact when you mention people by name.

And don't forget that old adage, 'Praise in public, criticise in private'. People like receiving compliments from their boss in front of their colleagues or on other public occasions.

Management Memo

Praise can be a powerful motivator. It can cost you very little but the rewards can be extraordinary... The old saying 'No news is good news' does not always ring true. Probably the worst action you can take is to withhold praise. Many simply see no news as no news – but some interpret it as bad news. Meaningful praise is one way of removing any uncertainty. Let people know what they are doing well. Reinforce the admirable qualities of their work. Meaningful praise makes a difference. [96]

9 Show your appreciation in many ways.

In addition to complimentary asides and spontaneous acknowledgements, effective managers never forget the power of silent compliments, in other words, they use a variety of nonverbal gestures such as nods, smiles and 'pats on the back'. As well, a short written note or a mention in the staff newsletter or at a staff meeting can have a dramatic effect. And nothing pleases a person more than to learn of the manager's admiration of his/her work from other people: so occasionally express pride in your individual staff members to colleagues, the boss or customers.

10 Don't use praise to sugar-coat a reprimand.

Never try to soften criticism by wrapping a few items of praise around it. Keep praise and criticism for separate occasions, or your staff member will become confused and suspicious of all future praise.

 See also: 192-194, 200

How to say thank you

Saying 'thank you' has been called the neglected art. Indeed, there is a reluctance among some managers to express adequate appreciation for a job well done. A few simple, well-placed thank yous, however, can do wonders for improving the performances of your staff. To maximise the benefits of this powerful word, here are a few useful suggestions...

1 Speak up.

Don't cheapen the value of a well-earned thank you by being embarrassed or by mumbling the words, and don't mistake your warm feelings and beaming smiles for the art itself. Think about what you're going to say and how you're going to say it. Even simple thank yous sometimes require preparation.

2 Say it - and mean it.

Every time we express sincere appreciation, we give value to the other person. Our words say, 'You are important to me and to our organisation.' Remember:

They who thank with the lips
Thank others but in part;
The full, the true thanksgiving
Comes deep from within the heart.

So, say it as if you mean it, not just because you're expected to. Routine and ritualised expressions of thanks often lack any real impact.

3 Be specific.

A vague, sweeping thank you is nowhere as effective or as flattering as a clear-cut: 'Thanks for drafting that letter to Joe Thompson, Judith. The reply was spot-on and it saved me heaps of time.' Don't leave people confused about what you're thanking them for.

4 Make eye-to-eye contact.

Look directly at the person you're thanking if you're serious about what you're doing. You might like to reinforce your appreciation with a casual pat on the elbow or shoulder.

5 Know the person.

With experience, you will get to know the different ways your various staff members like to be thanked. Some like public appreciation; others don't. Some appreciate flowers or chocolates;

others prefer a written note of thanks. Consider your options; consider your people.

6 Thank them by name.

A generalised 'thank you, everyone' carries little weight. Be generous and thank people individually whenever possible.

7 Surprise them.

Top managers everywhere practise daily the winning art of appreciation. They do it in offices, in corridors, canteens and carparks, over the telephone and in writing. And what they find is that a thank you has much more impact if it is given when a person least expects it. A small surprise gift and an accompanying thank you from the manager goes a long way to making an employee feel appreciated.

Management Memo

Any time you see someone doing something right, recognise it. We don't need employees of the month as much as we need to celebrate a multitude of employees of the moment. [97]

8 Do it in public.

People usually appreciate the thank you if you acknowledge their individual efforts in front of their colleagues. When people feel they matter, morale is high. When extra effort is recognised publicly, self-esteem soars.

 See also: 192, 202, 304

How to gain staff commitment

High levels of staff commitment to individual projects or to the organisation as a whole are considered to be indicators of an organisation succeeding in its purpose. Commitment, however, cannot be assumed. Rather, it requires continuing, credible and confident actions that result in employee trust and support. Although there is no one way of gaining commitment, there are, however, some key considerations…

1 Be clear about what is required.

You can't expect employees to be committed to something that they, and perhaps you, don't understand. Before people commit their time and resources, they have every right to expect to know exactly what it is they are letting themselves in for. Any confusions you have will be immediately communicated to employees. Your track record will be a factor also. There are many examples in history of the lengths people are prepared to go in support of causes that have their commitment. Authenticity will win through every time.

2 Focus on action goals.

Gather together employees whose commitment you are seeking, explain the situation as you see it, and describe the outcome(s) envisaged. Establish with them any short-term goals accompanied by specific actions for their achievement. Outline benefits – what's in it for them – to be derived from successful accomplishment of those goals. The noblest dream and the most appealing strategy are worthless until those involved make a commitment to make goals happen.

3 Adopt a problem-solving approach.

Use group facilitation skills, a force-field analysis perhaps, to identify blockages preventing goal achievement. Engage employees in planning for the elimination or reduction of those blockages. Allocate responsibilities for agreed actions and confirm individual commitment. Document all agreed upon actions and circulate to those involved.

4 Adopt measures to determine achievement.

If possible, decide on how goals and their progress can be measured. Rarely will employees be prepared to make or maintain a commitment when there are no measures of what their involvement has achieved. You, too, will need to use measures as a means of assessing levels of commitment. Sound management advice is: If you can't measure it, you can't manage it.

5 Give it time.

Employees will be waiting to see what you do. Even if employees give the impression of being ambivalent to your proposal or project, your subsequent actions will be under constant observation. Gaining and building commitment cannot be rushed and your actions will lead the way. The American Indians encapsulated it with 'You can't push the river'. If you find that commitment is not forthcoming, you will need to decide either to persevere, adopt another approach, or scrap the idea.

6 Foster interdependence among staff.

The development of strong links among employees is of real benefit to you and the organisation. One of those benefits, for example, is a decrease in absenteeism because staff realise how others are affected by their non-attendance.
Interdependence helps to build ownership, trust and commitment among employees as they see how their individual contributions affect, or are affected by, fellow workers.

Management Memo

Successful organisations require the 3Cs – that's creativity, competition and commitment. [98]

7 Develop a work environment where commitment grows.

Make your work place one where employees want to be. A harmonious working environment helps to bring out the best in people. People will be prepared to commit themselves to a project or organisation that they feel part of.

8 Recognise achievements.

When employee commitment has resulted in goal achievement, provide rewards and other forms of recognition that are valued by individual employees.

Recognition should cater for individuals, work groups and even families. After all, the success of many projects depends, in part, on the nature of the support provided by life partners and other family members.

How to reward your staff for a job well done

People like to receive recognition for a job done well. It's nice to have one's efforts appreciated. From management's point of view, it's smart to reinforce desired behaviour by acknowledging the behaviour with an appropriate reward. Rewards play an important part in job performance, motivation and productivity. Now you can recognise your employees' achievements and make your workplace a haven for high productivity by considering these suggestions...

1 Ensure performance and reward go hand in hand.

An organisation's incentive scheme can only be effective if it is seen by staff as truly acknowledging good performance. If staff know that top performance, by individuals or teams, will be acknowledged in some way, then those rewards and their efforts will have meaning. In this regard consider such points as these:

- The size of the reward should reflect the size of the effort. An employee or team idea that generates a big return for the company should be rewarded accordingly.
- Rewards should be tied to an individual's contribution, not simply to the length of time with the organisation.
- Participating staff must be aware of the criteria being used to assess performance.

2 Devise a workable scheme.

Develop a set of principles which could form the basis of an employee reward system for your organisation. In doing so, you might consider the following:

- Establish a committee of innovative managers and, in time, previous award winners to administer the scheme. Rotate membership to maintain the flow of fresh ideas.
- Ensure the scheme spreads the glory to all parts of your organisation and to all levels, from senior executives to back-room operatives.
- Avoid granting rewards at fixed intervals, such as end-of-year or at performance appraisal time. Employees need to be motivated throughout the year.
- Recognise the achievements of teams as well as individuals. In this way you heighten team spirit, downplay the nasty side of individual rivalry, and recognise the project-based nature of your organisational structure.
- Have supervisors nominate awardees in writing by noting and documenting specific accomplishments.
- Seek input from staff in designing their own incentive programme. Keep it realistic of course, but be aware that performance will peak when participants are involved in proposing their own rewards.
- Actively support the scheme, even participate in it. This means the CEO and top managers too – if they don't make the effort to make the scheme work, neither will staff.

3 Select rewards that employees value.

Incentive schemes must provide rewards that are valued by staff. Different things motivate different people. For example, one researcher has identified those incentives which improve productivity most and they include, in priority order:

opportunities to advance, good pay, opportunities to develop new and old skills, pay on merit, recognition for good work, opportunities to be creative, interesting and challenging work, having a say in decision-making, responsibility, fringe benefits, equal workload.

In other words, not all rewards need to be monetary or materialistic in nature.

Brainstorm the types of rewards worth considering in your organisation, for example:

reduced working hours or nine-day fortnights, tickets to sporting events, company vehicles, praise, in-house fitness centres, housing loans, a weekend away, a trophy, plaque or certificate, choice of work hours, feature article in company newsletter, a week in the company villa, flowers or wine delivered home, catered breakfast or lunch, team 'conference' at a coastal resort, overseas research trip, job security, movie tickets, paid development or training course, promotion, permanent part-time work, letter of appreciation from CEO, name a space in the building after a winner, donation to a charity of the employee's choice, restaurant dinner…

Variety is appreciated by most staff who will often choose to focus on particular endeavours for which they find the reward most appealing.

4 Reward performance immediately.

We've all been brought up to respond to instant gratification so, whether the reward is individual excellence or team success, give it immediately wherever possible. Reward for performance long forgotten is of little value.

Management Memo

It is the practice of many organisations to reward their sales performers with incentives, bonuses or other inducements for sales achievements. Unfortunately these rewards are usually made on an individual basis to the 'star' who excels. Now there is nothing wrong with this; however, in my experience what this usually produces is an 'every man for himself' outcome. This 'me first' incentive creates unhealthy competition, even division and disharmony, as disputes over territory and the spoils mount.

This is the antithesis of real team harmony, the spirit of mutual support, and the business principle of co-operation.

And what about the back-room people who produce the product, provide the service, maintain the facilities, send out the accounts and bank the money? Don't they deserve to share in the rewards that success and profit bring?…

So share the glory and use incentives, not to promote individual (and potentially self-serving) achievements, but to build real team spirit and team esteem. [99]

5 Make a big deal of the presentation.

Publicise a winner(s) widely, as well as the reasons for the choice. Ensure that the recognition is delivered in a personal and honest manner. Avoid slick ceremonies which offend some employees as being artificial. Instead, consider tasteful alternatives such as lunch with the CEO, a brief presentation in the workplace, acknowledgement in the company newsletter, a short ceremony at a senior staff meeting. Sincerity counts.

See also: 334-336

How to develop staff cohesiveness

Cohesiveness is the feeling of unity that holds a group together voluntarily. Staff will operate better as individuals if they consider themselves to be part of a well-functioning, supportive team to which all are happy to belong. As committed participants in the group, they in turn are more productive, communicative, trusting, motivated and loyal. If you want to ensure your staff develops into a winning team, then you should consider these suggestions to foster that vital ingredient – cohesiveness...

1 Be aware of the features of a cohesive team.

What are the characteristics of the cohesive self-supporting team you are striving to establish? According to Douglas McGregor, the ideal team displays these features:

- The atmosphere is informal, comfortable and relaxed.
- There is lots of discussion in which everyone participates. Members listen to each other. Every idea is given an airing.
- The goals of the group are well understood and accepted by all.
- There is constructive disagreement. The group seeks resolution rather than domination of the dissenter.
- Decisions are reached by consensus.
- Criticism is frequent, frank and comfortable. All members are free to express their personal feelings.
- When action is agreed upon, clear tasks are assigned and willingly accepted.
- Members share beliefs/values, and seek each other's support and recognition.
- The group displays a united front.
- The leader does not dominate, nor does the group unduly defer to him/her.

2 Promote interaction between staff members.

Effective teamwork will occur when group members feel positive towards each other. Act as a catalyst to create and maintain a network of interpersonal relationships among group members. Arrange regular meetings that are either work-related or social. Organise an annual 'get-to-know-your-colleagues-better' barbecue or similar function.

3 Set clear, attainable goals and priorities.

When everyone in the team knows 'where we are going and why', and helps set those objectives, there is a greater potential for cooperation and high morale.

4 Clarify and negotiate roles.

Just like a team of rugby players, your staff members need to know who is playing in what position and how to play together confidently and effectively. The way they play will be determined by their beliefs about the group, its members and their place in the scheme of things. To clarify such roles, you might consider this approach:

Have team members share this information with others in the group: What I get from you that I want; what I get from you that I don't want; what I don't get from you that I want. Where disagreement exists among members regarding their role, this needs to be discussed so that the situation can be resolved. Some role expectations may need to be modified so that members are clear about their role and the expectations others have.

In this way members will see that their performance depends on the performance of someone else and this understanding creates a strong sense of unity and loyalty within the team.

5 Stress teamwork and ownership.

Show your commitment to the team principle at all times. 'I don't care who gets the credit as long as we achieve our goals' is the attitude to be fostered in the group. Talk about '*we*', '*our* company', 'what *we* hope to achieve' – positive suggestions that reflect a cohesive unit.

6 Provide leadership support to the team.

How can you increase and maintain each member's sense of personal worth and importance as a group member? Consider these strategies:

- Work with everyone. You may work very well with some people – but don't let this lead to the exclusion of others.
- Give everyone a piece of the action, something they can be identified with and recognised for.
- Keep the group informed.
- Look for opportunities to tap the talents and develop the skills of each member.

Management Memo

As a manager you will play a crucial role in building the team, and then in maintaining its effectiveness. Some of this team building work will be high-profile and visible, but much of it will be behind the scenes, self-effacing work that receives no recognition and often little credit – your reward will be the private knowledge that without such work the team would not be so effective. [100]

- Explore ways to let everyone publicly share the glory of achievement.
- Rotate jobs in the group if possible so that members identify with the team as a whole rather than with their own jobs.
- Ensure that all members are free to express their views to the group.

As team leader you must foster the trust and confidence of all members of your team. This may take time but without this rapport group cohesion may fail to materialise.

7 Facilitate task accomplishment.

Ensure that team members are provided with the equipment, facilities, work methods and timetable for accomplishing group goals. Focus too on solving those problems that interfere with goal attainment and building team identity.

8 Acknowledge good work.

Your task is to build a group of willing, cooperative people who work together in a climate of acceptance, support and trust. Recognition and appreciation of every member's contribution are vitally important in that regard.

 See also: 74-76, 110, 222

How to get on well with other people

We all want to be accepted and well liked by our staff and colleagues, if for no other reason than it makes our task as managers so much easier. In most situations, managers should be easy to get along with and be understanding of other people. If you want to win friends within your organisation, then here are some well-proven principles for you to consider...

1 Always be open and honest with people.

Get a reputation for being a straightshooter. To be open with people, there are three qualities you will need:

- React honestly to incoming information. Indeed, where an important decision is required from you, disagreement is often better than indifference.
- Express your own views openly and accept responsibility for your own actions.
- Make sure the other person is quite clear where you stand on a particular issue.

2 Empathise with other people.

If we make a practice of putting ourselves into the shoes of other people, we will appreciate far better the feelings of our staff members and colleagues. While we can't 'own' another person's feelings, we can say that we understand how we'd feel under the same set of circumstances. We win points for empathising with others.

3 Be known as one who espouses equality.

Do all you can to ensure that your workplace is one which recognises that all people are worthwhile and valuable, and that everyone has something important to contribute to the organisation's success.

4 Listen to what people are saying.

People will know if you're really concerned about their welfare. Showing an interest in what they're saying is one clear indicator of this: pay attention, maintain eye contact, concentrate on what is being said, and respond warmly.

5 Try not to impose your expectations on others.

One of the most common causes of tension in any relationship is when other people do not meet or satisfy our expections. If you have particular expectations of others, and these are important to you and the organisation, then make certain you share them with your staff. You can but ask them to do their best.

6 Gain a reputation for being supportive.

People work best together in a non-threatening environment, one in which they feel free to say what they think rather than what they think you want them to say. They need to feel that your relationship with them is openly supportive. When you offer this support, they will make every attempt not to let you down.

7 Be positive.

A positive attitude will affect all those with whom you come in contact. In this regard, there are three steps you can take right now:

- Think positively about yourself. Believe that you're OK. Others will respond to you in the same way.
- Get others to feel good about themselves too.
- Encourage a favourable exchange of communication amongst all those with whom you come in contact.

8 Embrace these classic principles for gaining the esteem of others.

For over half a century, the advice of Norman Vincent Peale has worked for many people. There is no reason why it wouldn't work for you too…

- ☐ Learn to remember names. Laziness in this area may indicate that you are not sincerely interested in other people. Names are very important to some people.
- ☐ Be a comfortable person so there is no strain in being with you – be an 'old shoe' kind of individual.

Management Memo

Strive deliberately after popularity and the chances are you will never attain it. But become one of those rare personalities about whom people say: '(S)he certainly has something', and you can be certain you are on the way to having people like you. I must warn you, however, that despite your attainments in popularity, you will never get everybody to like you. There is a curious quirk in human nature whereby some people just naturally won't like you… But the fact is that popularity can be attained by a few simple, natural, normal and easily mastered techniques… [101]

- ☐ Acquire the quality of relaxed easy-goingness so that things do not ruffle you.
- ☐ Don't be egotistical. Guard against being a know-all. Be natural and humble.
- ☐ Cultivate the quality of being stimulating and interesting so that people will want to be with you and get something from you.
- ☐ Determine and eliminate the scratchy elements from your personality.
- ☐ Sincerely attempt to heal every misunderstanding you have had or now have. Drain off your grievances.
- ☐ Practise liking people until you learn to do so genuinely. Will Rogers said, 'I never met a man I didn't like.' Try to be that way.
- ☐ Never miss an opportunity to say a word of congratulations upon anyone's achievement, or express sympathy in disappointment.
- ☐ Listen more than you speak, smile more than you frown, laugh with rather than at others, and watch your manners whether you feel irritated or not.

How to get on with people you don't like

People behave the way they do for two main reasons: they don't know any other way of behaving or they believe that behaviour gets for them the outcomes they want. Managers are likely to come across at least one employee whose behaviour they don't like, with whom they don't see eye-to-eye, or whom they dislike for some other reason. The challenge resides with the manager: is she/he sufficiently flexible to bring about desired changes in the employee and the relationship? Here are a few considerations…

1 Try to adopt a tolerant approach.

The fact that you don't like certain employees should not be allowed to affect the way you relate to them. You have to be tolerant and positive in your attitude toward such people. Try to exude a relaxed, confident, easy-going style to demonstrate that you are not put off by people who can be hard to get on with.

2 Practise liking people.

Will Rogers adopted the famous line, 'I never met a man I didn't like' as his way of getting on with people. Other successful ways include:

- Create opportunities to recognise an individual's achievements.
- Remember people's names.
- Treat all people with respect.
- Concentrate on the work context only.
- Focus on the person's good points and don't be too critical. Remember Richard Burton's description of Elizabeth Taylor, 'Her arms are too fat, her legs are too short, she is too big in the bust, she has an incipient double chin, and she has a slight pot belly'. He still married her – twice.

3 Be flexible about how you respond to the behaviour of others.

If you learn to be flexible in the way you react to people who are difficult, you'll learn to live with their unpleasantness. The secret is to choose an appropriate response to particular behaviours. For example,

- If the person always reacts aggressively, give responsibility and encourage ownership.
- If the person carries a personal grudge, avoid discussions about pet peeves.
- If the person never admits to being in the wrong, avoid direct criticism, sarcasm and ridicule. Deal with it in private.
- If the person is argumentative, stay calm and cite hard facts and figures to present an alternative position.
- If the person is overtalkative, have someone 'interrupt' you at a

prescribed time, or plead another appointment, or start to move away.

- For additional examples and advice, consult 'How to deal with difficult people' on page 242.

4 Keep your work relationship formal but friendly.

Being formal does not mean avoiding the employee altogether. It means that you confine your interest in this person to work-related matters. In fact, by dealing with the employee in this way, interactions will be kept to a minimum and will not interfere with work outcomes. Let the employee make the first move to discuss any matters not specifically related to the job.

5 Never let a relationship cloud your managerial responsibilities.

Do not let a testy relationship with a difficult person inhibit your managerial role. Indeed, it's important that you try extra hard to involve these people by delegating appropriate tasks, inviting their participation on committees and working parties, and in other essential organisational activities. Managers who set out to be liked by everyone all the time are heading for problems, just as those who do not attempt to patch up differences will in time inherit a similar batch of managerial headaches.

6 Talk to the employee.

Life is too short to get trapped into playing games such as 'I don't like you' or 'I'm not talking to you'. If there's a problem with an employee, talk about it with him or her in a mature, non-threatening manner. You will have taken the first step to a possible resolution of any conflict.

Management Memo

Don't chop the other guy's liver any finer than you have to. The future is an enigma. None of us can be certain that we'll never need something from a former boss, competitor, co-worker, customer, employee, neighbour, supplier, or anyone at all whom we've had contact with. That something might be a recommendation, a crucial vote, an order, or a vital piece of information. It might even be your job. [102]

7 Make changes.

As a result of talking over the matter with the employee, you may be able to recommend some changes. If you are in the wrong in any way, admit it and resolve to do something about it. If the employee is in the wrong, reach agreement about particular changes that will follow. Let the person see that you are anxious to operate in a friendlier manner than in the past.

8 Develop coping skills.

Your desire to get on with all behavioural types will require that you improve some existing skills and take on new ones. By your actions you will demonstrate your intention to get on with all people, even those you don't like.

 See also: 116, 222

How to establish rapport

Rapport, an harmonious relationship of trust and confidence, is the essential ingredient in any meaningful communication. Where rapport does not exist, most efforts to communicate effectively will be in vain. Managers, therefore, need to be skilled in the process of establishing rapport, either on a one-to-one or on a group basis. Although there is no one technique for building this rapport, there are some general principles to be observed...

1 Know what outcomes you want.

All behaviour is outcome-related – people act the way they do to get what they want. Before entering into conversation or a meeting, you need to know what you want, and have the flexibility to adopt the appropriate behaviours to achieve that outcome – through the building of confidence and trust in your colleague(s).

2 Encourage conversation.

In the early stages of most conversations, get-togethers or meetings, some people can be reluctant starters. The best approach is to get them talking – the topic or content is not important (though we do know that most people like talking about themselves). Talk, and laughter, help to establish a breathing pattern that helps to relax the person, making them feel more at ease in the situation. So that's your initial agenda: maintain eye contact, listen attentively, nod your head intermittently to match the tempo of the person's voice, and demonstrate your interest with an occasional 'a-hum' or 'a-ha' to match voice tone. Your encouraging behaviour will be appreciated.

3 Listen and observe.

Most meaning is transmitted non-verbally – more than 80 per cent, according to some experts. We are particularly aware of incongruence, that is, when there is a conflict between what people say and what their body language communicates. That incongruence could alert you to the fact that something is wrong and you may decide to pursue that uncertainty further by asking appropriate questions.

4 Use getting-to-know-you activities if necessary.

In a group context, brief, well-structured ice-breaking activities can play an important rapport-establishing function. The right activity can help to remove any inhibitions people may have about participating actively in a group and to focus attention on the task at hand. If you decide to develop your own icebreaker, rather than select from a plethora of commercially available ones, focus on three main points:

- The activity has to be simple, straightforward, fun, and encourage people to participate.
- Activity, involving interaction among group members, is required.
- The activity can be linked in some way to the main purpose for the group being assembled in the first place.

Examples of simple ice-breakers would include:

- *This is me!* Participants in turn give their name, where they're from and one other brief fact about themselves. The facilitator suggests what this third fact might be: a recent accomplishment, their most embarrassing moment, their finest hour.
- *Round the Circle.* To help remember people's names, people sit in a circle, the first person saying, 'Hello, I'm…(name)'. The next person says, 'Hello, I'm… and that's…'. And so on around the circle, each person introducing themselves and all those who have gone before. A fun, rather than a competitive, activity.
- *Pairs.* People split into pairs of strangers. Person A interviews Person B for three minutes: name, origins, interests, strengths, and so on. Person B then interviews A. Using the information gathered, they then introduce each other to the re-assembled group.
- *Biographical Name Tags.* People are given a name tag or card on which they write their name and several other facts that can be fun things: favourite food, film, resort, book, sport or items relevant to the meeting. People then mill around looking at each others' tags and talking to people as they wish.

Management Memo

Total rapport is where you feel comfortable with another person, comfortable enough to trust them. You feel it because they seem to understand your viewpoint and your way of thinking or doing things. [103]

5 Test and re-test for rapport.

The main indicator of rapport being established is 'feel'. As if instinctively, you will know when a feeling of trust and confidence exists between you and another, or among people in a group. The existence of that feeling is the precursor to continuing with the main business. Occasionally, particularly in a group setting, you will need to re-test for rapport. If you are operating in a didactic mode, for example, pause and ask the group, 'How am I going?' Encourage and listen to their feedback. Another approach is to involve the group in an energiser – a brief, high-energy activity designed to stimulate and re-focus attention.

6 Act 'as if'.

By adopting an attitude that there is nothing that can happen in a group that you can't handle, your actions will instil confidence in others around you. And that is easily achieved: by acting 'as if' (i.e. in control), you can become just that. So start behaving 'as if' establishing and maintaining rapport is one of your special qualities.

How to negotiate a better deal

Negotiation is an essential management skill; that process of arriving at mutual satisfaction through discussion and bargaining with another party. Managers negotiate to settle differences, to determine the value of services or products, or to vary terms or agreements, and it is the smart manager who goes into the negotiations with a clear strategy in mind. The following behaviours are certainly worth considering if you want to become a better negotiator…

1 Know exactly what you want and draw two lines.

This is the key. Determine your bottom line position before beginning negotiation, by identifying your goal specifically, with dates, numbers, prices, and so on. Imagine yourself drawing this proverbial 'baseline in the sand' and then drawing a second line a few steps in advance of it. The second will be the line at which you begin negotiations. In this way, at worst, you'll be negotiated back to your first line in the sand.

2 Make sure this person can say yes.

You don't really want to get into a situation where the other party has to okay with a superior an agreement you have worked long and hard to negotiate. So how do you know if this person can negotiate the deal? Just ask. Do whatever you can to negotiate directly with the person who *can* say yes.

3 Enter negotiations with a win-win attitude.

If you win at the expense of the other party, the deal will invariably return to haunt you. Continually adopt a win–win attitude because the only truly successful negotiation is one in which both parties believe their needs have been met.

4 Apply proven strategies.

Bearing in mind that you'll want to secure the best deal for yourself without making the other side feel that it has lost, consider these strategies for clinching the deal:

- Always allow yourself negotiating space by asking for more than you expect to get – you might just get it!
- Resist the first offer – you can't have the other side thinking they were too generous.
- Learn to flinch – your reaction, real or sham, will be noticed and perhaps encourage concessions.
- Be a reluctant seller. Your perceived caution will encourage a higher offer.
- Look for ways of solving the other side's problems first. Then sit back and watch them meet your demands because they'll be wanting you to follow through on your end of the deal.
- Talk about the potential for future deals (or lack thereof) by making

sure the other side sees the long-term benefits of sealing the deal *this* time.

5 Apply pressure by playing games.

A great deal of successful negotiation is game-playing. Try these games:

- *Play Dumb*: a game that allows you room and time to manoeuvre. You might indicate your agreement with the deal but state you will have to pass it by a higher authority. Return the next day with the news that the higher authority wants more concessions.
- *Time Trap*: a power game exploiting the fact that the closer you get to the deadline the greater the possibility of concessions being offered. When both sides are facing the same deadline, the least powerful side is going to feel the greater time pressure.
- *Goodies and Baddies*: a game that shifts the blame to another, leaving you smelling like roses. You indicate that you want to do the deal but your partner or boss won't buy it. Apologise and suggest concessions from the other side that may get the negotiations back on track.
- *That's It*: a game of bluff in which you walk away from a deal, either forever or to encourage the other side to make concessions. It is never a 'take it or leave it' ultimatum. Be prepared to say, 'I'm sorry, we won't be doing business after all.' If they come back to you, don't drop everything to re-start negotiations – over-eagerness could lose the day for you.

6 Make power your partner.

Negotiations are also power games. Understand and use these five main sources of power, either separately or combined:

Legitimate or positional power: achieved through symbols like titles, address, physical presentation and office setting.

Management Memo

There often seem to be two types of negotiations: the battle of wills and wits, in which at least one of the parties is motivated by a desire to win, and the kind that is really non-combative because at least one of the parties does not want a conflict to continue and is therefore motivated by the need for harmony and agreement. Very often these negotiations do not leave a particularly good taste in the mouth: the winner may not have achieved his or her real goals, and the conceder may feel embittered and exploited despite having reached agreement. [104]

Exploit all of those symbols, but guard against falling for theirs.

Reward power: achieved by the other side knowing what they will get from doing business with you. Make sure they know what's in it for them.

Coercive power: achieved by the other side knowing that they lose out by not doing business with you. Third-party testimonials can be extremely coercive.

Reverent power: achieved when others know that there are some things you will never deviate from – your core values, for example. You can always be relied upon to respond in a particular way.

Situation power: achieved when one side only has the power. Ever tried to get the attendant at the ticketing counter to provide you with a pre-booked ticket when you have no identification?

7 Remember also...

- Never make a concession without getting one in return.
- Focus on needs, not on personalities. Keep egos out of it.
- Never deal when you must – it's the worst possible time. If you don't have the luxury of negotiating well in advance, then at least feign a lack of urgency.
- Establish a clear and specific agreement that leaves no room for confusion or reneging.

 See also: 90, 98

How to lead others to your way of thinking

Verbal brawling shows a lack of control and an inability to use those vital skills of persuasion. Managers must be able to present their particular point of view or to express an opinion about an issue, without being too emotional or engaging in a bout of verbal fisticuffs. Here's a peaceful way of winning people over to your way of thinking...

1 Avoid arguing with extremists.

You can hope to persuade rational people but, if someone is a fanatic to a cause, you'll be unlikely to convince them.

2 Analyse your stance before you get involved.

Be convinced that the subject or issue is worth arguing about. Will you be going on the defensive or the offensive? Will it be worth the emotional effort?

3 Prepare your case in advance if you can.

If the opportunity arises, make ready for the discussion by considering the following:

- Understand the issue clearly. If you don't, you're disadvantaged from the start.
- Reflect on the issue and clarify your side of the argument.
- Organise your thoughts. Tease out the issue. Jot down salient points.
- Consider your opponent's possible argument and build up ammunition to counter such views in a rational way.
- Rehearse.

4 Listen to what the other person has to say.

Speed of reply counts very little in an argument, so let your opponent express an opinion without interruption. Besides, how can you compose a telling reply if you don't know what's been said? So listen carefully while having your own case at the ready. If you really listen, you'll be able to throw back in attack the faulty points in your opponent's argument.

5 Give the impression of giving the other side a fair go.

Don't signal your impatience by responding too quickly. Pause and reflect. Give the impression that at least you are interested in your opponent's point of view and that you are giving your considered thought to those opinions. In return, a rational opponent will return your courtesy, and that's important if you want to win the day.

6 Keep your cool and present your case logically and calmly.

Calmly stated facts are more effective weapons than intimidation, raised voices, immoderate language and table thumping. If you allow the debate to degenerate into emotional out-pourings and name-calling, a satisfactory conclusion is unlikely. If your opponent resorts to such statements as 'Nonsense!', 'Ridiculous!', or 'That's crazy!', insist on knowing why. Make your opponents destroy your line of reasoning logically. If they can't, your case is almost won.

7 Consider these valuable weapons in winning your case.

- If you can, make use of a third person to state or support your side of the debate. After all, that's what lawyers do in court.
- Resist attacking the conclusions of your opponents. Instead, attack the reasoning that got them there. You have to erode the foundations upon which their conclusions are built.
- Establish the basic principles that underlie your argument and your opponents'. Defend yours. Attack theirs.
- If you attack your opponent's character or name-call, you've all but lost the debate.

Management Memo

All communication is persuasive to some extent... Any attempt to influence the actions or judgements of others by talking or writing to them is being persuasive.[105]

8 Let your opponents retire gracefully.

If you sense it is hard for your opponents to admit defeat, give them the chance to save face. For example, say: 'Seeing that you didn't have all the information at your fingertips, I can see why you felt the way you did...'

9 Move on.

Don't dwell on your victories, or your opponents may dwell on their defeats. You've won the day, so your next challenge will be to work with your former adversary. Forget about trying to assert your authority – that's already accepted. Having led others to your way of thinking, it's now time to lead on.

 See also: 124-128, 334, 338

How to help reduce stress in your employees

Stress goes with the job – most jobs. And the signals of stress include apathy, fatigue, tension, frustration, detachment, boredom, irritability, hopelessness, a sense of not being appreciated, deteriorating health and absenteeism. Your staff are not immune to stress – in fact, you may well be the cause of it. But, as a manager, you can help to alleviate employee stress in a number of ways...

1 Be reasonable in your expectations.

Don't make unreasonable demands on employees. Extra duties take them away from core tasks and make their goals more difficult or impossible to achieve. Often we apply too much pressure on our staff to satisfy our own values or ambitions.

2 Be decisive, clear and unambiguous.

When managers inappropriately delay making decisions or reverse previous decisions, employees report that they experience more stress than when firm, timely decisions are made. So collect relevant data, set achievable deadlines, and make decisions at the appropriate time. As well, lack of timely information about rules, standards, evaluative criteria and goals causes confusion, uncertainty and frustration. Effective communication is vital.

3 Create a supportive work environment.

Some work environments often isolate workers from one another and make it difficult for them to receive the encouragement and support of colleagues. Foster a supportive network to allow your staff to share problems and resources, because colleague support softens the effects of stress on staff members' lives.

4 Be alert to the value of self-esteem.

Many workers suffer frustration from wondering how effective they are as practitioners. They report stress from lack of feedback, especially if they feel they do not get due recognition for any extra effort. Be liberal with meaningful praise and encouragement.

5 Plan ahead.

Stressful situations can be avoided with a little foresight and planning. Alert your staff to special events, projects and meetings well ahead of time so they can plan their schedules accordingly.

6 Involve employees in the decision-making.

When staff are given the opportunity to participate in decisions affecting their work, they experience more clarity, fewer conflicts and better relations with others. But don't ask for input and then ignore it!

7 Be consistent in disciplinary matters.

Be consistent in enforcing policies governing the conduct and performance of your staff.

8 Communicate with each staff member.

Communication is the key to building trust, a healthy atmosphere, team spirit and a sense of community within your organisation. Seek out your employees whenever possible and talk with them. Sponsor small group discussions or retreats away from the workplace. Use bulletin boards and in-house newsletters. Keep everyone informed of changes, however small those changes may be.

9 Provide adequate resources.

Lack of supportive supplies, equipment and facilities can be quite stressful for enthusiastic workers. Make every attempt to fund existing programmes before allocating moneys to new programmes or activities for which employee commitment has not yet been secured.

10 Always follow through.

Implement only important innovations for which you can muster sufficient time, skills, resources and commitment. Managers are often criticised for initiating new programmes and then failing to follow them through adequately.

Management Memo

Stress is not limited to any one level in an organisation. Although typically we have assumed all the heart attack candidates come from the executive ranks, it is now known that middle and lower levels have their own unique problems, making stress an 'equal opportunity' opponent... By massive popular vote, the leading cause of stress at work is the bad boss... [106]

11 Provide variety in an employee's life.

Burnout can occur from a feeling of being locked into a routine job. Identify potentially exhausting jobs and wherever possible have your staff switch assignments, projects and departments to find new challenges and a fresh environment.

12 Be an effective gatekeeper.

Protect your staff. Control the rate of innovations entering the workplace. Some you will be unable to delay or exclude, but you can control your own initiatives. Protect staff from angry customers, and support your staff when speaking with others.

13 Check your personal style for defects.

Your own managerial style may trigger feelings of anxiety amongst staff. Be alert to such defects as: delegating too little or too much, blaming others, playing favourites, not delivering on promises, discouraging creative thinking and frankness, hogging credit, nit-picking, being cheap with praise, setting unreasonable deadlines, and showing lack of concern for others.

 See also: 150, 192, 218

How to encourage and keep innovative people

The trouble with having innovative or entrepreneurial people in your organisation is that they're often hard to keep. They get frustrated with all those organisational rules, controls and restrictions which impact on their creative spirit, and such frustration often leads to their departure to set up their own enterprise. Can you afford to lose such creative talent? What can you do to foster and keep these internal entrepreneurs or *intrapreneurs* as Gifford Pinchot termed them? Try adopting the following strategies...

1 Let them select themselves.

Management cannot appoint an employee to become an intrapreneur, tell him or her to become passionately committed to an idea, and then expect success. Instead, look at every level for intrapreneurs with ideas – not just for ideas alone, because an idea without someone passionate about it is sterile. Find these people, then empower them to follow their dream. And if *you* have a bright idea, but not the time to carry it through, expose potential intrapreneurs to it and see who begins building on it and making it his or her own. In other words, it will pay to go the extra distance if you can locate self-appointed intrapreneurs.

2 Keep them on the job from go to whoa.

Unfortunately in many large organisations, new ideas are handed from group to group during the course of development. We often forget that intrapreneurs become dedicated to an idea and that this commitment is the primary force behind successful innovation. By all means involve other people, but remember, with each handover, it is likely that a less dedicated person will become involved and the intrapreneur will drop a notch in enthusiasm. You must find ways of keeping your intrapreneur fired up, and on the job from start to finish.

3 Let them get on with the job.

An intrapreneur's job is to create a vision of a new business reality and to make it happen. The major problem with many large organisations is not blocking that vision but, rather, blocking the action. So, are the innovators in your organisation permitted to do the job in their own way, or are they constantly having to stop to explain their actions and ask for permission? Are you willing to allow them to make decisions and take action themselves?

4 Make sure you give them enough rope.

Company resources are usually committed to what is planned and nothing is left over for trying the unplannable. But innovation is inherently unplannable. Intrapreneurs need discretionary resources – funds, people, time, materials – to explore and develop their ideas. If you put a tight lid on the bucket so that nothing is available for the new and unexpected, then the result will be nothing new, and you'll end up with a creative and very frustrated employee.

5 Be tolerant of risk-taking and failure.

You can't innovate if you don't take risks. In organisations that succeed with innovation, and retain their creative people, a tolerance for blunders, false starts and failure is built deeply into the everyday activities of the company.

6 Be patient.

One of the drawbacks of innovation is that it takes time. Once you've decided to try something new, the challenge for you will be to stick with the experiment long enough to see if it will work, even when it may take several years and several false starts and many hiccups on the way. Intrapreneurs require more patient support than they generally receive.

7 Prevent people from protecting their own turf.

Because new ideas almost always cross internal organisational boundaries, e.g. research, personnel, finance, marketing departments, the potential for people to protect their own interests and territory exists. 'Turfiness' blocks innovation. Your challenge is to find ways to allow your intrapreneurs to travel with their ideas across territories, and to get all involved to value innovation more than politics.

Management Memo

Intrapreneurs are the 'dreamers who do', those who take hands-on responsibility for creating innovation of any kind within an organisation. The intrapreneur may be the creator or inventor but is always the dreamer who figures out how to turn an idea into a profitable reality... Intrapreneurs will make all the difference between your firm's success and failure. The cost of losing entrepreneurial talent is more than just losing a skilled technologist or effective marketer. Intrapreneurs are the integrators who combine the talents of both the technologists and the marketers by establishing new products, processes and services. Without them innovation remains potential, or moves at the glacial pace of bureaucratic processes that no longer suffice in an environment filled with entrepreneurial competition. [107]

8 And remember...

To take full advantage of the innovative streak which may be lying dormant in your organisation:

- Make sure your company's vision for the future is clearly understood by all staff so that your intrapreneurs can work on creating innovative ideas that relate directly to the strategy of your company.
- Make it known that the greatest opportunity in your organisation lies in becoming an intrapreneur.
- Replace red tape with responsibility.
- Reward intrapreneurs with new career paths that fit their needs.
- Know your innovative people and nurture them – or lose them.

 See also: 150, 192, 216

How to unleash the creative potential in your staff

As a manager, you can increase the effectiveness, productivity and competitiveness of your organisation if you take steps to establish a more creative working environment for your employees. There are innovative people in every organisation if only they are given a chance to display their creativity. They can be one of your greatest assets, but only if you know how to get the best from them...

1 Understand the creative process.

People won't be creative unless they want to be creative and they must work in an environment that encourages them to be creative. If people are given the opportunity to participate in planning their work and are encouraged to make decisions about how it should be done, they will want to be involved. A positive attitude, ownership and commitment are the key ingredients of creativity. Creativity is a fluctuating process – there will be fallow periods during the incubation stage when little happens. Wise counsel will rekindle the creative spirit, so the manager must keep the communication lines open and provide a flexible, supportive environment.

2 Appreciate that all staff can contribute creatively.

Nobody has a monopoly on creativity. Good ideas can come from the receptionist or the managing director. The trick is to create an environment where everyone in your organisation is encouraged to have a say. Set in place procedures where the views of all staff members are welcome and considered.

3 Set the example yourself.

To foster a creative work environment, you need to be a 'Theory Y' manager; you see your staff as creative, imaginative, hardworking and responsible. You need to favour informal organisational structures and encourage supervisors and employees to share ideas, information and resources. You need to set the norm for creativity by occasionally coming up with an outlandish idea yourself. You need the ability to inspire, to 'work them up', to relax the controls, to demonstrate a positive attitude of confidence, and to offer praise and support.

4 React warmly and positively to all ideas.

Ideas are easier to tame down than to think up, so welcome those way-out ideas and toss them around, because often one idea will lead to another. Remember, criticism kills an idea faster than anything else, and creative people are usually very sensitive to criticism. Listen to yourself next time someone comes up with a new idea. Do you thunder 'No – that wouldn't work here!' or do you say 'Sounds promising. Let's see if we can do something with it.'? And if ultimately the idea must be criticised, your objective should be to nourish, modify and nudge the idea along, not kill it, and its originator's enthusiasm, outright.

Management Memo

William McKnight, who helped turn a failed corundum mine into a flourishing sandpaper and grinding-wheel business that grew into 3M, told his colleagues: Listen to anyone with an original idea, no matter how absurd it might sound at first. Encourage; don't nitpick. Let people run with an idea. Hire good people, and leave them alone. If you put fences around people, you get sheep. Give people the room that they need. Encourage experimental doodling. Give it a try – and quick. [108]

5 Identify and encourage creative individuals.

Spend time with people, observe the quality of their work, talk to them about their views of things, and listen to what other staff and colleagues have to say. Words like 'risk-taker', 'leader', and 'exceptional' are variously used to describe people who are more creative than others and they are the ones who should be particularly nurtured:

- *Recognise that innovators on staff are apt to be 'different'* and may need to be treated differently.
- *Innovators should be free to associate with their opposite numbers in other organisations.* Enlightened managers see the value of an interchange of ideas among professionals working in the same field. Such people should be encouraged to network, to attend conferences, and to join professional associations.
- *Innovators should be allowed to select their own projects whenever possible.* Creative people produce better results if they can identify with the project they are given to tackle.
- *Establish challenging assignments.* Creative individuals are too hamstrung when tied to tried-and-proven concepts. They thrive on adventure and experimentation.
- *Acknowledge individual achievement.* Many innovators are 'loners', rather than team players, and are often encouraged more by individual accolades rather than praise directed at a team's achievements.

6 Reward usable ideas.

3M stages its own annual Oscars night when, with considerable fanfare, several of its creative staff are honoured by peers. Devise strategies for rewarding or at least acknowledging creative contributions by your staff. In this way, others will also be encouraged to have an input.

7 Set aside time for creative thinking.

Remember that most ideas do not come in a flash of inspiration, but rather in a lather of perspiration. Focus meetings, brainstorming sessions, and think-tanks in relaxed settings, as these are often the sources of the best creative ideas. As manager, you are in a position to remove the weight of everyday, routine duties and to set regular time aside for such creative activity.

How to ask questions

The best way to solve a problem is to ask the person who has the key to its solution. Asking the right people the right questions is the pathway to real information about your workplace, your employees and your customers. Whether you're solving problems, establishing a better working relationship, shaping your vision, motivating, interviewing, or negotiating, asking the right questions is a vital management device. Here are the essentials of effective questioning...

1 Understand the purpose of questions.

Questions are used for a variety of purposes:

- to get information
- to clarify a point
- to keep discussions going
- to communicate feelings
- to make the other person feel good
- to gain insight.

Your task is to understand the purpose of your questioning, then to use the types of questions that will deliver the desired outcome. Remember, the more senior your position within the organisation, the more questions you should ask. By asking questions, rather than attempting to provide answers, you help to keep your organisation 'open', tap into others' accumulated wisdom and insights, and conceal your own agenda.

2 Use the right type of question.

The type of question you ask can influence the response, and in the hands of a skilled interviewer, a question can be a powerful tool. For example:

Open-ended questions (Why?, How?) explore opinions and attitudes, encourage others to keep talking, and avoid a yes-no response.

Closed or *yes-no* questions ('Did you see...?') establish specific fact, obtain a pattern of agreement, or force an unambiguous response.

Leading questions ('Don't you think...?) suggest the required answers.

Reflective/probing questions ('Are you saying that...?') restate or reflect on what you've heard and invite the disclosure of other information.

Rhetorical questions ('Have you ever wondered why...?') are used for effect; you do not expect an answer.

Directive questions ('So you agree that...?') focus on desired outcomes.

'*Dumb* 'questions ('I don't follow. Could you go over it again, please?') test the rationale of why things have always been done in a certain way.

Summary questions ('So what you're saying is...?') check understanding and confirm your interest.

3 Keep your questions simple and direct.

Good questions are direct and to the point, worded in such a way that the listener has no difficulty in understanding exactly what the questioner wants. If the response to your question is 'I'm not quite sure what you're asking…', then your question was not simple nor direct.

4 Ask questions that are focused.

Questions should emphasise only one point at a time. Avoid complex, double-barrelled questions. If you keep them concise and brief, you'll cause no confusion and you'll get the answer you're looking for.

5 Move from general to specific.

In situations where you seek detailed information, if you get too direct, too soon, you run the risk of creating a defensive attitude rather than one encouraging open communication. Start with the general issues and gradually focus on specifics. And if you start with difficult or delicate questions, you will only cause discomfort for the other person. A person at ease will respond openly and without animosity.

6 Ask the question, then pause.

There's nothing wrong with silence. It places the onus to respond on the other person. So, after you ask a question, pause, and use your body language to let the person know that you're waiting for a reply. By nodding your head, and minimising your verbal response through the use of 'mm' or 'yes', you can encourage the other person to keep talking.

7 Don't telegraph an answer.

Don't be bluffed by an answer. Remember, sometimes we inadvertently word our questions in such a way that the listener can guess what answer will satisfy us; they give it to us and we are happy. Be alert when asking your question. You want an answer based on facts and information, not on guesswork.

Management Memo

The higher you climb in your organisation, the more people will come to you with their questions, expecting answers. And the higher your level in the hierarchy, the fewer answers you should give, and the more questions you should ask…

By bringing the views of different people to bear on a situation, you create the opportunity to reach new solutions. Only by asking questions can you bring a degree of confidence and trust sufficient to elicit these different, perhaps radical, points of view. [109]

8 Refuse to accept inadequate answers.

Be persistent when answers are vague. Seek out the specifics until you are satisfied with the information provided. Remember that powerful word *why?* If a response is a simple 'yes/no', ask 'why?'. This three-letter follow-up is very potent and often elicits information that leads to better decision-making.

9 Don't baulk at unsettling responses.

When seeking information, or in an interview situation, avoid evaluating answers and showing your disapproval, verbally or non-verbally, when someone responds incorrectly or displeasingly. In fact, such answers can help to identify gaps in your knowledge, or indicate to you specific areas where further probing is warranted.

How to listen actively

Listening accounts for well over half of a manager's communication time and it is unquestionably the weakest link in the communication chain. We simply don't listen well enough. The failure is not in the hearing, but in our inability to attend to what we hear. Listening is hard work. It's so easy to 'switch-off'. If only we listened attentively and with empathy, we would eliminate so much in terms of misunderstandings, arguments, delays and mistakes. Become a better listener by adhering to the following advice...

1 Commit yourself to each individual act of listening.

Whenever you need to hear everything someone is saying, commit yourself, really commit yourself, to that. Say to yourself, 'The most important thing in my life at this moment is to understand this person's feelings and views.' Accordingly, focus *all* of your listening capacity on the speaker for the next five, fifteen or fifty minutes. Actually *want* to listen better. It's a small investment of your time that can pay enormous dividends.

2 Neutralise your biases.

Don't let your personal biases turn you off, despite what you may feel about the speaker's voice, character, appearance, reputation or the subject being discussed. Don't let your feelings distort the real message. Stay calm, don't get upset, and keep an open mind.

3 Really concentrate on what is being said.

When listening, listen. Listening is not a passive activity. Unless you're concentrating solely on what is being said, you're not listening. If you've heard it all before, hear it again. Fight the 'switch-off' syndrome. The more you work at concentrating while listening, the more your powers of concentration will develop and the easier listening will become.

4 Encourage the speaker.

Show the speaker you're listening. This can be done by nodding, facing the speaker, through eye contact, leaning forward slightly, smiling and repeating key words or points. Don't interrupt the speaker's train of thought by interrupting with a response until the speaker has finished.

5 Ignore all distractions.

Particularly if the speaker or the topic is dull, or once we get a rough idea of what is being said, we readily allow distractions to interfere with our listening: noises, ringing telephones, our own thoughts, the speaker's mannerisms, daydreaming, passing employees, a memo you're working on… Giving in to distractions is a bad habit which could have you not hearing something worthwhile or vital.

6 Focus on the main ideas.

Good listening involves separating the verbal grain from the chaff. Learn to identify the major points to which the facts adhere, for good listeners are concept listeners rather than fact listeners. Finally, search for the implications of what is being said.

7 Test your understanding.

Ensure that you really understand what the speaker is trying to say. Ask for repetition, clarification, amplification and examples. Summarise from time to time. By doing this, you will also indicate to the speaker that you are really listening.

8 Delay formulating your arguments.

Since brain speed works at about 90 times the rate of the speed of speech, we sometimes allow our mind to soar ahead of what we're hearing, by working on our response. In doing this, we don't hear what is being said. So try not to let your attention wander too soon in formulating a reply.

9 Suspend judgement.

Listening is a separate task to interpreting and evaluating, both of which can hamper the listening process. Make sure you comprehend before you judge the message, so resist the temptation to debate, mentally and prematurely, the message instead of listening. Your time would be better spent checking and re-checking the information through questioning. Delay the act of processing for later.

Management Memo

We receive little training in listening, and probably spend little time evaluating or refining our listening behaviour or practising our listening skills – unlike the time we spend in reworking or rehearsing our public speeches. But studies of management activity have shown that those in leadership positions may spend up to 60 per cent of their time listening and it is, therefore, important that we focus more of our attention on the way we listen. [110]

10 Don't talk too much.

You can't talk and listen at the same time. If you're seeking information, you shouldn't say much – you already know what *you* think. You should be more interested in what the other person has to say, so let them dominate the discussion, allowing you to stay focused – listening.

11 Remember: listening is a key to personal success.

Recognise that listening is something you do if you want to succeed. Listening earns you power and respect, and gets you the information you need to be an effective manager. But listening is a sophisticated skill. It requires self-discipline, and you'll need to work on it.

How to communicate with someone who doesn't speak your language

As managers increasingly employ people from diverse cultural backgrounds and pursue global markets, they will inevitably be required to communicate across language barriers. Learning to speak the languages of one or two other countries would certainly help, but even this would never eliminate the need. Here are some helpful hints which will increase your flexibility when having to communicate with someone speaking another language...

1 Do your homework.

If you have advance warning of a meeting, find out all you can about expected attendees: their cultures, their languages, their companies. No one expects you to be an expert but it wouldn't hurt to buy a book on the basics of the country and its language. You will impress your guests or hosts when they see that you have made the effort. Although interpreter services may be available, think carefully about introducing a third-party, particularly without the consent of the people with whom you are planning to meet.

2 Test for understanding.

The people with whom you are meeting may have developed 'survival skills' and use often-used phrases in your language, so ask them. This can be done either in your language or you can create a favourable impression by asking this question in their language. There are many books available containing the most commonly used phrases and sentences.

3 Be patient.

Meeting and communicating will be equally as challenging for the other person, so progress slowly to avoid any confusion and frustration. Remember, most meaning will be communicated non-verbally and impatience will be easily detected. The speed at which you progress will be dictated by the other person and you will be aware of that speed if you're patient.

4 Note the responses.

The response to your communicating will indicate the meaning the other person attaches to what you've said. If the response is not what you expect, it probably means that your message has not been understood. Begin again, speaking slowly and clearly, making certain that you do not raise your voice.

5 Avoid jokes.

Your attempted humour may be misunderstood; it may even be taken as an offence – a joke at their expense. Seek eye contact with the person, smile, use open-hand gestures, mirror posture, but never attempt to provide the comedy. When in doubt, don't.

6 Chunk-down.

Break instructions into smaller manageable pieces. Provide the information at a rate that can be taken in and comprehended. It is far better to get your communicating right the first time than to have to repeat it.

7 Seek feedback.

Don't be afraid to stop occasionally and ask, 'Do you understand what I am saying?' or 'Is it clear what I am saying?' A blank response will convey information about the meaning attached to your communication efforts. Remember, response is meaning.

8 Be aware of your non-verbal messages.

You can't not communicate, so ensure that the non-verbal messages you are giving off – gestures, eye contact, use of space – are those that are in harmony with your message. All people are highly aware of incongruence between what is said and what is communicated non-verbally. Remember too that, in some Asian countries, making eye contact could be considered disrespectful. Staring or pointing could also be seen as offensive. And in some countries, our simple thumbs-up signal for 'A-okay' is an obscene gesture. Be aware!

Management Memo

Managers must increasingly understand intercultural communication – the customs, etiquette and methods of communication in other countries. A rudimentary knowledge of cultural variations in values and work attitudes helps in the supervision of a culturally diverse workforce.[98]

9 Avoid the no-nos.

If you've done your homework, you will be aware of some of the 'no-nos' observed by the particular cultural group. Avoid our jargon and slang, and certain topics of conversation: religion, politics, personal issues.

As well, interaction can be difficult. We can sometimes come across as rude, pushy, assertive and impatient. In other cultures, people may prefer to hint at what they mean, will not communicate bad news or rejection, and will tell you what they think you want to hear rather than what they actually believe. Competition is valued in some cultures, collaboration in others. It is difficult to encourage people to behave in ways that contradict cultural conditioning. Be prepared to learn, adapt, adjust.

10 Consider taking lessons.

If you find that expanding business interests require you to hold frequent meetings with business people whose first language is different from yours, consider enrolling in a course to learn that language and the culture. You will be pleasantly surprised at the developments that have occurred in language teaching, even since your school days, so give it a try.

 See also: 90, 190, 246, 338

How to handle your critics constructively

How should you react to criticism of yourself or your organisation? Ignoring the criticism may be one way, but that often solves nothing. On the other hand, if you are able to build a co-operative, supportive environment in which criticism can be given and received with little pain, then you'll be perceived as an effective communicator and a highly effective manager. One of the hallmarks of success is being able to react to criticism constructively. Here are a few ideas that may help…

1 Acknowledge that you will be criticised.

Recognise that you, as a leader, will have faults. Someone will always be out to put you on the defensive – it's a hazard of your position. Awareness of this will make criticism easier to accept. Remember the saying: 'They who shrink from criticism cannot be showered safely with praise.'

2 Face your criticism as soon as possible.

Criticism is often the result of faulty communication. Whether you believe the criticism is fair or unfair, it's important if possible to make personal contact with your critic. Open communication will prevent the build-up of resentment and help defuse a potentially damaging situation.

3 Listen to the criticism with an open mind.

Let your critic get the criticism out in the open. Resist the temptation to interrupt with defensive counter-arguments. Don't let your emotions block your listening. Weigh the words as you hear them. Be courteous. An angry critic in particular needs to be listened to before she/he will be prepared to hear your point of view.

4 Keep your cool.

Don't raise your voice and wave your arms about. There are other occasions for that but dealing with criticism is not one of them. The way you visibly respond to criticism will be remembered more vividly later than the argument you present in reply.

5 Clarify the criticism.

In order to understand fully your critic's perspective, seek further details if necessary. 'What exactly is it about my decision that bothers you?' 'Are you saying that my decision means that I am critical about the way you're tackling your job?' And it's sometimes sobering to consider if you, in your critic's place, would not have responded in a similar fashion.

6 Seek out any hidden causes for the criticism.

Don't overlook the identity, credentials and motives of your critic. Is he passing the buck in order to save himself from criticism? Is she criticising merely to vent her rage or compensate for her own faults? Is he criticising from a genuine impulse to help you improve your performance? Is she a chronic complainer? Answers to such questions will help frame your response.

> **Management Memo**
>
> We learn from criticism. Many of our most productive actions come from a recognition of areas of our lives that need improvement. We look back fondly at events that revolutionised our thinking, perhaps even made our careers, and find they usually started with someone's constructive advice. Criticism of any kind is never fun, but it loses its bite as time separates us from the circumstances that bring it about. Resign yourself to criticism. Think of the poor unproductive fool who has nothing in his or her life to criticise.[112]

7 Encourage a solution from your critic.

How might you have better handled the situation which generated the criticism? Invite your critics to participate in working with you towards finding a workable compromise. Ask what they are prepared to contribute towards it. Often such discussion can bring about a clarification of roles, a change in priorities for certain activities, and a sharing of responsibilities.

8 Take appropriate action by responding positively.

Admit to shortcomings without self-castigation. Being able to wear a mistake is enormously stress-reducing for you and your organisation. The ability to offer a simple, 'Yes, perhaps I could have done that differently', reduces staff defensiveness and creates goodwill all round. But, in admitting your shortcomings, it is also appropriate to set limits: indicate perhaps that you cannot be everywhere at once and that problem solving involves others showing responsibility as well.

If the criticism is justified, tell your critic what you intend to do to remedy the situation. On the other hand, if the complaint is unjustified, be calm and firm in telling your critic just that. Explain why nothing can be done and why.

9 Acknowledge criticism with courtesy.

Thank your critics for pointing out the negative aspects of your behaviour that upset them. Don't sulk: view justified criticism as a way of improving your performance. As Andrew Sherwood, author of *Breakpoints*, advises: 'Treat all criticism as friendly and with good intentions. This professional outlook will enable you to recognise the value of legitimate criticism and ignore the rest. By conceding the critic's goodwill, you can turn an attacker into a friend and, as you climb the career ladder, all friends are welcome.'

10 Follow up.

If your critics' grievance or suggestions were valid and helped you perform better, let them know about it, because criticism often does improve overall efficiency.

See also: 168, 188, 270

How to criticise other people constructively

No one likes to be criticised; even justified criticism has the potential to demoralise a person. But there are times when managers have no other choice and, indeed, not to criticise or to overlook errant behaviour is sometimes even worse than to do so. However, it's possible to criticise staff so that they actually feel good when you've finished. It's a very sensitive management skill that can be learned, particularly if you view criticism as an investment in your colleague's future...

1 Know when and where to criticise.

Criticism should follow errant behaviour as soon as possible, while the experience is fresh in the person's mind and before anxieties begin to fester or the mistake is repeated. Except in emergencies, such as a factory worker endangering the life of others, criticise in private, at a time which allows for the minimum of interruption. If possible, allow for a second contact later in the day, when you can show by your amicable attitude that your regard for the individual has not diminished.

2 Know why you are criticising.

Before confronting the person, understand the real reasons for your criticism and make sure they're valid. Are you criticising to let off steam? to put her in her place? to show him who's boss? Or are you criticising for valid reasons: to motivate to greater effort, to indicate how performance is being judged, or to prevent the recurrence of a particular pattern of behaviour?

3 Get to the root of the problem and gather your facts first.

Find out what went wrong, when and how, before you talk to the person. Be sure of your facts before you criticise and your criticism will be more convincing. And don't forget to investigate the 'why' and the 'who', because it may not be the fault of the person it seems to be, or the fault may be shared.

4 Be prepared to criticise the act, not the person.

One of the functions of criticism is to prevent the recurrence of a particular pattern of behaviour. Since personal attacks make people defensive and it is easier for people to change their behaviour than their personalities, stick to the facts of the act and people will be more responsive to your message. To accuse a person of 'having a poor attitude towards work' or of 'being an irresponsible professional' could buy into a heated argument. Instead, stick to the facts of the errant behaviour: always late for work, rude to customers, failure to meet deadlines, and so on.

5 State your concerns as you see them.

Confront the person and share, from your perspective, all information relevant to your criticism. Listen to his/her side of the story... but you can go no further until you both agree that a problem exists and you are sure that the person understands clearly what you find objectionable.

6 Make clear your expectations.

Despite the fact that some mistakes are stupid and it sometimes requires a superhuman effort to avoid sarcasm or invective, the only valid purposes of criticism are positive in nature. Having both agreed that a problem exists, you are now at the constructive stage of your criticism, where you can demonstrate a sincere desire to help your colleague. Seek his/her ideas in working towards future improvement. Talk about the next step: discuss what can be done to rectify the errant behaviour. Don't leave the person confused about what action is required.

7 Provide back-up support.

Providing back-up is a way of re-establishing your confidence in the person and that person's confidence in you. This doesn't mean re-opening the topic (unless it is raised again by your colleague) and it doesn't mean nagging. It means keeping in touch and being available to help if needed.

8 And remember...

Here are a few more important suggestions to keep in mind when next you must criticise another person:

- Do not use humour; too often it is mistaken for sarcasm.
- Never criticise people in the personal areas of their lives, such as drinking or home life. Relate such transgressions only to the effect they may be having on performance in the workplace.
- Never criticise when you're angry: you need to be calm, rational and objective. Never act in haste. Never raise your voice. Never let the discussion turn into an old-fashioned chewing-out or tongue-lashing – that simply crushes egos, creates tension, triggers hostility, and generates aggression.
- Try to create a climate of reasonableness in which your colleague will be encouraged to work with you against the common foe: an error.
- Commend before you criticise. By prefacing your criticism with an honest compliment, you are assuring your colleague that you still think highly of him/her, and you indicate that you view the errant act as an untypical departure from the norm. With this inferred assurance, your colleague is liable to be receptive to what you say.
- You'll make the criticism a lot easier for the other person if you share in some way at least some part of the responsibility for the mistake.
- View criticism as an opportunity for you to learn as well, for you may indeed be part of the problem.

Management Memo

Criticism is not only recognition, proof of the boss's concern; it can be a vital learning experience for both boss and subordinate... Criticism can provide an occasion for growth and development, provided it is not the only thing subordinates hear from their boss. But it must be used thoughtfully if it is to serve as an incentive. [113]

 See also: 232-234, 246

How to handle an angry person

When an angry employee or customer bursts into your office, rarely do you have time to prepare yourself. Often, you are not the target of that anger but you must be able to bear the brunt of the emotional onslaught. How do you normally respond? Do you become confused? defensive? disoriented? Are you always tempted to return anger with more anger? What is needed is self-control, a sense of calm, a touch of assertiveness and, most importantly, you must show a sincere desire to solve whatever problem lies at the source of the outburst. Here is a proven technique which will work with most angry people in most situations...

1 Acknowledge the person's anger upfront.

Nothing adds more fuel to the fire of anger than to have it brushed aside, ignored or challenged. Anger is a symptom of a greater problem so make it clear immediately that you realise the person is upset: 'I can see that this is important to you, so it's important to me too. Let's go and have a talk about it.'

The message you thus send is twofold: first, it says that you're interested in helping with the problem and, second, it makes clear that you're not going to combat rage with rage. Your supportive comments don't condone anger, but drive home the need to redirect these emotions constructively.

2 Be calm and confident.

It is essential when confronted by an angry person to remain calm, dignified, express confidence in your face and body language, and to speak in a steady voice that says you are concerned but not intimidated. It's vital not to respond aggressively to another's anger. If faced with shouting and profanity, draw a line: 'I have no intention of raising my voice during our discussion, and I ask that you extend the same courtesy to me'. No one can win with an angry exchange of words.

3 Provide a non-threatening environment.

Your aim is not to shut them up or outshout them, but to devise a solution for their problem. The search for a solution can only begin in a non-threatening environment, so move any confrontation to a private setting such as your office. Get the person seated (it's harder to continue an outburst from a sitting position) and at ease.

Come out from behind the barrier created by your desk. Try a less formal setting such as adjacent, on one side of a table.

Management Memo

Anger is a healthy, normal human emotion that warns us that something is wrong. It can bring attention to injustices and it can force people out of complacency. But it's also an uncomfortable emotion – especially when expressed at work. Fortunately, anger can be managed. The key is to deal with it in a way that solves problems instead of causing them. [114]

4 Listen to what the person has to say.

If the other party is still fuming, let him/her get it all out before you start responding. If you maintain eye contact and listen actively without saying anything, the angry person will run out of steam much sooner – it's not easy to keep yelling at someone who doesn't respond. By letting the person get it off their chest, you are going a long way towards defusing a volatile situation.

5 Ask questions.

As anger subsides, to get at the seat of the fire you'll need to smoke out the real problem, which the person may not readily be honest about. You may need to ask lots of questions; you're now moving the discussion more clearly into the objective, rather than the subjective, phase.

6 Summarise the situation as you see it.

Without being aggressive or defensive, work through the facts as you now understand them, being as objective as possible. The other party can confirm, correct or add to your understanding of the issue.

7 Work towards a solution.

By now you will know if you are dealing with a reasonable person or not. If you've heard him (or her) out calmly, asked questions in a courteous and concerned manner, and are now about to explore solutions, then his anger should have cooled so that you can talk rationally with him. However, if he's still too angry to consider solutions, it may be best to postpone the discussion, allowing time for him to reflect and regain composure.

But if discussion is now possible, explore with the other party the various options for a fair and equitable solution. Finally, agree on the solution that meets your mutual needs as fully as possible within the bounds of any existing constraints.

8 Act on the solution.

If the organisation or you are to blame, admit it. Apologise and assure the person that it will not happen again. If the other party is in the wrong, be firm in stating this without overreacting. If another person is involved, state your intention to gather further information before deciding on any action. Indicate that you will advise later of your decision. Above all, demonstrate fairness and an interest in the person and the problem.

9 Express appreciation.

Thank the other party for sharing the problem with you and guarantee your continuing interest, concern and intention to use the opinions of customers/staff in serving their best interests as well as the interests of the organisation.

 See also: 208, 230, 234

How to take the heat out of a confrontation

Confrontations can be unpleasant episodes but they are inevitable. What is important is that they can provide valuable opportunities to identify and deal with problems that otherwise could have remained undetected and simmering. But there is a technique to handling them constructively. When you find yourself in face-to-face confrontations, here is what you can do to defuse, resolve and profit from that potentially explosive situation...

1 Make confrontation constructive.

For a confrontation to become a beneficial episode, it should provide the following outcomes:

- The other person's behaviour changes in the manner desired.
- The self-esteem of the other person is preserved.
- Your relationship with the other person remains intact.

These outcomes can be realised if you remain objective about the other person's undesirable behaviour, listen to the other person's response, identify the effects, describe future expectations, and commit or agree to future behaviour.

2 Choose the time and place.

Don't fuel the fire by initiating any conflict in public. Also avoid confronting people after a hard day, before an event at which they have to be at their best, when they are dealing with a mistake or loss, or when they're working under the cloud of an imminent deadline. Choose time and place carefully. Sensitivity to the other person's circumstances is always important, but in a conflict it is critical.

3 Keep your cool and listen.

Listen to everything the other party is saying and not just for what you want to hear. Don't let the other person's tactics unsettle you. Give yourself time. Keep calm and tell your adversary that you would rather discuss the observable facts and not personal opinions. You'll find that your actions will enable a focus on solutions rather than an attribution of blame.

4 Develop strategies to cope with confrontation.

Learn to accept conflict as inevitable and develop tactics to handle it when it occurs. Coping mechanisms include:

Count to ten. Deep breathing helps to lower your emotional temperature, and can even cool the other person's anger.

Take 5. If you're not getting anywhere, postpone the encounter.

Set a time. Regroup, get your house in order, and resume.

Go for a walk. It is often easier to talk about difficult issues during a long walk. It also solves the problem of what to do with your hands and any difficulty you have with eye-to-eye contact.

Use 'I-language'. State your case in terms of your own feelings.

Agree. If appropriate, agreement defuses most confrontations.

Side-step. Maintain strong and confident eye contact for a second or so, then move on.

Rehearse responses. Thinking afterwards, 'I wish I would have said that', indicates you weren't prepared.

Control voice tone, tempo, volume and nonverbals. It's not what you say, but how you say it.

5 Switch from content to process.

You *talk* about 'content'; how you *deal* with content is 'process'. When no progress is being made with content, it is often because the process is not working. Try to negotiate a better way of dealing with the process. You might say, 'John, I'm getting a bit frustrated because I'm not getting anywhere. You don't wait for me to finish what I'm saying, and I don't believe I'm conveying what I want to say to you. I can't operate that way. Can we work out a different way of doing it?'

6 Settle it now or postpone it.

If you can resolve the issue without attempting to allocate any blame, do so. But, if necessary, don't be reluctant to call a halt to things and set a time and date for resumption. Your actions will show that you're taking the problem seriously and want to resolve it in the fairest way possible.

Management Memo

By bringing conflicts out into the open and overcoming them, we develop honest, forthright, and loving relationships with ourselves and others. We turn heat into light. [115]

7 Consider involving a third party.

A 'win–lose' outcome is really 'no-win' because it usually means that people are locked into their set positions, any goodwill is gone, and the goal is only to win. You need to break out of that mind-set by considering other options, like using a third party. Often the dynamics of a situation will change in the presence of a third person. If there is someone who is trusted and respected by both you and your adversary, seek his or her help to see the problem through to a successful conclusion.

8 Arrange a follow-up.

Just as it is helpful to keep your conflict focused on the specifics of the problem, it pays to keep the solution focused on the specific *action* that will be taken. Set a follow-up date to meet again to discuss progress, and to strengthen any shaky bridges.

 See also: 230-232

How to mediate in a staff dispute

In a dispute between staff members, attitudes tend to polarise, perspectives usually get set in concrete, the middle ground is ignored, and a feeling of 'win-lose' dominates the confrontation. To prevent this conflct from reaching such an impasse, you may find it necessary to intervene as a third party mediator (as opposed to an arbitrator who makes the final decision after both sides have presented their cases). Your aim as a mediator would be to defuse the emotionality of the combatants and to catalyse their efforts to reach, themselves, a mutually acceptable resolution...

1 Intervene before it's too late.

You need a reason to get involved in a staff dispute. Clearly, if you allow the conflict to get out of hand, it will disrupt the workplace and impact eventually on total staff harmony and effectiveness. State your concerns to both parties, either separately or together, and indicate that you wish to meet with both to establish, at least, a better working relationship.

2 Prepare both parties for the mediation process.

Explain the process to both staff members and inform them how the session will be conducted. Emphasise your role: you are not there to judge who is right or wrong; you will not be telling them how they will resolve their differences; you will not be taking sides. Your role is as a catalyst, to help the parties generate a solution for themselves with which both parties are comfortable and to which they can commit themselves.

3 Get the issues out into the open.

'Getting it off one's chest' is a very important part of the process. There are various approaches that might be considered. For example:

(a) Have each person explain the dispute from his or her perspective without interruption. Encourage open and honest expression. After each has concluded, you then summarise the facts (not the emotions) of what you have heard from both parties. Confirm with them the accuracy of your summaries.

(b) Alternatively, have both parties complete two lists responding to, firstly, 'What I like about your behaviour and want you to continue', and, secondly, 'What I don't like about your behaviour and want you to change'. This information is then exchanged one item at a time so that each person understands the other's perspective. You dictate when each party responds, using this process:

- Sue takes one item from one of her lists and outlines it as clearly as she can and, if possible, without blame, criticism or demand.
- Ken then seeks clarification, if necessary, before responding to Sue's statement.
- When this sequence is complete, Ken

- then presents one item from his lists and the above procedure is repeated in reverse with Sue responding.
- Continue this process through the lists.

Follow such approaches until all relevant information has been exchanged and understood. Even if the conflict remains unresolved, a better understanding of the problems by both parties will have resulted.

> **Management Memo**
>
> When all other approaches to conflict resolution fail, conflicting parties can have a mediator intervene. Mediators have no power to make decisions, but they can help clarify the issues, urge participants to cooperate, establish ground rules for interaction, and serve as impartial aids to help the conflicting parties settle their own dispute... By intervening, the manager seeks not only to help resolve the conflict, but attempts to develop rational, effective conflict management skills in others. [116]

4 Identify the issues.

Because you are not directly involved, you are in a good position to help both individuals see the conflict as a difference of issues rather than personalities. Separate the people from the problem. Only when the issues have been isolated will both parties see the conflict as a shared problem that will require the cooperation of both to resolve.

5 Generate solutions.

Having pinpointed the real issues fuelling the dispute, encourage both parties to identify possible solutions to the conflict. Resist the temptation to put forward your own solutions or to evaluate their suggestions. Challenge both to consider what they want to see occur in the future rather than allow them to dwell on the past. If the process is in danger of getting bogged down, lead with 'Let me offer a suggestion...' or 'Why not consider trying...?' Continually express your pleasure at any shift towards resolution of the dispute.

6 Reach an agreement.

Write down solutions or areas of agreement as they are mutually accepted. Ensure that this record of agreement is clear and concise and that both parties have a mutual understanding of what each is promising to do to resolve the conflict. Congratulate both individuals for their ability to resolve the dispute cooperatively and productively.

7 Follow up the agreement.

While agreement is a major achievement, implementation is the key to success or failure. Discuss how the situation might be reviewed over an agreed period.

8 Remember also...

- Try to build the discussions around questions rather than demands or recriminations.
- When language gets strong, ask people to repeat the statement. The tone is usually less strident second time round.
- Don't speak on behalf of one to the other.
- Sometimes the process of mediation can take considerable time.
- Avoid 'I win–You lose' endings at all costs.

 See also: 42-44, 238, 270

How to overcome problems at meetings

As a manager you are often required to chair meetings. To be successful, you will need to keep your own involvement to a minimum, foster interaction amongst the participants and ensure that everyone makes a contribution. There are times, however, when awkward situations arise and you will need to call upon a repertoire of responses to maintain control. Here are some of the most common problems to arise in meetings and the strategies for handling them...

1 When the discussion gets off the track...

Meetings sometimes get bogged down in time-consuming, irrelevant discussions which lead nowhere. To get the meeting back on course, you can:

- re-focus the discussion by indicating how the group has strayed from its real objective.
- summarise the discussion to date and link progress to the objective.
- bring the discussion back into line by posing a question that relates to the agenda topic.

2 When the participants begin to lose interest...

Often caused by lack of concrete short term goals or successes, flagging enthusiasm can be halted in a number of ways:

- Propose a success-guaranteed, short-term task to be completed.
- List the achievements of the group to date.
- If the current topic lacks interest, introduce a related theme to encourage a more active response.
- If the group suspects that their recommendations will not be implemented, convince them that worthwhile ideas might well gain acceptance.
- Check whether the individual participants are still in agreement with the group goals.
- If participants believe that a decision has already been made, assure them that solid arguments from an interested group could amend or reverse the decision.

3 When there is uneven participation...

Reluctant speakers can be brought into the discussion by asking questions that you know they can answer. Compliment them for the views offered. Or, ask everyone, in turn, to express an opinion, before anyone else can discuss or evaluate the issue further. Restrain the talkative participants tactfully.

4 When the meeting gets overheated...

Your task here will be 'to stop the warring parties shouting at each other from the mountain tops and to bring them to the valley floor again to talk'. To this end, here are some strategies:

- Summarise the hot issue, giving combatants a chance to calm down.
- Appeal to other members, thus using

group pressure to restore order: 'Can anyone suggest a way of getting John and Tony out of their no-win situation?'
- Propose that the current issue be dropped for a while and another line of discussion be followed.
- Call firmly for order, stating that progress is being hindered through lack of objective or reasoned discussion.
- Call for a short coffee break.

5 When someone is distracting the group...

If you have a pencil-tapper, paper-shuffler or side-talker, then, chances are, they're unaware of their disruptive action, they've lost interest, they don't feel included, or the issues being discussed are irrelevant to them. Try:
- looking directly at the offender,
- calling the offender by name and asking a relevant question,
- tackling them in public, indicating that they're making it hard for the group to get through the agenda items, or
- taking a coffee break, and tackling the offender in private.

6 When an argumentative person takes over...

Often if a participant continually argues over minor points, the group itself will sometimes show its impatience. Failing this, you could:
- indicate that, unless positive and helpful contributions are made by all present, nothing worthwhile will be achieved,
- give him/her a job to do – taking minutes, recording on whiteboard, and so on,
- break the meeting into small work-groups, giving the offender a small group only to distract,
- speak with the offender outside the meeting or over coffee.

Management Memo

Meetings, like voyages through space, are strewn with potential problems. The Chair and members, their sights set on a successful conclusion, have to guide their way through uncharted territory with care without at the same time becoming too obsessed with the difficulties, as to do so will only slow down their progress and even perhaps distract them to such an extent that what they fear worst will happen – the meeting will self-destruct somewhere in space. [117]

7 When a long-winded participant dominates...

Here are four suggestions to quieten the long-winded, repetitious speaker:
- Politely interrupt the speaker and suggest that it's now time to hear from other participants.
- Say: 'I think we've been over this before.'
- Fire a difficult question at the offender to halt the flow of words.
- Discuss the problem in private with the talkative one.

8 When two people dominate discussion...

When two members engage in a back-and-forth contest, leaving others to look on, close the debate by:
- summarising their arguments: 'Is this what you two are saying...?'
- involving other participants: 'What do the rest of us think about this...?', 'So, everyone, is there some way all this helps us solve the problem at hand...?'.

9 When a decision can't be reached...

Make it easier for participants to evaluate the pros and cons of the issue:
- Summarise the discussion to date.
- Restate the issue or question clearly.
- Reiterate the goals or decision criteria.
- Take a short break or postpone the decision until next meeting.

 See also: 42-44, 90

How to deal with disruptive individuals at meetings

Meetings can be ruined by disruptive individuals who seek to dominate proceedings at the expense of others. They frequently interrupt, emotionalise issues, sidetrack, challenge, complain, engage in repetitious speechmaking, threaten, discount the contributions of others, personalise issues and, in general, throw a pall of gloom over proceedings. Managers must minimise such disruptions and regain control over the meeting. Here are several strategies for handling the disruptive individual...

1 Create a smaller audience for them.

Give the disruptive person only one or two people to influence. Break the meeting into smaller groups and instruct each group to generate statements by consensus, prior to reporting back to the full meeting.

2 Get the disruptive person to confront the issue.

Ignore the content of the individual's remarks and openly tackle the problem. For example, say: 'You seem particularly upset or disruptive today, John, especially when someone disagrees with you. Is there any way the rest of us can help you?' Alternatively, gain the support of the rest of the group by becoming a little emotional over the issue, by stating precisely how you feel about the situation. For example, say: 'As chair, I feel powerless to accomplish anything at present and I get upset when you try to take over the meeting by attempting to ramrod through your own ideas. John, is there any way we can get this meeting back on to an even keel?'

3 Attack the content.

Two strategies could be adopted here to force the person to focus on content rather than disruption:

- Turn the disruptive individual's questions, pessimistic asides, or veiled threats into statements. This procedure will force him/her to take responsibility for expressing a point of view rather than blocking the proceedings through questions or disparaging comments.
- Reduce his/her position to absurdity. Adopt an interrogative stance to get to the bottom of the argument being put forward.

4 Pre-plan the meeting to defuse the disruption.

Various tactics can be used if you know in advance that the disruptive individual will be in attendance:

- Give the disruptive person a special task or role in the meeting, such as recording the views of others on the whiteboard, or taking the minutes.
- Structure the meeting to include frequent discussions of progress to

date, thereby providing the opportunity for others to highlight the lack of progress due to this person's ongoing obstruction.

- Remove all vulnerable items from the agenda.
- Get others on your side before the meeting, by seeking their support in dealing with the anticipated disruption. For example, they can be asked to refuse to argue or to openly confront the disruptive behaviour either verbally or through expressive non-verbal reactions.
- Seek the cooperation of the disruptive individual beforehand. Ask him/her not to argue.
- List disruptive behaviour as an item early on the agenda for discussion.

5 Suggest a role reversal.

If the going gets tough during the meeting, try these suggestions:

- Invite the disruptive individual to argue the other side of the issue for a while.
- Have the disruptive person summarise proceedings to date.
- Offer to vacate the chair in favour of the difficult individual.

6 Listen – just in case.

Don't ignore altogether what is being said because the disruptive individual, despite the objectionable approach, may indeed have something useful to contribute to the meeting's outcome.

> **Management Memo**
>
> Disruptive behaviour in meetings is almost always a symptom of some defect in the organisational system that the meeting is designed to support. Leaders need to consider that every meeting is, in reality, an organisation development session, and they should facilitate it in ways that isolate problems for remedial action. [118]

7 Pull the plug.

When all else fails, and the meeting's real purposes are being thwarted, drastic measures may be called for:

- Indicate how the meeting has degenerated, and that the only way out of the chaos is for closure and order. Adjourn the meeting.
- Leave the meeting, disavowing any responsibility for what has occurred; remembering, of course, that follow-through action will be required on your part if you are to retain your authority.

8 Remain calm and in control.

All of these strategies demand that the chairperson adopt a cool, unruffled exterior. If you become angry, you give away power. Remember also that, if you use these tactics as part of your routine style, then there is a danger that you could prevent less bold participants from contributing to the meeting for fear of being confronted by you.

See also: 74, 222, 244

How to help your staff with their personal problems

Staff members with a personal dilemma usually work at their problem and it goes away. But sometimes the problem is not easy to cope with and, as an effective and sympathetic manager, you will frequently be approached by people with problems which might be affecting their work, or home life, or both, and they will ask you for help or advice. Here are some useful suggestions which will assist you to improve your counselling skills...

1 Set aside time for the counselling session.

Once the need for a counselling session has been identified, you have to create the right conditions: in private, unhurried and free from interruption. Put the employee at ease by offering coffee and assurances of confidentiality. Make the setting relaxed by getting out from behind your desk; sit next to the person. Take time to establish rapport early because the success of the session will depend on it.

2 Encourage your colleague to talk.

Use the early stages of the session to let your colleague talk. Often all she/he needs is someone who will take the time to listen. Here are some techniques to encourage your colleague to unwind:

- **Listen actively**. Show that, at the moment, your colleague is the only one that matters. Maintain eye-to-eye contact. Demonstrate that you're listening by making 'listening' noises ('yes' and 'uh huh'), and by rephrasing and summarising.
- **Be reassuring**. Be supportive. Show that you are not being critical or disapproving... 'Yes, I can see how that would get you down...'
- **Ask questions**. Relevant, open-ended questions will make it easier for your colleague to open up, to disclose feelings, and to begin exploring and clarifying the problem... When did you first become aware of the problem? How does the problem affect you? When do you tend to get most angry? Why do you think the problem has arisen? Who else is involved? Such questions should emerge gradually as natural stepping stones during the session.

At this stage your behaviour is the key to a successful session. Encourage your colleague to talk freely; be empathetic, non-judgemental and supportive.

3 Observe.

Your colleague's oral communication will provide you with other useful insights into the person and the problem. The speech will be full of hidden meanings. Take particular note of tone, expression, mannerisms and body language.

4 Isolate the problem.

Having now worked your way through the web of emotions and detail, and having extracted the facts of the case through listening and questioning, the core of the problem can now be identified and the possible cause isolated. The one person who has the answer to the current problem is the person you are counselling. It is up to you to assist your colleague to identify the true problem – not just the symptoms – and to analyse the situation.

5 Work towards a solution.

Remember: your aim is for your colleague to arrive at his/her own solution. Consider these approaches:

- Ask questions to solicit ideas and explore various ways of solving the problem, e.g. 'So what are the options?', 'How can we improve the situation?'.
- Make your suggestions as tentative questions, e.g. 'I guess one option might be...', 'What about trying this...?'.
- Make encouraging noises but avoid being specifically approving or disapproving of anything.
- Get your colleague to work through the pros and cons to come to a decision, unaided by you, on the best course of action.
- Your aim is to help and support your colleague, so accept his/her solution even if you may have a few misgivings. The solution must be seen by your colleague as his/her own.

Management Memo

You will often need to give people clear guidance and advice when you are counselling them. You may even need to take action to solve someone's problem – say by separating two workmates who are not getting on together. Such a 'directive' approach is not always appropriate. Much in favour nowadays is the so-called 'non-directive' approach. Instead of telling the person how you think they should solve their problem you let them talk it through, come to terms with it and find their own solution. In many cases the person will be unable to 'own' and implement a solution unless it is the one they feel they have arrived at for themselves.

You will need to decide which approach is more appropriate to the problem of the particular person you are counselling. [119]

6 Follow up if necessary.

If your colleague seeks specific help with implementation, agree to do so. If the problem does not appear to be resolved down the track, another meeting may be warranted.

7 And finally...

These points should also be considered:

- If you feel insecure as a counsellor, don't try. Suggest that your colleague approach a more qualified person.
- Counselling, to be effective, must be conducted carefully and sensitively.
- Never betray a confidence, or your colleague will never trust you again.
- When you counsel a colleague, you must suspend your professional authority persona for the duration.
- Always stay calm and do not show any dismay at what is revealed.
- A 30-minute counselling session should be adequate. A longer interview could be protracted and purposeless.
- Seek professional help if required.

How to deal with difficult people

According to Napoleon, the driving force behind behaviour is either self-interest (people doing what they do principally in their own interests) or fear (doing what they do because they fear the consequences, perceived or otherwise, of not doing something). That's what makes managing others a unique activity because outward expressions of such basic drives differ from person to person. Most people are easy to get on with, but some difficult individuals will require that we dig deep into our people-skills bag...

1 Know why some people are difficult.

If Napoleon can be believed, the main motivation of difficult people is fear: fear of loss, of embarrassment, ignorance, inadequacy, and so on. Although fear is a natural phenomenon, you are not to know its cause; that is, what is it that individuals are fearful of. To complicate the matter further, individual behaviour changes according to context; an aggressive person at work may be a gentle, loving parent at home, or a person you find shy may be open and out-going in the company of others. When people display behaviours you identify as being difficult, ask yourself these questions.

- What is that person afraid of?
- Where did he or she learn that behaviour?
- What response do I need to achieve the outcomes I want?

2 Be familiar with difficult behaviour types.

Most organisations have difficult employees in varying numbers and degrees, but the most common types include:

Extra-sensitives – desiring their own space and rarely taking risks.

Fuss pots – taking an eternity to produce top-quality results.

Excuse-makers – using any reason to account for their poor performance.

Deadline-missers – leaving things until (after) the last minute.

Can't-doers – insisting 'we've always done it this way' to avoid change.

Careless-cavaliers – believing that near enough is good enough.

Lazy-loafers – doing just enough to get by.

Pig-heads – resisting change by locking into one way of doing things.

Thin-skins – overreacting to anything that sounds like criticism.

Shrinking-violets – avoiding social contact at all costs.

Big-bullies – seeking power by throwing their weight around.

Grim-reapers – expressing dissatisfaction with self and the environment.

Nit-pickers – finding fault, no matter what.

Cross examiners – questioning everything.

Chatter-boxes – talking about little or nothing to anyone who can be cornered.

Know-it-alls – being closed to others' information.

Snail, *mule* and *clown* metaphors may be used to describe other types.

The list is limited only by your experiences in dealing with people. *Sexual harassment* and *substance abuse* also pose difficulties and are dealt with separately.

3 Embrace key behaviours.

Different types often require different responses from management, but there are some useful management maxims common to most behaviours…

- Behaviour that is reinforced, rewarded and recognised is likely to be repeated.
- Behaviour that is not reinforced, rewarded and recognised is likely to diminish gradually.
- You don't have to be liked by everyone; that's only your ego getting the better of you.
- Make sure people are aware of acceptable standards – all customers won't want a 'Rolls Royce' version.
- Performance should be clearly monitored; employees should know when you expect greater effort.
- Pressure brings out the worst in people. Control the flow of work or employees will feel snowed under and react accordingly.
- You must follow up on promises.
- Ensure communications are clear, open and made available to everyone.
- Acknowledge contributions in ways that are valued by the individual.

4 Avoid the pitfalls.

There are definite 'no-nos' in dealing with difficult types. If people are…

Aggressive, don't argue. Encourage them to look at a proposal from both sides.

Shy, don't force them into things. Get to know them so they feel comfortable in your presence.

Slow, don't be overbearing. Be more patient and negotiate tighter deadlines.

Negative, don't get involved in their discussion. Present a reasonable optimism by asking for a worst-case scenario or using a lesser-of-two-evils argument.

Obsessed with detail, don't get into a debate about quality. Emphasise overall objectives and suggest a logical step-by-step approach.

Lazy, don't try to push more work onto them. Assign them more challenging tasks and monitor progress.

> **Management Memo**
>
> If we select people cavalierly, let them wander around in a disoriented state, assign them to someone who hasn't made a contribution to management in ten years, don't match their skills with the demands of the job, give neither encouragement nor opportunity for new learning, provide no feedback, allow no avenues for personal problem handling, and make no effort to match rewards to performance, the result is guaranteed. [120]

5 Identify new behaviours and skills you'll need.

The one behaviour you have most control over is your own. To become more skilled in dealing with different types of people, you'll need to increase your level of flexibility. Some of your new skills may be patience, assertiveness, reframing, authoritativeness, listening and self-confidence. When you're in control of your actions, your level of personal power greatly increases, reducing the nature and number of difficulties confronting you.

 See also: 74, 222, 240

How to comfort a grieving employee

The death of a close relative or news of a terminal illness in the immediate family can be the source of considerable emotional strain for an employee whose work habits and performance are usually affected. It is also a difficult time for the person's manager and co-workers. But by providing a supportive climate, a manager can help the employee through this difficult period by considering the following points...

1 Discuss any crisis in private.

It is important that the employee feel at ease and able to talk openly and frankly with you, so choose a comfortable and non-threatening setting for any conversation.

2 Be empathetic.

The impact of a personal loss can be traumatic. An employee can exhibit a range of emotions: shock, disbelief, numbness, disorientation, denial, helplessness, guilt, anxiety, fear, anger, a sense of futility. In all discussions, you must be aware of such possibilities. Listen attentively, repeat and reflect the emotions revealed to you, and ensure that the employee feels free to ventilate any built-up emotions in your presence. Empathy fosters openness and trust. Help the person identify and express feelings. Reassure your colleague that these feelings are natural, will ease with time, and help them to become aware of the ways they got along before the loss, trauma or onset of the terminal disease.

3 Demonstrate your support.

Discuss with your staff member strategies for providing support at this critical time. For example,

- Reveal how you might be able to bend the rules for the employee during these difficult days.
- Work with the employee to list ways of accommodating any problems during this time. 'Forget about your project while you're away. We'll take care of it.' or 'Would you like me to call anyone for you?' or 'We'll ease your work load for the next few weeks by sharing it around the office' may be all that the employee needs to hear from you.
- With any particular difficulties, a problem-solving approach is a useful counselling technique; your organisational and decision-making skills will prove useful here.
- Seek the views of the employee. Have your staff member suggest what levels of performance can be expected from him/her at work during this period. Find time to discuss these anticipated needs.

4 Provide advice on available resources.

Where necessary, refer the employee to specialised counsellors and supporting agencies within your organisation and the community. Make the employee aware of your company's policy with respect to compassionate leave and the like.

5 Seek progress reports.

From time to time and as appropriate, show your interest, concern and support by asking how the patient is progressing and how the employee is coping under the circumstances. In so doing, you are also gathering information which reveals how the employee is handling the work situation and what other action you might need to take in the workplace.

6 Don't be afraid to raise the subject.

There is a tendency for fellow staff members to avoid the grieving employee during this difficult time. Often, however, the employee would prefer the opposite. So, if the opportunity arises, don't be reluctant to bring up the name of the terminally ill or deceased person with the employee. Be prepared to listen to his/her stories about the loved one, even though you may have heard them before.

7 Keep other employees informed.

Within the constraints of confidentiality, keep other appropriate staff members informed.

Management Memo

Discussions with troubled employees require sensitivity on the part of a manager. The worker needs to feel that his or her company and manager will be supportive during this period... The employee will remember your good faith efforts, and this recollection and the assurance of a supportive climate may well increase the employee's loyalty to the company and commitment to do a good job. [121]

Your staff are perceptive and they will notice if you are supportive, sincere and caring. Your sensitivity will foster positive feelings and loyalty among staff.

8 Expect grieving to be a long and difficult process.

The scope of 'normal' grieving behaviours is wide and people grieve in different ways. If the loss is significant, the adjustment in rebuilding one's life will usually be a painful and quite lengthy process. Even with considerable support during those first few weeks, the healing process can take years. It is important, therefore, to accept that grief can be a slow process and that during this time a wide range of behaviours, symptomatic of grief, can be considered normal. However, if the individual is particularly or persistently distressed – for example, severe depression, agitation, fear, guilt, memory gaps, disorientation, self-neglect, disturbed sleep, inability to function normally and drastic personality changes – or does not have a strong emotional support network in place, then referral to specialist counselling or a support group may be of assistance.

How to deal with complaints

The way that managers deal with complaints or grievances can make the difference between satisfied, cooperative complainants and those who end up being a constant source of irritation and trouble. Your response to complaints must demonstrate two things: your interest and willingness to get involved, and your commitment to a fair deal for everyone. Here are some basic principles which will leave complainants with positive feelings about how you've handled their concerns...

1 Show your concern and remain calm.

Complaints are important to the aggrieved, so give them a chance to let off steam and to express their feelings. If they have a problem, you might have one too. It's okay for them to be upset, but you need to remain calm, in control, tactful and ready to respond.

2 Be objective.

Your job is not to judge – the issue is not really about who is right. The complainant is simply seeking satisfaction. You must make it clear that you are interested in the problem and are concerned with fair treatment. Often the opportunity to complain is just as important to some people as any resolution of the issue.

3 Be prepared to listen.

Every story has at least two sides, and you are about to hear one of them. Listen to, and empathise with, the complainant. This not only shows respect, it may also enable you to find out what is the real problem, including any hidden agenda, and the depth of feeling associated with the complaint. Your considered response will demonstrate that you have taken the matter seriously. If you are particularly busy at the time, make an appointment to meet within a day or two. Never allow people to gain an impression that you're not interested.

4 Assemble the facts.

Although you will want to avoid any escalation of the perceived problem, you should resist making a decision until you've probed for the facts. Complainants may attempt to minimise their part in a problem by selectively omitting certain details, so search beneath the surface to understand what is involved without trying to manoeuvre them into admitting the complaint is unfounded. Finally, state your interpretation of the key issues and allow the complainant to clarify where necessary. Effective handling of the complaint at this early stage could avoid complications later.

5 Direct the complainant to the right person.

Sometimes the best help you can give complainants is to put them in touch with the person who can help to solve their problem. You should make the necessary arrangements for discussions to take place.

6 Use creative techniques.

Complaining is a form of attention-seeking. By understanding the complainant's motivation, you will be able to adopt an appropriate strategy; for example:

- *Passivity.* Respond when you're ready; just sit; let the complainant exhaust the verbal tirade to the point of repetition before responding.
- *Positive reframing.* Change negatives to positives. Whatever someone complains about, counter with a good point. You might get the complainant to stop and think, even back off.
- *Monkey manoeuvring.* Avoid taking care of other people's monkeys by asking them, 'What are *you* going to do about it?' or 'Do *you* have a workable solution?'

7 Adopt and follow a grievance procedure.

If you have ISO 9000 certification, you will have in place documented procedures and accompanying work instructions for reporting and handling 'non-conformances', including complaints. If not, develop procedures for handling complaints and educate employees and customers about those procedures. Though not every complaint will require strict adherence to formal, documented procedures, you can't afford to ignore a grievance or complaint.

Management Memo

There's not much use in paying attention to people and listening to their complaints unless you honestly do care about them, unless you really do want to help them, unless you won't feel right until you do. I can't tell you how to do this one; it has to come from inside.[122]

8 Address the complaint; advise of the decision.

It's safe to assume that anyone coming to you with a complaint or grievance would like a direct answer. Either give it in clear, definite, understandable terms, or guarantee a response by a certain time. If further time is required to investigate, unanticipated delays should be communicated to the complainant. Once you've made your decision, tell the person yourself. Any misunderstanding can be clarified at this point. Though complainants may not always agree with your decisions, they should understand that their complaints were given very serious consideration.

9 And don't forget...

Other important points worth remembering include:

- Avoid 'off-the-cuff' remarks.
- Practise patience.
- Concede any point that you can.
- Admit any errors.
- Never laugh off a complaint.
- Help people to voice their complaint.
- If you're at fault, admit it, apologise, take steps to ensure it won't recur, and move on.
- Alert your superiors if you feel the grievance could escalate.
- Review your procedure to see if you could have handled the process better.

See also: 388-390

How to keep contact with hard-won customers

If every sale you make had to be made to a new customer or client, you'd soon buckle under the weight of it all. Whether you're offering a service or selling a product, repeat business is the best business – it allows you to build on contacts you have already made. The really productive and satisfying relationships, in business as in life, are the ones that last, and usually they take a little work to remain so. Here are some of the ways you can build long-lasting client relationships.

1 Make a contact soon after the initial sale.

The key to holding customers is to give superior customer service. Remember when you bought a washing machine and the sales person said to you that this is the cycle, this is the switch, and this does something, and this does something else? When you got the machine home, chances are you probably forgot just about everything that was said. Imagine how nice it would then have been if the sales person had rung to ask you how the machine was going and to refresh your memory with user instructions…

The message is clear. A day or two after you make a sale, make a brief phone call to your customer to check that everything is in order. If there's a problem, do something about it immediately.

2 Make a second contact two weeks after the sale.

A fortnight later, make another telephone call. This is not a courtesy call. Its purpose is to check once more on the customer to ensure that she/he is having no problems with the product or service. Attend to any concerns immediately.

3 Stay in regular contact.

During the year, give customers a call for no reason other than to touch base with them. This is an important part of relationship building, demonstrating to customers that you value them as individuals. If you feel apprehensive about giving them a call, it could be an indicator that the relationship needs working on. Find out what they like and don't like – an initial discussion of their individual interests is a useful entrée into a conversation on matters of business.

4 Take an interest in family successes.

Your customer's favourite pastime is likely to be family and the achievements of its members. Get to know those areas of interest or expertise and find opportunities to recognise their achievements. Monday's papers usually record results of weekend activities that may have involved members of the family. Your recognition of those achievements will enhance your relationship with the customer.

5 Encourage customers to contact you.

Show you care by giving your home and mobile numbers to customers. Let them know that you don't consider it an imposition if they call you outside of business hours. Research indicates that your chances of successful sales are increased fourfold when the customer calls you.

6 Drop in when you're in the area.

Help customers to see that you have an ongoing interest in them and their businesses. Rather than plan the minimum number of times you must make face-to-face contact with customers, exploit every opportunity to increase your contact.

7 Keep them informed.

Write to inform your client about any new product or service, or just send a brochure with your business card attached. Often bulletins and other readings that come across your desk are likely to have applications for some individual customers. Mail or fax them copies, attaching a personal note. It's often those little things that will make the biggest difference.

8 Play Santa Claus.

Every now and then send the client a small inexpensive gift with a personal note or labelled with your business inscription (key ring, coaster, calendar, diary, year planner). Occasionally you'll receive referrals from such items. Establish a mailing list for Christmas cards or birthday greetings.

> **Management Memo**
>
> Everyone likes to be remembered. So remember them. Everyone is flattered by attention. So give them attention. Everyone values reliability and trustworthiness. So be reliable and trustworthy… Show that you care about your clients, about your product and about your reputation. Do that and they'll still be talking to you in the morning. And next month. They'll probably come back to you again and again. Perhaps you will have formed a relationship for life. And wouldn't that be nice? [123]

9 Provide networking opportunities.

Many business people are too busy to devote time to getting together with other business people of similar interests. You can help by providing those opportunities: boardroom lunches, seats at the football, and so on. Customers will look to you to provide networking opportunities – and remember you for it.

10 Develop your own after-sales strategy.

Using some of the above ideas, establish a follow-up action plan of your own. Keep an after-sales diary. As soon as you make a sale, record when you intend to contact your new client and what type of contact you intend it to be. Make subsequent entries in accordance with your follow-up strategy. Selling never finishes with the sale!

How to hire a consultant

The decision to hire an outside expert to help your organisation in a specific area is always an important step. Although good outside consultants can provide you with invaluable service, the big hurdle is actually selecting the right person for the job. There are consultants, and there are consultants, and they can also be expensive so, in choosing one, always remember to apply the well-proven caveat: 'Let the buyer beware!' As well, the following advice will prove helpful...

1 Know exactly why you are using a consultant.

External consultants are brought in for a variety of reasons: to solve problems, give advice, perform specialised services, inject expertise that the organisation currently lacks, bring about change, and so on. Presumably no one in your organisation possesses the required knowledge or expertise and, for that reason, you are prepared to pay for this short term service. Consultants are usually able to see the wood through the trees, are usually seen by employees as being more credible and impartial, and their recommendations are often more readily accepted by the rank and file. But remember this key point: the consultant's job is to provide you with the best advice to enable *you* to make the final decision.

2 Identify your needs and what you want from the consultant.

To consider using a consultant, you must first take the time to determine the following:

- Why are we using a consultant? Identify a problem or a need. In this regard, remember that it is important to define your problem in enough detail to target the kind of consultant you'll be requiring. And be warned: in the process of defining, you can also fall into the common trap of dictating, or partially stating, a solution to the consultant. Never use consultants to substantiate preconceived points of view, practices or ideas. Simply determine the problem you want solved and set about hiring an expert to find the best solution.
- What are the specific areas of the project or effort the consultant will work on?
- What are your expectations of the consultant?
- How will the consultant's performance be evaluated?
- Who will be working with the consultant?
- What are the roles of those working with the consultant? What is the role of the consultant?
- What is the timetable for the project?

3 Shop around.

Finding the right consultant means playing detective: some are self-employed, some are associated with large consulting firms, others are affiliated with universities. Don't accept any old consultant who comes along. Be wary of those offering standard or prepared packages which might not be able to meet your specific needs. Check out the Yellow Pages, your network of colleagues, directories of consultants in libraries or on the internet, professional or technical associations and universities.

4 Screen potential consultants.

Matching the right consultant with the task at hand is the key to success. If necessary, call tenders from two or three firms and seek details on such criteria as:

- technical competence and training
- ability to carry out the task
- back-up available
- recent experience on similar tasks
- availability
- testimonials
- compatibility with your staff
- their understanding of your problem
- fees.

Don't be misled by a smooth-talking principal who is the firm's salesperson. You want doers, not sellers; so check out specifically the particular consultant to be assigned to your project. Perhaps hire on a small trial project first.

Management Memo

Independent consultants are not supermen who can pluck ailing businesses from the jaws of liquidation, nor fairy godmothers to suicidal chairmen, who with one wave of a magic wand will make all problems disappear. But usually they are highly qualified business professionals with extensive experience at the sharp end of business, having worked at director or senior executive level. In addition, they may have worked in the same or in a similar industry as the ailing company, since many independents tend to specialise. [124]

5 Be clear on fees.

Don't be shy when talking about money. Understand precisely how the fees are to be charged: by the hour, on a predetermined scale, flat fee, contingency basis, and so on. Ask what preliminary work can be done by your staff to reduce costs. Never make a decision on the basis of cost alone: often the lowest bid simply provides a shoddy quick fix. Good solutions often take time – and cost money.

6 Pay particular attention to the contract.

Make sure the contract covers the nature of the project, who will perform the actual work, deadlines, number and type of interim reports, when, where and how the final report will be made, and the total cost of the project. Don't assume related services or 'expenses' are included. Be thorough before commissioning the project: ensure all of your specific requirements are part of the written agreement.

See also: 250

How to work with a consultant

A cynic has described consultants as 'those people who borrow your watch to tell you what time it is and then walk off with it'. Maybe that used to be the case. Provided that you have wisely selected a consultant to start with, and that you abide by certain rules during the consultancy period, then the highly specialised services of an outside adviser may well prove to be one of the best decisions you have ever made...

1 Make sure both parties understand the brief.

Having hired your consultant, you should have in place a written contract that specifies the expectations of both parties: who will do what, by when, how and for how much. Written contracts vary in detail but, initially, the early interactions between you and your consultant should be characterised by explicit statements. Over time, as trust develops, the relationship may continue to thrive on oral agreements. Either way, it is essential that both parties are clear on the details of the objectives, resources, deadlines, costs, and so on.

2 Develop a sound working relationship.

You and your consultant are a team working together to solve a problem. Both parties should appreciate the collaborative nature of the relationship, being willing to exchange opinions and information freely and to make mutual decisions on the way. You have to be open and honest with each other.

A typical client–consultant relationship might build on the following steps:

- Agree on what aspects are to be investigated.
- Decide on what investigative methods will be used: study of reports and files, interviews, surveys, observation, research, measurement of deficits…
- Select those to be involved in the project to assist the consultant.
- Advise staff of consultant involvement to allay fears of probing activities.
- Analyse the data. Work with the consultant in this analysis to see firsthand what's happening and to learn the skills of data analysis.
- Have the consultant present results and make recommendations.
- Decide on what actions should be taken in response to the recommendations proposed.

3 Do not expect miracles from your consultant.

Consultants are employed to *help* solve an organisation's problems. They rarely *solve* the problem. They have no magic wand. Change in organisations comes slowly and will depend not only on the quality of your consultant's advice, but also on your ability to implement the advice.

4 Try not to become too reliant on your consultant.

A consultancy is a short-term, temporary relationship so you should remember that your aim is to work towards the successful completion of the project and then put an end to the relationship. Resist the temptation to cling too long to your expert adviser. Be aware also that some consultants create circumstances or systems to foster this dependency.

5 Insist on regular meetings.

Keep in touch with your consultant. Consultants shouldn't be left to their own devices for too long. Regular reporting to clear roadblocks and to discuss progress and direction is vital to the success of the project.

6 Be careful not to hamstring your consultant.

You will cripple your consultant's effectiveness if you place too many restraints in your adviser's path. The consultant will need to access freely all people, records and information in your organisation. On the other hand:

- Do not allow the consultant to change the agreed programme without consultation.
- Insist on making the decisions yourself when it comes to spending money.
- Ensure that the final outcome takes the form of a practical proposal which you can implement yourself or with the minimum of help.

Management Memo

Consultants are not miracle workers. Consultants summoned to fix emergencies are at a disadvantage. Pro-active clients call consultants when opportunities for improvement exist – not when the patient is dying. Consultants' fees are better spent on preventative measures rather than damage control. [125]

7 Get the most for your money.

Capitalise on the outside adviser's expertise, knowledge and skills. Minimise wastage of your consultant's time, and your money, on those components of the project that your staff can do in-house. Appoint a member of staff to chase up basic information, to liaise or even work full-time with the consultant.

8 Remember: the final decision is yours.

In the end, the consultant will provide advice and recommendations that may challenge many cherished notions. It is your responsibility to act on those suggestions that are workable – and to reject those that you consider to be, after objective evaluation, unrealistic or contrary to your organisation's best interests.

How to use a business lunch to your advantage

There's no such thing as a free lunch – or any other meal for that matter, so be prepared to pay in some way. Whether you're the guest or the host, mealtime meetings are the business of doing business. And with today's hectic schedule and work loads, combining meetings and mealtimes can be a productive and enjoyable use of your time. All you need to do is choose the type of meeting that will deliver the outcomes you want. Here's what's required to get the most from your next mealtime meeting...

1 Plan your meeting carefully.

Mealtime meetings must achieve the results you're looking for, be it in furthering business relationships and social contacts, or improving your business. Without a plan, the meeting might become little more than a social get-together. If you're the guest, think about the likely reasons for the invitation but set *your* goals anyway. While you're at it, plan your exit beforehand. If you think the meeting may go over time, and you don't want to be delayed unnecessarily, have your secretary phone you at a predetermined time.

2 Create the right impressions.

If you're the host and it's an important meeting, make contact with the restaurant beforehand. Find out the name of the waiter who will be responsible for your table. Introduce yourself and explain the importance of the meeting and that *you* will be settling the account. Tell the waiter how you would like to be addressed and provide some general information about your guest(s) that will add to positive recognition. If necessary, discuss special meals and seating arrangements. You may consider offering to pay an additional amount, say 10 per cent, for very personal attention. This preliminary planning will convey the impression of a 'club' atmosphere and that you are a valued patron.

3 Dine – to your advantage.

The meeting must make the best use of everyone's time. If you sense a reluctance on the part of the invitee to have a business lunch, provide some options – breakfast, dinner, coffee. Perhaps the other person may prefer a brief office meeting with lunch being brought in. If you're the host, or guest, try to suggest the time and place for the meeting that's most suited to *your* purpose.

4 Select the appropriate mealtime meeting.

Your goals and your guest's availability will generally determine the type of mealtime meeting you will choose. A summary of the main types is as follows:

Breakfast meeting. These can be held in a restaurant or at your office and their purpose is primarily to talk business. Their advantages are:

- you're fresh and wide awake
- a simple menu and quick service
- there is no temptation to drink anything stronger than coffee
- there is a work-imposed time for completion of the meeting.

Luncheon meeting. Lunch meetings, either in-house or at a restaurant, provide for a high degree of flexibility in timing and location. If you want a serious meeting, and privacy, have it in your office. You may even consider having the meeting first, then going to lunch. Luncheon meetings provide:

- a chance to impress with good food, responsive service and a quiet atmosphere
- a convenient and pleasant way to talk business
- an opportunity to be seen in a business-social environment.

Dinner meeting. These are more of a social event to 'wine and dine' an important client. Very few big deals are ever closed over dinner, but you can ensure you set a specific date for an office appointment or another less social meeting at which you can get down to business.

Other options.

- Try a coffee break: it feels good to take a break and get out of the office for a little while.
- Order in: if you're lunching with a colleague co-worker, why go out at all?
- Pay your own: a chance to discuss ideas and plan areas of mutual interest – and share the bill.
- Let your hair down: a night on the town for clients and their partners.

5 Keep the conversation moving.

Intersperse the conversation with issues of common interest: family, mutual friends, issues peripheral to your industry, sport or some other interest. Never lose sight of your objective, however. Encourage your guest to talk about him or herself, their business, their goals and their aspirations. Remember, the old saying, 'Bores talk about themselves, gossips talk about others, perfect conversationalists talk about me.'

Management Memo

Remember the 3Cs: your calories, the cost and the clock. [126]

6 Play your cards slowly.

Get to the point of the meeting by letting your guest see your position step-by-step. Encourage discussion, and make sure they're listening. Try to have your guest study your proposal and arrive at your most favourable conclusion by themselves, as if it was their idea.

7 Use a note pad to jot down important issues.

A blunt pencil can help a sharp mind. Don't be embarrassed to jot down some notes to act as memory joggers. Always have business cards and business brochures on hand just in case. After the luncheon, immediately write a brief note of appreciation and make diary notes on the outcome of the meeting, including dates and future deadlines.

8 Stay focused.

You're not in the business of buying people meals; you're in business to do business. If the other person seems reluctant to schedule a follow-up meeting after your lunch meeting, she/he is probably not interested in doing business with you.

 See also: 70

How to get your staff to read material that matters

Research shows that independent reading of manuals, books, trade journals and other professional literature remains the most fundamental, reliable and efficient way of keeping up-to-date professionally. Unfortunately, many of us are reluctant readers. As a manager, you can use several strategies to promote systematic reading habits in your staff members. In so doing, you will contribute to their personal development and to the advancement of your organisation…

1 Work towards bringing about a change in attitude to reading.

Reading is essential for personal and professional development. It expands our interests, introduces new and challenging subjects, and exposes us to the latest ideas, trends and issues in our field. As a manager, your main contribution will be to foster a positive attitude in your staff towards reading for their own benefit and for the advancement of your organisation.

2 Encourage your staff to set aside time for reading.

The time devoted to reading is a measure of its value to the employee and to the manager. The usual excuse provided by people for not doing more professional reading is that they simply 'don't have the time'. The way around this is to make sure that appropriate reading material – journals, books, manuals, policy documents, handbooks, references – is readily accessible *and* that time is set aside for reading it. Are you, as a manager, able or sufficiently motivated, to find ways of doing this?

3 Urge employees to be discriminating readers.

If your staff can't find the time to read sufficiently, the solution is to trim from their reading focus the unwanted and unnecessary reading matter that currently swamps the marketplace. This selection process can be accomplished as follows:

a. Determine those areas of interest so important to the work task that they must, and can only, be explored in depth and thoughtfully.
b. Determine those developments and ideas which must be kept up with on a broad and less intensive basis.
c. Compile and consider two lists of journals/books which cater for your specified interests in a and b above.
d. Decide what *minimum* combination of journals/books will best serve your needs in these two areas and focus on these only.

4 Establish a staff library.

Most employees, if left to their own initiative, are unlikely to purchase or subscribe personally to professional or trade literature. You can combat this reluctance by setting aside a small budget to maintain and upgrade a reading resource centre within your organisation.

5 Experiment with a variety of strategies.

Be pro-active in your approach to the fostering of active staff reading habits. Consider these ideas:

- Locate reading materials centrally.
- Establish a staff committee to select and purchase materials for the library.
- Scan items of interest to particular staff and distribute these.
- Display details of useful items on staff bulletin boards.
- Set aside time at staff meetings to discuss useful articles and ideas.
- Delegate some of your own essential reading to staff members for summarising and reporting back to you or to a staff meeting.
- Acknowledge those staff members who initiate discussions on issues or topics of interest.

6 Target the young employee.

Research reveals that young employees do not read the available literature as frequently as their older colleagues. Make a special effort to engender a respect for the literature in these younger employees.

7 Advise publishers of your organisation's needs.

Many journals do not always give readers the information they are seeking. Often we must read so much to find anything of real value that we end up turning away from the literature. Tell the publishers what you want. They want to know.

Management Memo

All professionals should be aware of the need for keeping up to date. We either progress or become obsolete. Growth is not easy; it takes work and discipline. Some people develop professionally by attending society meetings to learn the latest developments and to talk with able professionals. It is not practical, however, to attend all meetings of interest and there is not enough time to talk to all the capable top people in one's fields of interests. Therefore, through the ages, people have relied on studying the written word as input to growing knowledge. People must read to grow. [127]

8 Encourage your staff to write for publications.

Encourage your staff members to get involved in writing for publications. An enthusiastic involvement in this type of activity not only advances an employee's personal development and profile, but also raises the status of periodical literature in the eyes of the employee and colleagues.

9 Set the example yourself.

Once upon a time there was a manager who had three basic rules for employees wishing to see him in his office. 'If I'm on the phone,' he declared, 'wait until you hear me put down the receiver, then come in. If I'm poring over paperwork, knock and enter. But if I've pulled out my bottom drawer, I've got my feet up, and I'm reading my latest trade journal, come back later!'

Here was a manager who valued the importance of keeping up-to-date through professional reading. In what ways do you indicate to your staff the value of the trade literature?

 See also: 260-262

How to support your boss

Your career prospects often rely on how effectively you interact with and support your boss or others further up the organisational ladder. In front of every competent person there will eventually be a vacant chair and it will be your boss who will have a major say in determining who gets to sit in it. Often, your success will depend on your boss's success, so he or she will need your continuing support. Keep these suggestions in mind if you hope to support your boss...

1 Get to know your boss.

Find out all you can about your boss: likes and dislikes, quirks, expectations, interests and prejudices. By observing and by asking others, get to know how she/he likes things done. Learn your boss's style of writing, for example. Does she/he prefer a succinct proposal on one sheet of paper, or a detailed argument? Find out what's really important to your boss and make sure she/he gets it.

Or, as James Cribbin suggests, 'Study them to understand what catches their minds, stimulates their souls, and turns their stomachs.'

2 Keep your boss informed.

Keep your boss up-to-date on all matters for which you are responsible, as well as other items which you have established she/he requires. In other words, always anticipate your boss's information needs and questions. Press clippings and media releases can provide valuable data. Be sure to include a 'compliments' slip with your signed, personal but business-like message. Never let your boss hear good or bad news from others when it's your job to provide it.

3 Find out when and where your boss is most approachable.

If your boss is an early starter, then this may be the best time to meet for discussions. If your boss takes some time to warm up, the end of the day might be a better time. Learn to read changes of mood. The boss's secretary is often a valuable ally in this regard. Timing can be vital.

Is it best to tackle your boss in the office, or over lunch, after work, or even at home?

4 Deliver the goods.

When you're given a task by your boss, do you see it through to completion, or do you turn in a half-finished job with all the tricky bits left for your boss to tidy up? If you're asked to do something, do you do it promptly and thoroughly?

Successful people are usually busy because they agree to take on tasks that others find too challenging or too demanding of their time. If attracting the attention and respect of your boss is a priority, then manage your time to give these additional tasks the priority they deserve.

Don't offer promises, just deliver; don't make excuses when something goes wrong – just deliver next time. Be a tough self-critic and be persistent at delivering the goods promptly and well.

5 Focus on solutions not problems.

Just as Henry Ford is supposed to have said, 'Don't give me a problem, give me a solution', you should also adopt this approach. Make it a personal rule to provide solutions, or at least options for consideration, but never problems for the boss to solve. Bosses don't need messengers conveying bad news; they want to hear what you've done about it. So, gain a reputation in your boss's eyes as a 'doer', not a 'gonna'.

6 Demonstrate your loyalty.

When you honestly can, speak well of your boss to others, and be as loyal to your superior as you would wish him or her to be to you. Offer protection when necessary, serving as a buffer, absorbing some of the shocks when you can prudently do so. Always help your boss 'to be right'; you can do this without being subservient. If you are fortunate enough to have one who deserves it, don't be too proud to express admiration for your boss.

Management Memo

By learning to manage your boss, you can earn more job satisfaction, bring more motivation to the job and have more fun. To do this your relationship with your boss must meet your needs. You and s/he must work together in a way that complements both your styles. In an atmosphere of mutual respect, you should be able to communicate clearly your expectations of one another. You need to be able to trust one another and to be honest with one another... Your boss has a great influence on your job satisfaction. The steps you take to improve the way you are managed are part of your personal pursuit of happiness. [128]

(Remember, however, to show equal loyalty to and openness about your colleagues so that you don't earn a reputation as the boss's pet or the office crawler.)

7 Work towards gaining your boss's confidence.

If you're determined to support your boss, you should let him or her know that you can be relied on, not only to do your own job but to help your boss to do his as well. Whenever the opportunity arises, here are some of the messages you should try to get across:

- I'm happy to have you talk your concerns and problems through with me.
- I'm keen for you to allow me to take some of the load off your shoulders.
- I have certain strengths that can compensate for your inadequacies.
- I'm always available.

 See also: 258, 262

How to win the support of your boss

The art of management requires that you spread your influence upwards through the organisation, as well as downwards. If you want to achieve results and get on, you will need to gain the support of your superior. Most bosses can quickly detect flattery and manipulation, but there are other more acceptable strategies which will enhance your upward influence, and win for you the continued backing of your superiors...

1 Support your boss at all times.

If you give your boss loyalty and support, you can normally expect such support in return. You can make your support obvious in various ways, and page 258 provides details. Remember: in the wash-up, you exist to support your boss.

2 Take a long-term view.

To prove that you're worthy of your boss's support, you'll need to win that support over a period of time. It will require your continuing effort, culminating in the development of a positive working relationship. Be persistent and patient in working towards that goal.

3 Make sure your boss notices what you do.

Find ways to show your boss your strengths, your abilities and your willingness to take on responsibility. Being recognised by your boss as being very good at what you do is the best way to stand out from the crowd and win his/her support. Think about how you sell your ideas, present information at meetings, collect and collate information, interact with your boss and others, and so on. What differentiates you from your colleagues? And is your boss noticing? Consider providing your boss with a monthly one-page report of your achievements. Keep copies of these to use at performance appraisal time.

4 Try making your ideas your boss's ideas.

Present your proposals in such a way that your boss can contribute to them and thus feel some 'ownership' of them. Management consultant Derek Rowntree offers this advice:

- Show your boss how she/he can gain something of value from what you are proposing.
- If your boss makes suggestions that are at all practicable, incorporate them into your proposal.
- If they are not practicable, get your boss talking about the implications until *she/he* decides they are not.
- If your boss offers a better proposal altogether, acclaim it as such and *you* be the one to offer suggestions.
- If the only way of getting your ideas adopted is to let your boss believe

they were his or her own, you may sometimes decide to go along with this for the sake of the proposal.

The key is to win over your boss by working *with* your boss, and to gain your boss's confidence in your ability to create and develop cooperatively your worthwhile proposals, in which the boss believes she/he's played the major part.

5 Tackle conflict constructively.

From time to time conflict with your boss is inevitable. By all means disagree with your boss if you have a case to put, but don't dispute his or her authority – the ultimate decision is the boss's; nor provoke confrontation in the presence of others. It's smarter to retire to fight another day. Never beat your boss into the ground. If she/he loses face, *you'll* end up being the loser. Remember, 'in the end, the boss is always right'.

6 Gain a reputation for solving problems.

Keep minor problems off your boss's desk; sort them out yourself. If your boss must get to hear about problems you're having, make sure she/he hears about them first from you. Never let your boss be embarrassed by having to admit ignorance of a problem or crisis in your area. Whenever something is seriously wrong, tell your boss and indicate what you're doing to put the situation right. Make it clear that you have learned from the experience and that the error is unlikely to happen again.

Management Memo

Just as a successful marriage is the product of hard work and planning, a successful relationship with your boss also requires forethought and preparation... Your boss is the most critical person in your career. Whether you're fired, left alone, or promoted is dependent on your boss's judgement. Therefore, time invested in working with your boss is a good investment in your career. [129]

7 Be open, frank and honest.

Your boss needs to rely on you, to believe in you, if you are to gain his or her support. The faintest suspicion that you are not being perfectly honest, and the boss will rarely trust you again. Gain a reputation for honesty and straight-shooting.

8 And remember...

- Don't wait for your ship to come in; swim out and meet it. Look for opportunities to impress your boss and win support.
- Learn to play office politics. If you find this disagreeable, remember that those who do play the game may soon be above you.
- When your boss makes a mistake, tread lightly.
- Observe the chain of command. Never go over your boss's head.
- You'll gain your boss's respect if you refrain from spreading gossip or put-downs about colleagues.
- Help your boss look good if you want to win real support.
- Finally, heed James Cribbin's advice: 'Avoid crying on their shoulders, stepping on their toes, twisting their arms, and breaking their hearts.'

 See also: 258-260

How to deal with a boss who is a liability

Although a great deal of a manager's time can be devoted to improving the performance of staff, bosses upstairs can also be difficult to work with. Like many other people, they too can be lazy, incompetent, bullies or arrogant. Coming up with successful ways of coping with poor-performing bosses can tax the resources of the most talented managers. Here are some suggestions that will help you handle a boss you have a problem working for...

1 Recognise the problem.

There are a few perfect bosses in this world, but many are less than great performers. If you have trouble with your boss, you can try to tackle the problem only if you know exactly what your problem is. For example, bosses can be:

Inconsistent – warm, supportive, and encouraging one day, aloof, rigid and uncompromising the next.
Inflexible – unable, or unprepared, to change when it is obvious to everyone that a new direction is required.
Closed – reluctant to provide oral feedback leading others to deduce meaning from a mix of non-verbal messages.
Manipulative – getting people to 'perform' by resorting to using carrot or stick approaches to motivation, and by making promises that they have no intention of honouring.
Exploitative – continuing to assign tasks to those who never complain.
Inactive – demonstrating a lack of control of people and of projects; even lazy.

In *Never Work for a Jerk!*, Patricia King identified the really difficult bosses: scoundrels and liars, slave drivers and bullies, ignoramuses and incompetents, cheapskates and skinflints, blowhards and egomaniacs. Can you pinpoint the problem (if there is one) with your boss's behaviour?

2 Take your choice.

If you have a boss who's a liability, you have three choices: cope with the situation, try to improve the way you're managed, or look for another job elsewhere. The choice is yours...

3 Consider coping with the current situation.

You can handle this in two ways: by moaning, complaining, becoming stressed, even ill, a martyr to the cause; or by making the most of the situation, by being positive, and using the following approaches:

- *Keep things in perspective.* Make it a practice not to take things personally. Remember, in the wash-up, your boss has the problem, not you.
- *Keep your cool.* Others, too, are likely to be affected by your boss's actions, so let your responses to the boss's actions set an example for others to follow.
- *Learn from your boss.* Problem behaviours will identify for you the way *not* to do things, thereby saving

you from falling into similar traps.

- *Get as much satisfaction out of your job as you can* by doing your job well. Find other competent people in your organisation and work with them to try to absorb into the system the most destructive influences of your boss.
- *Learn to play the game the boss's way* – grin and bear it, but take a stance against unethical or rude behaviour, harassment or bullying.

4 Consider trying to improve the situation.

Some bosses may be unaware of any problem. Most would be eager to address those faults if they knew about them. Only if you have the kind of boss who's approachable, then do so, but remember, you must focus on the behaviour, not the person. Describe the problem as you see it, indicate its impact on others, including customers, and on productivity. Bosses who are committed to the organisation and its goals, will welcome your concerns and respond positively. Offer your help if you're in a position to do so. If the boss is not prepared to commit to changes, talk to other managers who are likely to be experiencing similar problems. Even talk to the boss's boss if confidentiality can be assured.

If the up-front approach is inappropriate in your situation, then consider ways of changing your boss's behaviour in small ways over time:

- *Make the most of your relationship* with your boss by concentrating on common aims and mutual gains.
- *Understand your boss.* Compare the way you like to work with your boss's style of management and find workable links.
- *Help your boss achieve common goals* by focusing on each other's assets and finding a mutually acceptable style of interacting.
- *Strengthen your people skills.* Your ability to get along with others, including the boss, should be one of your most important qualities.
- *Take a more active role to make up for the boss's inadequacies,* but always work through your boss so that your actions are not seen as undermining.
- *Be diplomatic in how you say it…* Don't say: 'You never invite me to Monday morning management meetings.' Say: 'I'd like to come to the Monday morning management meetings because with my financial background I think I can make a useful contribution to group discussions…'
- *Record everything,* especially if your boss is the type who denies or distorts what you have discussed.
- *If your boss lets you down,* let him/her know that you feel let down and why.
- *Discuss strategies with fellow managers* on how to deal with his/her undesirable behaviour.
- *Consider any machinery* that exists for lodging an official complaint.

Management Memo

By learning to manage your boss or taking the trouble to find a good boss, you can earn more job satisfaction, bring more motivation to the job, and likely make more money and have more fun. [130]

5 Consider looking for another job.

Always keep your options open but, if your situation is intolerable and unlikely to change, get yourself another job, either a transfer within the company or a new job elsewhere. Having made that decision, regard your current state as temporary. Once you have made the decision to go, make sure that your energies are focused on your next step.

How to prepare someone to take your place

At some point in time, you will find the need for an assistant who is capable of slipping into your management position at a moment's notice. In all likelihood, she/he will come from the ranks of your experienced employees whom you have identified as potential leaders. Indeed, your own promotion may well depend on having someone who can step immediately, in an acting or permanent capacity, into your key role with minimum disruption. How can you find and prepare someone for this responsibility?

1 Be aware of the benefits of training a successor.

It is astute for a manager to select and develop a top assistant for a number of reasons. Consider the following:

- *There'll always be someone to take over when you're absent.* With peace of mind, you can be absent through unexpected illness, accident or vacation, knowing that a well-trained replacement is in charge back at the workplace.
- *You'll have more time for other things.* A trained successor can take on some of your managerial duties during your busiest periods, and take care of some of those tasks you never seem to get around to.
- *You'll always be ready for promotion.* If you are given the opportunity to move up, you'll be able to guarantee there's a trained person capable of taking over your old job immediately.
- *You can devote more time to public relations activities.* Step out and improve the image of your company and yourself in the community, safe in the knowledge that there's someone capable of 'minding the store'.

2 Make the decision today.

For some managers, it can be a tough decision electing to hand over the reins of responsibility and authority for their organisation or department. But if you're in doubt, weigh the balance by making two lists. In the first, list those things that might happen if you *don't* train a successor; in the second, list those things that might happen if you *do* develop a replacement. Compare both lists, and you'll be convinced of the need to prepare for succession.

3 Know what you're looking for in a successor.

A capable assistant is most often the one whose strengths match your weaknesses rather than one whose strong points match yours: two dynamic and assertive individuals are apt to set the wrong kind of sparks flying. Make a list of the qualities you're seeking, for example, loyalty, a healthy attitude towards the job, the company and staff members, good communicator, relevant skills, experience, common sense, intelligence, a self-starter, ambition, energy, popular... With these qualities, plus initiative, your candidate can readily be taught to cope with the additional authority and responsibility of your position.

4 Select the right person for the job.

The advantage of selecting an employee from within your organisation is that you have a knowledge of his/her work over time, have access to his personnel file and performance records, and you can test his potential on some trial assignments before making your final decision.

5 Develop your successor over time.

In working closely with your potential successor over many months/years, you will find the following suggestions useful:

- *Devise a programme of development.* This could take the form of regular discussions, on-the-job practice in management, formal study, reading of trade and professional publications, frequent contact with suppliers, customers, colleagues and trade associations, and so on.
- *Outline what the job entails.* Outline what you do, and where your and his (or her) authority begins and ends.
- *Work with him on your job.* Tell him about your plans, progress, actions, projects, decisions and problems. Involve him in the daily details of these activities.
- *Ease him into the role.* Growth will come if he learns to handle the new responsibilities in small doses.
- *Don't stifle growth.* Hold a loose rein so that your successor can gain confidence. Constant checking on progress will inhibit initiative and development.

Management Memo

The most vital part of training will be gained on the job, since it is only by doing that the understudy actually learns to put to work the ideas and concepts. Since understudy training is the indoctrination of the subordinate into the supervisor's job, it must be accomplished through sharing your knowledge and experience and giving the opportunity to apply it. Such training must also include continual follow-up, evaluation of progress, and communication with him concerning growth and performance. [131]

- *Provide appropriate authority.* Through delegation of relevant roles and tasks, your assistant will develop, but only if the necessary authority accompanies the responsibility.
- *Use tried-and-tested techniques.* Coaching, mentoring, delegation, project management and decision-making are among the many techniques treated in this volume which can be referred to and applied in working with your successor.

6 Make sure you don't lose your protégé.

There are those organisations, of course, that don't take the time to develop potential leaders, preferring instead to poach from those that do. Having trained a successor, you must guard against such corporate plunderers by letting your successor know what his (or her) prospects are, and that your plans are to reward his efforts as your company grows, with salary increases, opportunity to buy into the business, bonuses, stock options, junior partnership, and so on. If you don't take care of him, someone else might.

 See also: 270, 372

How to deal with dishonest staff

Once upon a time, if an employee was caught stealing in the workplace, this would have been sufficient grounds for instant dismissal. Staff members actually caught 'red handed' were found to be In breach of their duty of good faith to the employer and termination of services was an expected outcome. But these days, industrial legislation can give employees protection in this area and employers must, therefore, tread carefully when dealing with dishonest employees...

1 Be scrupulously fair in any investigation.

Even if you believe that theft can be proven beyond doubt, a court could find the dismissal to be harsh, unreasonable or unjust unless you have treated the employee with 'procedural fairness'. To ignore this just process could mean that you may have to suffer dearly in terms of time, aggravation, back pay, damages and compensation, even continued employment, if the terminated staff member seeks court judgement on unfair dismissal.

2 Gather clear evidence of your employee's dishonest behaviour.

Remember that, for dismissal, you will need to show:

- that the theft was so serious as to suggest that the employee be no longer bound by the contract of employment
- that the employee's behaviour was not subject to any mitigating circumstances or alternative explanations.

3 Be aware of any mitigating circumstances.

Consider any underlying causes for an employee's dishonest actions. Were there any personal problems? Or major concerns with family? Or stress factors which may have affected the staff member's conduct? Courts have even favoured employees who actually showed no sense of guilt – who 'didn't realise that I wasn't supposed to take the item from the site'. So check out any underlying causes for the dishonest behaviour.

4 Put your allegations to the employee clearly.

State in clear terms your findings to the employee and provide the staff member with the opportunity to respond to your statement and to explain his/her side of the story. It is important that you encourage the employee to respond and for you to listen sympathetically to that explanation. If the employee admits to a serious offence and shows little remorse, then there may well be a case for dismissal on the grounds of seriousness and a breach of duty of good faith to the employer. Remember, 'procedural fairness' is an important consideration in this process.

5 Provide the contrite employee with a second chance.

On the other hand, if the employee admits to an indiscretion, expresses genuine remorse, and can provide a sincere explanation for the dishonesty, then this should be noted and the employee given a second chance. Courts have been very sympathetic to employees who express genuine contrition and legal actions have gone against employers who have ignored such pleas.

6 Ensure the employee receives a written warning.

A written warning that an instance of employee dishonesty has been identified and that the employee's future behaviour will be carefully monitored, should be provided to the employee. This will ensure that a further breach will make the employer's case for dismissal so much stronger.

7 Become familiar with legislatory provisions.

Forewarned is forearmed. Industrial relations legislation is ever-changing. It is important for employers to become familiar with the latest laws and requirements on dismissal. By knowing your local provisions, you will be prepared to act promptly and legally in cases of employee dishonesty.

> **Management Memo**
>
> Employee pilferage causes more businesses to close or go into bankruptcy than any other crime. Studies by the US government and by a variety of business organisations indicate that employee pilferage accounts for 38 – 75 per cent of business losses. I need to add that business owners and management often resist the idea that employees steal from them. Others know or suspect it but ignore the problem, believing it's only a temporary situation. [132]

8 Eliminate the opportunity, eliminate the crime.

If you want to reduce the discomfort of having to deal with dishonest staff members, then take steps to eliminate, or at least reduce, theft by employees. Consider this advice:

- Acknowledge the problem. Dishonest staff could be costing you money. US government studies show that employee theft from manufacturing plants alone amounts to $8 million a day nationwide!
- Conduct regular pilferage vulnerability assessments in your business operations.
- Recognise the many techniques dishonest employees use to pilfer your assets; devise effective counter-measures.
- Create an effective inventory system that will alert you to a potential problem.
- Include your employees in the inventory control programme – participation increases awareness and responsibility.

 See also: 168, 240, 332-334

How to deal with continuing absenteeism

It is not unusual to find that ten per cent of employees account for fifty per cent or more of total absenteeism. Employees who continually let the team down by not turning up for work can cause real problems for management. Morale, productivity and profits are affected, but it can also irritate managers who are called on to make alternative arrangements to cover for employees who fail to show. Here's how you can deal with the problem...

1 Focus on interdependence.

Research shows that the greater the reliance employees have on each other, the lower their absenteeism. Employees are less inclined to take time off if they know that workmates will be affected because of their actions. To foster interdependence, you might consider the following strategies:

- Use work-teams to get employees involved.
- Involve employees in decisions on issues that affect them.
- Engage employees in project-based activities that require participation among colleagues.
- Encourage employees to tell you in advance when they will be absent.

2 Be alert for the warning signs.

Most employees will have legitimate reasons for their absence. Others will absent themselves because they feel their jobs lack challenge, or are just plain boring. By keeping in regular contact with employees, you are able to nip problems in the bud and take corrective actions.

3 Look for patterns.

Errant employees are usually easily identified because their absenteeism often follows a pattern. It may be that their absenteeism coincides with major events or is tacked on to weekends. The employee often telephones in with an excuse, but you find it increasingly difficult to believe the excuse that is offered.

4 Keep accurate records.

Maintain a record of patterns of absence because that information will be essential if you choose to tackle the employee about the problem. Indeed, you will need such evidence to prove that you didn't discipline or terminate for discriminatory reasons.

5 Conduct post-absence interviews.

Don't let suspicious absences go by without an interview. Ask for a second explanation of the absence and plant suspicion in the employee's mind that you are sceptical of the excuse offered earlier.

More importantly, you want this discussion to convey the message that you are keeping an eye on the situation.

6 Be supportive of legitimate personal problems.

Before deciding on disciplinary actions, determine if the employee is experiencing personal problems: family crisis, genuine illness, low self-esteem, a general wish to avoid problems at work, and so on. Show empathy for those who have a genuine problem. Offer help which might include counselling, additional skills training or even paid leave to deal with a personal problem or domestic concern. Resolve the problem amicably and you'll generate long-term benefits for all parties.

7 Meet formally with the employee and act decisively.

If absenteeism does not improve and you are not convinced as to the legitimacy of the absenteeism, meet formally with the employee and reveal the evidence. Do you offer another chance to improve? Do you discipline or do you terminate? Whatever the identified cause of the absenteeism, take firm action to eliminate or significantly reduce the problem. If counselling or skills training is appropriate, schedule a time immediately. If a warning is called for, make sure that you record that warning and notify the employee in writing. If possible, have the employee sign the letter. If stern action is required, don't baulk at taking those steps either. Finally, feed the grapevine so that all employees become aware of management's firm stance on unwarranted absenteeism.

> **Management Memo**
>
> Employee absenteeism is one of the most pervasive, persistent and challenging problems confronting organisations... Many organisations fail to measure the real costs of absenteeism and erroneously conclude that it is just a minor annoyance. Some companies recognise the costs, but apparently are resigned to accepting high absenteeism as they do not take meaningful actions to reduce it... It is only after absenteeism is accepted as a costly and serious problem that meaningful efforts to reduce it can be initiated and implemented. [133]

8 And also...

Consider the following strategies in the ongoing battle to improve attendance in the workplace:

- Establish attendance standards and communicate these to employees regularly.
- Reinforce the input poor attendance has on work, peers, the organisation and the individual.
- Reward good performance.
- Make jobs more interesting.
- Counsel poor attendees – absenteeism is often the symptom of other problems.
- Consider also flexible working hours, child care centres, fitness programmes, accrued sick days and incentives for good attendance.

See also: 154, 184, 208, 220-222

How to lay down the law to a staff member

Most employees act with their organisation's best interests at heart. Inevitably, however, occasions arise when managers are required to take disciplinary action against an errant employee. In such situations, it is important that the disciplinary action achieves a positive response from the employee involved. Any retaliatory, get-even, disgruntled reaction is a clear indication that the manager did not handle the matter well. The following guidelines will better prepare you for reprimanding employees in future...

1 Make sure the rules are known and understood.

Not only must you be thoroughly familiar with the organisation's rules and policies, but you must ensure that your employees know and understand them as well. Don't fall into the trap of assuming they know the rules because they once received a printed copy of them. You must make sure that employees are reminded of them from time to time.

2 Get the facts before you act.

Before you take any disciplinary action, make sure you know what happened, when, why and how. Never make a hasty decision. Be aware of the employee's past record and know how similar situations were handled in the past. Don't accept hearsay evidence or go on general impressions.

3 Know your authority and operate within it.

What actions can you take without checking with anyone higher up? What can you only recommend to higher authority? Can you send an employee home, with or without pay, while an investigation is carried out? Are there others who should be advised of any actions: your boss, an equal opportunity officer or personnel officer. You should know these things before taking any action. And finally, remember the advice of General Norman Schwarzkopf: 'Rule 13: When in command, take charge.'

4 Raise the issue in private.

Avoid open confrontation with the employee. If you censure a person in public, you can blow an issue out of all proportion and create unnecessary resentment.

So broach the subject with the employee in private, outlining your concerns and the problems created by the errant behaviour. Let the person know the general charge and the specific details of the offence. Reveal how you feel about the situation and invite an explanation of anything you might have misinterpreted.

5 Be calm, constructive, and consistent.

Discipline is not meant to be retaliatory; it should be constructive and consistent. Don't lose your cool. Be as objective as possible. If you're too emotional, postpone the confrontation until you regain your composure. What you say and how you will say it must influence the other person's response. The purpose of a disciplinary encounter is not simply to relieve your feelings of anger and frustration.

6 Act decisively and fairly.

Managers can't afford to be indecisive or wishy-washy and risk paying the price for their inaction. Laying down the law implies leaving the employee in no doubt of your feelings, concerns and disapproval, and that changes are required. The matter can be handled firmly but fairly by you, without any embarrassment and unpleasantness. The employee's dignity should be maintained at all times.

7 Offer assistance and end on a positive note.

The aim of a disciplinary action should be to teach, not to punish. If necessary, arrange for coaching and counselling. Set down what the employee should do differently in the future. Conclude by expressing your confidence that the employee will make adjustments. Work towards the elimination of any feelings of resentment and bitterness. Motivate, encourage, and communicate optimism. Conclude with a clear understanding by both parties of what changes are required. Secure a commitment to future action.

Management Memo

Although there will undoubtedly always be a certain amount of reprimanding and bawling-out of subordinates as long as one person works for another, as a general means of management it's on the decline.

This is only in part because we've become more civilised and considerate. The principal reason is that new strategies that work better in getting people to excel in their work have proven more effective. More rational organisation of work, more participation, and the breaking down of class and status systems carried into the workplace from the outside, make temper tantrums less and less acceptable.

In the light of this trend, it behooves the manager who uses rage and personal tyranny as a system of motivating others into action to have a serious look at himself and his techniques of management. [134]

8 Keep a written record.

Make notes on what happened and what you did about it. But remember, Freedom of Information legislation allows access by individuals to any details recorded about them. Your records must be objective and not prejudicial in any way. If possible, ask the employee to sign the record of the meeting.

9 Follow up.

You must follow up within a reasonable time to determine the success of your intervention. An informal chat on a friendly, positive note is probably all that is required.

 See also: 208, 220-222

How to conduct an exit interview

Employees leave organisations for a variety of reasons: a desire to pursue other career paths, offers too good to refuse, imposed retrenchments or dissatisfaction with their current positions. Exit interviews are conducted just prior to an employee's departure. They not only provide valuable information that can benefit the organisation, but also attempt to foster an harmonious end to the relationship...

1 Develop and implement an exit procedure.

Exit interviews are a valuable management practice that should occur for every employee leaving the organisation. Make sure that all employees know the importance you place on such interviews. Assign the responsibility to one person: the general manager, the human resource manager, or their nominee.

2 Plan for the interview.

An exit interview is more than an informal chit-chat. It allows an employee the opportunity to explain reasons for resigning or to reflect on the period of employment. The interview procedure should focus on a detailed list of questions designed to get the information you consider relevant to organisational improvement. General headings might include 'leadership', 'my management', 'training', 'unfulfilled expectations', 'policies', 'morale', 'customer service' and 'salary'. The employee responses will provide valuable data for use in improving operational effectiveness.

3 Schedule the interview.

You want an open discussion, so the timing and the venue will be most important. For a senior employee, for example, you or your nominee may decide to conduct the meeting over lunch. During the last week is a good time for that meeting. Tell the departing employee that you intend to take notes so that you will consider and perhaps act on relevant comments. The number of times a similar item is recorded during other such interviews indicates a direction for your follow-up actions.

4 Assure confidentiality.

When people are leaving the organisation they are likely to be open about issues that may have impacted on their decision. Assure them that anything they have to say will be held in strict confidence.

5 Find out about the former employee's new job.

This topic will not only get the person talking but also provide useful information about reasons for leaving. You will gain valuable information about what is so attractive elsewhere, as well as what is so unattractive about your organisation, and what it has failed to offer.

6 Ask, ask, ask.

If there is something you want to know, ask. The exit interview allows you to be as probing as you like. That's why you should try to ask open-ended questions (those that do not encourage straight 'yes' or 'no' answers). And remember that examples help to communicate meaning, so ask, 'Can you give an example of that?'

7 Check feedback on outplacement services.

If you are paying for outplacement, ask for a summary of the value of assistance given thus far. The employee's satisfaction with the service will also provide a useful assessment of the service being offered by the contracted firm.

8 Settle money and security matters.

Be prepared with all necessary arrangements made regarding back pay, entitlements, references and security issues. Err on the side of generosity if there are any doubts about any issues. If you are not the person to settle those matters, make sure the right person is available immediately after your meeting.

Management Memo

What could be the advantages of exit interviews? A more accurate picture of the duties and difficulties each job entails, insight into internal problems, and first hand suggestions on procedural improvements.

But there *may* be a price to pay: it may be just a waste of time. The employee may give only answers he feels are acceptable – perhaps because he thinks they may affect any reference inquiries, or because he sees no benefit in speaking frankly. Either of these reservations can be overcome by proper preparation and tactful handling. [135]

9 Offer to act as referee – but...

Guard against providing a reference carte blanche. Instead, offer to act as a referee by asking that you be contacted with specific details of the position being sought. You are communicating to the employee that you want to provide a reference of substance, but you are also ensuring that your general reference is not being submitted in relation to a position for which the employee may not be qualified. You can then opt to provide a verbal reference.

10 End the interview positively.

Employees leaving your organisation can provide a source of positive advertising, so ensure the departing employee does so with the message your organisation hopes to communicate in public. Wish the employee well in any new career choices and make every attempt to part on a friendly basis.

 See also: 160, 166-168, 228

How to terminate a person's employment

Termination – sometimes referred to as 'firing' or 'giving the sack' – is the act of concluding a contract of employment. It can be an unpleasant task for a manager, compounded by the fact that you must comply with relevant legislation, guaranteeing that a 'fair go all round' is afforded to all parties. Here are some key considerations to ensure the process is handled competently...

1 Make sure of your facts beforehand.

Termination can no longer be a matter of managerial whim. You must do your homework and make sure your actions satisfy the relevant legislative requirements of the day.

In the South African context, a person's employment may be terminated:

According to the Labour Relations Act (no. 66 of 1995):

- for reasons of misconduct (related to the employee's behaviour, e.g. absenteeism, insubordination, theft, etc.)
- for reasons relating to the employee's capacity (e.g. incapacity due to continued illness)
- relating to the employer's operational requirements (redundancy or retrenchments).

According to the Basic Conditions of Employment Act (no. 75 of 1997) on giving the appropriate notice in writing, which is:

- during the first four weeks of employment, one week's notice;
- after the first four weeks and for the remainder of the first year of employment, two weeks;
- thereafter four weeks, as well as for domestic and farm workers who have been employed for four weeks.

As a consequence of other events like the death of the employee or the sequestration of the employer.

2 Ensure procedural fairness.

It is no longer sufficient to dismiss an employee with only the requisite period of notice. You must make sure that the employee is

- given a valid reason for the dismissal,
- notified of the reason,
- given a chance to reply to allegations,
- warned previously in writing about his or her conduct, and
- given another opportunity to meet stated performance standards.

Where an applicant's termination is deemed to be unfair, the Courts may order reinstatement and payment of lost wages or other compensation.

3 Guard against unfair and unlawful dismissal.

In South Africa, the Labour Relations Act makes provision for an employee who alleges unfair or unlawful dismissal to refer the case within 30 days to the Commission for Conciliation, Mediation and Arbitration (CCMA), and in certain circumstances to the Labour Court.

The CCMA will first attempt to conciliate the matter and the results of the efforts could lead to arbitration. Unfair dismissals will usually go to the Labour Court for adjudication.

The difference between unfair and unlawful dismissal is that an unlawful termination means that the terms and provisions relating to the giving of notice have not been complied with, or that the contract was summarily dismissed for an insufficient reason under the law.

Unfairness of the dismissal relates to the procedure followed and the reason for the dismissal.

A dismissal will be automatically unfair if the reason for the dismissal is:

- on the basis of the employee's membership of a trade union (contravenes the employee's right to freedom of association);
- that the employee participated in or supported a strike or protest action;
- that the employee refused or indicated an intention to refuse to do any work normally done by a striking employer, unless that work is necessary to prevent an actual danger to life, personal safety or health;
- to compel the employee to accept a demand in respect of any matter of mutual interest between the employer and employee;
- that the employee exercised rights in terms of the Labour Relations Act;
- the employee's pregnancy, intended pregnancy or any reason related to her pregnancy;
- discrimination.

4 Arrange termination payment.

Termination payment should be prepared as part of the termination interview and is likely to include some, or all, of the following:

- Payment of work done to date
- Payment in lieu of notice
- Payment for accrued but untaken leave (at the ordinary rate of pay at the date of termination)
- Payment for fully accrued but untaken long service leave, or pro rata long service entitlement
- Job or employment protection payments, sometimes called 'severance pay', when an employee is dismissed as part of a retrenchment of employees caused by redundancy.

5 Meet with the employee.

Select an appropriate time for the meeting and a suitable private location to allow you to call a halt to discussions if things become difficult.

If termination is the issue:

- Be brief, clear, firm and to the point.

Management Memo

The law does not prevent employers from dismissing employees, providing the dismissal is dealt with in an appropriate manner – 'a fair go all round'.[136]

- Stick to the facts and information documented.
- Provide all necessary documentation – including termination payment.
- Empathise with the person, but stay firm and calm.
- Be precise as to the exact termination date – the sooner the better.

If retrenchment is the issue:

- Make it clear that the decision is non-negotiable, and that the decision was taken in view of the current financial circumstances in the organisation.
- Assure the employee that there is no implication of deficient performance.
- Communicate what severance will be paid and what outplacement support is offered. This should be made clear in a written letter handed to the employee at that time.

In both cases:

- Institute security procedures promptly. Stop access to credit cards, purchase authorisations, computers, security numbers, keys to car park, building, and so on. Terminations should be escorted from the building and retrenchments given access only to those limited areas related to any task being completed.
- Provide the person with a way to save face by agreeing on a common story that will be communicated both internally and externally.
- Nip rumours in the bud. Inform all relevant staff but respect the employee and the confidentiality of the interview.

6 Document the event.

Following the interview, ensure that all data relevant to the dismissal is recorded, signed and dated. If you have a concern that a dispute may arise, seek additional counsel from your professional association.

Managing the Organisation

Organisation is what you do
before you do something,
so that when you do it,
it's not all mixed up.

Christopher Robin in
A.A. Milne's *Winnie the Pooh*

 See also: 280-284, 316

How to articulate a vision for your organisation

It is so easy for an organisation to busy itself with daily activity and to become oblivious to its future, without reflecting, without having a vision or developing a sense of direction. Your organisation may be active in the short term but, without this vision of the future, it will lose direction, purpose and control, those essential ingredients for success in the long term. Here is one way of articulating a vision for your organisation which links values, purpose and mission...

1 Get 'vision' in context.

Visionary organisations have two distinct, outstanding features: an enduring character that transcends all other things like products, bosses, management fads and technological breakthroughs; and visible, vivid, real futures as yet unrealised. Vision helps to bring those two features to life. In *Leaders*, Warren Bennis and Bert Nanus defined an organisational vision as:

> 'A mental image of a possible and desirable state of the organisation... a view of a realistic, credible, attractive future for the organisation, a condition that is better in some important ways than what now exists.'

2 Understand the contributing factors.

In *Built to Last: Successful Habits of Visionary Companies*, James Collins and Jerry Porras identified three components that contribute to the articulation of a vision:

- *The core values*: the three to five guiding principles important to those in the organisation.
- *The core purpose*: the organisation's reason for being, its *raison d'être*.
- *A desired future* (or *mission)*: a clear, compelling, unifying and enduring statement that you believe distinguishes your organisation from others, a catalyst for team spirit.

By reflecting on these three areas, you will be well on the way to articulating your organisation's vision, a vibrant, energising and specific description of what it will be like to achieve your mission.

3 Isolate core values.

Only a few values can be considered as 'core' – those that define what you stand for – and are likely to be meaningful and inspirational only to those in the organisation. Ask a small selection of highly credible representatives from groups within your organisation such questions as these:

- If you were to start a new organisation in a different line of work, what core values would you build into the business regardless of the industry?

- If you won the lottery and decided to retire, what core values, held in our organisation, would you continue to live by?
- What would you tell your children are the core values that you hold at work and that you hope they will hold when they are working adults?

4 Identify core purpose.

Core purpose captures the soul of the organisation, why it exists. Though the purpose does not change, it inspires change. Walt Disney's core purpose, for example, is 'To make people happy'. 3M's is 'To solve unsolved problems innovatively'. Core purpose differs from a goal because purposes will never be totally fulfilled.

One way of identifying purpose is to ask selected, individual representatives what activity they are engaged in. To their response you ask, 'Why?' To their next response ask, 'Why?' After the fifth 'Why?' (the approach is called 'The five whys') you are close to identifying the core purpose.

5 Picture a desired future – your mission.

This picture of the future serves as a unifying focal point of effort and acts as a catalyst for team spirit and inspiration. Though the mission needs to be visible, vivid and real, it communicates unrealised dreams, hopes and aspirations. The mission needs to stimulate and encourage forward momentum.

Management Memo

We shall not cease from exploration,
And the end of all our exploring
Will be to arrive where we started
And know the place for the first time. [137]

To arrive at this picture, you might ask your organisation's representatives: 'Imagine sitting here in twenty years' time. What would we love to see?' What should our organisation look like? If someone were to write an article for a major business magazine in twenty years, what would it say?' Would the picture painted raise a goose bump or two, and cries of 'aha!'?

6 Now articulate your vision.

Now is the time to paint a larger picture with words by bringing together all your reflections about core values, purpose and the desired future, to create the vision – the big picture. As it describes what it will be like to achieve the mission, the description should attempt to be vibrant and energising, and capable of arousing passion and emotion.

Sony is a good example of a company with a clear vision that inspired the organisation over the decades that followed. In the 1950s, its vision read: 'Fifty years from now, our brand name will be as well known as any in the world… and will signify innovation and quality that rivals the most innovative companies anywhere… "Made in Japan" will mean something fine, not something shoddy'.

Will your vision inspire such achievement?

 See also: 278, 282-284, 344

How to develop a mission statement

Leaders of today's organisations are faced with the challenge of trying to transform their companies, to adapt to increased competition, deregulation, downsizing and the globalisation of markets. The starting point for dealing effectively with such issues is the organisation's mission statement. By considering the following guidelines, you too can develop a mission statement that instils inspiration among your staff and truly reflects their dreams, hopes, aspirations and reasons for being...

1 Understand the purpose of mission statements.

Mission statements are not simply slogans or mottoes. They are the operational, ethical and financial guiding lights for organisations. They articulate the goals, dreams, behaviour, culture and desired future of companies. A mission statement is a key component in an organisation's entire planning process. Strategically, it is a tool that defines a company's business and target market. Culturally, it serves as the 'glue' that binds the company together through shared values and standards of behaviour. It must inspire and stretch staff to higher levels of performance.

2 Form a task force to draft the mission.

Gathering the right words, setting the tone, and finding the main theme should involve individuals whose commitment to the final statement is expected. Establish a working party comprising representatives from various departments. Select wisely, for people's hearts as well as their heads are required.

3 Write a first draft.

Conduct a situation or SWOT analysis to identify where your organisation stands today, how it came to be where it is, what external forces will probably influence its future, and what it hopes to become. Be sure to get input from the CEO and other senior people. With this background, the working group can brainstorm to compile a collection of ideas that can be synthesised into a draft statement.

In preparing a first draft, bear in mind the following cardinal rules for writing a mission statement:

- ***It can vary in length.*** It can be very short (*Total customer satisfaction* – Motorola) or several paragraphs long, where the mission is supported by vision statements, values, objectives, principles or philosophies to provide guidance. Most would average 25 words in length.
- ***It must be clearly articulated.*** It should be easily understood, pithy and to the point, free of empty phrases and complex terms or jargon, espousing principles and values that will guide the stakeholders in their day-to-day and future activities.The mission of this US airline was succinct and readily understood: *The mission of Southwest Airlines is dedication to the highest quality of customer service delivered with a sense of warmth, friendliness,*

individual pride, and company spirit.

• ***It should be written in an inspiring tone.*** It should encourage commitment and energise all staff towards achieving the mission. It should be elegant, positive, colourful and inspiring. Consider Intel Corporation's mission: *Do a great job for our customers, employees and stockholders by being the preeminent building block supplier to the computing industry.*

• ***It must be relevant and current.*** It should echo your organisation's history, culture and shared values, focus on the present but look to an attainable future. But in an ever-changing, competitive environment the mission should be regularly reviewed and subject to revision to retain your company's current focus and direction.

• ***It must reflect your organisation's uniqueness.*** It should set your company apart from others, establishing your individuality. Consider the mission statement of Celestial Seasonings: *Our mission is to grow and dominate the US speciality tea market by exceeding consumer expectations with the best tasting, 100% natural hot and iced teas, packaged with Celestial art and philosophy, creating the most valued tea experience…*

• ***It must be enduring.*** Mission statements should guide and inspire for many years, challenging, yet just short of total achievement. Disneyland's mission, for example, will be forever, provided there was 'imagination' left in the world.

• ***It must cater for all audiences.*** The statement must convey your message clearly, concisely and strikingly to all your stakeholders, who universally understand and accept its meaning.

4 Review, revise, validate and seek acceptance.

A statement that is hurried, or does not reflect the input of those who must carry it as their standard into the community, will rarely inspire nor involve those whose input matters most. The process may take a few weeks, a few months – even a year. During that time you should circulate drafts to any who were not present at drafting meetings and whose commitment is required. Display the mission statement for employees to see, inviting them to add any minor finishing touches.

Management Memo

A mission statement is worthless if it does not truly inspire and challenge the energy of every employee in the same direction. Everyone has to believe the mission is reasonable and doable and not just empty rhetoric. Business leaders need to 'walk the walk' by setting the example for all employees. They don't just talk the mission statement, they become examples of the new philosophy; they live it every day. A mission statement is a key to guiding the firm in these turbulent times and to creating a competitive advantage. [138]

5 Operationalise the final version.

When you're confident that the mission statement has received and benefited from stakeholders' input, produce a final version. Hold meetings to gain commitment to the mission and to turn its message into reality. Agree on the other uses to be made of the mission, on posters, publications, business cards, T-shirts, coffee mugs, products, calendars…

6 Keep the mission under review.

Developing a mission statement is just the beginning. It must continue to have meaning for all employees. Periodically refer to it on the agenda at staff meetings, Board, and other groups. An annual revisit should occur as part of the review of your organisation's strategic plan.

 See also: 278-280, 284

How to get started on a strategic plan

There's more to strategic planning than arranging for a select few to lock themselves away for a couple of days each year to develop a document they hope will lead their organisation to new levels of profitability. Preliminary deliberations and detailed preparation involving a range of people are required. Among the issues for your consideration during this preparatory phase are the following...

1 Be aware of strategy and what it has to offer.

In the organisational context, strategy is the design of integrated management systems to effectively serve the needs of carefully chosen sets of customers or clients. As you would expect, management strategists differ in their interpretations of strategy and how it applies to individual businesses. Strategy guru Michael Porter says strategy comes down to either doing different things or doing things differently. Gary Hamel uses the 'revolution' metaphor urging that strategy be used to radically reinvent the industry. Adrian Slywotsky coins the phrase 'value migration' as the driving force associated with an entirely new way of doing business. David Maister, on the other hand, advocates a more conservative interpretation of strategy as it applies to professional service firms like lawyers and accountants.

2 Be sure your organisation is ready for it.

Drafting a unique and effective strategic plan takes effort, so be prepared for a busy and eventful time. One of your first considerations will be whether your organisational culture is one that is open to a detailed exploration of business opportunities. Exploring strategy must challenge the comfort zones of all members within your organisation – especially those at the top. If senior management is resistant to any change, its stay-put attitude will limit what can be achieved. If true commitment is lacking, gaining the necessary support will need to be at the top of your to-do list.

3 Gain the agreement of your key people.

Bottlenecks occur at the top of the bottle, so be prepared. Those with a vested interest in keeping things as they are have become experts at derailing threats to their comfort and security. They realise that their experience counts only if the future is the same as the past. Spend time with senior management and other key people to reach a shared view on strategy, what it involves, and what their contributions are expected to be.

4 Involve stakeholders.

Your discussions will focus on:

- identifying areas of uniqueness for the organisation
- deciding on a strategic position to exploit that uniqueness
- considering trade-off areas that do not contribute to that difference
- constructing a fit among all parts of the organisational process.

The process must involve as many stakeholders as possible: usually long-serving, highly credible employees' representatives and perhaps selected clients. You may decide to conduct a series of group meetings designed specifically for that purpose. In this regard, two approaches might be:

- Ask the group to identify the 10 to 20 most fundamental beliefs that people in your business or industry share. In the hotel/hospitality industry, for example, one such belief may be that everyone checks out by 10 a.m., even if they only checked in at 1 a.m., and everyone pays the same price irrespective of the time they spend up to 24 hours. Have the group challenge those beliefs as a means of identifying new opportunities. New horizons, such as late check-outs and variable rates, are explored as opportunities to help improve services and profitability.
- Or, conduct a SWOT analysis of the organisation by having participants consider the organisation's internal *S*trengths and *W*eaknesses, and identify *O*pportunities and *T*hreats external to the organisation. The compiled lists can be used later in a planning workshop to determine issues crucial to the organisation.

There are other approaches, of course, like Slywotsky's 'radar screen', as a way of identifying as yet distant potential competitors. Having completed a preliminary audit of the organisation's operations, the group should be in a position to assemble its ideas about a suitable mission (refer to page 280). A first draft could be used at the subsequent planning workshop.

> **Management Memo**
>
> To invite new voices into the strategy-making process, to encourage new perspective, to start new conversations that span organisational boundaries, and then to help synthesise unconventional options into a point of view about corporate direction – those are the challenges of senior executives who believe that strategy must be revolution. [139]

5 Report outcomes to senior managers.

Either you deliver these documented preliminary deliberations from the group to management, or have elected representatives meet for that purpose with top management, preferably somewhere other than the boardroom to avoid any feelings of intimidation. The documentation will form the basis of the next phase: a workshop to develop the strategic plan.

6 Document and disseminate results.

Share the outcomes of this preliminary process with everyone who participated. Where possible, this should be done by reassembling the groups. Indicate to contributors those suggestions you have taken on board and those you have not – and why not. Outline briefly the next steps in the planning process (see page 284) and how their contributions to that initiative will be sought. Make a commitment to report future outcomes in a similar way.

How to develop a strategic plan

If you have completed the necessary preparations as suggested on the previous pages; taking note of culture and context, and involving as many individuals or groups as possible in that preparatory process, you should now be in a position to develop a documented plan which will map out your organisation's direction for the future. The steps leading to the development of this plan, possibly conducted as a two-day workshop, are as follows...

1 Establish rapport and outline the programme.

Get the group together, welcome participants, engage them in activities designed to build trust and confidence with fellow participants, then introduce the programme outline (which follows), detailing areas to be covered with time estimates. Invite participants' comments, offer explanations, and make additions or deletions as necessary.

2 Articulate a vision.

Using information already compiled from the preliminary sessions and the expertise within the group, work through the following process which focuses on articulating a vision. This process, adapted from James Collins and Jerry Porras, and outlined on page 278, requires that you:

- isolate the three to five *core values* held in the organisation
- identify its *core purpose* or reason for being
- draft a *description of that future* in the form of a vision statement.

The process will also influence the development of a mission statement.

3 Consider existing and new opportunities.

Whichever approach you adopted under '4' on page 283, you need to encourage the group to consider the information compiled as a result of that preliminary exercise. If you used the SWOT approach, for example, consider the following:

- Invite participants to work alone to consider and record any additional strengths, weaknesses, opportunities or threats not recorded. This encourages participation by everyone.
- Form into pairs to discuss individuals' lists and compile one list representing combined contributions.
- Repeat the process in groups of 'fours', then 'eights'.
- Group and categorise the final refined lists under broad headings such as 'production', 'marketing', 'communication', 'management/ administration', and so on.

Your final list will contain those issues that are considered crucial to the organisation's growth and profitability over the ensuing period, the next few years, say.

4 Develop a mission statement.

Using the information generated and refined thus far, you will now be in a position to develop a mission statement (refer to page 280). It is likely the result will be considered as a second draft (the first draft having being prepared already as part of the preparation for the workshop). A sub-committee could be formed to polish that draft for presentation to the group at a later date.

5 Construct action matrices.

Now is the time to consider the specific actions that need to be taken. For each issue, develop action matrices detailing goals, necessary actions, individuals' responsibilities, timelines and estimated costs. Not only does this activity outline the necessary actions, but it also instils ownership of those actions.

6 Form think-tanks to overcome blockages.

If you find that discussion on a particular issue becomes bogged down, and goals and step-by-step actions are not forthcoming, you may decide to conduct a brief think-tank on the particular issue. By opening up the meeting for a brief (say, ten-minute) discussion on a specific topic, you will find that participants arrive at decisions and begin again feeling refreshed and ready to deal with the next issue.

Management Memo

A company can outperform rivals only if it can establish a difference that it can preserve... The essence of strategy is choosing to perform activities differently than rivals do. [140]

7 Link the plan to structure and budget.

Strategy must inform structure. Analysing the structure of your organisation may take longer than workshop time allows, so an appropriately briefed sub-committee may be formed for that purpose. The budget provides the funding necessary to convert plans into actions. It must be simple, straightforward and workable. It, too, may be compiled by a sub-committee formed for that purpose.

8 Document, disseminate and implement.

A final plan should be produced within fourteen days of the workshop; any longer and the exercise will become a fading memory only. If possible, reassemble the group to distribute the document. Arrange meetings of other groups to communicate outcomes to all parties. You may decide that the completion of such an important document is worthy of a celebration involving all participants. Ensure that the plan becomes a 'living' document by insisting that it is used, referred to and reviewed regularly.

See also: 282-284, 374-376, 380-386

How to develop a business plan

If a strategic plan is the 'where' of the planning process (where you plan to be at some point in the future), the 'how' is the business plan (how you are going to achieve the 'where' of the strategic plan). The business plan usually focuses on a 12 to 18 month period, setting out in operational terms what must be done. Again, the planning process, and the commitment it brings, is the key. Here are the main steps in the business planning process…

1 Consider adopting a strategic approach.

A useful strategic approach to adopt in drafting a business plan is to see the plan as comprising three main sections: the NOW analysis, the WHERE analysis, and the HOW elements of the plan…

- *The NOW analysis* outlines where the organisation is now and would consist of a business diagnostic or situational analysis.
- *The WHERE analysis* contains essential information linking where you are now and where you want to be.
- *The HOW analysis* details actions required to achieve desired outcomes.

Given that your plan will be read by organisational support persons like bankers and investors, give it a title page, a table of contents, an executive summary, and a general description of the business and its history. Supporting materials such as brochures, articles, research summaries may be included, but they must be brief.

2 Conduct a diagnostic – the NOW.

The diagnostic component involves coming to grips with the key issues in the organisation as it presently operates, referred to sometimes as an operational audit. In addition to your personal observations, you may decide to include in this analysis customer surveys, attitude surveys, questionnaires and other information gained from staff interviews. A financial analysis will give an indication of how the business is travelling. A diagnostic may be run in parallel with the development of the strategic plan.

3 Investigate realistic futures – the WHERE.

Though the business plan is a 'how' document, your process must ensure that due consideration has been given to the 'where'. Here you will need to consider vision, mission, SWOT and crucial issues – aspects which will no doubt be investigated in compiling strategic information for other components of the plan. Try to involve as many stakeholders as possible in this process. If people's commitment is required in implementing the plan, their involvement in its development should be encouraged.

4 Prepare action plans – the HOW.

Consideration has to be given to marketing, general operations, human resources, innovation, finance, and the actions required to convert ideas to actions. The action plans will indicate 'who' will do 'what' by 'when' and any costs associated with those actions. The inclusion of a financial component is essential to show the viability of the plans.

5 Provide realistic cash-flow projections.

The financials may include monthly cash-flow projections, quarterly or annual order projections, profit and loss projections, and capital expenditure projections. Cash-flow projections are based on the difference between the money that you expect to take in (your cash receipts) and the money you expect to spend (cash expenditures). In a start-up phase, cash flow will be negative but that number gives you and an investor an idea of the financial support you will need. Projections can never hope to be precise, so aim at raising 25 to 50 per cent more than what your projections indicate. But remember: excessively optimistic projections can ruin your credibility as a responsible business person. Be conservative, but don't use the word 'conservative' – it's a tip-off that you actually think you'll do much better.

6 Consider adopting a more traditional approach.

The key to developing a business plan is to make it simple, yet businesslike in its approach. The alternative traditional structure comprises five sections:

- *Executive Summary.* An overview statement.
- *Product Profile.* A description of the product: what, where, how.
- *Organisational Structure.* Present and proposed venture structure and who is involved.
- *Operational Plan.* The strategy and basic financial forecasts.
- *Appendix.* Market research data, product brochures, CVs, assets and liabilities, competitive information...

> **Management Memo**
>
> Most business plans waste too much ink on numbers and devote too little to the information that really matters to intelligent investors – the people, the opportunities, the context, the risks and the rewards. [141]

7 Make sure the plan is usable.

Your business plan needs to be a working document and be kept under regular review. Its format should be simple and straightforward, contain essential information only, and have an in-built flexibility to respond to organisational and marketplace changes.

8 Maintain confidentiality.

The business plan is not for public display and should be kept in a secure place. As appropriate, your employees can be advised of the plan in broad terms, but it is not the kind of information you would want in the hands of your competitors.

 See also: 290

How to set goals that can be achieved

Goal setting has been described as 'the inner technology of success' and is one of your organisation's most important activities. Unless taken seriously, this vital planning task will be a futile exercise, an activity that can produce several high-sounding intentions which, for various reasons, are soon forgotten. If you want challenging goals that are, importantly, achievable, then you should consider these basic principles…

1 Make sure your goals are realistic.

A goal that aims too high, or offers a great deal of risk, with little chance of achievement, leads to frustration and surrender. It's easy, for example, to say that a goal for the year is: 'To increase production by 150 per cent', but quite unrealistic with inadequate resources and uncommitted staff.

2 Keep your goals simple.

If goals are complex, it is unlikely they will be clear and specific enough to focus effort and marshal the necessary resources. Clear simple goals give your staff an unmistakable vision of what needs to be done.

3 Develop your goals participatively.

When goals are imposed, rarely does anyone become committed to them. Develop goals with those who will be responsible for achieving them – your staff. The goals become a matter of record and, through personal involvement, everyone will be more motivated to work towards their attainment.

4 Know why you have set each goal.

For every goal you set down, ask *why* you believe that goal is important to the organisation. Be persistent in getting an answer. If reasons don't measure up to your expectations, revise the goal until it warrants inclusion – or get rid of it.

5 Make your goals specific and measurable.

Goals should be specific rather than vague, and quantitative rather than qualitative. For example, rather than proposing that you should 'become more visible' around the factory or office, it is much easier to get a handle on such aims as 'I will spend at least one hour a day mixing with staff in the workplace' and 'I will meet weekly with those in positions of responsibility'.

6 Write goals with accountability in mind.

The successful accomplishment of goals usually depends on someone being held responsible for each goal. This often creates a sense of urgency and purpose, especially when personal reputation or career advancement is involved.

7 Make your goals timely.

There should be a time dimension that specifies when the goal is to be achieved. Tying a specific deadline to a goal along with individual accountability usually leads to a more pro-active approach to its achievement.

8 Write down your goals.

By committing your goals to paper, and making them public, you not only convert dreams into tangible targets, but also work harder for their achievement – or risk losing face.

9 Align goals with the corporate mission.

Remember to link individual goals to group goals, which ultimately should be linked to organisational or corporate goals.

10 Review progress regularly.

Schedule regular meetings to review progress with colleagues. Be honest and forthright in your assessments and don't expect 100 per cent achievement. If you find that a specific goal is unreachable, that it was too ambitious, then modify it to a degree that is attainable. It's a good idea to set and monitor subgoals as a means of giving an ongoing sense of achievement and keeping people motivated along the way.

Management Memo

Goals serve an important function in the continuing existence of organisations. Realistically developed, stated and implemented goals can be the guiding principles for increased effectiveness and continued growth. On the other hand, unrealistically developed and/or improperly implemented goals can lead to questions about the level of performance or even the survival of the organisation.[142]

11 Make your goals challenging.

A goal that is too low, too easily reached, offers little challenge or interest. Add 'stretch' to encourage performance. Striving for our goals takes us out of our comfort zone and causes us to grow with each accomplishment. The best goals are beyond our grasp, but within our reach.

12 And remember also…

- Goals should focus not only on ends but also on means.
- People can attend to just so many written goals. Don't go overboard.
- The total set of goals should be mutually reinforcing – one goal should not have to be achieved at the expense of another.
- Face your goals with determination and resolve to never give up. Persistence is important for achievement.

See also: 288, 344

How to conduct a goal-setting session

Managers determine what they want to accomplish and how they plan to achieve it by setting goals: for individual projects, short- and long-term strategies, production, sales... Given the importance of goal setting to an organisation, you will often be called upon to conduct regular goal-setting sessions with the participation of selected employees. This process can be readily facilitated by adopting the steps suggested here...

1 Establish rapport.

As with any individual or group process, gaining others' trust and confidence is essential. You may decide to use an ice-breaking activity, engage participants in conversations about areas of individual interest, or use a more structured strategy. Whatever the approach, you should not proceed until you feel that rapport has been established.

2 Develop an initial set of group goals.

It is important that all participants contribute, so have individuals work alone to list two goals that are important to them. Work around the group recording first-choice goals on a whiteboard, then record others not previously listed.

3 List those affected by the goals.

Identify those people who will be affected by the goals. These stakeholders are likely to be either shareholders, customers or colleagues, including members of the group. This action may require that some new goals be written taking into account this additional information.

4 Identify the motivators.

Work down the list of goals identifying the motivations for each. What exactly is the purpose of each goal? Why has it been included? If no good reason can be given, it's doubtful if it should be retained. Consult with the person who contributed the goal in the first place regarding its continued inclusion.

5 List constraints.

Constraints, sometimes called 'blocking forces', can inhibit the ultimate achievement of a goal. Such constraints may be rules, regulations, policies or any other factor that may limit goal accomplishment. For example, inadequate funding or staffing may severely limit the extent to which a goal can be achieved. Seek suggestions regarding actions that will eliminate or reduce constraints. Explore briefly the tasks and timelines necessary for accomplishing each goal.

6 Revise and collapse the listed goals.

After taking into account the motivations, constraints and timelines, you may now need to revise your list of goals, rewrite those that are considered similar, and collapse the list to a manageable number.

7 Distinguish between primary and secondary goals.

Primary goals typically relate to the products or services affecting profits. Secondary goals are achieved as a by-product of pursuing the primary goals and relate specifically to satisfaction and achievement. By differentiating between these two types, you will be better placed to take the necessary actions.

8 Collate a final statement of goals.

Record each goal statement to include both a primary and a secondary component. Each statement should be written so that as a primary goal is achieved a secondary one is accomplished as well.

> **Management Memo**
>
> Some form of goal setting is necessary for proper performance by the organisation and for the manager's job. Goals, the product of environmental analysis (internal and external), serve as guiding principles for planning, organising, leading, controlling, and change. Goals are among the major factors in the management process. [143]

9 Seek consensus for the listed goals.

Given the participative approach adopted, consensus can be expected. However, you still need to give participants an opportunity to suggest adjustments. Prioritise the final list.

10 Follow up.

Arrange for participants to get a copy of the goals as soon as possible after the session. Indicate that any adjustments to the list can be made prior to the commencement of the next session when specific actions, timelines and responsibilities will be developed.

 See also: 184, 298

How to develop a plan for action

Here is the situation: You have agreed on a solution to a particular management problem and you now want to convert that solution into a step-by-step approach for action. In simple terms, 'who' is to do 'what' by 'when'? You will need to develop an action plan, and you can be assured of success if you follow these steps during an action-planning session...

1 Express your solution as a series of goals.

Having agreed on a solution to a particular problem within your organisation, you first need to define that solution in terms of a number of goals or objectives. For example, each goal could be expressed as follows: 'For us to... , we would need to...' Record each goal at the top of a whiteboard or sheet of paper.

2 Generate a list of actions for each goal.

Use brainstorming to compile a list of actions to achieve a particular goal and record these below that goal. Arrange this list of suggested actions in sequential order.

3 Prepare a timeline.

Beginning with a time point labelled 'Now' and ending with a point labelled 'Goal achieved', build a timeline on which you allocate dates by which you intend to complete each of the sequential actions listed under a particular goal. It is important that you get both sequence and timing right if you are to reach 'Goal achieved' effectively.

4 Allocate resources.

Financial, physical and human resources must be allocated to each action step. If resources are limited, or fall short of requirements at any stage, it may be necessary to return to an earlier step and revise the action plan.

5 Identify possible problems.

Consider all of the things that could go wrong in the process of achieving a particular goal. List these problems and identify causes and suitable actions to resolve them. If necessary, these actions might need to be added to appropriate slots on the timeline.

6 Develop strategies for monitoring progress.

List ways in which the progress of the action plan can be monitored. These monitoring stages should also be included on the timeline.

7 Assign tasks.

Take each point on the timeline in turn and ask: 'Who will do what, by the date set, to bring about the specified action?' Allocate these tasks to appropriate individuals or teams.

8 Estimate costs.

Give consideration to any expenditure required to complete the tasks. All costs will have to be taken into account when preparing a budget. If funds are not available, tasks will have to be reviewed and, where necessary, revised or eliminated.

Management Memo

It has been said that if you do not know where you are going, any road will get you there, although it might well be asked how you will know that you have arrived. From the point of view of any organisation, planning is deciding where to go, how to get there and how to know when you have arrived...

Planning is also preparatory to action. Analytically at least, planning must be separated from implementation so that the major policy decisions can be taken and their implications understood prior to action.

Unfortunately this can lead to a situation in which vital revisions are not made because the planning process, mistakenly, is thought not only to be preparatory to action, but also to conclude once implementation commences. [144]

9 Implement the plan.

Translate all your information to a clean copy, listing the actions required, the person responsible for a particular task, and when that task is to be completed. Having now finalised the plan for action in specific terms, this information can now be made available to all involved.

One final comment from Peter Drucker to put your action plan into perspective. 'Sooner or later,' he said, 'all the thinking and planning has to degenerate into work.'

See also: 290, 344

How to develop policy using collaborative and consultative processes

Many companies often have written policy statements to clarify certain aspects of organisational life and to prescribe an outline for consistent and coherent behaviour by staff and management. Policies can relate to a range of issues: leave, training, discipline, incentive schemes, recruitment, and so on, but often become dated and decrepit. You can turn your policies into fresh and workable statements by actively involving your staff in the process of creation or revision – and gain commitment at the same time...

1 Determine a need for the new policy.

The most effective policy stems from a grassroots need for it. For example, concern among staff that on-site training is inadequate and neglected, creates a feeling that 'We need to do something about this'. It is often difficult to create commitment to a training policy when it is management that senses the need, and then compiles and imposes a written policy statement. When presented with it, employees are likely to become defensive and resistant to the new policy's implementation. In short, there must be a clear articulation of need, preferably from the staff members themselves, if a policy is to have both credibility and direction.

2 Establish a representative policy committee.

As well, the more a policy statement is seen as the outcome of representative review and drafting, the more likely it will be approved and accepted by the employees. The process of formulating a specific policy should be outlined to all relevant groups prior to their participation and input through representation on a small policy committee. Ensure that the members of this committee possess skills in information-gathering, managing an extensive consultative process, writing policy statements, and communicating with the organisation. The committee is responsible for carrying the development of the relevant policy to completion using collaborative and consultative processes.

3 Gather data through wide involvement.

Opportunities for wide discussion of the topic being reviewed can be instigated by the policy committee. Established strategies for encouraging staff involvement could be meetings, workshops, discussion sheets, morning teas and consultations. Group discussions should be held at times convenient for all participants and include relevant special interest groups; for example, in a discussion of a possible change to the company uniform policy, a local uniform manufacturer could be represented. Seek agreement first on a clear three to five line rationale to underlie the final policy, then raise all relevant issues: in discussions relating to uniforms, for example, consider such aspects as the existing dress code, the case for and against uniforms, availability, equity issues, relevant legislation, design, cost, and so on. Outline the decision-making process to be adopted.

Management Memo

Good policy identifies and articulates the values and the basic principles to be applied to specific needs in an organisation... Effective policy sets direction, but it does not give directions. Staff and administrators are left to apply the policy with discretion required by circumstances and their own professional judgement. Professionalism is given guidance. If effective consultation has occurred, that guidance will be welcome and professionally enhancing. [145]

4 Draft the policy statement.

Having obtained data and views from organisation-wide consultation, the policy committee should now produce a draft policy statement. Key points to consider would include:

- Ensure the statement is concise, unambiguous, readily linked to identifiable practice.
- Limit the document to two to three A4 pages.
- Group the details logically and as numbered cumulative points.
- Make sure each point can be adequately addressed by this question: 'How can we put this into practice?'
- Consider drafting two or three alternative policies to stimulate discussion and ensure that the final adopted policy will indeed result from active consultation.

5 Gain support for the policy.

A consensus policy statement should be arrived at only after reasonable consultation and debate. Publicise and promote the document through presentations at staff meetings, leaflets, or items in the company newsletter.

These are the important questions to address when considering the appropriateness of the policy statement:

- Does the policy statement convince me that the topic needed to be addressed?
- Does the statement give me a clear message? If so, what is it?
- Is the statement easy to follow? Do I clearly understand the language used?
- Is there enough information in the statement to guide me in implementing this policy? If not, what is missing?
- Does the statement cover all important issues? What other issues should have been treated?
- Are there any other documents or resources needed to help me understand the policy more fully or to implement it effectively?
- How will the policy benefit me? How can I use it?

Support for the drafted document can be obtained through resolutions passed at meetings or forums, or through negotiation, surveys, ballots or petitions. Circulate the refined policy statement.

6 Convert the policy into practice.

An accepted policy must be linked to short-, medium- and long- term implementation plans. These should outline roles and responsibilities of those involved, timelines for the introduction of the various components, and procedures for periodic review and evaluation.

 See also: 208, 292, 300, 344

How to help groups reach decisions

Group decision-making is an effective management practice which involves a group of people collectively making a decision. A major benefit is that the process increases the participants' ownership of and commitment to the decision. Helping groups reach those decisions, therefore, is a key management function that requires a working knowledge of the most popular decision-making tools...

1 Ensure the group knows when a decision is made.

There are five ways in which a group can make a decision. Agree early on which approach is to be adopted:

- Decision by unanimous agreement, with no dissenters.
- Decision by consensus. The decision has the support of the whole group, and while some may not agree with the decision, they have had their say and are happy to accept the will of the group.
- Decision by majority. The proposal attracting most votes is carried.
- Decision by minority. People agree, following their input, to allow those with greatest expertise or power, to make the final decision.
- Decision by chairperson, following input from all in the group.

The approach adopted by the group usually depends on the situation or the significance of the decision. The techniques on page 297 will assist in working towards a decision based on agreement by the majority or by consensus – an ideal group result.

2 Avoid the traps of group decisions.

Busy managers can sometimes 'push' too hard for decisions and, in the process, create additional problems. So steer clear of such hazards as these...

- Interpreting silence as consent – making a decision by default.
- Settling for majority rules – believing that a win/lose result is better than no result.
- Letting minorities decide – 'Trust us, we know what others want'.
- Accepting that those who make the most noise are the most knowledgeable.
- Accepting opinions as facts.

3 Select the best tool for your situation.

When decision-making involves having to determine the relative importance of several different issues or priorities under discussion, a choice of techniques is available:

Brainstorming** or **Brainwriting. Decisions can only be based on ideas and information. Brainstorming or its alternative, Brainwriting, is often the first step in group decision-making. It is able to equalise involvement, generate excitement, and result in a range of ideas or items for addressing the problem in focus. Refer to page 300 for details.

Management Memo

Where a meeting has to reach a decision, the team leader should make this clear from the very beginning. It should also be made clear how any decision will be made. This may be done by a majority vote or, at the other extreme, it may be done entirely by the team leader after 'getting a feel of the meeting'. Ideally, of course, the leader should seek to obtain a consensus of all team members. But when the decision is finally reached, it should be announced in such a way as to leave no doubt in the minds of those present about what has been decided. [146]

3 for - 3 against
This ensures that all sides of an issue are heard. When an issue is being discussed, the group is asked to give three reasons why the issue should be supported and then three reasons why it shouldn't.

Spend a Dollar
For prioritising a set of five to 15 issues, you need enough slips of paper for each participant to have one slip per issue. Distribute slips and have them write one issue on each slip. They have R1 to spend on the issues according to their relative importance. They must spend and record a minimum of 5c on each item. All spendings are recorded from the slips to a wall chart, and the totals, percentages and rankings can be calculated.

Multivoting
Number each item in the set requiring prioritising, then follow this procedure: 1. Choose one-third of the items on the list and discuss them. 2. After discussion, members vote by show of hands (or secret ballot) as each item is called out. 3. After voting, reduce this list by removing some items with fewest votes. 4. Repeat steps 1 to 3 on the remaining items and continue until only the most-voted-for items are left. If no clear favourite emerges by this time, repeat the process on the most-voted-for items.

Merging Priorities
The group breaks into pairs. Each pair discusses the set of items and agrees on the top two priorities. The pairs then join to form groups of four, which discuss the four priorities (although there could be overlap), and reduce the four items to two. The fours join to make eights, and again agree on the top two priorities out of the accumulating set. Continue the process until you merge into one whole group with two surviving agreed-on priorities.

Nominal Group Technique
This is a fancy name for a simple procedure designed to involve all group members. Issue the following instructions to the group participants:

Each person must think carefully about the set of items or issues requiring prioritising. From the set, each person must select the five most important items, and write them as a list on a sheet of paper. Put a 5 next to the item you think is most important. Put a 1 next to the item that is least important. Put a 4 against the item that is the second most important, then a 3 beside the next item of importance, and a 2 against the remaining item. Collect the sheets, shuffle, and tally the scores against a list of all items on a master chart. The group considers those items with the highest scores to be the most important.

Force Field Analysis
This technique helps groups to make decisions about change. It assumes that the current situation is the result of counteracting forces. One set is pushing the situation towards a more desired state (helping forces) and a second set is acting to restrain movement in the desired direction (hindering forces). Brainstorm to create two lists: 'helping forces' and 'hindering forces'. Examine each completed list to delete, add or integrate as required. Identify and underline those forces that are most important and most able to be influenced. For each underlined 'hindering force', think of a list of action steps that will reduce or eliminate the effect of the force. Repeat for the 'helpful forces'. Finally, develop a plan for action (see page 292).

How to plan and manage a project

What makes a project different from your day-to-day work is that it has a beginning and an end. To get from one to the other, a project manager must follow a sequence of steps, regardless of the task. Some projects can be highly complex activities, involving numerous sub-tasks, intricate scheduling and detailed monitoring. They can range from planning a company conference, to producing a video, to building a factory. Here then are the steps to follow when tackling a new project...

1 Establish your objectives.

Define clearly, in concrete terms, the purpose of the project. Write down the project specifications or the criteria for a successful outcome and ensure they are agreed to by all parties involved. These specifications define your objectives for the project.

2 Set a deadline.

Some projects must be completed by a certain date. Your planning will hinge on this final deadline. If you have not been given a completion date, set one for yourself.

3 Identify the tasks to be done.

List everything that needs to be done on the way to final completion. It could be a long list, but it must be a complete list. Ensure nothing is missing. If you are not sure of all the tasks, go to the experts for advice. If you do not have a complete breakdown of jobs, you will have difficulty organising the project's timeline, developing a budget and handing out assignments.

4 Organise the tasks in sequence.

Arrange the tasks into their order of performance. What happens first? What comes next? Then what? Timing becomes a vital factor: projects can have a sequential line of development (do one job before moving on to the next), or a parallel line of development (several jobs can be taking place at once), or both. Understand the sequence clearly by creating a logical diagram: a PERT chart or a critical path network.

5 Allocate a time for each task.

Using your logical diagram, estimate how much time each task will take (try estimating an optimistic time, a pessimistic time, and then take the average). Factor in a little extra time to cover delays or problems.

6 Create a schedule.

Using this information, you can now place a target date for each task on to your logical diagram. It is sometimes wise to also set specific review dates to evaluate progress and to modify your course if necessary. Remember, if you have a definite completion date, it is often helpful to work backwards from that date, providing you with an indication of how much time compression must be applied to get the project finished in time.

The creation of a horizontal bar chart might also be useful at this stage. List the tasks sequentially down the side of the chart and appropriate calendar periods across the top. Create a bar of the calendar period that each task is expected to take.

7 Assign tasks.

Delegate appropriate tasks to project members, not forgetting to allocate time to yourself for overall project management duties. Look for the full range of experience and expertise when putting your project team together. Ensure all team members are available at appropriate times, and are fully briefed as to their responsibilities and deadline dates.

The creation of a project team matrix might help you keep track of who's doing what, and to keep you from overloading some members. This matrix lists the tasks vertically, team members along the top and responsibilities below each name.

8 Establish a budget.

Project budgets are normally activity-oriented. Estimate all costs associated with each task and prepare a spreadsheet with tasks listed vertically and cost factors (expenses, labour, resources, and so on) listed horizontally, totalled at the right of each line.

Management Memo

The major responsibility of the project manager is planning. If project planning is performed correctly, then it is conceivable that the project manager will work him/herself out of a job because the project can run itself. This rarely happens, however. Few projects are ever completed without some conflict or some trade-offs for the project manager to resolve. [147]

9 Monitor the project to completion.

Supervise the progress of the project, in particular…

- *keep track of progress.* Refer frequently to the project charts.
- *communicate regularly.* Keep on top of what's happening through status reports and formal and informal meetings with your team members.
- *become a troubleshooter.* Identify trouble spots and emerging gaps between scheduled and actual performance.
- *take corrective action.* When necessary, step in to develop alternative solutions, take remedial action, and follow up to ensure your solution is effective.
- *use your managerial skills.* Check out those essential skills of motivation, conflict resolution, team leadership, meeting facilitation, persuasion, and so on. You'll need them.
- *evaluate the project.* On completion, hold debriefings to review problems and successes, and make recommendations for future projects.

 See also: 218, 292, 296

How to generate creative ideas through brainstorming

If you're short on ideas, or you want a large number of ideas quickly, then you should use the classic group process called 'brainstorming'. The process encourages divergent thinking among group members as they collectively address an issue confronting the organisation. Here are the steps to follow...

1 Explain the process to the group.

Outline broadly the brainstorming process to your group after having read the steps listed on these pages. If the approach is new to some participants, begin with a simple practical exercise. For example, 'To what other uses might a common house brick be put?' Encourage the group's creative input, with a recorder listing all the suggestions offered.

2 Discuss the rules for brainstorming.

The brainstorming process has five basic rules which can now be elicited from your group following the introductory exercise. These are:

- Keep an open mind: suspend criticism of anyone's idea.
- Let yourself go: 'free-wheel' in terms of using your imagination. No discussion of any item is permitted in the process.
- Generate as many ideas as possible: all ideas are acceptable; quantity is encouraged.
- Try to build on the ideas of others by hitchhiking.
- All ideas are visible to everyone: up front on a whiteboard or flipsheet.

3 Present the problem to the group.

Preliminaries over, you are now ready to generate ideas which focus on the problem at hand. Make sure that participants have a clear understanding of the issue to be addressed. If necessary, spend some time talking about the issue as you see it and encourage the views of others before moving into the idea-generating stage. 'Why', 'how' and 'what' questions are appropriate here.

4 Appoint a recorder.

Select a person to write down the ideas mentioned, preferably on a whiteboard or flipsheet which can be seen by everyone. By having someone else record the ideas, you are free to lead the process.

5 State the problem in clear terms and begin.

People often see an organisational problem through different eyes, so it is important to state the focus issue in terms which all participants understand clearly. List various statements of the issue at hand before selecting the one that expresses the issue most succinctly. Display the selected statement in bold letters before the group. Give everyone a minute or two in silence to think about the question, before calling on the group to begin brainstorming ideas. All suggestions, no matter how 'off-beat', are recorded and numbered for ease of reference later. Allow no discussion at this point or the flood of ideas may be suppressed.

6 Synthesise similar ideas.

When the creativity of the group has been exhausted, have participants identify statements or ideas which are alike, for example, 'Numbers 4, 7 and 14'. Compile and record a new statement which incorporates these points and remove the superseded statements or ideas from the list.

7 Group the ideas.

In grouping the ideas listed, you will find they probably form into three groups:

- The impossible: those about which very little can be done (often these are the 'off-beat' ideas).
- The unlikely: those with little hope of implementation but which cannot be ruled out completely at this stage.
- The possible: those you can address and which can be given immediate attention.

8 Give priority to the best ideas.

When you have identified the 'possibles' and eliminated the 'unlikelies', place the ideas in priority order, using one of the techniques outlined on page 296 if necessary.

Management Memo

Brainstorming is a technique often used in connection with idea-getting which has produced some amazing results. The term and its application grew out of advertising man Alex Osborn's attempts to improve the creativity of copywriters, and has been adopted wholesale by industry. Many firms report amazing success in the use of this stimulating technique, which uses the group approach to idea-getting...

Continental Can Company found some profitable savings through brainstorming the question of how to use the angle irons which came to guard corners of tin plate from the mill. Previously these had been scrapped, and sold for a fraction of their value. Through brainstorming, over 50 usable ideas for commercially producible items or money-saving uses came out of the scrap-iron piece.

Ultimately, ideas must be evaluated from the viewpoint of their value and practicality. This ordinarily falls to a few people who have the broad picture of the needs and procedures of the firm, and can fit new ideas into operations.[148]

Finally, develop an action plan to address the problem under review.

9 Consider the alternative – brainwriting.

If members of the group are shy or intimidated by the competitive or open nature of brainstorming, brainwriting is an alternative. Each member lists four ideas on a sheet of paper which is placed on a central table in exchange for another's completed sheet. Fresh ideas foster more ideas. Participants continue to add ideas to the sheet taken from the pool, exchanging it for a new sheet whenever additional stimulus is needed. All the sheets are later collected and processed as outlined in 6–8 above.

How to establish work teams in your organisation

There is no 'I' in 'T-E-A-M'. Teams are made up of people with complementary skills, committed to a common purpose, performance goals, and an approach for which they hold themselves mutually accountable. They may be established *ad hoc* as project teams or as more permanent work groups. Although most teams can outperform individual people, it's the 'people issues' that cause most of the problems. So when you believe a team is required in your workplace, consider these points...

1 Establish clear, achievable goals.

In *Why Teams Don't Work*, Harvey Robbins and Michael Finley identified that one of the main reasons for the failure of teams is that they don't know where they're going or why they've been put together. A team works best when members clearly understand its purpose and its goals.

2 Set a clear plan.

Having established a team for a specific purpose and made that purpose clear, the next step in the process is to ensure that the team is not left to 'muddle through'. Help the team determine what advice, assistance, training, materials and other resources it may need. Develop a flowchart setting out the required steps of a project and the required resources, including the training budget.

3 Define roles clearly.

Effective teams empower their members and demand their contributions, so performance expectations are essential. Focus attention on 'who' is to do 'what'. Shared roles, too, need to be clearly stated. An added advantage of ensuring clearly defined roles is that it limits the possibility of the same people getting stuck with the same tedious tasks.

4 Insist on clear communication.

An effective team is interdependent: each member makes significant contributions, and each depends on the other. In the team context, good discussions depend on how well information is passed between and among team members. Insist that members' communications are succinct, that they listen actively, explore opportunities rather than debate them, and share information.

5 Encourage team behaviours.

T-E-A-M means Together Everyone Achieves More, so make sure the climate of your workplace encourages all members to use their skills to make work an even better place to be. Behaviours will include initiating, seeking information, suggesting procedures, clarifying, elaborating, summarising, compromising and recognising the contributions of others. Collaboration replaces competition as the team's *modus operandi*, with clear boundaries set so that teams are aware of any limits to their autonomy.

Management Memo

Psychologist B.W. Tuckman identified the four stages of a team's formative process:
Forming – learning to deal with one another.
Storming – conflicts are brought to the surface and must be resolved.
Norming – team members settle into their roles and a team feeling begins to develop.
Performing – the team is united and working on the task at hand. [149]

6 Agree on decision-making procedures.

Ultimately, a team will have to make a decision, and the way it goes about that will be an indicator of its effectiveness. Group decision-making considerations are outlined on page 296. Be prepared to intervene in any group process by providing the required leadership.

7 Increase awareness of group processes.

If individuals are to become fully-functioning members of a team, they must be aware of group processes – how the team works together. You need to demonstrate the important role played by group dynamics, draw attention to non-verbal messages, and be aware of changes in the group's behaviour.

8 Expect participation.

Most people are goal-directed, social beings and teams provide ideal opportunities for more people to be involved in decisions, especially decisions whose outcomes are likely to affect them. So all members should participate in discussions and decisions, share commitment to the project's success, and contribute their talents. Understandably, that participation will be balanced according to factors like knowledge about the topic under discussion, investment in the outcome, and the level of commitment the person is prepared to make. People who are not prepared to participate should not be considered for a team project or work team.

9 Establish ground rules.

Have the team set rules or norms for what will, and will not, be tolerated in the group. It's too late to consider ground rules after the team has been operating for some time.

10 Insist on the best available information.

Reliance on good data for problem solving and decision-making makes it much easier to arrive at solutions to problems that have a greater chance of succeeding: failure to use quality data seriously compromises outcomes. Opinions should be supported by, or at least defer to, data. An added advantage is a decrease in group problems and disagreements. Strong opinions – even dominance – are quelled by the presence of real data.

 See also: 334-336

How to enhance your organisation's culture

Culture comprises those tangible, intangible and symbolic elements in organisational life: those customs, stories, practices, assumptions, values, symbols, ceremonies and traditions that are shared by all members of an organisation. The culture specifies how employees should dress, think, work, behave, communicate and make decisions in the workplace. It can be a most powerful influence and leaders must work to enhance their organisation's culture, through maintenance, sustenance or change...

1 Do not underestimate the role of culture.

The culture of your organisation is the set of beliefs that are shared, often subconsciously, by people in your organisation. It is a powerful influence that shapes behaviour, influences morale, and creates your organisation's identity. For example:

- It determines how individuals act and what they should value. Do men wear ties? Do superiors get called by their first names? Are meetings formal affairs? Staff who fail to come to grips with your organisation's culture will have trouble fitting in.
- It helps you understand employee motivation, performance standards and actions. Your company rewards individual effort, and yet you still wonder why some people have trouble working in a team?
- It can explain the presence of intergroup conflict. Do you ever wonder why your slow, analytical, patient, deliberate R&D people have trouble working with your action-oriented, flamboyant marketing group?
- It explains why change is so difficult to bring about. The targets of change are invariably those deeply embedded cultural values, habits, behaviours and images.

2 Appreciate that culture is not easy to change.

Organisational culture is usually so deeply rooted and pervasive that it is very difficult to change. However, because of a perceived need for more effective management approaches, a major restructuring or changing market conditions, a decision to consciously reshape the corporate culture may be warranted. But remember, change could take years to achieve, be expensive, and create disruption for management and employees alike.

3 Begin with a vision.

The successful creation of a new organisational culture goes hand in hand with strong and respected leadership. Such leaders always have a vision of the type of company they want to develop, and devise workable strategies to actively reshape the culture of the organisation.

4 Be patient in bringing about cultural change.

What steps might an effective leader

take to bring about a change in the organisation's culture? Consider:

- *Intervention strategies:* such as team building, organisational development or training.
- *Role modelling:* through your own behaviour, reveal the values and practices you want others to adopt.
- *Deliberate action:* such as participative decision-making, greater delegation of responsibility, management-by-walking-around.
- *Recruitment:* hire and promote those people with the sought-after values and beliefs.
- *External consultants:* these are often needed to help your organisation cope in periods of confusion, upheaval and anxiety.
- *Visible support:* particularly from top management, committed to change and clearly prepared to assist staff through a difficult period.
- *Resourcing:* equip the organisation with skills and materials to cope with change.

Management Memo

Every organisation, small as well as large, new as well as old, has a particular culture, determined by the individual values and experiences which each person brings to it, the ways in which its people act and interact, and the footprints they leave behind them... A unique culture will be apparent in any ongoing organisation. [150]

5 Focus on the elements of organisational culture.

If managers are seriously concerned with excellence and quality, then they cannot avoid becoming involved in maintaining or reshaping the elements and outward symbols which express what their organisation stands for. If you intend to examine, retain, change or nourish your organisation's culture, the following aspects should be your focus:

- **Values**. Values are guidelines for behaviour. When operationalised, they permeate and shape the company. Strong leaders know what values they consider to be important: creativity, teamwork, persistence, accuracy, quality, and so on, and over time these become embedded in the organisation's culture. In turn, they are reflected in outward manifestations like customer creeds, slogans, mission statements, policy documents, logos, ceremonies, even architecture.
- **Tradition**. An organisation's culture is an accumulation of the influence of its major leaders and landmark events of the past, apocryphal stories, hero figures and colourful characters, and how these personify the values that the organisation wishes to sustain. The past invites emulation and helps to maintain group entity. The key is to capitalise on a rich history if it's there.
- **Procedures**. Decision-making processes, communication patterns, power-authority relationships, reward systems – every new and existing procedure should be consistent with the organisation's values.
- **Symbols**. Organisations have emblems, symbols, signs and slogans to represent what they stand for. Furniture, buildings, uniforms, company literature, letterheads – they all contribute to organisational identity and should be a source of pride and loyalty.
- **Rituals and ceremonies**. What image do these public displays of culture portray and what values do they embody?

 See also: 282-284, 370, 374

How to develop a strategic asset management plan

Physical assets provide the platform from which an organisation delivers its services. Those assets have a life – they are planned and created, used and managed and, where no longer required, prepared for disposal. The management framework through which that asset journey or life cycle occurs is strategic asset management – aligning physical assets with service demands, and promoting better practices in all stages of the journey. Consider these key points to help you improve your asset management...

1 Decide on a strategic approach to asset management.

In the past, asset management has been associated with 'accountant-speak' and policies governing purchases, disposals, periodic stocktakes, custody, physical security, maintenance, transfer of assets and reporting losses.

A strategic approach, however, has much more to offer the long-term development of the organisation. The guiding principles are:

- Assets exist only to support the delivery of services.
- Asset planning is a key corporate activity that must be undertaken along with planning for human resources, information systems, knowledge creation and transfer, and finances.
- Non-asset solutions (enhanced technology, technological alternatives, reskilling), full life-cycle costs, risk and existing alternatives must be considered before investing in building assets.
- Responsibilities for assets should reside with the elements that control them.
- Asset management at the organisational development level should reflect the organisation's overall asset policy framework.
- Waste must be eliminated.
- The full cost of providing, operating and maintaining assets should be reflected in the delivery of services.

2 Develop individual 'plans' leading to a strategic asset management plan.

The strategic asset management plan will consist of most or all of the following components:

Capital Development applies to all capital 'built' assets including buildings, building services and plant, and the infrastructure necessary to support these assets.

Maintenance applies to maintenance or restoration of non-current or capital physical assets to their original condition. Parts of this plan comprise: statutory maintenance (required by legislation), preventative maintenance (generally manufacturers' requirements), corrective maintenance (breakdowns, for example), and deferred and backlog maintenance. Deferred and backlog information is derived through a comprehensive facilities audit.

Facilities Management aligns the physical workplace with the people and work of the organisation. Examples include energy management (lighting, air conditioning) and the management of other utilities, environmental management, cleaning, waste removal, and recycling, cleaning, workplace health and safety, and training. The facilities management plan is the area most often associated with asset planning.

Organisational Management ensures facilities management activities are aligned with the strategic direction of the organisation. It will be the organisation's culture and structure that ultimately determine the success of any facilities management.

Disposal/Adaptation uses all assets to best support the mission of the organisation.

> **Management Memo**
>
> This new responsibility – Facility Management – has emerged as organisations both large and small (private or government) have realised how much capital is involved in their offices, factories, warehouses, and everything that is associated with them – building costs, rent, maintenance, running costs, manufacturing, computer equipment, furniture, lighting, power, heating and air conditioning, and people in their practical workplace. [151]

3 Apply a similar structure to those features.

The following structure could apply to each 'plan':

Definition – what you mean by 'maintenance' or 'facilities', and so on.

Objective – what the plan hopes to achieve

Scope – what is covered by the plan

Benefits and Risks – benefits of having and the risks of not having the plan

Statutory Requirements – those that impact on the process

Responsibilities, Roles and Functions – what is to be done, by whom

Performance Indicators – how you will measure the effectiveness and efficiency of the plan

Competencies and Training – what core competencies and associated training are required.

You will find a flowchart a valuable tool in illustrating how each element contributes to individual plans.

4 Compile an asset register.

Your asset register will be one of the outcomes of a comprehensive facilities audit. The register should provide some or all of the following details: location, original cost, current cost insurance replacement cost and any deferred maintenance. That register should be upgraded on a regular basis to incorporate new purchases, adaptations and disposals. Labelling-bar coding, a simple numbering system or similarly appropriate procedures should be used to ensure accountability and that the register remains current.

5 Prepare budgets, but...

A strategic asset management budget must be a working document affected by the direction set by the strategic plan – a good reason for including facilities managers in boardroom discussions. Remember:

- For many organisations the value of physical assets far exceeds the total annual operating budget, making decisions on only an annual budget impractical because you will be neglecting part of your assets.
- Effective facility management ensures that areas like energy and waste management are not interpreted as overheads but as manageable items. Waste management, for example, may include recycling, negotiating with suppliers like computer hardware providers to collect and dispose of packaging accompanying orders; or other innovative management approaches.

How to achieve operational effectiveness

Operational effectiveness means performing similar activities and practices better than your competitors and making the best use of your resources in doing so. Although operational effectiveness alone will never lead an organisation to greatness, it is important to be able to choose the appropriate tools or techniques that can help your organisation to a sustainable competitive advantage. Here are some of those tools and techniques...

1 Begin with the right attitude.

Be wary of management fads. Many organisations, in adopting new management thrusts, meet with only limited success – although that may not be the fault of the programme itself. Involvement in any of the following techniques demands commitment from yourself and your organisation in terms of time, cost and energy...

2 Consider what TQM has to offer.

Total Quality Management (TQM) is an evolutionary strategy for focusing on process improvement. TQM preceded reengineering and became associated with getting products and services right the first time, rather than waiting for them to be finished before checking them for errors. It does not, however, question whether or not a particular process should exist. TQM emerged from leading business philosophers, Joseph Juran and W. Edwards Deming. The impact of TQM has been so great, that quality procedures usually associated with it have become more of a basic necessity rather than a competitive advantage.

3 Explore the possibilities of reengineering.

Reengineering, also referred to as business process reengineering, also emerged from the work of Juran and Deming, and is a revolutionary process challenging the operation and even existence of fundamental processes. It is aimed at radically redesigning processes in order to dramatically improve an organisation's competitiveness. Hammer and Champy first introduced reengineering in 1990 as a response to the failure of traditional business tools to make an impact on costs, quality and service. Despite its offerings, reengineering has become associated with cost-cutting – particularly labour costs.

4 Focus on benchmarking.

Benchmarking involves finding and implementing best practices. David Kearns, while CEO of Xerox, defined it as, 'the continuous process of measuring products, services, and practices against targeted competitors or those companies regarded as leaders'. Its goal is to reinvent operations to achieve significantly better performance and is best accomplished as part of a restructuring or reengineering process. Benchmarking's one main downside is that the more organisations benchmark one another, the more they come to look like each other. Rarely, therefore, does benchmarking provide any sustained competitive advantage.

5 Contemplate change management procedures.

Change is a measure of life in progress, so a key role for managers is to promote that need for change – more often as a result of pressure from outside rather than as a result of planning. Making change happen, therefore, is a key management function that involves tasks as varied as recognising and articulating a need for change, to selecting the right process for it. Quality management, benchmarking and other operational tools contribute to effective change management.

6 Consider outsourcing.

According to Al 'Chainsaw' Dunlap, much of the work that organisations do doesn't add value to production or selling a product or service. His advice is to identify what gives you competitive advantage, focus on that and outsource the rest. Outsourcing should provide access to specialist skills, free up management time to focus on core business, and provide cost savings, improved service quality and reduction in staffing. The main steps involved are to assess the risks, decide whether the cost difference is worth it, then act. The main problem with outsourcing is that the more rivals outsource activities to efficient third-parties (often the same ones), the more alike those activities become. Outsourcing provides savings – but at a price.

Management Memo

Differences in operational effectiveness among companies are pervasive. Some companies are able to get more out of their inputs than others because they eliminate wasted effort, employ more advanced technologies, motivate employees better, or have greater insight into managing particular activities or sets of activities. Such differences in operational effectiveness are an important source of differences in profitability among competitors because they directly affect relative cost positions and levels of differentiation. [152]

7 Try time-based competition.

Time-based competition is a competitive strategy that seeks to compress the time required to propose, develop, manufacture, market and deliver products. Though initially applied to manufacturing contexts, the approach has been successfully applied to non-manufacturing environments as well. Providing products or services in significantly less time can improve service quality and increase your organisation's profitability. Any reduction of product cycle times by improving processes can have a significant impact on your organisation's performance.

 See also: 308, 316-318

How to improve your organisation through total quality management

Total quality management is a business philosophy, devised by W. Edwards Deming and enthusiastically embraced worldwide, which helped to lift Japanese industry to achieve world-class standards of quality. TQM is based on the belief that change for the better will occur through dedication to continuous improvement and sharing a constancy of purpose by everyone in the organisation. Here's how you can put TQM to work in your organisation...

1 Rally your organisation around the quality banner.

The Deming philosophy requires that a strategy for pursuing quality be formulated collegiately throughout the organisation. Total quality requires a commitment to improvement by everyone in your company. It ends up as a dominant cultural value, becoming a part of 'how we do things around here'. TQM challenges managers to empower all participants to discover the joys of their labours, to improve continually, and to celebrate change that *they* devise and direct.

2 Focus on the process not the product.

Deming's hypothesis is that, if we focus solely on the product, we may never find out what is working or not working in the system. Rather, TQM focuses primarily on the quality of processes. For example, if we judge a high school solely on the tertiary entrance results of its graduating students, without looking at the quality of relationships, or morale, or teacher training, then this is contrary to TQM principles. Managers must emphasise processes in their organisation: goal setting, communicating, decision-making, image building, staff training, and so on – not just the final product.

3 Commit your organisation to continuous improvement as a way of life.

One of TQM's tenets is that *kaizen* (Japanese for 'continuous improvement') must become ingrained as a value in the organisation's culture. Toyota used kaizen to become a leader in high quality vehicle production. For Toyota, the term meant 'rapid inch-up': small, ongoing improvements that eventually result in outdistancing the competition. Over time, the cumulative effect of endless small improvements will generate pride, commitment and confidence in all stakeholders.

4 Acknowledge the sovereignty of your customers.

One definition for quality in TQM

terms is 'meeting or exceeding customer expectations'. Who are the 'customers' in your organisation? Does each employee have the same 'customer'? The storeman? the typist? the regional manager? the salesperson? the driver? In many cases, their customers are fellow employees! It's vital that everyone knows who his/her customers really are and what their needs are. In TQM their needs drive the organisation, for they are seen as partners in your organisation's success.

Management Memo

Total quality management is, as the name implies, a management system. Its main feature, in intention at least, is that it is a comprehensive system, even, its proponents claim, a philosophy. Quality has to be everyone's business. According to its advocates, some of the key features are that there should be obsessional commitment from the top, understanding from the bottom, that there should be well-developed systems and training, supportive management, and that policy objectives should be clear. The ultimate aim is to achieve zero defects: failures will not be accepted. [153]

5 Build in quality and then adjust as required.

It often costs more to fix a problem than to prevent one. TQM demands we constantly assess processes and adjust those that appear to be out-of-synchronisation. A pro-active rather than a reactive approach is required. TQM means addressing quality at the mission and strategic planning stages. It may mean working to eliminate mistakes and waste: cutting back on those unnecessary memos, files and photocopying, or removing those time-consuming and superfluous meetings, or not mismatching staff to tasks.

6 Foster mutual respect and teamwork.

Fear, says Deming, creates an insurmountable obstacle to any improvements and it must be driven out of the organisation. There is no place for hierarchy-dominated structures where employees fear ' bosses' and inflexible policies, for this fear, he says, detracts from high-quality, collaborative work. The alternative is a system where the integrity of each person is respected, where the importance of each person's work is recognised and rewarded.

7 Train and empower all stakeholders.

TQM stresses the importance of empowering the stakeholders by giving them more responsibility, autonomy and participation in decision-making. Encourage the generation of improvement ideas – and give the authority to carry them out. Provide opportunities for staff to undertake programmes of self-development. TQM requires that managers become partners, mentors, coaches and co-learners. It calls on them to recognise, nurture and use the talents of others through empowerment if they are to maximise stakeholder satisfaction and to gain the competitive advantage.

 See also: 308, 314-316, 346-348

How to use benchmarking to improve the performance of your organisation

Benchmarking is the process of measuring against, and improving on, the products, the services and the practices of your toughest competitors or those organisations regarded as leaders in a particular practice or business area. Its goal is to reinvent operations to achieve significantly better performance and is best accomplished as part of a restructuring or reengineering process. If you want to be the best-of-the-best in your field, benchmarking can help. Here's how...

1 Identify what you want to benchmark.

Xerox identified American Express as providing the benchmark for effective and professional telephone services. The Port Authority of Singapore provides a benchmark for similar organisations contemplating operational improvements. A high achieving real estate agency in one area may be a valuable benchmark for another office seeking to improve sales success. Know your field of concern and the areas in need of improvement in your organisation.

2 Find out the leaders in that field.

The organisation identified as providing the benchmark need not be a competitor. In fact, it is possible that the organisation will be operating in a different field altogether. You can identify leaders in your field of inquiry through observation, word-of-mouth, reading or published surveys.

3 Set realistic targets.

Best-of-the-best or best-in-class are not absolutes. You need to:

- formulate criteria that define a 'class' of companies of interest
- define measures that can be used to compare companies to determine the 'best'
- find companies that meet your 'class' criteria and that appear to be the best performers to defined measures.

4 Collect the information.

Some organisations would be flattered to know that they have been selected as providing a benchmark and may invite you to send an individual or a small group on a fact-finding mission. The saying that, 'If you never ask you'll never know', certainly applies when it comes to collecting valuable information. Alternatively, the key people in the organisation identified may agree either to be interviewed or to respond to a simple survey or questionnaire.

5 Talk to customers.

Improving customer service, presumably, is one of the main reasons you have decided to benchmark; so don't neglect to seek customers' views about the services you are wanting to improve. You may even decide to ask the permission of the benchmark organisation to speak to its customers about the area of its business that interests you. Customers experience outcomes of processes, so it's important you get their views.

Management Memo

While a benchmark is the mark old world craftsmen used for manufacturing – all production and construction was compared to 'the benchmark' to assure it would fit – the practice of benchmarking is a bit more sophisticated. As a management tool today, benchmarking is a means to improve your company against the most successful companies, both in and out of your industry.[154]

6 Plan the process to overcome differences.

The key is to learn and discover why some operations are better, some are worse, and how both got that way. Having gathered your information, develop plans and decide on schedules to enable you to implement the best-of-the-best throughout your organisation by continuous improvement. Update your position and status constantly.

7 Do it quickly, or don't do it.

People, their positions, their interests and the organisational context are all subject to constant change, so implement new-found practices promptly. You can help speed up the process by:

- allocating adequate resources
- using experts as required
- preparing well in advance
- biting off manageable chunks.

8 Manage the change.

Continuous improvement is essential if you're going to continue to prosper. The good thing about using a benchmark as the focus of the change process is that a successful working model already exists for you to emulate. Remember, benchmarking is a process, so keep stakeholders informed and supported throughout the process or you'll risk having your proposals collecting dust on the shelf. If indeed employees are having problems with change, act on those problems – perceived or actual – immediately.

9 Make measurement part of the process.

Selecting critical success factors – the things that must go right and can be measured – must be part of the process. These factors will influence the scope of the project, determine the key measures, help to identify benchmark partners, develop benchmark questions, and be valuable in your preparation of the final analysis and recommendations.

10 Set new benchmarks.

Continuous improvement means just that: once you have created the momentum, encourage employees to be on the lookout for winning ideas and organisations succeeding in particular practices. Always listen to what customers have to say; they will tell you other areas you need to be focusing on.

 See also: 308-312, 316, 346-348

How to use what reengineering can offer your organisation

To compete in today's business world, you must provide customers with quality products and services otherwise they'll go elsewhere. To compete, you may have to abandon outdated notions about how your organisation does its work and start afresh. This is the essence of reengineering: a process of improving the old ways of doing business and seeking to create new and better ways. Here's how your organisation can benefit from reengineering...

1 Consider 'reinventing' your business.

Look critically at the way things happen in your organisation. Ask yourself, 'If we were starting again from scratch, how would we do (whatever we are doing)?' That's what reengineering encourages – redesigning selected processes to dramatically improve competitiveness and productivity. And it may require making tough decisions including selling off, combining or closing down areas of your business that don't fit with where you want to be.

2 Focus on processes.

Processes become the new basic building blocks of the organisation. Improving processes or practices (what people do and how they do it) is the way to decrease turnaround time. By reducing turnaround time (and improving quality), you become increasingly competitive: more work-in-progress should mean greater profits. Remember, more than 85 per cent of problems in most organisations are process-related.

3 Emphasise the need for change.

Reengineering reconstructs work into multi-task jobs, and that inevitably demands a fundamental shift in employees' perspectives. Change is a measure of life in progress, and others will be expecting you to be fostering ongoing, planned change. Don't disappoint them. Your never-ending pursuit of best practices in the fields in which you operate provides an ideal catalyst for meaningful change. But one of your principal roles will also be to act in a 'gatekeeper' capacity, to control the introduction of change processes. Your task will be to build in a change process enabling staff to respond positively.

4 Gain the support of your employees.

You may be the visionary with the BIG picture and the ideas about how to achieve best practice, but you won't be able to achieve your goals single-handedly. You'll need to enlist the support of your bosses and of your employees. And there is no rule to say how long this should take.

What we do know is that you should hasten slowly until others share your vision of identifying the problem, redesigning the process, and fixing the problem.

5 Identify areas for improvement.

If you're tempted to take on too many areas at once, don't – your change initiatives may simply get bogged down. Initially, identify and select a few key areas for attention. If your company is involved in, for example, product development, manufacturing, sales and order fulfilment, develop process maps or flowcharts of the existing processes followed in those areas. Let value-adding be a key focus. Specific projects can then be identified to address process improvements. As processes improve, the boundaries – perceived or real – will disappear, heralding a more flexible and responsive organisation.

6 Create project teams.

Having identified specific projects, form project teams – one team per project – to research, report and implement changes over an agreed time (usually between four and 16 weeks). Include outsiders if necessary to inject fresh ideas. Early scores on the board are essential, so monitor the progress of project teams so that they achieve early successes. Remember to focus on business practices, aim for more than modest results, anticipate resistance, and spend time and money to make the new procedures work. The focus becomes results, not performing tasks.

Management Memo

Business reengineering means starting all over, starting from scratch. Business reengineering means putting aside much of the received wisdom of two hundred years of industrial management. It means forgetting how work was done in the age of the mass market and deciding how it can best be done now. In business reengineering, old job titles and old organisational arrangements – departments, divisions, groups, and so on – cease to matter. They are artifacts of another age. What matters in reengineering is how we want to organise work today, given the demands of today's markets and the power of today's technologies. How people and companies did things yesterday doesn't matter to the business reengineer. [155]

7 Encourage employees to identify reengineerIng opportunities.

One measure of the success of a reengineering process will be that employees will identify new areas in need of attention. A reengineering culture encourages continual improvement to all parts of the organisation. Your efforts to reengineer the organisation are rewarded with the emergence of professional work groups.

8 Learn from others.

A study of 47 American and European companies that had successfully completed reengineering programmes identified best practices, including:

- Recognise and articulate a compelling need to change.
- Use a structured framework.
- Link goals to strategy.
- Pick the right process before redesigning it.
- Plan for continuous improvements.

 See also: 284, 310-314

How to apply the principles of best practice

In an age of increasing deregulation, technological change, and new competitive attitudes, organisations must become nationally – even internationally – competitive. To do this, it is essential to pursue 'best practice'– a comprehensive, integrated and co-operative approach to the continuous improvement of all facets of an organisation's operations. Leading edge companies achieve world class standards of performance in this way. The general principles of best practice which you should consider adopting are...

1 Develop a shared vision and strategic plan.

Central to achieving best practice is a vision of world class performance, shared by everyone in the organisation, translated into action through a strategic plan.

2 Ensure that your bosses are committed.

Committed bosses are essential to drive and support change processes. And one of their key roles is not only to provide leadership but to recognise and encourage leadership at all levels of the organisation.

3 Provide a flatter organisational structure.

Competitive organisations respond to customers' needs in a time frame acceptable to the customer. Flatter organisational structures are better able to deliver a quick response. They are usually characterised by devolution of authority – particularly via team-based activities, empowerment of workers and improved two-way communication strategies.

4 Work towards a cooperative industrial relations environment.

Best practice workplaces promote effective communication and consultation throughout their structures. Enterprise bargaining, for example, is an effective process for introducing and institutionalising best practices.

5 Create a learning environment.

Two key qualities of a learning organisation are its commitment to continuous improvement and a recognition of the contributions of everyone in the organisation.

6 Develop and implement innovative human resource policies.

Occupational health and safety, equal employment opportunities, career-path planning, new remuneration systems, flexible working hours, part-time work, work-based child care and literacy training are just a few examples of innovative workplace initiatives.

7 Focus on your customers.

Customers determine the success of any enterprise, and organisations responsive to customers' demands will profit in a variety of ways – increased market share, increased staff and customer satisfaction, and a reduction in the need for marketing.

8 Develop closer relationships with your suppliers.

Leading-edge organisations involve their suppliers as an integral part of their change processes. These links can cut inventories, create innovative opportunities, and ensure a higher quality of end product.

9 Pursue innovation in technology, products and processes.

Market leaders have developed and employed integrated technology to ensure continuous improvement of production systems. Technology is not viewed in isolation, but as part of the whole system.

10 Use performance measurement systems and benchmarking.

If you really want to compete, you will have to match and improve on the performance of the nation's or world's best. Benchmarking is an essential tool for organisations committed to achieving top standards of performance.

> **Management Memo**
>
> The major lesson to emerge from our company's experience with its best practice project has been the need for total commitment on the part of everyone. Unless everyone realises that all parties are determined to instigate the necessary changes, the program will be treated as another fad.[156]

11 Think 'green'.

Increasingly, the integration of environmental management to all operations is becoming a component of competitive strategy.

12 Develop external relationships.

Networks can enhance an organisation's competitive capabilities through the sharing of information, by gaining access to services that individual organisations may not have been able to afford, in developing new technology or products, by exchanging staff to defray costs associated with entering new markets, and so on. Networks are valuable in the pursuit of best practice programmes.

 See also: 304, 334

How to turn your organisation into an empowered workplace

Increasingly today, the manager's role is becoming one of empowering the workforce to reach new levels of performance by means of participative work practices and the delegation of authority and responsibility. Empowerment, however, can't simply be conferred. It has to grow. Conditions must be nurtured to create it. How can you foster conditions which will lead to empowerment in your organisation?

1 Tackle the barriers to empowerment.

One of the first steps in empowering your staff is to deal with blockages to the empowering process and to overcome them. Examples of such barriers would include:

- Doubt that the system is sincerely committed to empowerment.
- Suspicion that 'empowerment' is simply another fad or buzzword. A feeling that 'what we do won't make any difference anyway'.
- Unhappiness with new roles that may be required. Reluctance to accept added responsibility without additional pay.
- Dislike of frequent meetings.
- Lack of time to take on the extra load.
- Unwillingness to give up authority and a preference for the comfort of routine.
- Concern that others may not carry their weight or share the increased workload.
- Fear of failure or, for some, success.

Many of these fears can be overcome if you strive to cultivate conditions which foster a climate of empowerment. But remember, as Ken Blanchard says: empowerment is not something you do to people, but with people.

2 Develop a climate of trust.

Trust is the mortar for the bricks of empowerment. You can't have empowerment without trust at every level of your organisation. Trust breeds a climate of mutual respect which is conducive to open, frank discussions. Set the example: build trust by keeping your word and discussing your concerns openly.

3 Open up the channels of communication.

Communication is the key to empowerment. As an empowering leader you not only need to communicate well yourself, but you also need to facilitate communication among all staff. You must foster not only the movement of ideas and information to and from yourself, but also to, from, and between every other unit within the organisation. And by sharing feelings, goals and information you ultimately build a sense of community within your group. So, practise empowering communication:

- Share your knowledge and skills.
- Offer and welcome constructive

criticism or suggestions.
- Work with others in planning projects and initiatives.
- Respect the views of others by listening attentively.
- Form a network with others to hear and offer new ideas and information.
- Keep everyone in touch with news, ideas, suggestions and information.
- Reduce the isolation of individuals and groups, a factor which can inhibit trust and empowerment.

4 Foster creativity and risk-taking.

Empowered people are willing to take personal and professional risks. By so doing, they gain new insights about themselves, meet challenges, stretch their limits, solve problems and test their mettle. They grow in self-assurance and, in turn, are better able to empower others.

Listen to and support new ideas in your organisation. When people feel they can experiment, receive encouragement, and be defended – not penalised – for making honest mistakes, creativity and innovation are likely to flourish.

5 Be aware of your changed role.

In sharing power, you may feel you are giving up long-held authority. But you are, in fact, increasing your power because power shared is power multiplied. In an empowered organisation, instead of 'controlling subordinates for the good of the organisation', you now embrace a consultative and consensus-building role. Individuals and teams within the organisation coordinate with and support each other, while you facilitate the process and intervene only when problems occur.

Management Memo

Empowerment is not an external event but rather an internal one; that is, not something that I ' do to someone' but rather something that they decide to 'do for themselves'. From this point of view, management's role shifts to supporting, coaching and teaching empowerment skills from trying to delegate them. [157]

6 Be supportive.

Show ongoing support for your staff:
- Focus on results and acknowledge personal improvement.
- Foster a climate in which people enjoy what they do and are recognised for their contributions to the organisation.
- Help staff succeed. Be tolerant, sympathetic and encouraging.
- Ensure resources are readily available.
- Promote understanding and support of staff efforts by focusing public attention, through media, newsletters and ceremonies, on outstanding work.

7 Encourage personal and professional development.

Knowledge and skills are power – so personal and professional development is important for empowerment. Consider such strategies as these:
- Consult with staff about the types of professional development and training they need and provide it, along with the necessary time.
- Give staff time to think, plan, share and learn from each other.
- Involve staff in discussions about budgets, staffing, resourcing, and so on.
- Encourage them to share with others what they have learned from training courses and reading.
- Provide technology along with adequate training and technical support.

 See also: 316, 346-348

How to manage a learning organisation

A movement which has entranced management gurus and practitioners in recent years is ' the learning organisation'. Such an organisation encourages everyone who works in it, or who has contact with it, to learn. It focuses on the ' learning habit' so that actions taken for reasons of production, marketing, problem-solving, or customer service also yield a harvest of learnings, reflections, insights and new issues for action. To turn your company into a learning organisation, take account of the following points...

1 Learn to learn – or you won't survive.

Mike Marquart writes that our large dinosaur organisations with pea-sized brains that flourished in the past, cannot breathe and survive in today's new atmosphere of rapid change and intense competition. The survival of the fittest is quickly becoming the survival of the fittest-to-learn, he says. The advocates of learning organisations warn that traditional models won't cope in today's rapidly changing and increasingly technological society. The real issue today is one of knowledge management.

2 Focus on your people.

A learning organisation is achieved only if its people are eager to learn new ways of thinking. Peter Senge's argument in *The Fifth Discipline* is that people should be encouraged to put aside their old 'mental models', learn to be open with others, understand how their organisation really works, agree on a shared vision, and work together as a team to achieve a common purpose.

From hiring the right people to creating an environment in which people are free to fail, your influence as manager will be vital. You will need to win the hearts and minds of your employees, who will need to be:

- flexible, and able and willing to do the new jobs
- creative, and able and encouraged to think beyond apparent boundaries
- healthy, with a balanced rather than stressed approach to responsibility.

3 Reflect on your new leadership role.

Senge sees the manager of a learning organisation as a 'servant leader'. The concept is an ideal, appealing to deeply held beliefs in the dignity and self-worth of all people and the democratic principle that a leader's powers are given from those led. The manager and staff together must develop towards a shared vision based on mutual trust and risk-taking.

4 Identify the knowledge you want to cultivate.

Three main types of knowledge will be present in your organisation – public knowledge (what everyone knows), industry-specific (what most people associated with your industry know), and firm-specific (what your people know about their own place). You need to define 'knowledge' for your organisation and consider how it can be converted into products and true competitive advantage. Intelligence, like any other asset, needs to be cultivated through action.

> **Management Memo**
>
> In learning organisations people continually expand their capacity to create the results they truly desire, where new and expansive patterns of thinking are nurtured, where collective aspiration is set free and where people are continually learning how to learn together. [158]

5 Promote learning as a way of life at work.

Work and learning should not be seen as separate forums. For example, it is your task to ensure that you transform into your organisation's 'way of life' such values as 'people are valuable resources', 'people must be nurtured and developed', 'people are partners in our enterprise', 'people need to be empowered' and 'structures which manipulate and control people are demeaning and outdated'. Unless such values are lived and modelled daily, they remain platitudes and a growing source of cynicism.

6 Encourage growth of 'human capital'.

Knowledge can grow in two ways: unleash the human capital already in existence, and channel talents to where they are needed and are most productive. The first can be achieved by using more of what people know and minimising mindless tasks, meaningless paperwork and other unproductive activities. The second implies applying knowledge. Interdisciplinary teams, for example, are one way of capturing, formalising and capitalising on individual talents that might otherwise be lost to the organisation.

7 Promote a passion for experiment and risk.

Encourage learning through a work culture in which experimentation is valued and mistakes are accepted and promoted as learning experiences. Reward risk-taking. Though it may be difficult at times, in the interests of learning and progress, you need to be prepared to take a back seat.

8 Make a note...

Be familiar with and work towards the development of the attributes of a learning organisation. You should:

- have everyone reflect on practice
- consciously evaluate and live the company's goals, norms and values
- have everyone experiment and question, searching for new strategies for innovation and action
- use teamwork and group approaches
- focus on self-esteem, self-discovery and self-directedness
- value the whole person, including feelings and emotions, in learning
- motivate through empowerment
- foster continuous, informal, on-the-job learning
- focus on service and contribution to the whole
- give control to get control
- encourage people to act as if the business is their business
- recognise that the manager is the leading learner.

How to negotiate and implement an enterprise bargaining agreement

An Enterprising Bargaining Agreement (EBA) is an outcome of consultation among management, employees and unions (if they are on-site or their involvement is requested by employees). It focuses on delivering real productivity benefits for the organisation through workplace reform, thereby benefiting employees, customers and the organisation. The process is best suited to companies which have a good management-worker relationship and a high level of mutual trust. Here are the basics...

1 Decide what you can get out of an EBA.

An EBA provides an ideal opportunity to look critically at your organisation to eliminate its inefficiencies, and to increase its level of responsiveness to the benefit of all those associated with it. The EBA process integrates strategic workplace reform programmes with the corporate planning process, so it will require the support of all key stakeholders – management, employees and unions. Relationships at all levels, especially at the senior management level, will need to change from control- to commitment-driven.

2 Establish consultative structures.

Developing an EBA requires a highly consultative approach to replace the adversarial, stratified systems of industrial relations traditionally used to manage workplace change. Although, initially, you may opt for a top-down approach, a structure must be in place that allows for consultation among all stakeholders. Larger organisations may need to establish a joint sponsored project team made up of stakeholders' representatives. Consultation is a slow but essential process requiring the following steps:

- invite input from employees
- collate their feedback
- identify issues
- discuss those issues with stakeholders
- conduct workshops involving those affected
- present a draft agreement to all concerned
- produce a final agreement, vote on it, and get it registered.

3 Build incentives into the agreement.

Opportunities exist for group and individual bonuses to be built into the agreement. By operating from a position that all salary increases are tied to achievement of key performance indicators, consultation among those directly involved will identify bonus opportunities. Employee gains would include:

- more interesting jobs with more responsibility
- more pay for more effort and skills
- the possibility of tailoring working hours more to their requirements
- job security for the term of the EBA
- increased voice in all things affecting the workplace.

Conditions and benefits for worker negotiation might include:

product/service discounts, child care, health/recreation facilities, job redesigning, flexitime, counselling, company cars, relocation/transfer expenses, parental leave, uniforms, training, job security, journal subscriptions, provision of tools, employee participation, insurance, multiskilling, expenses (telephone, power, travel), rostered days off, annual leave, membership of associations, superannuation/retirement benefits...

Employees need to know that, in return, such issues as these may affect them: pressure to keep improving productivity, some jobs may vanish, and changes to conditions of service, including hours of work, removal of restrictive work practices, no strike clauses, and so on.

4 Agree on the measures.

When the EBA is in place, the idea of a productivity scorecard, to record how well the reform process is progressing against agreed targets and to determine wage increases, is a useful measurement tool. Scorecard indicators may be customer service, employee satisfaction, and savings against budget. Like any other expenditure, wage increases must come from the budget. A more refined system of measurement could include key performance indicators applied to areas like service, quality and costs. Targets must extend employees.

5 Promote the benefits.

The normal employee response is initially 'What's in it for me?' If you make your EBA link productivity and efficiency improvements to a fair and equitable outcome-sharing model which can form the basis for wage determination, then everyone profits from increased productivity. However, individuals vary in their response to organisational change, so there'll be some employees who will prefer to observe before committing themselves to the agreement. For this reason, it's important to have a support infrastructure in place to respond to employee queries and uncertainty: a telephone hotline, printed information and trained facilitators.

> **Management Memo**
>
> The age of control, obedience and conformity is over... Leadership, independence, autonomy, initiative, diversity, questioning, provoking and debating are just some of the qualities and characteristics successful organisations recognise are essential to their future. [159]

6 Implement the agreement.

The success of the agreement will be in its implementation. Increasing empowerment of employees commensurate with their skill development, their involvement in decision-making, and ownership of organisational functions must be promoted as part of any strategy.

7 Keep your EBA under constant review.

Keep your EBA under constant review relying on stakeholders' representatives to identify and act on problems before they're allowed to develop into major issues. Consult the Labour Relations Act (no. 66 of 1995).

 See also: 224, 316, 326-328

How to embrace the concept of equal employment opportunity

As well as being sound, ethical management practice, assuring Equal Employment Opportunities (EEO) is a legal requirement of most governments. In South Africa this is also going to be a statutory requirement with the introduction of the Employment Equity Act. This Act makes specific provision for the introduction of an Employment Equity Plan and Affirmative Action to redress the inequalities of the past. The Act stipulates the employers' obligations in terms of the new labour legislation...

1 Adopt and circulate an EEO policy statement.

Inform your employees that your organisation has adopted or reaffirmed a policy commitment to EEO, thereby ensuring that staff will not be disadvantaged in any way on religious, gender or racial grounds when it comes to employment within your company. Your chief executive or boss should endorse that action, for it is difficult to comprehend a situation in which a boss will not be an advocate of equal employment opportunity. Use that support to enact your policy.

2 Appoint an EEO officer for your organisation.

Appoint a person or persons to be responsible for ensuring adherence within your organisation to any EEO legislation. EEO officers must have sufficient authority and resources to enable them to carry out that role effectively. Given the importance of assuring equal employment opportunity, it is likely that your chief executive officer will feel obliged to assume overall responsibility. Group ownership of the plan, however, will be achieved by involving all those affected.

3 Consult with those whose support is required.

Unions and employees are likely to be the two affected groups. A consultative committee comprising representatives of staff and unions should be considered. Additional consultation with employees can occur through meetings and surveys. Target relevant group networks, for example, indigenous people, single parents and the disabled, use newsletters to get your message across, and establish a 'help desk' for quick response to individuals' queries. Consultation is invariably a time-consuming, but essential, activity.

4 Construct an employment profile.

To manage something effectively you must understand it, and a statistical picture will help that process. In fact, comprehensive statistical data will prove to be one of the essential ingredients in evaluating the effectiveness of an

EEO plan. Most organisations will not have all of that information immediately available, but the picture will become clearer over time through surveys and using other information already in existence.

5 Review existing policies.

Make sure that existing personnel policies and practices do not contribute to any systemic discrimination. If you identify areas of incongruence, make the necessary amendments and include those as part of your overall EEO management plan.

6 Set objectives and make forward estimates.

Having now gathered all relevant information, you should now be ready to formalise your EEO plan or policy statement. The plan's objectives should be clearly stated to give the plan direction and structure. Time frames for achieving the objectives and responsibilities should be assigned. The corporate and strategic goals of the organisation should be taken into account, so close consultation with senior management is essential. A clear, concise, usable plan is what's required if you are to give direction to your company in terms of EEO policy.

7 Prepare your plan.

A typical EEO plan might comprise the following elements:

- an executive statement outlining organisational support for the plan
- an overview of the plan, its scope and its content
- a clear statement of objectives
- a time frame for the achievement of those objectives
- a statement of how the policy will be implemented and monitored.

Management Memo

EEO is linked to the important issue of social justice and helps organisations to fulfil their equity and fairness obligations. Employees and the community have every right to demand fairness and impartiality; that they will be able to compete for employment and will not be excluded on grounds such as gender or race that have nothing to do with their ability to do the job. [160]

8 Monitor and evaluate the programme.

Review the operation of the plan annually to monitor and evaluate its progress and to set the objectives and forward estimates for the next year. Its progress can be measured against the stated objectives and forward estimates. If your organisation fails to meet its goals, then a satisfactory explanation should be sought and relevant corrective actions should follow.

9 Use your plan to promote your organisation.

Your organisation's commitment to equal employment opportunity can prove to be a useful tool in attracting the right people to your organisation. Your EEO plan will help to further differentiate your organisation from others, so advertise your commitment to EEO whenever the opportunity arises.

 See also: 220-222, 234, 270, 324

How to handle harassment in the workplace

Legislation today requires that companies must be responsible for creating a working environment free from harassment and must have procedures for dealing with any reported incidents of harassment. What mechanisms do you have in place to tackle workplace behaviour that attacks, verbally or physically, an employee's sex, colour, creed or race? These suggestions may help...

1 Establish and publish a policy.

Familiarise yourself with your organisation's policy on harassment. If no policy exists, campaign for one. It should define harassment, provide clear examples of harassment, and explain the organisational procedure for reporting and dealing with complaints. Provide copies of your policy to all employees.

2 Educate your employees.

A policy alone may not be sufficient. Provide training to clarify the issue, to show management support in preventing harassment, to encourage staff to discuss the matter, and to teach employees how to deal with offensive behaviour in the workplace. Managers themselves also need to know how to detect signs of harassment, how to intervene, and how to process complaints received.

3 Establish investigative procedures.

Knowing how to conduct a fair investigation can ensure you take action appropriate to the offence. Consider these guidelines:

- *Interview the complainant.* Determine what happened, when, who else might be aware of the incident, the background, and attitudes towards the accused.
- *Interview the accused.* Have a third person present and allow the accused to choose that person. Tell the accused what she/he has been accused of doing and make sure the nature of the claim is understood. Again, seek the facts of the incident.
- *Interview **all** key witnesses.* Discretion is insufficient reason not to interview someone. Be aware that third parties often tend to take sides, so seek and document facts rather than opinions.
- *Mediate a meeting between the complainant and the accused* if such a meeting would not be too traumatic or sensitive. This can clarify perceptions, reveal management's concern, and often resolve the incident.

- *Make an objective decision.* The final decision must be based on facts, not personal attitudes or relationships. Weigh up the evidence. Objectivity is essential.

4 Consider the range of disciplinary measures available.

Once a complaint has been judged to be accurate, disciplinary action is required. Decide on whether the action was one of deliberate, recurrent harassment or a one-off act of thoughtless behaviour. Depending on the nature of the incident, disciplinary action might include a warning, close supervision, reprimand, transfer, suspension or termination. Some organisations also act against employees who knowingly file false allegations or against managers who do not follow established procedures in handling reports of harassment. Note also: if you unfairly dismiss someone accused of harassment, the courts may be forced to send them straight back to the workplace.

5 Remember...

- You must act immediately when any harassment issue is brought to your attention.
- When collecting the facts, do so assertively and confine your investigation only to those involved and to witnesses.
- For minor offences, warn the offender promptly in writing.
- Seek legal advice if serious disciplinary action such as termination is warranted or if an employee threatens legal action.
- Legislation usually demands that you must ensure harassment does not take place. An employer cannot claim ignorance. You are, by law, responsible for providing an harassment-free work environment.

Management Memo

One outdated approach to sexual harassment is that harassment does not occur in 'our' company and that women who accuse men of sexual harassment are overreacting to or misinterpreting certain types of behaviour. That view trivialises the subject, maintaining that allegations of sexual harassment stem from romances that have gone sour, from women taking offense at well-intentioned compliments, or from overly sensitive women employees who are not tough enough to handle a normal work environment. Managers who hold this view will dismiss reports of sexual harassment by indicating that boys will be boys, that the accuser must have behaved provocatively, that women have no sense of humour, and that no harm was intended. In short, sexual harassment is regarded as nonexistent, as an overreaction, or as a misunderstanding between two people. By perceiving harassment as an interpersonal rather than an organisational matter, managers who adhere to this school of thought either refrain from getting involved or try to protect the accused party.

Although some organisations seem to operate smoothly with this perspective, there is no way to determine the costs of absenteeism, medical benefits claims, turnover, or decreased morale or productivity resulting from unresolved incidents of sexual harassment. Such organisations and their managers clearly expose themselves to financially disastrous lawsuits, in light of contemporary EEO guidelines. [161]

 See also: 324-326

How to manage diverse ethnic groups

An increasing number of employees come from different countries, cultures and social backgrounds. The more managers learn about, understand, and become sensitive to those differences, the more positive the influence they will have over discriminatory and politically incorrect practices in their organisations. Here are some important guidelines for dealing with diverse cultures...

1 Find out about ethno-cultural backgrounds.

No one can be expected to know everything about every cultural group, but there is no excuse for not doing your homework about your own employees' cultural backgrounds. You should know about their preferred ways of greeting, sense of humour, emotions, perceptions of time and punctuality, particular gestures, attitude towards authority and the opposite sex, and status symbols. Good bookshops carry a wide selection of information to help you improve your knowledge of different cultures. Government agencies can also assist.

2 Adopt politically correct behaviour.

By being aware of cultural traits and idiosyncrasies you will become an even more effective communicator – and your flexibility will be acknowledged and admired by others. Set the example. Use terminology that is not offensive when referring to race or cultural background. Never let racial slurs in the workplace go unchecked. Language can be potentially a powerful vehicle of discrimination because through language we can, intentionally or unintentionally, describe people in derogatory, hurtful, condescending or alienating ways. Be prepared to demonstrate your commitment to equal employment opportunity by always employing and promoting the best person for the job.

3 Understand the idiosyncrasies of communication.

'Communication' means different things to different people; and its interpretation differs across cultures. In Australia, for example, criticising the Prime Minister (the person elected to that position) seems acceptable. In some countries, however, such criticism would be seen as a criticism of the position and, therefore, would be totally unacceptable – and punishable.

4 Encourage social events.

Every opportunity should be taken to encourage employees to get to know one another through formal or informal social activities. When new employees join your organisation you may use a 'buddy system' or mentors as part of the induction process. Later you may celebrate their various national days – even include information about cultural groups in your organisation as part of your staff training. Much more will be achieved from building on individual differences rather than ignoring them.

5 Recruit, promote and train.

Your organisation can only improve by virtue of the high calibre of your people. Employees representative of a variety of cultural groups can add a new dimension to your organisation – if you take the time to identify and use their particular skills. Don't pay 'lip service' to equal employment opportunity; let your actions do the talking.

6 Be aware of your non-verbal signals.

Experts tell us that our body language communicates more than half of the meaning when we communicate face-to-face. So we need to be not only aware of our body language but also to use it to ensure that we communicate appropriate messages. Use all of your skills to eliminate any chance of mistaken perceptions of prejudice.

7 If in doubt – don't.

If you're unsure how something will be interpreted – don't do it. It is far better to err on the side of conservatism than to create an embarrassment. Take humour, for example. What may be seen as fun in one culture may be taken as a personal affront in another. Similarly, an assertive stance may be interpreted differently in different cultures. Consideration of an individual's cultural sensitivities will always remain a key management quality.

Management Memo

All people hold cultural beliefs – norms, rules and values, which have developed through their experiences at home, in school and in the wider community. Most people also, perhaps unconsciously, believe that their own particular set of values is the 'right' set – the idea of 'how things have always been'. The resultant actions or non-actions from this prejudice affect relationships with those who hold different values. An awareness of one's own conditioning and sense of values is required if one is to grasp the significance of and understand the values held by others. An awareness of the effect of cultural conditioning on behaviour will increase sensitivity to both clients and colleagues whose behaviour and values are different. [162]

8 Recognise and deal with problems immediately.

Inevitably, problems among minority groups will occur. Denying prejudice if it exists in order to avoid problems, is unrealistic, stressful and could be, in terms of anti-discrimination legislation, disastrous. Never try to handle such problems by ignoring them or believing that they will just go away. Let employees see that you are committed to dealing with problems as they occur. You will gain the respect of all people for your actions.

How to ensure a healthy and safe workplace

Today there is a legal and moral responsibility for managers to attend to their employees' health and safety in the workplace. Managers are required to introduce and apply safeguards and procedures which will guarantee the physical security and welfare of employees and, should an accident occur, be in a position to provide the appropriate assistance. The following strategies might be considered in this regard...

1 Make workplace health and safety a priority.

Consult the Occupational Health Act (no. 85 of 1993). Advise your employees of these requirements, provide the necessary training, and demonstrate clearly your commitment to a healthy and safe work environment.

2 Make use of any available advisory services.

Most government agencies are only too willing to advise you on the legislatory requirements and will usually accept an invitation to review your procedures and help you develop workable policies.

3 Appoint a workplace health and safety officer.

Find an employee willing to assume the role of a health and safety officer – some legislation actually demands that. Relevant training programmes are usually available through tertiary training institutions. The trained employee will play an invaluable role in implementing the health and safety programme for your organisation. A safety committee may provide a support option.

4 Involve employees.

A healthy and safe workplace is the responsibility of everyone in the organisation, so provide opportunities for employees to be involved in a consideration of this initiative. Employees must know that management is committed to occupational health and safety, and that all staff are empowered to act in the organisation's best interests.

5 Keep records.

Your safety record is one measure that others will use to judge your organisation. Many potential employees are reluctant to join an organisation that is not serious about the safety of its employees. Reviewing statistics is one way of making sure that health and safety issues have been dealt with satisfactorily.

6 Prevent problems before they happen.

Document your procedures and train employees to follow them. Start with your staff induction programme. An Australian study, reported by the Australian Institute of Management, claimed that it is six times more expensive not to train than to train – findings which would be conservative when the costs resulting from accidents are calculated.

7 Be ever vigilant in seeking solutions.

Be wary of quick-fix solutions. If employees are required to engage in excessive overtime, this could be indicative of inadequate staffing levels or ineffective procedures. Remember that productivity levels not only decline when employees are required to work long hours but workers are also adversely affected on the following day. Procedures also need to be in place to ensure that areas of non-conformance are identified, addressed and monitored through a management review process.

8 If an accident occurs, take immediate action.

Make sure that documented procedures are carried out during any accident. Your first concern must be the health and safety of staff and any customers. Review the procedures after the accident and make any changes that will improve accident prevention, and that will deal with any accidents should they occur. Keep a detailed record of the incident for possible workers compensation claims, litigation or future corrective action. Provide any rehabilitation necessary, and recognise any significant staff achievements in coping with the incident.

> **Management Memo**
>
> Companies that have turned their attention to health and safety at the workplace, have found rewards surpassing their expectations. Gains include enhanced productivity, improved industrial relations, cost effectiveness, a more skilled workforce, efficient communities, greater flexibility, and better informed decision making. [163]

9 Conduct regular checks.

Work closely with your Health and Safety Representatives and insist on regular audits and reports (as required by the Occupational Health and Safety Act (no. 85 of 1993)). One of the added benefits of management-by-walking-around is that you keep your own close check on health and safety issues in your organisation.

10 Focus on continuous improvement.

When (or if) problems occur, initiate corrective actions that will ensure there is no recurrence of that problem. The importance of documented procedures cannot be overemphasised.

 See also: 78, 166, 240, 270

How to deal with substance abuse in the workplace

When it comes to dealing with drug and alcohol abuse in the workplace, managers are today expected to take on increasing responsibility in an area for which they have little or no formal training. The problem is exacerbated further because drug dependency does not discriminate according to status – anyone can be an addict, from your CEO to your back-room employee. Here are some practical ideas that will help...

1 Adopt and circulate a substance abuse policy.

By having a policy, employees know what is acceptable behaviour, the consequences of abusing drugs and alcohol at work, and the level of support provided by the employer in the event of a problem. The policy should contain information about where employees need to go voluntarily for help and advice on drugs and alcohol abuse, about time off for treatment and counselling, whether drug and alcohol abuse is a disciplinary matter and at what level that issue will be addressed, and the employees' rights under the disciplinary procedure.

2 Be aware of tell-tale symptoms.

Drug or alcohol impairment is more than an isolated incident. Indicators usually include performance problems, physical appearance, lack of coordination, mood swings, excessive tiredness and/or thought disturbance. These are usually 'flagged' by

- excessive absenteeism, particularly on Mondays
- regular tardiness
- diminishing performance and declining productivity
- increased injuries and accidents
- personal problems – legal, financial, or family
- constant and/or suspicious phone calls
- physical deterioration, dilated pupils, slurred speech, runny nose, scratching and dry skin
- changes in interactions with others
- increased isolation from or conflict with peers
- rebellious behaviour towards authority
- erratic behaviour, moodiness, disorientation
- increased visits to the washroom/toilet.

3 Record observations.

If you suspect impairment, you must act on it and document signs and obvious patterns. If the person is performing a dangerous task, they must be removed from that task. Engage them in conversation to assess for slurred speech or disturbance in thought. Involve others if possible to verify your observations. Be careful not to make accusations until you've collected the facts, particularly if the employee tries to deny that there is a problem. Ultimately, you may be left with no other option than to tell the offending employee that disciplinary proceedings will be instigated unless their performance improves.

Management Memo

A major U.S. survey showed that employees were taking drugs in one in six firms, and of the 1 500 personnel professionals surveyed, nearly one-third reported alcohol and drug problems in their organisations. [In the U.S., an approximate cost to industry from productivity loss and absenteeism is about $30 billion per annum. In Australia, the amount is considered to be in excess of $600 million.] [164]

4 Act in the best interests of all persons.

Chemical abuse affects more than just one person. As the manager responsible, it would be wrong for you to:

- ignore or excuse unacceptable behaviour
- take on the person's responsibilities
- make excuses to others, cover up the problem, pick up the slack, or fill in for them
- feel responsible
- enable the person to get away with poor job performance.

5 Confront the person with your evidence.

This should be done privately and in a supportive manner. Be firm but positive, have your facts on hand, don't label, and give the employee a reasonable amount of time to address the problem, insisting that help be sought if necessary. Additional guidelines are:

- Avoid blaming, using guilt tactics, or getting sidetracked with the person's personal problems. Stick to work issues.
- Clarify goals and standards set in your policy document. The person should refocus on what is expected of him or her.
- Let the person know the consequences of poor performance. If the employee has been involved in drug offences outside the workplace, it is likely that you will be able to act only if you can show that the employee's actions have damaged the organisation in some way.
- Refer the employee to a professional to deal with personal problems. Programmes exist to deal with these issues.
- Don't counsel on your own.

If performance does not improve, follow disciplinary steps according to company policy which may involve a union representative.

6 Provide internal and external counselling.

Use the resources available to offer help – sooner is better than later. One of the conditions of your disciplinary actions may be that the person attends counselling sessions conducted by a qualified counsellor. An in-house substance-abuse prevention programme could be considered for the entire staff.

See also: 304-306, 336

How to build a workplace where employees want to be

An environment where employees want to be will be far more productive than one where they literally force themselves to come to work. One of the most powerful and basic of all elements necessary to attract and keep the right people is happiness. Employees who are happy in their jobs will work hard and well – and will be reluctant to leave. Here's how you can build a happy and encouraging workplace...

1 Create the right environment.

Given the cost of hiring new employees, and the destabilising effect of a high turnover of staff, you can't afford not to make your organisation a happy place to be. You need to look critically at the physical, social and achievement environments to ensure that the mix of those three promotes a place where employees want to be. Ask staff periodically what they need to improve their person comforts and productivity and, where possible, undertake to have those needs met.

2 Know what makes people happy–and unhappy.

Research tells us if we were asked to remember the last time we felt unhappy, chances are we were thinking about what we don't have. As a manager, therefore, your task must be to affirm the positive, reinforce individuals' and groups' accomplishments, and share successes. Keep employees focused on achievements and discourage dwelling on what could have been or what they don't have. Napoleon's description of leaders as, 'dealers in hope' seems appropriate.

3 Develop a pleasant management style.

Managers who enjoy their work will do their job in more positive and constructive ways than managers who are unhappy or frustrated in their jobs. You and your attitude help set the tone. Employees are happier in a workplace run by managers who enjoy themselves, their work and their employees – and vice versa. Target these things:

- *Manage your thoughts.* Think positively, choose to think the thoughts and stories about your work that you enjoy thinking about–and avoid thinking about the rest.
- *Enjoy your work.* The most important thing for you and for all those around you is that you like what you're doing. If you're not enjoying work, do something about it.
- *Act spontaneously.* Share those qualities that make you special.

4 Promote openness and trust.

An open, trusting environment provides a platform for growth, so authentic behaviours must be encouraged, even if you don't agree with that particular behaviour. There will always be plenty of opportunities for you to discuss the appropriateness of particular behaviours on a one-to-one basis. You must be able to rely on your employees at all times.

5 Recognise contributions.

One of the most common reasons for employees leaving an organisation is because they did not receive adequate recognition for their work. Employees' expect recognition and won't be happy until their expectations are satisfied. Your recognition will get the best results when it is of a type that is valued by the employee. Remembering an employee's birthday, for example, may be valued more by that person than a pay rise.

6 Involve families.

Families help to provide balance in people's lives. When things are going well at home, people are usually much happier and more productive at work. So you should take every opportunity to involve employees' families in the organisation's incentive bonuses scheme, at out-of-hours conferences and training sessions, and in social get-togethers. Keeping life partners happy is a productive investment. They, too, become committed to seeing the organisation succeed.

Management Memo

In order that people may be happy in their work, these three things are needed: They must be fit for it, they must not do too much of it, and they must have a sense of success in it. [165]

7 Encourage team identity.

The adage, 'a champion team beats a team of champions', proves itself in organisational as well as in sporting life. You can promote the team identity by referring to your staff as a 'team', using 'we' instead of 'I' when talking about things to be done and, wherever possible, encouraging decision-making by those likely to be most affected by the decisions.

8 Empower your employees.

Make empowerment more than just a management 'buzz word'. Give people the authority and associated responsibilities to make decisions considered to be in the organisation's best interests. But remember that empowerment does not mean that you, as manager, can abrogate responsibility.

See also: 198, 202, 334

How to boost flagging morale in your organisation

'Low morale' are two words most managers don't want to hear when the *esprit* among their employees is being discussed. Organisations where morale is considered to be low usually lack achievement motivation, a sense of real purpose, and experience a high turnover of their employees. Though effecting a turnaround will take time, you can be assured of success if you act on the following suggestions...

1 Become a morale missionary.

Morale is a group phenomenon, but an individual matter. We speak of good morale in a group – meaning that most of the people in the group have a good sense of *esprit*. Group morale depends on the morale of each individual in the group. Thus, improvement in *esprit de corps* must be achieved by improving the morale of every individual in the group. And this is best done through the personal missionary work of the manager. Group initiatives such as projects, services, clubs and inspirational talks can help, but without the manager in there working with individual staff, group morale will not improve.

2 Identify issues– not the outcome.

Morale is the outcome. Issues are the things contributing to that outcome. Employees may attribute the cause of low morale to the turnaround time on decision-making, the constant changing of priorities without consultation, the lack of training, inflexible procedures, the incorrect mix of resources and people, or poor communications. By focusing on identifying the issues, you will have a much better chance of improving the situation and boosting morale.

3 Measure before trying to manage morale.

You may decide to use commercially available 'tools' to measure the impact the issues have on productivity or you may opt to design your own. Whatever your decision, you will need to use measurement tools to get an accurate picture of the issues and the associated problems. As gurus of management tell us, 'If you can't measure it, you can't manage it.'

4 Build self-confidence and security.

Job security and a feeling of confidence in one's ability to handle the day-to-day incidents of life and work are key elements in good staff morale. You can provide this feeling – by training staff to do their jobs effectively, showing them the importance of their jobs to the organisation, and demonstrating your own confidence in them.

5 Set priorities.

Establishing priorities helps to make molehills out of mountains for people. Issues will generally fall into three broad categories:

- those that you will not be able to influence at all
- those over which you have very little influence
- those that you can influence.

Help people to live with those things you cannot change. Take specific actions to remedy those things that can be changed. Communicate your feelings to the people who can change those other things.

6 Establish work groups.

The essence of good morale is participation and the feeling of being wanted. The interdependencies created by people working in groups help to build bonds and enthusiasm among group members that affect other aspects of everyday life, like reducing absenteeism, increasing cohesiveness, and improving morale.

7 Encourage action.

Nothing succeeds like success, so get runs on the board as soon as possible. Empower groups to recommend and act on a variety of issues. This is not to suggest that you abrogate all responsibility to the groups; but if a group has been formed to deal with an issue, lend your support and acknowledge achievement.

8 Keep people informed.

Communication is the lifeblood of any organisation, so make sure that employees have all the information they need to function effectively. An open, honest and caring environment promotes a feeling of *esprit de corps.*

Management Memo

Morale might be called the spirit of a company – the sum total of the attitudes of its people. It is influenced more from the top down than from the bottom up. No single condition will consistently explain good or poor morale, for it is a 'mix' of many related elements operating together at any given time. [166]

9 Remain alert to the morale factor.

Morale changes even on a daily basis, so you can't rest on your laurels when you think a crisis has been averted. Stay in touch with day-to-day events, and watch for ups and downs in morale.

10 And, don't forget...

- Establish fair policies and administrative practices.
- Encourage staff members to discuss their problems.
- Help staff through encouragement to guard against a sense of failure.
- Protect staff against unfair criticism.
- Develop a sense of purpose and solidarity.
- Keep jobs interesting, with new challenges, new authorities and new responsibilities.
- Be friendly and appreciative of staff effort.
- Recognise the impact on morale of reassignments, redundancies and dismissals.
- Encourage promotion from within.

How to conduct a gripe session

Whingeing occurs in most groups at various times, but its existence in your organisation should not necessarily be interpreted as a personal criticism of your management approach. Constant complaining indicates the likelihood of perceived problems, the presence of negative energy that needs to be redirected and refocused, and opportunities to use those gripes to bring about meaningful changes. Here's how you can derive maximum benefit by having your staff air their gripes...

1 Learn to capitalise on complaints.

Gripes can be blessings in disguise, alerting you to existing and potential (and imagined) problem areas. If particular kinds of gripes are universal among your employees, some company procedures or practices may require changing, or they may be precursors to other gripes to follow. You should always look on all complaints – including employees' gripes – as springboards to better performance. Chances are you will become so sensitive to employees' needs that you will know their complaints almost before they express them.

2 Adopt a structured approach.

Gripes can be indicators of the existence of group problems that can get in the way of organisational development. Never try to apply a 'bandaid' or cover-up. Instead, embrace a pro-active, structured strategy by, firstly, assembling a group made up of those with gripes and any others with an interest in hearing and acting on them.

3 Generate a list of gripes.

In a group situation, have individuals work alone and compile lists of gripes. Then have individuals form pairs and compile combined lists. Similar gripes are rewritten to form descriptions that satisfy both people. Pairs are then formed into fours and the process continued. Fours then become eights. Each eight presents its list and the whole group is engaged in producing one list representing all contributions. Number each item for ease of reference.

4 Categorise the list.

Classify the list into four categories based on the control the group has over individual complaints. A useful classification is:

- *Acts of God* – those over which we have no control and will have to learn to live with.
- *Acts of lesser gods* – those which we will probably have to live with, but we can, at least, let those gods know the group's feeling.

- *Shared issues* – those we share with others (organisations, divisions, departments) and can resolve in cooperation with them.
- *Individual issues* – those that are ours alone and can be actioned immediately.

Save time by listing numbers in each category.

Management Memo

Gripe sessions are an excellent tool for demonstrating your listening skills, proving you're serious about getting honest feedback, and confirming that you'll do everything possible to correct the problems that are discussed.[167]

5 Address each category.

Have the group assign actions to each complaint in each category in turn:

- *For the 'God given' category*, write statements in the form of, 'Learning to live with...'. They have acknowledged the problem and that's all they can do about it.
- *For the 'lesser gods' category*, they may decide to draft a letter or memo, signed by all members and directed to the person(s) responsible for that situation. They have alerted the other(s) to the problem; the ball is then in the others' court.
- *For 'shared issues'*, the group decides which of those it wants to address. Meetings with the identified 'others' are arranged for a time when each party is able to devote full attention to reaching solutions. That may require putting this step on hold until the fourth-category issues have been addressed.
- *For individual issues*, the focus is on those items which the group considers it can begin to work on independently. By using a simple voting procedure to establish a priority, the group can work its way down the list starting with the number one priority. In the process, actions should be assigned to individuals.

6 Develop plans for action.

Action plans are best constructed in matrix form containing goals, timelines, expense allocation, individual responsibilities and support persons. The action plans should be reviewed regularly and individuals held accountable for their completion. Ensure that members are satisfied that all items on the list have been adequately addressed. The first draft of the plans should be returned to participants within three days of the workshop. Encourage a twenty-four hour turnaround on corrections so that completed plans can be delivered to participants the next day. For credibility, strike while the iron is hot.

 See also: 192, 198, 336

How to help your staff overcome complacency

Most people prefer things to continue in their same old predictable way. If change is to take place, such people will probably argue that it should happen at some point down the track – when their routines will not be affected. Such complacency needs to be transformed into a sense of urgency, or your organisation will stagnate and you won't get the staff support you need to make change happen. You can overcome staff complacency if you...

1 Set performance standards that demand effort.

Never accept low performance standards. Set productivity, revenue, sales and other performance targets so high that staff cannot afford to rest on their laurels. Goal-setting literature often places too much attention on words like 'achievable' and 'realistic' – words that have been interpreted by some employees as a 'softer' approach to performance standards. Your organisation's standards must encourage employees to extend themselves.

2 Insist on S-T-R-E-T-C-H goals.

It's not hard for employees to accomplish goals when they state them in easily 'achievable' terms – such as 'contact five new customers each day'. Steer clear of statements of *minimum* acceptable competence, because these soon become accepted as *maximum* standards. Make sure that *you* have a say in what are acceptable goals. You will find that employees will appreciate your involvement.

3 Make employees accountable.

The success of the entire organisation should be the aim of all employees. Even if your staff have become used to focusing on their own individual divisions or departments – almost as if their area is all that matters – they must be encouraged to think in terms of being accountable to the wider organisation. If the organisation prospers, they too will share in the recognition.

4 Share external feedback.

Employees need to hear feedback of all kinds, not only from satisfied customers but also from dissatisfied clients, angry stockholders and frustrated suppliers. If the only feedback employees receive is 'good news', then they may consider complacency acceptable behaviour.

5 Encourage honest discussion.

Employees sometimes fear that honest disclosure of information will not be well-received if the news is 'bad'. You can't afford *not* to encourage open and honest discussion of problems. You should come down heavily on those attempting to conceal information.

6 Adopt a 'What's next?' attitude.

Your staff should be encouraged to be constantly on the lookout for opportunities. And if every opportunity is not grasped, or if things don't fall into place as one would hope, don't linger, lament, and engage in unproductive analysis. It is far better to ask, 'What's next?' and move on to the next opportunity.

Management Memo

People rest on their laurels and never notice that they're losing ground. I don't know how many times I've seen very talented people get short-changed on a promotion or new job because they rested on their laurels. They think that because they're doing a great job, it should be obvious to the people who control their future that they deserve success. This is a most dangerous type of complacency... Paul Austin, the late chairman of Coca-Cola, once told me. 'The worst thing that can happen to a CEO is to enjoy his company's position in the marketplace – especially if it's the dominant position. Anytime you become content with where you are, then that's like issuing a corporate decree to stand still.' [168]

7 Remove unhealthy messages.

If your organisation has all of the outward signals of success: lavish parties, boardroom bashes and other events that convey the wrong messages, employees can't be expected to be overly concerned about the organisation's future. Get rid of these obvious examples of excess. Communicate to employees instead the messages that will encourage them to lift their game.

8 Find or invent a crisis.

If the organisation isn't losing money, or no lay-offs are on the horizon, employees don't see any visible threats and thus don't feel any sense of urgency. If there isn't a crisis, create one, even a minor one. You'll find that crises help people to regain focus.

9 Look to the future.

Focusing on past successes may serve some purpose, for example, when you're coping with a one-off rejection. However, you should not dwell on past glories for too long. What you focus on grows, so concentrate on working towards the future and not on something that's history.

How to implement a training programme in the workplace

When there is a gap between what an employee *can* do and what that employee *should* be able to do, then there is a training need. Most learning takes place on the job and success will depend largely upon the effectiveness of the training method and the ability of the manager, or his or her delegate, to instruct the worker in that new skill. Here is a proven strategy to help you master the training process...

1 Define the training need.

Be alert as to the need for training within your organisation. For example:

- Be aware of any plans for expansion or changes in technology which might require new skills within the organisation.
- Identify any operating problems, the outcome of inadequate performance, which would be corrected by training.
- Use job analysis and performance appraisal to identify individual training needs.

2 Prepare yourself for the training session.

Although you may be completely familiar with all aspects of a given job, it is essential to make adequate preparations before attempting to instruct others. For example, determine how much skill you want the trainees to acquire by what date. Break the job down into its various components. Isolate and write down the key points. Have the right equipment and materials ready, and make sure the workplace is in order.

3 Prepare the trainees.

Some employees do not necessarily want to learn; others may even have a fear of learning. Hence, it is essential to put the trainees at ease and to foster an interest in the task by explaining the purpose of the training, what is going to be done and how the trainees and the organisation will benefit from it.

4 Find out what the trainees already know.

Check on what the employees can already do, for then you can build upon that knowledge. You don't want to waste time teaching employees something they already know, but you cannot always assume that they *really* know what they say they know. Sometimes workers pretend, to impress you.

5 Present the task step by step.

Explain and, wherever possible, demonstrate what has to be done and how. Instruct clearly, completely and patiently. Pace your instruction carefully, one step at a time, and move on to the next step when you are sure each employee has absorbed what has been taught. Emphasise the key points. Encourage questions if something is not understood.

6 Check for understanding.

Having explained the task, let the trainees demonstrate the job to you, explaining each key point in turn. This is important. Unless they can tell you the key points as they proceed, you can never be sure they have grasped the message. If no errors are made – fine. If an error is made, interrupt there and then, and patiently go over that point. Continue in this way until you are sure the employees have mastered the entire process.

7 Have the trainees practise the skill.

Practice makes perfect. Under supervision, get the employees to practise each stage until the required standards of speed and accuracy are achieved. A progressive approach should be used. That is, when any two successive stages can be done separately at the required standard, have the employees practise them jointly until the standard for both steps together is reached. Then the third step can be added, then the fourth, and so on until the entire task is learned.

> **Management Memo**
>
> The basic purpose of training is the transfer of skills from those who have them to those who do not. Just having the skills is not enough to be an effective trainer. Anyone responsible for training should understand how best to impart knowledge or skills using proven techniques. [169]

8 Put the trainees to work.

When you feel sure that the employees have mastered the skill, put them to work on their own. Designate to whom they go for help if required. Check progress frequently, particularly in the early stages. Retrain wherever necessary and be friendly and encouraging in your manner. As the workers become more sure of themselves, the need for coaching should diminish and finally the necessity for follow-up on this task should cease completely.

Remember that if the worker hasn't learned, the instructor hasn't taught.

How to conduct a workshop

Workshops provide a forum for individuals and groups to get together to explore areas of mutual interest or concern – skills, problems or possibilities. And often the expectation is that you, as the manager, will lead and conduct the workshop, thus providing another opportunity for you to demonstrate your leadership and group skills – if you do it well. Here are some necessary considerations to help you prepare for when that opportunity next arises...

1 Do the hard yards early – get prepared.

Preparation is essential. If you are not prepared, postpone the workshop until you are. Preliminary considerations should focus on:

- Timing – the topic must be relevant to the period and participant needs.
- Establishing outcomes – fuzziness up front will create problems later.
- Deciding on essential knowledge and skills – pre-workshop training may be required to ensure effective participation on the day.
- Identifying possible attendees – 'wall flowers' are merely excess baggage.
- Developing materials to suit the audience – even the best materials will fail with the wrong audience.
- Liaising with any other providers – they'll be expecting to hear from you.
- Inviting participants, disseminating an agenda, arranging facilities, and providing directions if necessary.

2 Plan the format.

Sequence activities to help achieve your desired outcomes. Adult learning techniques should guide the approaches you use (Kolb, for example, advocated a balance between activity, reflection, theory building and consideration of any practical application). Ideally, the workshop should commence with an ice-breaker to 'unfreeze' the group, establish rapport, and help focus attention on the intent of the workshop. Plan to scatter energisers (short, sharp exercises or activities) throughout the session to help refocus attention on the tasks at hand.

3 Arrive early.

You must be the first person to arrive at the venue. Check all equipment. Arrange seating to suit the purpose of the first session – e.g. theatre style, U-shape, or round tables. Greet people as they arrive. Direct people to refreshments. Introduce people to one another and generally make them feel welcome. The work done now will make your task much easier later. Housekeeping issues may be dealt with here rather than at the start of the workshop.

4 Start on time.

Never penalise those who arrive on time by waiting for stragglers. If a senior executive does not want to get things underway, you do it. Act and sound authoritative, but warm. Use an ice-breaker, if necessary. Introduce yourself and ensure everyone knows each other's name, job, special skills, key objectives, and what they want to get out of the workshop. Make the objectives of the programme clear. Display them where they can be seen clearly. Review the agenda so people are aware of how you are aiming to achieve your objectives.

Management Memo

The first few minutes of a workshop are the most crucial. If they are interesting, relevant and pleasant, problems which may arise later can be resolved with a minimum loss to the learning. If the first few minutes are boring, pointless and unpleasant, the most precious gems of learning are likely to be lost in the mud of misunderstanding, incomprehension or apathy. [170]

5 Remain relaxed.

Adopt the attitude that there is nothing that can happen in the workshop that you can't handle. Your non-verbal and verbal responses will contribute substantially to the climate of the workshop. Be guided by these suggestions:

- If things don't go according to plan, there's no need to apologise. Move on.
- If you don't have an answer to a question, ask others. And if they don't have the answer, offer to get back to them later.
- Keep away from jargon. *Paradigms, parameters,* and other management mumbo-jumbo are a turn-off for many participants.
- Use visuals wherever possible; they're six to eight times more effective than verbal instructions.
- Make sure all material and language you use are culturally neutral. The need for cultural sensitivity cannot be overemphasised.
- Repeat or rephrase questions that are not heard by everyone in the audience.
- The attention span of most adults is about seven minutes, so vary your pace and presentation techniques accordingly.
- Cater for the anticipated 'slow time' after lunch. High activity will beat a video or lecture at these times.

6 End on time – with the right message.

Stick to your committed finishing time. Begin the wrap-up about thirty minutes before then. Provide a summary of accomplishments. Invite others' input. Evaluate the workshop by distributing a short survey or use a less formal approach like handing out small cards and inviting a positive comment on one side and an improvement suggestion on the other. Thank participants and outline further follow-up.

7 Review the workshop.

Use the planned outcomes, the feedback provided, and your own impressions to evaluate the success or otherwise of the workshop. Decide on your next step. Act promptly and programme further meetings if required.

8 Observe other workshop facilitators.

All presenters have their own unique styles. Watch other people conduct workshops and you will learn much. And by 'borrowing' ideas you can add to your repertoire of skills.

See also: 122, 348

How to prepare to bring about change in your organisation

Planning for change can occupy a great deal of a manager's time and energy, but it is not a process that can be left to chance because it can be tricky and disruptive if handled poorly. Whether it be implementing a new job rotation scheme, rearranging the office layout, introducing new technology, relocating your manufacturing operations to a new plant, or whatever, a manager must embrace a preliminary, systematic planning approach to bring about successful change later...

1 Be convinced that change is necessary.

Are you sure that the intended change is sound and that there is every likelihood it will succeed? Is it practical, ethical, cost-effective? Will it solve more problems than it will create? Is it based on untested theory or speculation, on fashion or a whim? Are the risks acceptable? Has it proven successful elsewhere? Can you specifically identify projected improvements in productivity? There is little to be gained from adopting a plan that is doomed to failure before it gets off the drawing board.

2 Analyse the change in terms of the present and the future.

Get a clear picture of your present organisation *without* the change in place. Visualise the situation as it will be after the change is implemented. Now would also be the time to question what might happen if you did nothing. By visualising a future state, you're able to put a new perspective on the present, and be assured that the proposed change is worthy of support. Without a vision, change efforts dissolve into a list of time-consuming, incompatible and confusing projects going in different directions – or nowhere at all.

3 Understand why the change might be resisted.

Resistance to change is a natural response because we usually prefer stability and feel comfortable and satisfied with habit and routine. If anything diverging from the norm is introduced into our environment, it will be seen as disruptive. As well, change is often resisted because of –

Self interest: I will lose money, status, privileges and authority. I will have added responsibility with no adequate recompense.

Fear: I don't have the skills and experience to adapt. I'll be worse off than I am now.

Uncertainty: I don't understand the specifics of the change. What does it all mean? How secure is my job? Will it mean more work?

External pressure: I resent external interference and want to be in control of my own destiny. I have had little to say in the change.

Past experience: I've become too cynical about change. It's been too disruptive and ineffective in the past.

4 Consider how staff fears might be addressed.

As a manager, you must put yourself into the shoes of your employees and prepare yourself to tackle staff fears head-on by developing strategies to assist in the implementation phase.

Begin by assembling facts and arguments to answer the concerns of employees and to dispel their fears. With a little creative thought, potential objections can be turned into advantages. Plan how to communicate your vision and this information, and how to offset any objectionable aspects of the change initiative which cannot be eliminated.

5 Develop a tentative but detailed plan.

Draft an outline plan by identifying and listing each task or element of the change. Arrange the elements into their proper sequence or parallel relationships for implementation, construct a tentative timetable, allocate responsibilities, where necessary undertake critical path scheduling, and consider resource requirements. Focus on the appropriate means of involving staff in the planning and implementation stages of the process.

6 Prepare to shake up your staff's complacency.

Change is a measure of life in progress; complacency is often what's holding it back. Consider how the following approaches might be used to reveal to your staff the need for change:

> **Management Memo**
>
> Modern organisations are never static for long. Neither the local primary school, the country-wide chain of retail stores nor the multi-national corporation can shelter from the winds of change that are constantly blowing, soft or strong. Sometimes you will be introducing changes yourself; at other times you will have them thrust upon you by your bosses. Whether it's just that new equipment is needed in the typing pool or that Head Office has introduced a new accounting procedure, you will need to plan for and cope with the effects and repercussions. [171]

- Create a crisis or crises to break staff out of their complacency
- Introduce goals that require action rather than wishy-washy acquiescence.
- Benchmark your most successful competitor.
- Survey and report on dissatisfied customers' and shareholders' opinions.
- Restructure to remove the 'comfort-zone'
- Raise performance standards for everyone.
- Visualise a lean and mean operation.
- Focus on opportunities, not on yesterday's successes.

7 Prepare for the involvement of others.

The key to successful change is for management to treat staff as part of the organisation, rather than as the opposition or target. For this reason, it will be essential to involve staff in the change process as soon as possible following this, your initial preliminary planning. How this is to be accomplished is considered on page 348.

See also: 122, 346

How to implement change

Change has been an inevitable feature of the last decade or so – an unending flow of new technologies, new policies, organisational restructurings, downsizings, redundancies… Many employees are beginning to buckle under the weight of it all. Change might offer a promise of improvement, but it doesn't guarantee it, with the result that many people now approach change with scepticism, fear or frustration. How can a manager best introduce change in such an environment?

1 Note the basics of good change management.

The mere thought of change can be a real 'turn-off' for many people and, if you ignore the following change essentials, you'll find the process of implementation even tougher:

- People will change when they see the need for change.
- People will change when they know how to change.
- People will change when they are involved actively in the change process.
- People will resist surprises.
- People will change when they are secure in changing.
- People resist being treated as things.
- People do not necessarily change on the basis of new knowledge alone – attitudes, feelings and status are just as important.
- People change some attitudes slowly.

Keep these tenets in mind throughout the implementation phase.

2 Involve your staff in the process of change.

If your employees participate actively in the change process, they are more likely to feel ownership and less likely to resist. In this regard:

- *Involve staff in the processes* of planning, implementation and evaluation. They are more likely to see the initiative as their own, not as one imposed by outsiders.
- *Gain the support of opinion leaders* in the organisation. Others soon follow their lead, for people tend to model the behaviour of others, especially those they admire or trust.
- *Concentrate on the doers,* not the doubters; the risk-takers are more likely to support your efforts at change.

3 Ensure your staff clearly understand the change.

To alleviate staff anxiety and stress, you must explain fully the logic of the change, emphasising both the benefits and risks. New ideas are often misinterpreted, so make ample provision for discussion of reactions to ensure complete understanding and to alleviate any related concerns and fears. During implementation, chart the activities completed and those yet to be undertaken. Report periodically to all staff on progress to date. Up-front information and understanding help people feel more secure with the change.

4 Sell the benefits.

How will the changes benefit me? my unit? the organisation? Will the change mean more satisfying work, greater security, an opportunity to show what I can do, less confusion, less fatigue, greater autonomy, improved communication? Motivate your staff to embrace the change by putting benefits on as personal a level as possible. It would be dishonest not to point out some of the difficulties and disadvantages as well.

5 Present the change enthusiastically.

Resistance to change is sometimes due to the fact that change is half-heartedly presented in the first place. Introduce and implement the change with enthusiasm. Enthusiasm is catching. Remember the saying: 'I cannot kindle a fire in others until it is burning in myself.'

6 Provide them with tools, resources and support.

Give your staff the necessary implements and information so that they are able to feel confident with the change process. Remember:

- If you are unable to resource a new initiative, don't offer it.
- Train staff in the knowledge and skills needed to adapt to the change.
- Listen to frustrations and give time for them to be aired at meetings with staff.
- Arrange visits to locations where the change is operating successfully.
- Show that you understand the feelings and fears of those affected and take steps to relieve unnecessary concerns.
- Praise those who approach the change with a positive attitude. This will encourage others to follow.

Management Memo

Supervisors often face the task of helping their staffers accept changes over which they have little control. If employees can be convinced that they do have control, they'll feel less stressed and they'll allow themselves to adapt. They may even begin to believe in the changes, and their commitment will be reflected in increased productivity.[172]

7 Build a track record.

Concentrate on one project at a time and make it successful. Success, more than any other factor, will show those who might have a tendency to resist, that there is nothing to fear. Always be able to explain convincingly and without artificial justification why something new is necessary or desirable. If you develop a reputation for not leaping on every bandwagon, this too will add to your credibility as a change agent. You will be perceived as a thoughtful, deliberate manager so that when you do move in a new direction, there is confidence in your judgement.

8 Foster a climate in support of change.

Stimulate an ongoing positive attitude to change by regularly discussing new ideas, initiatives and issues with your staff. Celebrate the achievement of goals in the change process. Be flexible and experimental in your approach to the ideas of others, and encourage the risk-takers and innovators on staff. People constantly exposed to ideas and new practices are more likely to favour any call for change in the future.

See also: 306, 346-348

How to introduce new technology into your organisation

New and emerging technologies such as computers, printers, telecommunications, CD-Rom and multimedia are flooding the business marketplace. But there's a lot more to introducing these technologies than simply purchasing the hardware and the supporting software. To avoid costly mistakes, remember that the success of any technology purchase in your organisation is directly proportional to the time and effort you spend on the planning you do prior to purchase and implementation...

1 Develop a rationale for the use of the new technology.

The first step in planning for the introduction of any new technology in your organisation has little to do with the equipment at all. Before considering hardware and software, spend some time thinking about your organisation and what you want the technology to do, what software will help you meet those objectives, and what hardware will best run the software.

Here are some ideas to help in the process of developing that rationale:

- Do an audit. What technologies are currently being used, and for what reason, in such areas as:

  personnel, payroll, record keeping, library administration, word processing, scheduling, stock control, budget, communication networking, transport...
- How effective is current usage? What skills do staff currently possess? What staff development opportunities are available? What consultants are available? Who is responsible for the company's overall technology use?
- Verify the audit findings with the users.
- Formulate a plan which specifies how the new technology will facilitate more effective training, production or administrative practice.
- Establish a reasonable time frame for implementation.

Never purchase hardware and software before having identified clearly the purpose to which the technology will be put.

2 Build ownership of the initiative with key participants.

Any new initiative or purchase must be owned by and reflected in the beliefs and actions of the participants if it is to lead to altered professional behaviours. Without involvement and commitment, successful implementation will be difficult. Develop strategies for involving relevant staff members in the appropriate decision-making processes. Consider task forces, committees, regular communication, mentoring and awareness sessions.

Management Memo

Technology planning is not an isolated activity, but needs to be viewed in the context of the entire organisation. Planning is a people process which needs to involve the stakeholders... And just because technology *can* be used for an activity doesn't mean it *should* be used or even provides the best solution.[173]

3 Examine fully all budgetary considerations.

Funding for technology initiatives extends beyond the initial purchase costs of expensive hardware. Consider also maintenance, replacement and upgrading costs, as well as the costs of software, ancillary items and training. Ideally, a three to five year fiscal plan should account for these costs and incorporate such alternative financial strategies as lease or buy back agreements.

4 Develop a strategy for staff training and professional development.

Training and professional development are separate requirements when introducing new equipment or a technological initiative. Training makes staff competent users of the technology, and users need training time to become familiar with the use of the new technological tools, such as copying files adding graphics, crashing disks, losing files and operating printers. Professional development allows staff to successfully incorporate the technology into the workplace environment or into administrative practice.

5 Guarantee access to technical and professional support.

Staff require access to a range of support services which enable them to integrate the technology into the workplace environment. Without such support, the technology can become little more than another imposition on staff, rather than a catalyst for improving workplace performance. Explore the variety of opportunities: networking, journals, consultants, professional or trade associations, and the technology suppliers themselves.

6 Evaluate the initiative.

An evaluative process must accompany any new initiative in order to enhance further programme decisions. In essence, did the initiative contribute to more effective workplace or administrative practice? What were the positives? What were the negatives?

7 Appreciate the value of people.

Remember: a successful initiative depends on more than the mere injection of new technology into your organisation. It's the commitment, dedication, enthusiasm, skills and knowledge of your employees and other users that matter. Take steps to foster their involvement.

 See also: 202, 264

How to build and lead an effective executive team

People are our most valuable resource – a cliché perhaps, but it's true. To achieve all of the things you want for your organisation, you will need to surround yourself at the top level with the best people: an effective management or executive team. Having a good team is a very smart way of magnifying your own abilities. Here are a few ideas on how to assemble that team and then lead it...

1 Develop an inner circle.

Whatever your management situation, you need a trusted inner circle of colleagues; not ones who always agree with you, but ones who really contribute to the process and the end result. Smaller groups, often established on an *ad hoc* basis, are much more productive than larger ones. Entry to, or exit from such groups occurs according to performance and the specific task.

2 Select the best people.

To arrive at a good team, you will need people who –

- can get things done
- have leadership qualities
- are able to create useful ideas
- analyse problems effectively
- are good at oral and written communication
- have technical expertise
- can control the workflow
- can think and evaluate logically.

Select or build a team of people with compensating strengths and weaknesses. If you inherit an existing team, then reshuffle or reinforce as required.

3 Use time to drive decision-making.

People are often reluctant to make tough decisions, preferring to put off such action to another meeting. When you get your group together, get into the habit of setting specific timelines and targets – and don't let yourself be talked into extending those deadlines. Your actions will gain the support of group members tired of attending endless meetings that simply transfer agenda items to other occasions.

4 Keep it simple.

The old 'KISS' principle (Keep It Simple, Stupid) has been overdone, but simplicity *is* the key to achievement. Look critically at decisions and their planned implementation. If the required actions are not dead-set simple, complications will often result, and additional work will be required.

5 Set goals that challenge.

Think in terms of S-T-R-E-T-C-H goals. Setting minimum standards for an executive team results only in that minimum becoming the accepted maximum. Hold your colleagues accountable for achieving those stretch goals. If people are to be recognised for their performances, often in the form of bonuses, make sure they earn that recognition.

6 Maintain focus.

Remember the old saying, 'What you focus on, grows.' Once you have agreed on the action goals, stick with them until they have been achieved. Resist adding extra ones until you have succeeded with the existing ones. Too many goals reduce the focus and stifle real achievement.

7 Insist on value for time and energy.

If you're having a meeting, insist on results, especially action in the form of decisions. Meetings are important, but every meeting does not have to involve onlookers or passengers. Only those who can contribute should be involved in any discussion.

8 Focus on the can-doers.

Quality people are sometimes hidden in organisations. Often such people may have chosen to avoid the game-playing and corporate politics. You can't afford not to identify them, involve and encourage them. At the same time, rid your team of the excuse-makers and the 'we've always done it this way-ers'. You must surround yourself with those who can show you what has to be done – then do it.

Management Memo

A team is not a self-contained motor that continues to whirr smoothly as long as you supply the fuel. A team is composed of individuals in a dynamic relationship, both with one another and with their immediate environment. [174]

9 Think 55.

The Rule of 55 states that, 'fifty per cent of an organisation's products usually produce only 5 per cent of its revenue and profits'. This means that half of your business represents only 5 per cent of your profitability! The challenge for you and your executive team is to identify that underperforming 50 per cent and apply the strategy made famous by Jack Welch, then CEO at General Electric: find ways to fix it, sell it or close it down. That's what your executive team is for.

10 And remember...

- Executive team members must be very familiar with your organisation's goals and priorities.
- Members must know what actions are expected of them and their responsibilities in implementing team decisions.
- Members should be able to influence team decisions appropriately.
- Discussion is encouraged regardless of how critical it may be. Views that differ are not taken as indications of a disloyal or uncooperative colleague.
- Members must be skilful in expressing ideas so that others clearly understand their intent.
- Members share equitably in the workload of the team.
- Members are able to present team decisions to client groups in a manner that generates understanding and support for implementation.

 See also: 38, 292, 300

How to solve a major problem in your organisation

Managers are faced with a never-ending flow of problems and decisions. During the course of a week, hundreds of spontaneous, minor problems are usually tackled with the minimum of fuss using years of accumulated knowledge and experience. However, at times, a major problem will arise. On such occasions, the wise manager resorts to a classic problem-solving strategy, one of which is outlined here. When you have a serious problem to grapple with, why not try following these nine steps...

1 Identify the symptoms.

When you sense that trouble is brewing in your organisation, it's usually the symptoms of a problem that surface first: changes in behaviour patterns, bickering between staff members, uneven performance, missing petty cash, litter, poorly attended staff meetings. Be on the lookout for such clues for they are the indicators that a major problem could be below the surface.

2 Define the problem.

You're aware of the symptoms – now try to define the problem but, be warned, it's not always easy to pinpoint. Unless you can state the problem in one sentence, you either still don't know what the problem is, or you are trying to deal with several problems at once. Don't confuse the symptoms, the causes and the problem.

3 Specify your objectives.

Be clear on what you are setting out to achieve in tackling the problem. Compare the existing situation with the desired state: where you are now and where you would like to be. Then state the transformation necessary to move from one state to the other.

4 Analyse the problem.

Firstly, get the facts. Ask questions of all parties, use your eyes and ears without prejudice, and read for guidance in policy handbooks, precedent files or the journals. You might never have all the facts but it is essential to have enough facts.

Secondly, order and simplify your information. Distil and reorder the material to get at the core of the issue, the real problem.

Thirdly, check your facts for accuracy and for relevance. Discard where necessary.

Finally, assess the data without prejudice, preconceived ideas or emotion.

5 Generate alternative solutions.

Problem-solving requires a choice of options. To find the best option, you must consider several possible solutions. By formulating many options, you will be less likely to overlook the best course of action. If necessary use brainstorming and creative thinking techniques to foster the free flow of ideas.

6 Evaluate the various alternative solutions.

Evaluate the options you have now generated. List the advantages and disadvantages of each. Mentally test each option by imagining that each has already been put into effect. Think of the consequences, anticipated and unanticipated, of each alternative. Focus on the two or three that look most promising.

7 Choose the best solution.

You may now have come up with 34 ways to skin a cat – but you want the best one. In making your final selection, you could call upon previous experience, advice from others, intuition, experimentation, or such scientific tools as linear programming or simulation modelling. Compare your short-listed alternatives, allocate values or points to each to arrive at a final decision.

Remember, the best solution will normally be the one with the most advantages and the fewest disadvantages. Often the best solution will be the one that is least undesirable.

8 Take the necessary action.

Now is the time to plan carefully how best to implement your decision. You will need an action plan. Since most decisions affect or involve people, you should communicate and consult with those affected to gain their support. Decide on what has to be done, how, by whom and when. What might go wrong? How will the results be reported or checked?

Management Memo

The toughest part of problem-solving is defining the problem. What appears to be the problem might at best be merely a symptom. It usually is necessary to delve deeper in order to locate the real problem and define it.

For example, a supervisor might believe that she is confronted with a problem of conflicting personalities when two employees are continually bickering and cannot get along together. After checking, the supervisor finds that the real problem is that she, the supervisor, has never clearly outlined the functions and duties of each employee – where their duties begin and end. Therefore, what appeared on the surface to be a problem of personality conflict was actually a problem of an organisational nature. Only after the true nature of the problem has been recognised can the supervisor do something about it.[175]

9 Monitor the impact of your solution.

Routine follow-up checks will ensure that you have solved the problem. Check the symptoms again – have they disappeared or at least been reduced? Set up control measures to compare actual with planned results. Take corrective action where necessary. If the problem has in fact not been solved, you'll need to go through the process once more from a completely new perspective.

 See also: 354, 404

How to manage a crisis

A bomb threat, the recall of a defective product, a shooting, a wildcat strike, a plant explosion, a security alert of any kind – are you ready to handle a major crisis in your organisation? Those first few moments are going to be crucial in gaining control over events. Good crisis managers are decisive, and have a process in place to ensure the safety of customers and employees and to minimise disruption to the day-to-day operations of the organisation. Here are some guidelines to help you prepare for the unexpected...

1 Prepare for an emergency – now.

Now is the time to think about the unthinkable. It will pay off when you least expect it. Among the items you should consider immediately are:

- Have a crisis response team in place. Allocate specific responsibilities to team members (and their back-ups) and work together to outline each person's role.
- Imagine what crises your organisation might experience within and external to it. With the crisis team, develop skeleton plans for responding to those events.
- Ensure your records are always up to date – next-of-kin and contact names and telephone numbers for emergency services and helping agencies.
- Know where to access any information you will need in a hurry.
- Assemble the crisis response team periodically to review the overall plan and provide necessary training – handling phone calls, dealing with the media, alerting customers and staff.
- Be clear on how traumatic support services and care-givers will be used during and after the event.
- Check that your crisis plan is kept up to date with industry guidelines.

2 Analyse the situation.

When a crisis situation occurs, assess it as coolly as you can and consider:

- Is it really a crisis?
- What is its probable impact?
- How much time do you have?
- Who else is involved and who is likely to be involved?
- What resources do you have and what will you need?

3 Stay calm.

Now is an opportunity for you to demonstrate more of your unique qualities. Remember these three essentials for remaining cool in a crisis:

- *It's okay to be nervous.* Sports psychologists and athletes have exposed the myth that if you get nervous you'll perform poorly.

- *Relax*. This is a time when your mind and body need to be in sync. Breathe deeply, talk yourself through the situation, and repeat positive affirmations.
- *Remain calm*. Nervousness is okay; panic is not. Work through a process methodically, confronting problems rather than avoiding them.

4 Call your crisis team into action.

Your preparation will pay off when you are able to assemble your crisis management team in which members know their responsibilities. Discuss your preliminary plan and other contingencies, allocate roles, establish a crisis management centre, appoint a spokesperson, review the communication process, and enact the plan. The plan should include:

- specific timelines
- contingency plans to deal with new developments or emergencies
- longer-term solutions to be prepared and implemented at the right time.

5 Communicate the facts.

A quality communication strategy will allow you to weather the storm with integrity and credibility. Consider the following:

- Channel all communication through one spokesperson.
- Hold a thorough briefing for the entire staff: provide the facts and outline the coping mechanisms.
- Inform customers as soon as possible to combat rumours and gossip.
- Liaise with the media.
- Keep your bosses informed.

Management Memo

Crisis management is essentially about decision-making. The difficulty is in making quick, but effective, decisions under conditions that demand immediate solutions. The lack of a workable crisis strategy can lead to monumental errors in judgement and ill-conceived snap decisions. [176]

6 Provide counselling and follow-up support.

Depending on the nature of the crisis, staff and any customers directly involved can experience wide-ranging, distressing and emotional reactions. Counsellors and other support professionals should be made available. For employees, a critical incident debriefing is important to help stabilise the workplace after the crisis, hasten the return to work, lower the long-term incidence of generalised anxiety, and reduce the likelihood of litigation.

7 Evaluate actions and reactions.

Monitor progress continuously so that you can modify the plan and take corrective or pre-emptive steps. When the crisis has passed, assemble your crisis response team for a thorough debriefing and evaluation of procedures.

How to run a better office

Managing a modern office can be a demanding job. It requires some sensible and well-considered strategies to deal with people, resources, time and paper. Depending on the size of your organisation and your administrative style, your office and its adjuncts, can be Mission Control, the Fortress of Solitude, or something in between. Over time, it will become what you make it. In the meantime, here are a few basic suggestions which might start you thinking about running a better office...

1 Consider the premises.

It may not be possible to improve your existing office arrangement, but it's amazing how often people are prepared to accept an unsatisfactory layout just because they're used to it. Life is already filled with an ample supply of distractions and discomforts, so why make life in your office more difficult than it needs to be?

Take a look at your office. The office area should be efficient, neat, attractively arranged and business-like. The work environment should be well-lit, equipped with appropriate furniture, and easily accessible in terms of visitors and work flow. Are phones, equipment, files and materials conveniently placed? Do you have adequate privacy? Has all unwanted furniture or dated equipment been removed? Have you added some greenery and art?

And pay special attention to the reception area: it must be welcoming, comfortable and informative, after all, it is the first port of call for customers, clients and suppliers. Be imaginative with decor and setting.

2 Provide the appropriate equipment.

Research has shown that communication eats up over 70 per cent of a manager's time – phone calls, visitors, conferences, correspondence, writing, meetings, in- and out-trays, and so on.

For starters then, investigate the communicative tasks that you and your office staff are required to handle and determine if you have the appropriate tools to carry out this role in the most efficient manner. Focus for example on technology – phones (multi-feature units, conference, cellular), answering machines, computers, ancillary equipment, appropriate software, photocopiers, facsimile machines, modems, intercoms, electronic mail, pagers, security systems. Check out the many valuable and often inexpensive administrative aids now available: multi-purpose diaries, visual wall planners, modern filing, software programmes, pocket diaries, to-do lists, and the like.

Is your office equipment ready to carry you into the twenty-first century, or are you more appropriately equipped for the 1980s?

3 Focus on your office staff.

If you're lucky enough to have a secretary and other support staff, ensure that each has helped compile a clear list of responsibilities relating to mail, telephone, paperwork, appointments, visitors, filing, office organisation, human relations, typing, accounting, confidentiality and so on. How can you help your secretary make better use of time – by providing training? by improving conditions? by altering work schedules? Is your secretary an effective personal assistant?

Remember too that, for many people, their first impression of your organisation is the one formed when first greeted by office staff. When did you last discuss with your office personnel the importance of this up-front role – their appearance, and their manner and attitude in responding to public, customers, clients and suppliers.

4 Establish workable procedures.

When did you last analyse the way things are done in the office? Many 'procedures' aren't, they're just habits. What *are* your current procedures? How is mail, for example, best opened, screened and distributed? What procedure do you have for weeding out irrelevant files and records? Do you create work with endless forms? Have you recently checked the telephone etiquette? Or reception area courtesies? Take a look at each office task and ask:

- Is it really needed? If not, stop doing it.
- Is it being done at the right time?
- Is the right person doing it?
- Can the process be simplified without losing effectiveness?
- Can the process be computerised?

How effective are your office procedures for tackling the paper war? Does your office staff try to adhere to such basic rules of office management as:

- Never handle a piece of paper twice.
- Never leave the office until your desk is clean.
- Don't write it; phone it.
- Never stack paper.
- Work from a to-do list. And so on.

Management Memo

If your surroundings are depressing, your work may suffer. So brighten up whatever you can to create a pleasant and comfortable working environment... Paper processing, perhaps more than any other office function, depends on a responsive physical environment: easy access to files and equipment.[177]

5 Check the access to your office.

Do staff have ready access to you? Do you have an open door policy, or do you require appointments to be made? Just how accessible are you? With all the demands placed on a manager's time today, this can become a crucial factor in your relationships with employees.

6 Remember: the final image is important.

Courtesy, respect, availability, accessibility, appearance, efficiency – all vital elements for you to consider in fostering for your office a positive image within the organisation.

 See also: 358

How to save money by cutting costs

In tough economic times, it is vital for organisations to keep running costs to a minimum without jeopardising the welfare of employees or the productivity of the business. By examining some of the basic fabric of your organisation, such as telephones, photocopiers, lighting, office supplies and the use of outside services, it is possible to make considerable savings which, over a year, can have a marked impact on your financial bottom-line…

1 Recycle wherever possible.

By reusing whatever material you can, you save money, reduce waste disposal costs, and help protect the planet. Consider these ideas to begin with – ideas which will help save money and the environment:

- Reuse and relabel old file folders.
- Reuse letters or notes by drafting at the bottom or on the back your answer to the original correspondence.
- Staple scrap paper together to make handy memo or phone message pads.
- Reuse large envelopes if they are still in good shape.
- If you make a mistake on a sheet of paper, use the other side for future rough work or drafts.
- Take an inventory of the forms or standard letters you use and eliminate the unnecessary ones.
- Cut back on all those memos to staff. Instead, post memos on bulletin boards or circulate them.
- Styrofoam cups are a no-no. Have staff bring their own mugs instead.
- Prepare a small sign for bulletin boards and waste bins: 'THINK BEFORE YOU TOSS'.

2 Reduce your interior lighting costs.

Get the most out of your lighting dollar by considering the following:

- Replace old lighting systems with high efficiency fluorescent lights. They use less energy and last twice as long.
- Train staff to turn off lights when not in use and institute procedures which ensure all lights are extinguished at the end of the day. Colour-code switches for lights and equipment which must remain on at night.
- If rebuilding or remodelling, consider the use of natural lighting, skydomes, skylights, glass bricks, light paint colours and decorative mirrors.

3 Focus on the photocopier.

Photocopiers can be expensive technology in terms of purchase, rental, service charges, supplies and time. Consider these points:

- New technology is designed to save you money in the long term. So make sure your staff know how to take advantage of all the special features on modern photocopiers. Two-sided copying saves paper; automatic feeding, collating and stapling save time at the machine; reduction-enlargement options save time and money when used wisely. Staff training sessions are often offered as part of the purchase deal – so use this service.
- Consider cooperative buying with other businesses in your area for paper

and supplies. Buying larger quantities almost always increases discounts.

- Place a tray beside the photocopier to collect bad copies; the other side can be put to a variety of uses.
- Periodically, conduct an audit of photocopier use (or misuse) – you may be surprised at what you find.

4 Limit telephone usage.

Save on your phone bill by:

- letting your employees know you regularly review itemised accounts
- barring national and international calls
- scheduling national and international calls and faxes for off-peak times if possible
- charging clients for calls made on their behalf
- using an agenda for national and international calls
- purchasing or leasing equipment outright – it's cheaper than renting
- checking phone bills for errors.

5 Minimise expensive professional fees.

When using outside consultants and professional advisers, know clearly what services you are 'buying'. To minimise expenses, remember to…

- be sure you really need this service
- shop around for the best deal
- consider using less expensive services for routine matters, e.g. use a debt collection agency instead of a solicitor
- talk about fees beforehand, and be clear on how fees will be charged – by the hour, flat fee, varying scale etc.
- consider 'group actions' to share costs with other organisations
- do whatever preliminary work is needed to reduce costs, and ensure the adviser has relevant files to eliminate the need for expensive searches later.

6 Seek the advice of your staff.

Try asking your key employees where costs can be reduced and you'll generate some productive discussion. Ask: If you had to reduce business expenses in your area by 10 per cent, what would you cut? And where in other areas? Would any real value be lost? If we reduced just one expense each month by 5 per cent,what savings would accumulate annually?

> **Management Memo**
>
> Don't make occasional erratic efforts to get workers to reduce waste. Effective control happens only when continuous efforts are made until sensible economies become workplace habits. [178]

7 Check productivity.

Productivity leaks cost your business money. Consider the salary costs alone of starting meetings late, poor planning, duplication of effort, calling unnecessary meetings, non-essential overtime, socialising and keeping unnecessary records. Focus too on pilfering, loss of supplies through faulty equipment, and loss through worker confusion or incompetence.

8 Introduce your cuts imaginatively.

When introducing an unpopular cost cutting policy, try to get the message across creatively and, if possible, with a little humour – as did Nippon Steel several years ago:

> To reduce the excessive monthly phone bill, we tried a poster campaign to limit long-distance calls to three minutes. This failed. So a list of culprits was drawn up and each was presented with a gift-wrapped three-minute egg timer and call-monitor chart. Within a month, the plant's phone bill dropped 52 per cent.

How to reduce the number of time-consuming meetings

Meetings, whether they be one-on-one discussions or gatherings of five, ten, or twenty people, are an important part of working life – but they are so time-consuming. And often they are criticised for being unproductive, costly, boring, and sometimes unnecessary. Are they always needed? And so many of them? Check out these points, and you may find you'll be holding fewer meetings in future...

1 Be fully aware of the cost of your meetings.

Meetings consume valuable time – sizable chunks of time are often taken up with rambling discussions, excessive socialising, political manoeuvring, special interest conflicts and travelling. Nor is time the only casualty. When did you last check out what your organisation's meetings were costing in terms of salaries alone?

2 Consider why you hold so many meetings.

Meetings can be very useful tools for communicating ideas, clarifying information, solving problems, making decisions and building teams. But they can also be held for the wrong reasons:

Do you meet simply because the day of the week traditionally calls for it? Do you meet but are primarily socialising under the guise of work? Does your department meet once a week – only because another department does? Do you hold many meetings because you believe volume is indicative of the 'busy-ness' and productivity of your organisation or yourself? Do you hold a meeting simply because you haven't the courage to make a decision yourself? Do you hold a meeting to make a decision even though you've already made up your mind?

Spend some time thinking about *why* you hold regular and once-only meetings before considering the following strategies aimed at cutting back on unproductive meeting time...

3 Establish a workable review process.

So often regular meetings outlive their usefulness. Try to set a termination date whenever you establish a committee or, at least, review a committee's progress periodically, disbanding it if it is no longer productive.

4 Consolidate your meeting procedures.

One manager found she was spending hours each month in separate meetings with individual department heads, covering basically the same topics. She now holds a monthly group meeting – which also helps the department heads keep abreast of one another's activities and forges an *esprit de corps*. Are there any creative ways of consolidating your meeting times?

5 Limit the number of meeting participants.

Problem: The larger the crowd, the more the discussion, the longer the meeting. Solution: Limit attendance to those concerned with topics on the agenda. Schedule some participants to attend only that part of the meeting that they can contribute to. Make sure key people are present.

6 Define clearly the purpose of every meeting.

Have a definite reason for every meeting. Think 'reason' first, then 'meeting'. Legitimate reasons might include: solving a problem or making a decision where group expertise is essential; obtaining information from participants prior to group discussion and clarification; motivating people with common goals; generating new ideas through brainstorming; exchanging viewpoints; announcing new policies or programmes followed by a Q&A session to clarify the issues. Meetings are generally not an efficient way to dispense information; if that's the primary reason for the gathering, then you should rethink the need for calling the meeting…

7 Consider an alternative to calling a meeting.

Once you have specified the purpose of your meeting, consider if another alternative might not be a more efficient form of communication, e.g.

- Want feedback on a new proposal? Try a short survey or some quick phone calls.
- Need to disseminate information? Consider a memo, poster or news sheet.

Management Memo

There are many people who think that holding or attending a continuous string of meetings is a sign of their power and importance. The exact opposite is true. If meetings are merely routine or unnecessary, they are, in fact, a sure sign of bad management. [179]

- Trying to get your staff to know each other better? Run a barbeque after hours or on Saturday.
- Want some ideas on an issue? Put a large 'graffiti sheet' in the staffroom.
- Need to hear about problems? Try 10-minute one-on-one meetings rather than tying up *all* staff for two hours.

If you can achieve some outcomes without calling meetings, then you can save much time and the meetings you do call will become powerful, special events.

8 In addition...

- Occasionally cancel a regular meeting to test the need for it.
- Keep a folder of agenda items and, instead of having regularly scheduled meetings, only call a meeting when your folder has sufficient items. You'll find that many items will take care of themselves without a meeting!
- Question *every* item on an agenda. Could they be handled in other ways?
- To avoid losing productivity and time, work hard to make every meeting a very good one, for, as Peter Drucker reminds us: 'One either meets or one works – one cannot do both at the same time.'

How to compile a meeting agenda that really works

Call it a meeting plan or call it a simple list – but call it essential, because an agenda is the backbone of any successful meeting. The more care you take with its preparation, the more productive the meeting will be. If you want to gain a reputation as someone who conducts productive meetings, then take the time to compile a workable agenda beforehand. Here's how…

1 Be aware of the need for an agenda.

An agenda is a written promise from a meeting's leader to those in attendance. It is a commitment that, in the time allocated to the meeting, discussion will focus on the items listed. As well, the agenda is valuable because it provides the meeting with direction, purpose, confidence and control. A meeting without an agenda is a meeting without an end.

2 Decide on the degree of formality required.

There are meetings so small that a written agenda is inappropriate: the agenda is set in the first few minutes of discussion. Agendas are essential for larger gatherings, however. Formal meetings require formal agendas – including consideration of apologies, minutes of the last meeting, matters arising from those minutes, treasurer's report etc. For less formal meetings, the chairperson usually has a free hand to list and order the items to achieve the aims of the meeting in the most stimulating way.

3 List the items.

At least a few days before the meeting, decide on the items for discussion. Participants might also be asked to contribute specific topics for the agenda – often a pre-meeting discussion eliminates the need to put an item on the list. To restrict the length of the meeting, either limit the number of topics or the time to be spent on each.

4 Place the items in sequence.

The success or failure of a meeting can depend on the sequencing of its agenda items. Consider these points:

- If an item needs mental energy, clear heads and bright ideas, then put it high on the list.
- Hold back for a while any item of great interest to participants to get some other useful work done first. Introduce the star item when attention begins to lag.
- Less interesting items should come directly after a very challenging one, thereby giving members time to recover before the next tough topic.

- If a participant must arrive late or leave early, ensure an item requiring his/her input is placed on the agenda in a position suited to his/her arrangements.
- Items with potential for attracting conflict could be placed later when members have less energy to go for each other's throats. Then again, problems are probably best tackled when people are at their best. A tricky issue.
- Begin and end a meeting on a positive note, with items which unite members.

5 Structure the agenda.

An agenda should be more than just a list of topics. The features of a good agenda include:

- *Title, date, location* and, possibly, a list of participants.
- *Definite start/finish times.* This is an essential courtesy for busy participants. Note also, few meetings remain productive after two hours unless adequate breaks are provided.
- *Topics, the person responsible for introducing or leading the topic, the objective,* and *the time limit* set for that item (see accompanying box). Of course, the amount of time a topic will actually need can be very unpredictable, but without some indication, the meeting could go well over time, or several items will be neglected.

Topic	Person responsible	Objective	Time (mins)
1. Approve Agenda	Alan Fry	Decision	3
2. New information leaflets	Di Henty	Information	5
3. New requirements for leave requests	Alan Fry	Discussion	10
4. Changes to library	Phil Greer	Discussion	10
5. Increasing staff participation	Mary Gill	Problem-solutions	25

Management Memo

Think of the agenda as a device to focus your meeting. A meeting with no agenda will have no focus and the results will be fuzzy. Too many-sided issues slip into consideration and, finally, like the famous Caucus Race witnessed by Alice in her Wonderland dream, all the attendees end up chasing each other around in circles.[180]

- Where decisions need to be made, some chairpersons like to include as a guide on the agenda *the wording of the anticipated decisions.*

6 Assemble any background papers.

The agenda should be accompanied by any necessary background material. This will allow participants to consider the topic carefully in advance and to formulate useful questions.

7 Distribute the agenda in advance.

Distribute the agenda and background papers at least two to three days before the meeting. If it is circulated too far in advance, participants may forget it or lose it.

8 Use the agenda to monitor the meeting.

At the meeting, begin by seeking agreement for the agenda, then stick with the allocated order and times. Although the temptation will arise, it's important then to stay firm with the agenda if you are to gain respect as a productive chairperson.

How to get results from a committee you appoint

Committees are frequently criticised for their inability to accomplish a great deal, for being costly and time-consuming, for being unable to reach decisions, and for often producing mediocre decisions anyway. A committee's success or failure can often be traced back to the experience of the manager who appoints it and the extent to which the following guidelines are adhered to...

1 Be sure you really need that committee.

Sometimes the use of a committee is not the best strategy for tackling a particular task you have isolated. It might be wise *not* to use a committee if...

- you already have a solution, have made a decision, or will be hesitant about accepting the committee's recommendation. Remember, people resent spending valuable energy and time producing the axiomatic.
- there is not enough time or expertise available for the committee to operate effectively.
- the focus cannot be handled through group discussion. For example, policy formulation, problem-solving and planning are appropriate activities; managerial functions or research may be inappropriate.

In such cases, you might consider an alternative process, such as a survey, delegation, consultancy or a task force.

2 Define the assignment specifically.

A committee must know clearly its purpose, as defined through a written terms of reference, which in turn must be translated into a set of tasks or goals for completion within a set timeframe. Unless the committee's parameters and authority are specified, the members may not know whether they are responsible for a decision, a recommendation or merely inconclusive deliberation. To whom will the committee be reporting? By when? How will it report? What resources are available?

Try to resolve such matters before the first meeting is held.

3 Choose your chairperson carefully.

The chairperson is the key to avoiding many of the criticisms of committee work. An effective chair plans for meetings, prepares and distributes agendas and supporting material, presents proposals for discussion and action, conducts meetings efficiently, and guides the thinking of committee members. A committee's success is clearly linked to the skill of its chairperson.

4 Appoint good committee members.

In selecting members for your

committees, keep these points in mind:

- Seek voluntary membership preferably, since willing workers provide for greatest harmony and productivity in the long run.
- Appoint members according to the skills, strengths, energy and commitment required to accomplish the task.
- Select members who have a vested interest in getting the task completed.
- Attend to membership balance: consider age, gender, experience and positive and negative views.
- Ensure that the members are suitably representative of the interests they are intended to serve and that they possess the necessary authority.
- Select members who are able to perform well in a group situation.

5 Insist on effective recording and reporting procedures.

Agendas and written minutes of meetings are fundamental to a committee's ongoing productivity. They stimulate members to reach conclusions, call for follow-up actions, and provide a permanent record for future reference.

6 Evaluate regularly the effectiveness of your committees.

An ongoing programme of evaluation will show which committees are effective, which are not, how some could improve their operations, and when additional committees are needed. It is important to write an evaluation process into the life of all committees.

Management Memo

Productivity in a committee comes through its being given urgent problems, the power to make decisions or recommendations, easy communication between the members, an orderly system of treating problems, a skilled chairperson, and the intelligence and originality of the group... [181]

7 And, don't forget...

- Monitor overlapping areas of focus since there is always the danger that one committee might need to discuss an item on the agenda of another. Take steps to avoid conflict. In such cases, propose joint meetings on the common issue or refer the relevant recommendations of one committee to the other.
- Where possible, make your committees representative of all organisational groups: professional, clerical, support staff, workers, even customers.
- Check that, with time, your committees don't become more concerned with maintenance rather than developmental aspects.
- Provide feedback to the committee to preserve morale and to educate the members in relation to management thinking. Advise on how their deliberations were used, or how and why they were modified.
- Give credit where credit is due, even if a committee is having limited success.

How to make best use of the grapevine

Rumours and gossip are an inevitable part of everyday work life. Your organisation's informal communication network, the grapevine, draws groups together because of their common interests, fears and shared beliefs. Indeed, it is a perfectly natural organisational phenomenon which fulfils the members' desire to be 'in the know'. If left unguarded, however, malicious rumours in the grapevine can be very destructive. Conversely, properly managed, the grapevine can be used to your advantage...

1 Understand why rumours begin.

Your organisation's grapevine is very active and carries large amounts of information, at times inaccurate, with amazing speed. To deal with it, you must first know the conditions in your organisation which foster the spread of rumours:

- lack of information and news
- a situation loaded with anxiety
- the presence of faulty information
- prolonged delays in decision-making
- a feeling by staff that they have no control over circumstances
- serious problems in the organisation
- excessive personal antagonisms.

2 Assess the importance of any rumour.

Before planning corrective counter-measures, assess first the potential damage a particular rumour might cause. Often it is best to ignore it. Ask: 'What would happen if I did nothing?' On the other hand, if the spreading rumour is damaging, confer with those people primarily affected by it, assure them of your concern and reveal your plans to combat the story. Move quickly to 'debunk' the rumour by presenting the facts.

3 Combat misinformation – call a meeting.

It's always best to communicate face-to-face if possible. Written messages or those relayed via a third party aren't always understood. Conduct small-group meetings with staff or community if necessary. Present the facts. This up-front approach also provides for instant feedback and an opportunity to clarify the situation immediately through questions and answers.

4 Adopt a positive stance.

Don't risk reinforcing the rumour by restating it. Try to avoid references to it when disseminating the facts. Never be defensive. Most people can sense when someone is masking the truth or clouding an issue in such a way as to attempt to dissipate a problem simply because it is unpleasant. Respond in a calm, reasonable way with specifics to destroy the credibility of those who would make irresponsible statements without regard to consequences. Hide nothing if you have nothing to hide.

5 Encourage people to call you.

Through the printed word and at meetings, always encourage staff, if they hear something which appears to be particularly injurious to the reputation of the organisation or which is a severe departure from what has customarily been policy, to contact you immediately to check it out.

6 Keep key players on side.

Stay in constant touch with key subordinates and opinion leaders. Their friendship can be valuable when people are needed to support your position in a time of manufactured crisis. On such occasions, meet with these key players, and solicit their assistance to spread the truth via the grapevine.

7 Anticipate a rumour before it starts.

Likely staff, customer or client concerns should be anticipated and defused *before* they ever become a hot grapevine item. Meet with key players, give them the real story and guide their thinking. They can spread the facts before anyone else can spread the rumours.

8 Communicate.

Very few of your staff feel they get all the information they think they need. The grapevine is most active when information is scarce and demand for it is high. But when people believe that they are being kept abreast of every detail of your organisation's operation – maybe even more information than they want – the thirst for additional data from others is quenched.

> **Management Memo**
>
> The supervisor should always bear in mind that the receptiveness of any group to the rumours of the grapevine is directly related to the strength of the supervisor's leadership. If employees believe that their supervisor is fair and that every effort will be made to keep them informed, they will tend to disregard rumours and look to the supervisor for proper answers to be provided.[182]

9 Learn to use the grapevine yourself.

Alert leaders acknowledge the grapevine's existence and will try to take advantage of it, for example:

- Tune in to it and learn what people are thinking and feeling.
- Feed it yourself using trusted colleagues, opinion moulders and company advocates.
- Pass the word about some planned change in company routine and then wait to see what reaction comes back.
- Release good news into the system before it is officially released. This way you get a double effect: first, a good rumour increases morale and, later, the official confirmation gives another boost.

10 Learn to live with the grapevine.

Don't try to kill the rumour mill – that's futile. It will always exist. Devote your energy instead to know what's on it, to take appropriate action, and to foster conditions within your company which do not fuel the fire of rumour-mongering.

See also: 104, 356

How to guard against things going wrong

Things go wrong in organisations for a number of reasons – people do less than they are capable of, they misuse their resources, they choose an inappropriate time to act, or the wrong place... We misread situations, we take the wrong actions, we're often out-of-tune and out-of-step. But things could be worse – imagine if our errors were tabulated and published every weekend like those of a football team! You can reduce the number of mistakes in your organisation by considering this advice...

1 Learn from your previous mistakes.

Mistakes will happen. Murphy had it right when he said that if anything can go wrong, it will. The worst mistake is to make the same mistake more than once. Learn to analyse what goes wrong, make notes on what to do and what not to do next time – and make sure you get it right in future.

2 Remember the basics of mistake minimisation.

(a) ***Think ahead.***
Planning is the key to minimising mistakes. Think ahead, anticipate all eventualities, and make contingency plans to cover yourself. This might not make your initiative mistake-free, but at least you will be better prepared to handle any obstacles that arise.

(b) ***Don't be over-confident.***
Many managers are so certain that everything is okay that they make no attempt to foresee any problems or be prepared for the unexpected. You certainly need confidence, but don't let it blind you or your staff.

(c) ***Guard against carelessness.***
A simple act of carelessness, often the result of over-confidence, pressure or the belief that a task is easier than we think, can destroy a project and damage a reputation. Check every fact and figure in every important report, letter or memo – and get someone else to check as well.

(d) ***Tolerate no laziness.***
According to *Proverbs*, 'Hard work means prosperity; only a fool idles his time away' – basic advice for today's manager. Tolerate no fools, especially lazy fools, for they could cost your organisation time and money. All companies have lazy people. A few of them are lazy by nature. On the other hand, the manager may well be at fault, for many lazy employees are viewed as 'lazy' simply because they have been given inadequate leadership, insufficient supervision or a poorly-defined role. Provided you have done your job, and if one of your staff is indeed indolent, then sink the boot. Laziness cannot be tolerated.

(e) ***Take a stand against incompetence.***
It is said in sporting circles that dropped catches lose matches. A dropped catch can be the sign of poor skill development in the athlete, and under-developed skills in the workplace can similarly lead to disaster. But incompetency can be minimised if you take steps to refine employee selection processes, monitor and improve performance standards, and implement training and coaching aimed at correcting identified weaknesses in staff competencies.

(f) ***Be disciplined when delegating to others.***
A poorly delegated job can have a disastrous outcome, so ensure you always select the right person for the task, conduct a thorough briefing, train as required, hand over authority, and monitor appropriately.

(g) ***Supervise, supervise, supervise.***
Orders or instructions without follow-up or supervision court mistakes, even disaster. You can't be expected to check every detail of your employees' work personally, but supervisors and section heads can, and report progress to you.

3 Consider drafting a risk management plan.

Since planning is a management priority, a risk management plan will prove to be a valuable tool for minimising major mistakes. Corporate risk management applies common sense to identifying, evaluating, measuring and treating the broad range of risks confronting an organisation – especially its people, its assets, its profits and its reputation. The risk management process consists of:

- identifying and evaluating the risk
- controlling that risk
- financing the process
- delegating responsibilities
- measuring results or benefits.

A typical risk management plan may contain the following:

1. An overview, consisting of scope, objectives, evaluation criteria and asset description
2. Risk identification and analysis
3. Risk assessment – risks to be accepted; unacceptable risks
4. Risk handling measures
   - List actions for reducing, avoiding or transferring identified risks
   - Assign responsibilities for actions needed
   - Prepare a risk action timeline
5. A schedule for ongoing risk review and management.

Management Memo

When I was taking business administration in college, I learned how a business operates under ideal conditions. But I was never taught what to do when things went wrong. I've found that those perfect conditions my professor talked about don't even exist. I spend most of my time ... trying to set something right that someone else has messed up. [183]

Use of ISO certification and total quality management procedures will help put in place non-conformance reporting and preventative actions to eliminate or significantly reduce the chances of a problem recurring.

4 Finally, don't forget what Murphy said...

Murphy regaled us with several irrefutable laws of the universe (and of management) and we would do well not to forget his timely advice:

- If anything can go wrong, it will.
- Nothing is as easy as it first looks.
- If there is a possibility of several things going wrong, the one that will cause the most damage will be the one to go wrong.
- Left to themselves, things tend to go from bad to worse.
- Whenever you set out to do something, invariably something else will need to be done first.
- It is impossible to make anything foolproof because fools are so ingenious.
- Anytime things appear to be going better, you will have overlooked something.
- If you do everything right, nobody will notice. If you do something wrong, everyone will notice.

It's a pity Murphy is so often right. You'll need to do your best to prove him wrong.

 See also: 266

How to crime-proof your workplace

Offices, shops and factories everywhere are becoming increasingly vulnerable to an expanding variety of non-violent and violent crimes: pilfering, shoplifting, vandalism, burglary, embezzlement, bad cheque writing, insurance fraud, arson, assault, even murder... Just how far a security-conscious organisation can go without upsetting employees or losing customers is the question facing most companies today. Is it time for you to become more security-conscious?

1 Develop and distribute a security policy.

What type of environment fosters productivity for employees, openness for customers and protection of the business from fraud, theft and harm? This should be the basis of joint management-employee discussions in the process of preparing a security statement for your organisation. Having developed a statement, hold employee meetings to discuss reasons for the policy and ask for possible improvements or changes. Disseminate the final document.

2 Train your employees to be security-conscious.

Contrary to popular belief, your staff will not inherently know what they should do and how they should act to protect your business assets. You need to create performance standards to define the parameters of their jobs, inculcate honest work habits, and educate them in the basics of security relating to your organisation, e.g.

- the swift and certain consequences for dishonest employees.
- how to recognise and report all suspicious behaviour.
- awareness of personal security, such as after-hours safety and valuables.
- an anonymous in-house system for reporting possible crimes.
- the economics of crime and how it can affect pay-packets.
- the purpose of working in pairs in certain sensitive work areas.
- what to do if a break-in is discovered.
- what to observe when a crime takes place...

3 Protect your premises.

Whatever assets a business possesses, someone can always be tempted to steal them. To thwart overt and covert criminal theft or damage, you'll need to protect your premises. Consider the following precautions for starters:

- Keep all supplies areas locked.
- Use deadlocks throughout.
- Improve external lighting.
- Install movement sensor alarms.
- Install closed-circuit TV cameras in hard-to-see areas.
- Keep curtains closed.
- Re-key locks frequently.
- Reduce excess inventory.
- Limit the number of entrances/exits.

- Post signs outlining security and prosecution policies.
- Provide patrols in vulnerable areas.
- Seek neighbours' help in security awareness.

4 Review your procedures.

Slack operating procedures can make you vulnerable in terms of pilfering, theft, embezzlement, and the like. Think about how you can tighten up procedures. To begin with:

- Don't keep excess cash on hand. Adopt a 'no cash after hours' policy.
- Hold employees liable for money under their control.
- Mark equipment/merchandise with owner-identification information.
- Stagger work shifts to reduce the amount of unsupervised time.
- Monitor computer programs used by employees.
- Don't leave valuable material or tools in view of external windows or doors.
- Engage a reputable auditing firm to conduct regular audits.
- Consider potential problems with briefcases, purses, shopping bags…

5 Be cautious about whom you hire.

Many employee security violations can be averted through proper hiring procedures. For sensitive positions, screen potential employees carefully and make clear at this time the severe penalties for dishonest dealings.

6 Review employee tasks periodically.

'The weakest link in your business is your most trusted employee, because she/he is in a position to inflict the greatest damage.' Keep that often-quoted advice in mind. An employee who tends to blend into the background can be in a good position to defraud the company. By regularly conducting task reviews, you can keep your staff in check.

> **Management Memo**
>
> Effective supervisors today have to be security conscious and aware of crime-fighting techniques. Foremen and managers aren't trained to be sleuths or police; but they are expected to be the No. 1 crimestoppers in most businesses and industries. All supervisors must now learn the basics of crime prevention and detection. [184]

7 Use covert investigating techniques.

Most employees and customers are honest people. Any suspicion of wrong doing must be backed up with irrefutable evidence – and this should be obtained covertly. An overt get-tough approach will not only send a perpetrator to ground, it will upset loyal, honest employees/customers if they feel they are also under suspicion.

8 Seek assistance if necessary.

Remember, apathy is the friend of crime. Be vigilant, and seek help if necessary. Consider hiring a professional firm to conduct an audit of your internal and external security and your administrative procedures. At the very least, consult a reputable publication such as *Crimeproofing Your Business: 301 low-cost, no-cost ways to protect your office, store or business* by Russell Bintliff (McGraw-Hill, New York, 1994, 372 pp.). Don't ever think: 'It can't happen to me!'

 See also: 286, 376-378

How to prepare a budget

The great revolutionary writer, Thomas Paine, is attributed with the saying, 'People don't plan to fail, they fail to plan', and his words of wisdom can certainly be applied to budgeting. Planning (along with foresight) is acknowledged as the best way to avoid financial problems. A well-planned budget helps you to collect and use information about the day-to-day functioning of your business and to spot problems before they derail your business plan. Here are the steps to follow in developing your next budget...

1 See budgeting as a vital management tool.

Your budget process consists of three main parts: forecasting revenue and expenditure, recording actual revenue and expenditure, and reporting and acting on variance between the two. Budgets usually evolve from business plans and, therefore, will probably change over time. Your first budget may be nothing more than a statement of targets. In subsequent years, with established benchmarks and an improving track record, you'll be able to make more accurate projections. Eventually, your budget will provide a detailed, accurate comparison of your actual and desired performance.

2 Consider revenue and expenses separately.

Avoid trying to balance your receipts to expenditure in the first instance. Revenue is a product of your business plan and will have a 'lag' component – a start-up period before the cash starts flowing, anything from a couple of months to a couple of years, depending on your business. Expenses are your costs of resources and they will probably dominate in the early days.

3 Identify and list expenses.

The first step in costing your resources is to identify what those line items might be. A useful definition of a line item is one to which a monthly dollar value is assigned, such as accommodation, staffing, advertising, electricity... Many of these items are fixed expenses and this makes the task relatively straightforward. Begin by selecting broad headings and list in detail the line items or resources associated with each. Under 'Administration', for example, you might include stationery and office rental. Under 'Utilities' may be listed electricity and telephone.

4 Forecast revenue.

Revenue is sales. Using your business plan as a guide, make projections regarding the sales you hope to generate. Those projections will represent a target and should be broken down into monthly and weekly components – the smallest possible denominator, if possible. Don't ignore historical data when setting those targets and consider factors like the economy, inflation, whether or not your industry is growing, and any new technology that may improve productivity.

5 Prepare working papers.

Working papers are detailed calculations (cash-flow projections) that provide the monthly figures budgeted for each line item of revenue and expenditure. Produce separate working papers for each line item in the budget and this may be as simple as month-by-month predictions of revenue to be generated from one aspect of your business. Jottings may accompany individual papers as attachments. When a review of your budget is called for, your working papers will prove to be a valuable source of information. You may find, for example, that your revenue calculations were unreasonable and thus were contributing to a budget shortfall.

6 Check for variance.

Variance between your budget and your actuals must be identified and acted on regularly. Ensure that the person responsible for maintaining the financial records is provided with a clearly documented list of individual components designated as line items.

Using such information, this bookkeeper can logically record the actual transaction that can then be compared with the budget. Any variance, positive or negative, between actual and budgeted, is highlighted in a budget action list for follow-up actions.

Management Memo

A budget involves choices being made from competing demands for funding. In an ideal situation there would be adequate funding for all demands. In the real world this is seldom the case, and therein lies the challenge.[185]

7 Prepare a budget action list.

A budget action list is a result of the comparison (usually at month's end) of the actual versus the budget. Note any variance on the budget action list leading to a reassessment of the budget workings, to an amendment of the recording of actuals, or to action so as to address any variance.

8 Prepare a budget report.

A written budget report is a 'hands-on' summary, prepared on a monthly basis, setting out major variance between actual and budget items. The report should account for any variance and recommend relevant actions. The report is forwarded to the boss or nominee who will either confirm the actions recommended or suggest alternatives. 'What action is needed?', 'Who will take it?', 'When is it completed?' These are the outcomes of this reporting and review process.

9 Use your budget to help finance your business.

Potential investors or lenders will want to know how they are going to be repaid, and that's where your budget can help. Your budget gives you credibility, shows how your business is travelling, conveys the type of business needs you have to meet, and identifies the resources you must have to be competitive.

See also: 374, 378, 386

How to manage cash flow

Cash-flow is the lifeblood of any business. For this reason, it is essential that you have processes and procedures in place to ensure that you get paid on time, every time. Failure to adhere to these basic procedures will see your debtors' list grow, your cash-flow shrink, and your business days numbered. Effective management of cash-flow is needed, so here's what needs to happen in your organisation...

1 Agree on a price before work commences.

Make sure from the start that the customer is told what the job will cost – and agrees to that cost – *before* any work commences. You have plenty of other more productive things to do with your time than to work for nothing. If you have presented a reasonable quotation but the potential customer is not prepared to accept it, then direct them politely to someone who may be prepared to work for a much lower rate. The practice of writing off unpaid accounts usually becomes a thing of the past when both parties agree on an up-front price.

2 Build a sound personal relationship with customers.

Business is a series of relationships among people – the better the relationship, the more likely you are to win a customer's ongoing business. Your investment in getting to know more about individual customers will pay dividends when it comes to getting paid. Customers, too, who value the relationship, will feel an obligation to meet their commitments.

3 Adopt simple, straightforward procedures.

Customers and staff have to be educated to understand and follow a clear system of payment and collection. Three of the most basic requirements are:

- Send your invoice immediately upon delivery of the goods or completion of the service. The longer you delay in getting an invoice to the customer, the less urgency they will place on paying you.
- Set strict deadlines for payment of accounts – 14 days from date of invoice has the best track record.
- Use a no-fuss invoice and reply-paid envelope or phone payment option. Payment of your account must be as hassle-free as possible.

When you have your house in order, others will know it, and are likely to work with you to keep it that way.

4 Grab the attention of the debtor.

Lots of other creditors are competing for debtors' attentions, so it is important that your package – envelope, invoice and other information – gets the attention it deserves. Put yourself in your debtors' shoes and look critically at the material you send out. A simple initiative like offering incentives for prompt payment may be sufficient to distinguish your account from competing creditors. No job is complete until you get paid, so make every effort to get your money where it belongs – in your bank.

Management Memo

Getting your money from some people can be like extracting blood from a stone. Some act as if they've never received your account; others say they've misplaced it, or that it's just slipped their mind. Whatever the reason, *you* get no money to keep the wolves from the door... When it all boils down, the key to running any business successfully is cash-flow. In the end, that's the name of the game. And keeping the cash flowing demands that you get paid for your products and services – in other words, collecting your debts. Successful debt collecting is the key to staying in business. [186]

5 Be persistent.

Once you have decided that a debt is worth pursuing – and not every one will be – you must stick at the task like a blue heeler dog to a jogger's ankle. But remember Sun Tzu's (500 BC) advice: 'The purpose of war is victory, not persistence.' The focus of your persistence is results, so be flexible in adapting approaches to fit different situations. Making use of available technologies, phone and fax for example, can help you to be more flexible.

6 Deal only with the authorised bill-payer.

Heed the old saying, 'Don't waste time pow-wowing with the Indians when you know it is the Chief who makes all the decisions.' So, when it is time for you to follow up outstanding invoices, make certain that you talk to a person who can make a decision in your favour, the 'Chief'. 'Indians' can promise you everything but they are unlikely to have any decision-making authority. If the Chief is not available when you call, find out the best time for your follow-up call.

7 Set an example.

Make sure you practise what you preach. You can't reasonably expect others to pay you when *you* make no attempt to pay your creditors. So play your part in keeping money on the move. Where possible, adopt a habit of paying a bill as soon as possible after receiving it. With the bill out of the way, you can then focus all of your attention on the task at hand, and not waste time and energy carrying an overdue account with you.

 See also: 374-376, 386

How to collect outstanding debts

Every organisation, it seems, has its share of errant bill-payers and, although your formal management training may have not included debt recovery, you can be sure that others will look to you for guidance and assistance in bringing slow-payers to heel. By adapting the following simple suggestions to your own situation, you will go a long way towards satisfying those expectations...

1 Reject the myths of debt collecting – now.

Myths associated with debt collecting have plagued businesses for years. They're only myths. Reject them!

- *Bad debts are part of being in business. If you don't have them, you can't be doing too well.* The truth is: successful businesses ensure that their debtors' lists are minimal.
- *Pushing for payment of bad debts isn't good for business. Being too pushy will lose you a customer.* The truth is: who needs a customer that's costing you money?
- *Making people pay on time is difficult and expensive.* The truth is: it's possible to collect your money simply and inexpensively.

2 Decide if the debt is really worth pursuing.

Not all debts are worth chasing. Two variables to consider are the size of the debt in relation to your overall work in progress, and the time it will take to collect the debt. For example, a big business may be prepared to write off a R50 000 debt; a small business could go to the wall if it ignored such an amount.

3 Be persistent.

Once you decide that a debt is worth pursuing, then you must be prepared to persist, using a variety of techniques, until the money is recovered. Don't wait to see if something happens – take hold and make it happen!

4 Capture the debtor's attention.

If you want people to sit up and take notice, you must first attract their attention. When dealing with people who seem to have lost interest in paying-up, you must grab their attention, by fair means or foul, or your message will suffer a similar fate to previous reminders: collecting dust in their in-tray or filed in their wastepaper bin.

5 Be prepared to act decisively.

Never lose sight of the fact that it is *your* money, so be prepared to take decisive action to get it where it belongs: in your bank account. For example, if your initial reminder is unsuccessful, telephone or visit the debtor. Both approaches can be combined successfully in the following way. Telephone the debtor and say, 'I will be in your area tomorrow and will call in to say "hello" – and collect payment for my outstanding account.' Make sure you follow through the next day. Resist writing letters to debtors: the process is time-consuming, expensive, and rarely gets results for payment of long-overdue accounts.

6 Apply an appropriate carrot or stick approach.

We usually use a 'carrot' or 'stick' approach when motivating or dealing with other people. While encouraging behaviours (the carrot approach) are often the most successful, you may, on occasions, have to resort to engaging a third party like a solicitor or collection agency (the stick approach). Choose the approach that will deliver the results you want, but knowing that to engage a third party incurs an additional cost for you.

7 Think and act creatively.

If you send reminder after reminder, believing that these will eventually wear down an errant debtor, you may need to look for more creative ways of getting your message across, and collecting your money. Catch your debtor's attention creatively…

- *Vary approaches according to the length of time the account is overdue:*
- ☐ send your reminder invoice but add a couple of zeros! Your debtor will be on the phone in a flash, so be ready.
- ☐ courier a small birthday cake, with candle, and reminder invoice attached
- ☐ courier an old broom, with a note attached about 'sweeping things under the carpet – including my invoice'
- ☐ send a faxed reminder marked boldly 'PRIVATE and CONFIDENTIAL', so that *everyone* reads it.

- *Have your approach match your debtor's interests:*
- ☐ to a manager, send a 'to-do' list with every item scratched off, except 'Payment of (your) invoice'
- ☐ to a cricket fan, send a note using cricket metaphors – being bowled out, stumped, caught not paying your bill
- ☐ to a golfer, a golf ball and an appropriate reference to your invoice.

Remember: attract the debtor's attention, provide the information creatively (and with a touch of humour if that's your style), and make it easy for them to pay you (reply-paid envelope, credit card facility, payment by phone, etc.).

8 Build up a resource bank.

Nothing succeeds like success and some approaches will be more successful than others. So keep a record of those approaches that deliver the desired results. For dozens of creative ideas, consult *Creative Debt Collecting* by Neil Flanagan, Plum Press, Brisbane, 1992.

Management Memo

Every business has its own techniques for collecting debts, starting with the humble account reminder and developing into more innovative techniques. It's very much like a sporting contest. Businesses must continually develop their own collecting strategies to match the increasingly sophisticated debtor strategies. [187]

How to position yourself in the marketplace

The purpose of business is to get and keep customers – something that's difficult to do without a marketing plan. Such a document provides you with direction in terms of developing products or services which will satisfy customer demands, communicating the benefits of your products and services to customers, and guaranteeing satisfaction. In essence, it is a plan which enables you to encourage people to do business with *your* organisation. Here are some important aspects to consider...

1 Remember: marketing is everybody's job.

Everyone in your organisation is involved in marketing your company's products and/or services. They may not actually work in the marketing department, nor be directly responsible for finding customers, but they will all in some way be in a position to contribute to the organisation's success in keeping or losing customers. For this reason, you, and your key employees, should have some understanding of what the process of marketing involves in terms of your organisation...

2 Generate marketable products and/or services.

Do you have products, ideas, concepts or services which you have screened and tested to ensure they will satisfy customer need and which are potentially profitable? Have you analysed your product's life cycle in order to predict its sales pattern over a period of time? Do you continue the search for new products and services? If you don't have a durable, marketable product, then you won't build up and hold a customer base.

3 Profile your competition.

How well do you know those organisations that compete for your customers? Who exactly are your competitors? What are their strong and weak points? Gather as much information as you can on their marketing and communication strategies, types of advertising, their product, price and markets, and how they take advantage of changes in the industry. Identify any areas in the market which are not filled by your competitors' products or services and which could be exploited by yours. Remember, your competitors will probably be watching you also.

4 Analyse market opportunities.

Market research is essential. Assemble information on your organisation's current and potential markets, on the users of your products or services, and on those areas where your company has the competitive advantage when it comes to introducing new products, improving current products, or entering new market territories.

This market profile should include your current and future markets' size, growth potential, barriers, key players and the existence of particular niches. If yours is a small to medium business enterprise, remember that research tells us that 75 per cent of your customers come from within a five kilometre radius of your business.

Management Memo

The organisation must learn to think about itself not as producing goods or services but as buying customers, as doing the thing that will make people want to do business with it. [188]

5 Target your market.

Based on the information you have gathered, and on the skills and resources of your organisation, you should now be able to select specific target markets. If you are not in the mass marketing business, i.e. you don't offer your product or service to all-comers, then are you in a position to pinpoint those segments of the market at which your specific products should be targeted?

6 Develop an appropriate marketing mix.

Your preliminary research will now enable you to consider the 4Ps of marketing, that set of controllable variables that all companies attempt to blend into the right combination to achieve the dominant position in the marketplace. The four key factors are: Product, Price, Place and Promotion. In the long run, the success you have in addressing these four components will determine your success in the marketplace.

7 Forecast sales potential.

You will need to produce a detailed outline of your sales targets, a plan for achieving those goals, and costs to be incurred in attracting customers.

8 Develop a strategy for publicising your product.

If you have the products or services people want, and are prepared to pay for, then your next step is to bring these to people's attention. You will need to develop a strategy to address advertising and promotion of the product, new product launches, sales campaigns and distribution policies. How can you get value for your advertising rand? Are there more cost-effective ways to promote your product? Should you be using more than one method? Do you need to promote your product all year?

9 Review your performance regularly.

Unless you monitor the progress of your marketing plan, you will run the risk of not finding out until too late that the plan is not working. Check sales results constantly to ensure targets are being achieved within expenditure budgets. Amend your plan as required in the light of your findings.

 See also: 344, 380, 384

How to gain the competitive edge using focus groups

Successful managers are always on the lookout for ways to gain and sustain the competitive advantage over their rivals. One of the best sources of information to help identify those advantages are customers or clients: existing, potential, lost, and those of your competitors. If you want to discover the views of customers so that you can transform these views into a winning edge for your organisation, then you should consider using the focus group approach...

1 Decide on the focus for the group.

They're called 'focus groups' because they allow you to assemble a select group of people to investigate a specific issue – and there are many issues to consider: customer service, product reliability, responsiveness, company image, promotion, communication, and so on.

2 Target a specific group.

Focus groups can be conducted successfully for all the individual categories of customers or clients. Different customer groups can provide different information for you to transform later into specific actions. Consider inviting your participants according to your focus: for example, potential customers might be invited to participate in a group assembled to discuss ways that the organisation can attract new customers; former customers could be invited to contribute so that ways the organisation can retain its customers can be identified; current customers can identify ways existing services can be improved.

3 Plan to maximise the group's effectiveness.

Planning should take into consideration the following:

- Who should be invited? That often depends on the focus.
- How many should be invited? The ideal individual group size is considered to be seven to nine.
- When is the best time for the meeting? Its duration? After work, for no longer than forty-five minutes, can be a good time.
- Personal invitations. First contact should be by telephone, followed up with a letter or fax confirming the meeting.
- Should employees be invited? If so, which ones? This is your choice, but the guests must outnumber staff.
- Networking. Allow time to welcome guests and make sure they get to know one another.
- Who will act as facilitator? If you're comfortable leading the group, all the better.
- Seating arrangements. A round table configuration is best.
- Refreshments. Certainly.
- Record keeping. Arrange to have a

scribe who does not participate in discussions.

- Follow up. Contact every participant personally to express your appreciation and to provide a brief outline of the results of the meeting.

4 Start the meeting on time.

Get the meeting underway on time with a welcome and a brief description of the purpose of the meeting. Give an undertaking to conclude at a particular time. Explain how the meeting will proceed. If another person is acting as facilitator, introduce that person followed by an invitation to proceed.

5 Get people talking.

Slowly does it… you want contributions from every participant, not just the more vocal ones. A useful approach is to start with the broad picture and gradually focus on the issues of most concern to you. When you ask specific questions, try preceding those with 'softeners' like, 'I'm hoping you can tell me. . .' or 'I'm wondering if you know. . . '. Softeners not only encourage open questioning but also discourage the use of 'why'.

6 Don't become defensive.

You have invited guests to participate in an event that should improve your organisation, so you could well be receiving some bad news with the good. Disclosure of your company's faults is valuable information, and you should not get

> **Management Memo**
>
> Focus groups are ad hoc groups that are convened to discuss an issue. Good group facilitation and investigative probing skills are critical for conducting effective focus groups. [189]

defensive about such bad news. Indeed, you need to adopt an encouraging style by using prompters like, 'Would you be able to expand on that?' and 'Tell me what you mean by that' and 'Are you saying that…?'. Responses that surprise you, even upset you, could represent valuable information.

7 Summarise often.

Clarify comments by offering regular summaries. This approach keeps the meeting on track, ensures the group is proceeding in the desired direction, and helps your scribe keep up with the action. If individual participants disagree with your summary, seek their help in getting it right.

8 Wrap up, on time.

Participants are donating their time, so fulfil your part of the arrangement by ending on time. Summarise outcomes, thank participants, and make a commitment to provide a written summary within a set time, say 14 days. Thank each participant personally as they leave, then get with your participating staff for their general comments and a consideration of the lessons to be learnt by the organisation from the activity.

How to know what your competitors are doing

The military strategists refer to it as 'competitive intelligence', but, for the manager, it amounts to finding out as much information as possible about your competitors: what products they are developing, what the strategic thrusts of their businesses are for the next few years, how they are travelling, and their levels of profitability. If you want a more accurate picture of how your competitors are shaping up, here are a few tactical suggestions...

1 Attend trade shows and conferences.

Trade shows are excellent places to check out competitors' products and services. These exhibitions are more than just booths and displays. Most expositions also offer seminars, product demonstrations, and other special events that can be good sources of competitive information. If you play your cards right, you can even gain access to a competitor's senior management, often by simply chatting with the salesperson who works the booth. By networking in the right circles at conferences you will learn lots of useful competitor information.

2 Become a shareholder – of your competitor.

There are a number of perfectly legal and ethical ways to get information on your competitors. If your competitor is a publicly listed company, for example, you can purchase a limited number of their stock, making you a recognised shareholder. You'll be amazed how much financial and strategic information that this tactic will deliver to your door regularly.

3 Trade product with competitors.

Competitors may not let you inside their plants, but there are other ways to analyse their operation – as long as you don't mind reciprocating. You can start things rolling by offering to provide samples of your products in return for your competitors' samples.

4 Conduct a company search.

For a small fee, you can initiate a search of your competitors to see how they are travelling. The practice is legal and quite ethical. After all, it is possible that some of your smart competitors have already conducted a search to ascertain *your* position to help with *their* business planning.

5 Examine legal records.

Every time your competition applies for a patent or becomes involved in a lawsuit, a public record is created. These sources can tell you a lot about the health of their businesses. Your legal adviser will direct you to the best places to find this valuable information.

6 Subscribe to investment research.

In the United States, *Nelson's Directory of Wall Street Research* lists analysts that follow most major firms. *Fortune*'s *Company Profile* provides research on more than 8 000 US public companies. *McGregor's Who Owns Whom in South Africa* (1998) is a complete guide to listed and unlisted (on the Johannesburg Stock Exchange) companies in South Africa. Individual brokers provide for clients either specific or more general information on request. If your competitor is not a major firm, you will need to resort to other tactics – like requesting direct from the company copies of its Annual Reports.

7 Subscribe to a clipping service.

For a fee, these services will scan newspapers, trade journals and consumer magazines for articles on your field of endeavour or even on your competitors. You can be assured of keeping up to date with all reported competitor activities. And don't forget to check out the Internet too: your competitor may have an interesting home page.

8 Talk to former employees.

If a competitor has a high employee turnover or is laying off employees, and you can make contact with them, you can learn a lot. Keep in mind they may have an axe to grind and will be only too willing to provide information that will benefit you.

> **Management Memo**
>
> All warfare is based on deception. [All business is based on ingenuity.]...One who has few must prepare for defence; one who has many shall make the enemy prepare for defence... Thus, I can create victory. Even if the enemy is numerous, I can prevent him from fighting. Find out his plans to know which of his strategies will be successful and which will not. Provoke to agitate him and so learn the pattern of his movements. Force him to show his disposition and thus ascertain his strengths and weaknesses. [190]

9 Scan the employment advertisements.

Keep a check on the display and employment ads in your local newspaper. Jobs on offer and their descriptions are often good indicators of changes in strategies and organisational structures.

10 Don't rest on your laurels.

In the minds of many managers, the goal is to get the business up and running smoothly so that it will then 'run itself'. But such a model is deeply defective, because it assumes that it is possible to establish a pattern or system that can meet both present and future challenges. This may have been possible in the past, but not today. Today, there is no time to relax. Everything is in a state of flux: goals, personnel, procedures, customers, products, structures and, of course, the marketplace. No longer is anything predictable – and that includes your competition, so stay alert.

 See also: 286, 308, 374-380, 388-390

How to make your business grow

Managing a business is like being a top-flight athlete - always on the lookout for ways to become better and better. The general consensus among respected writers in the field of business growth is that there are three main ways for a business to grow successfully - get more customers, sell existing customers more products or services, and increase back-end sales. Here's an extension of those ideas...

1 Attract more customers.

Your customers are those people who buy from you at least once. So one way to extend your business is to get more and more people to buy from you or use your services – at least once. Although there are many different approaches to attracting more customers, the one thing those approaches have in common is that they must either satisfy an existing demand for what you have to offer or create a new one. Supply and demand are key considerations when it comes to attracting more customers.

2 Develop a marketing plan.

Creating or satisfying a demand involves more than a trial-and-error approach. Given the product or services you have to offer, you need to plan *how* to create a demand and *how* to satisfy it. A simple, straightforward marketing plan can achieve that. The plan needs to be sufficiently specific to provide the necessary focus and be flexible enough to adapt to changing circumstances. Remember, no one person can hope to know your product or service better than you do. By all means consult with outside marketing gurus if your strength is not in this area.

3 Sell customers more products or services.

It is considered to be five times easier, and much less expensive, to sell to existing customers than to find new ones. So focusing your energies and other resources on selling additional products to existing customers is a sound strategy. Accountants, for example, often provide information technology services, management consulting, and financial planning services in addition to their normal range of services. Successful organisations are finding that existing customers respond positively when asked for additional business or referrals to new customers.

4 Focus on adding value.

Adding value occurs when the service provider suggests additional products or services that dovetail with the selections already made. A laundromat, for example, might include phone and fax facilities, exercise machines, movie hire, dry cleaning and confectionery as add-ons to the basic laundry services provided. Wal-Mart adds value to the shopping experience with people-greeters at the door and distinctively friendly salespeople. In value-adding, the 'whole' is seen as being worth more than the sum of the parts.

5 Train, train, train.

Staff training is important if value-adding opportunities are going to be recognised and exploited. Selling customers additional products or services is going to require staff who can bring those products and services to the customers' attention. Recent research indicates that it is six times more expensive *not* to train than to train. If you're into the right training programme, additional sales made by well-trained staff will exceed associated training costs.

6 Increase back-end sales.

As your customer base increases and your relationship with those customers improves, you will get to know other services, not directly associated with your business, that customers would value and be prepared to pay for through you. Your main task may only require that you advertise the service or product and then act as the go-between, linking customer demand and the supplier. Video stores, for example, could offer a VCR maintenance, repair and hire service. That service, though provided by another party, would benefit the customers, and you, through increased customer loyalty and commissions paid to you by the third-party service provider. Back-end sales should be considered as a profitable growth feature by all organisations with a well-developed customer data base. And, of course, the approach fits in well with the whole idea of value-adding.

Management Memo

You have value when you meet customers' needs. You can count on those needs changing and, because they do, you have to change the way you do business – or your value will migrate to someone else. [191]

7 And finally...

The following advice from David Bangs Jr, US expert in small business management, is worth remembering:

- Put your customers first and the profits will follow.
- Give your markets reasons to buy your product.
- Look at what you sell through the eyes of your customers and prospects.
- Business is too competitive to allow your attention to lapse.
- 98 per cent of small business failures stem from managerial weakness.
- Businesses stand or fall on the strength of their personnel.
- The importance of establishing a market niche cannot be overstated.
- Increased sales do not necessarily mean increased profits.
- Keeping control of operating expenses is immensely important and easily overlooked, perhaps because so much emphasis is placed on generating sales.

 See also: 248, 390

How to provide exceptional customer service

It has been said that service management is a total organisational approach that makes quality of service, as perceived by the customer, the number one driving force for the operation of any business. But so often managers pay only lip-service to customer service – they're too tied down with the day-to-day concerns of production, union negotiations, meetings, paperwork, budget and personnel matters. What can you do to improve your organisation's service? Why not start with these basic ideas...

1 Let no customer wait more than three minutes.

Time is money – for the customer too. If you work at minimising customer waiting time to no more than three minutes, you'll gain more customers than you'll lose.

2 Do a little extra each time.

Always try to exceed customer expectations by providing an unsolicited little extra – it's called value-adding. When your car is serviced, and the dealer blackens your tyres at no charge and leaves a chocolate bar on the driver's seat, chances are you'll return.

3 Redress a customer concern immediately.

There are no 'little' problems when it comes to customer service. You must take action, without hesitation, to redress any shortfall in service or any product defect. Any delay in meeting a dissatisfied customer's needs could result in alienation and loss of business. On the other hand, prompt action can create a perception of a higher standard of company performance than if the problem had not occurred in the first place!

4 Take five seconds to answer the phone.

The telephone is often the first, and often the final, point of contact for some customers. Get that phone answered before its fourth ring. Any undue delay, any unanswered call, any engaged signal – and your company's goodwill could suffer, to say nothing of lost business.

5 Seek staff ideas on how to improve service.

Many of the best ideas for improving customer service come from those who deal with your customers – your staff. Implement their ideas whenever possible and provide encouraging feedback on suggestions that can't be used.

6 Attend to detail.

The ultimate test of a really caring attitude towards the customer is your attention to detail. It's been calculated that 80 per cent of customer alienation comes from getting 20 per cent of the detail wrong. While customers don't expect perfection, they do expect you to recover quickly and sympathetically.

7 Keep those promises.

Companies win customers by making promises about service – and retain customers by keeping those promises. The more promises you, your company or your staff make about quality, responsiveness, reliability, and so on, the more they must be kept. If a staff member promises to 'get back to' a customer today, they'd better do it – even if there's nothing to report.

8 Monitor those things you often don't notice.

How do your face-to-face people present themselves dress-wise and in terms of attitude? What about the appearance of that ageing sign, tired company logo or old-fashioned letterhead? Do your people smile and say thank you? How's your receptionist's telephone answering technique? Have you checked lately? Such basic outward signs are vital in securing a customer's confidence that the service you provide is reliable, courteous and of high quality.

9 Make sure your staff are 'in the know'.

Your company can only be judged as the best provider if your staff are 'in the know'. Are your employees familiar with the product? Do they know what service is really about? Do they know the company? How to get things done? How to solve problems? Do they know regular customers by name?

> **Management Memo**
>
> Customer expectations for... world-wide organisations are now coming through loud and clear:
>
> - Be efficient in giving me what I want
> - Be courteous and treat me with respect
> - Be responsive – react quickly when I need you
> - Use empathy – understand my needs and anticipate them
> - Treat me as an individual – my needs are very special
> - And above all, be reliable. [192]

10 Be confident that everything works.

A failure in the system is simply a breakdown in management. If you are guaranteeing a service, make sure the system works: the television set in the hotel room, the lift to your office, the car park barrier, the pay phone in the foyer, the photocopier, the escalator in the department store, the broken chair in reception, the cold drink dispenser…

11 Get to the customers before they get to you.

Things inevitably go wrong. Often it's not your fault, e.g. your serviceman gets held up in traffic. Sometimes it is, e.g. you underestimated the spare parts required. Whatever the reason, if you've made a promise to a customer that cannot be kept, it's essential that you inform the customer before she informs you. Chances are then that she'll be sympathetic rather than angry, and she might even thank you for keeping her advised.

 See also: 248, 388

How to provide responsive customer service

Without customers you don't have a business. So it is important that the focus of your employees should be to provide the best possible customer service – you can't afford not to if profit is your bottom line. Here are some more ideas for you and your employees to work towards in providing high-quality customer service and a sustainable competitive advantage...

1 Ensure your team is honest and open.

The foundation of strong customer relationships is trust. Truthfulness and integrity are essential qualities for exceptional customer service, because when you hide the truth, invariably the customer will find out (or at least suspect it). Nor should there be any variations of the truth: white lies, half-truths, distortions, excuses. In customer service, it's surprising what heights you will attain by simply being on the level.

2 Provide customer-service training for your staff.

In the long run, it is more expensive *not* to train than to train employees. You can't afford not to provide essential training that will lead to a more responsive organisation in terms of customer service. Identify those factors that affect customer service in your organisation and focus on improving those. Dealing with difficult customers, effective listening, problem-solving, courtesy, and using the telephone, are just some examples of the training required by all staff, even backroom employees. If your training is not making your organisation more responsive, don't scrap the training, change the programme.

3 Remember the key word – RESPONSIVENESS.

Whatever your business, responsiveness is the umbrella covering all organisational activities. Responsiveness is giving customers what they want, courteously, when they want it, at a price that matches their expectations. Customers are prepared to pay more for a product or service delivered when *they* want it – not when it suits you. Responsiveness is an individual as well as a group quality.

4 Empower employees.

You must give employees the decision-making powers that will allow them to always act in the customers' best interests and help them to solve their problems. Empowering employees does not mean that you are abrogating responsibilities, but making sure that customers receive a response in the minimum amount of time. Research tells us that most complaining customers will buy from you again if their problem is resolved on the spot.

5 Set the example.

Employees will not treat their customers any better than they themselves are treated. So make sure that you look after your employees. In addition, the way employees hear you talking about customers and the way they see you interacting with them will go a long way to determining the service culture at your workplace. In many ways, you and your actions set the standard for employees to aim for.

6 Establish benchmarks.

Emulating, even exceeding, leaders in the field of customer service is an established method of improving customer service. You will find that some of the approaches used by your competitors can be applied to your operations. Wal-Mart staff, for example, adhere to this principle: 'Every time a customer comes within ten feet of me I will smile, look her in the eye, and greet her, so help me Sam.'

7 Be accessible.

You need to remain informed about all aspects of the relationship between your organisation and its customers. Let employees and customers know that you value their feedback and encourage them to make regular contact with you. And when a customer takes you up on your offer and makes a complaint to you, resist going on the defence and accept the information as a way to further improve your service.

> **Management Memo**
>
> Customers perceive service in their own unique, idiosyncratic, emotional, irrational, end-of-the-day, and totally human terms. Perception is all there is.[193]

8 Add value, add profits.

A customer service focus will be one important way that you and your organisation can add value to the way you do things. Adding value goes beyond customer satisfaction to customer confidence. It will also improve the profitability and prosperity of your organisation.

9 Hold regular meetings on customer service.

Schedule regular discussions with your staff on service issues. Make 'The customer' an agenda item at all your staff and management meetings. Become aware of anti-customer policies and practices, and act to eliminate such things. Speak regularly about the importance of exceptional service. Create a company award which recognises excellent examples of customer service. Check that all in-house talk shows respect for the customer. Ban those negative stories, customer nicknames, and amusing but damaging jokes which are capable of eroding a positive customer culture. Your aim must be to have every employee live the service commitment culture.

How to get the most out of your advertising rand

Increased sales depend on a unified, coherent and consistent marketing programme, and advertising is one of marketing's major components. Since the success of many businesses depends on effective advertising which, these days, can be quite expensive, the guidelines which follow will help you to maximise your advertising rand...

1 Be aware that advertising can work.

'I don't believe in advertising. We ran an ad three years ago and didn't get one call!' Plenty of businesses say this each time the idea of advertising is raised – but they never get around to evaluating where the ad was placed, what it said, its size, its audience and particularly why they thought a one-shot ad would produce results. If only they had considered the following advice...

2 Get inside the customer's head.

In planning your advertisement or campaign, always start with the customer or prospect. You may need to seek the assistance of research to answer such questions as what problem can you solve for the customer? what does the customer want? what do you have on offer that other organisations do not? do you have a solution for the customer, or just a product?

3 Select the appropriate media.

The key to successful advertising is to use the right medium to reach the right people: national, state, and local newspapers and magazines, radio, television, letterbox flyers, posters, Internet, direct mailings, sandwich boards, and so on. Different media can reach different audiences, so again you'll need to do your homework to achieve the best result. Avoid basing your buying decision solely on the price of the advertisement. In fact, for best results, it might be best to advertise through several media outlets at the same time.

4 Use a quality advertisement.

It will cost you more money to produce a quality advertisement but, if results are what you are looking for, then investing in quality is well worth the cost. Remember, you'll be competing with other businesses for the attention of the reader, listener or viewer. The longer you can hold your potential customers' attention, the better your chances of convincing them that they want what you are offering – and you'll have more chance of doing that with quality advertisements. You may well require the services of an advertising agency to generate a quality ad.

5 Make it easy for the prospect to respond.

Whatever and however you're advertising, it's essential that you make it a simple process for an interested customer to seek further information or to make a purchase. Display a toll-free number prominently, or provide a credit card facility, or offer a pre-paid postcard or envelope for the reply.

6 Attract prospects with irresistible benefits.

The aim of your advertising should be to convince customers that they will derive immense benefit from what you are offering. In addition to old-fashioned 'reliability', 'dependability', and 'after sales service', we increasingly see attractive discounts, free steak knives, two-for-the-price-of-one offers, delayed payments, free gifts and a range of other eye-catching sweeteners. What can your business offer prospective customers or clients in terms of traditional values and/or sweeteners?

7 Plan and follow an advertising schedule.

If you run your advertisement once, it is highly unlikely that a majority of people will even see or hear it – let alone respond to it. And just because it appears does not mean that everyone is even ready to respond. The aim of advertising is to be out there just when someone needs you, your product or your service. Little wonder then that research tells us that to be effective, an advertisement must run three to seven times.

Management Memo

Most advertising doesn't actually sell a product or service (unless an order form is included), and it's not meant to do so. Advertising is intended to persuade, to convince, and to bring a buyer to the point of sale ... the sale still has to be made. [194]

8 Get value for your money.

Stretch your advertising rand by making each advertisement work and work and work. For example, be sure to reprint your advertisements and mail them, together with a personal note, to existing customers and prospects. Tell them where the advertisement appears and why. You'll be getting double value for your outlay as well as ensuring that those who missed it haven't after all.

9 Remember: advertising is only part of your total marketing programme.

Check out the opportunities to produce and distribute additional promotional materials to support your advertising. For example, M-Web is not only distributing its Big Black Box through Mr Delivery, but is following up with a 'peripherals package', that supports their Internet services. Classic fm has made a lot of people chuckle with their clever lamppost posters, supporting their campaign to make classical music more popular with the general public. Combine your advertising with press releases and media stories about your company and its services and products.

How to get the public image you want for your organisation

Sensible organisations are careful to develop and sustain a good public image. They strive to become 'a good neighbour', showing concern for the affairs of the community in which they operate. And if they don't live up to community expectations, then they will be rightly subjected to community criticism. Public support is therefore of utmost importance. But many managers expect this support without taking positive steps to win it. Here are some basic principles essential for winning a good public image...

1 Plan your programme.

Planning is essential. In devising ways to win community support for your organisation, you must take into account information that the public has, wants and needs about your organisation. Consider also such basic factors as your audience, programme timing, techniques you will use and potential media coverage.

2 Become a good neighbour.

Do your activities upset the local community in which you operate? If so, do something immediately about noise, fumes, smells, waste disposal, parking, visual pollution – things that can create antagonism locally. Or do your activities receive warm local acknowledgement because you support local development, contribute to local community associations, donate to charities, support schools, sponsor student awards, offer assistance with local sport, art and youth activities? Think about the many ways in which you can keep your local community on side by becoming a good neighbour.

3 Know your community.

No effective programme can be planned without a knowledge of the local community. What problems are of concern locally: lack of recreation facilities, youth unemployment, historic sites, pollution? What are your community's main interests – sport, culture, gardens? Who are the political leaders? Who are the opinion leaders? What is the current economic situation (the spending power of a prosperous mining town would be greater than that of a declining pastoral town)? Are there any special emotional issues, resulting from a racial, religious, industrial past? And so on. Only with such background information can your image-building efforts be directed into the correct channels.

4 Identify and assess all available avenues.

If you now know what it takes to be a good neighbour, and you know your community, then your organisation can now explore ways of demonstrating good citizenship and of developing the image of a good neighbour. List all possible options from which a balanced selection of programme strategies can be made, for example:

- *media relations:* keeping journalists aware of company projects which impact favourably on the local community
- *participation* in community activities
- *newsletters:* for distribution to staff, clients, opinion leaders, libraries, local businesses
- *speechmaking:* addressing schools, clubs, civic groups on activities of your organisation
- *sponsorships:* from financing the local pet show to purchasing a new bus for the local retirement village
- *product donations:* donating products or services as prizes in local raffles, at fetes or for other community fundraising events
- *open days:* inviting the community to view your facilities and featuring demonstrations, tours, exhibits.

Select your strategies in terms of the nature of your message and business, coverage required, cost, time and your particular situation.

5 Foster two-way communication.

Image building goes beyond advertising and is built on planned, systematic two-way communication. The greater the two-way flow of information, the easier it is to find out how effectively your message is getting across to the community. Encourage and welcome expressions of opinion, good or bad, for such views should be seen as opportunities for dialogue which can promote improved understanding and, possibly, even stronger local support for your organisation.

Management Memo

Put quite simply, image is the picture that other people have of you. It is also the picture you hold of yourself. If your organisation projects a true and attractive reflection of itself, you have a strong competitive advantage in the marketplace. A neglected, poorly communicated or outdated image can leave an indelible and damaging impression... Once an identity is created, it must then be continuously managed. Marketing, advertising and public relations are the tools for image creation and maintenance.[195]

6 Remember the fundamentals.

The nature, content and presentation of your message will vary with circumstances but there are basic principles which must be adhered to:

- *Be honest.* By all means accentuate the positive, but propaganda, dishonesty and exaggeration are rarely forgiven.
- *Be continuous.* By repeating your message in a variety of ways, you will produce a stronger community response.
- *Be comprehensive.* All the important aspects of your organisation's activity should be considered in planning an image-building programme. No activity should be singled out for undue emphasis, nor should others be ignored or minimised.
- *Keep it simple.* Language, content and presentation of information should be adjusted to the intellectual and interest levels of your particular community audience. Beware of mumbo-jumbo and jargon. Make things clear and interesting.
- *Present information rationally.* Your information should be presented objectively, constructively, unemotionally and without sensationalism. Such an approach is more likely to convince intelligent and reasonable people.
- *Timing is important.* Schedule your campaign for the greatest impact.

How to improve your organisation's visual image

Your company's visual image is often the first impression you give your customer or client – and it should therefore be a good one. Your logo, product brochures, signs, letterheads, business cards, leaflets, newsletters or newspaper advertisements all should have impact and increase sales. But to be effective, such visual images must be eye-catching and professional – and the best way to achieve this result is to engage a graphic designer. The following suggestions will assist you to make the right decision...

1 Resist the temptation to do it yourself.

Graphic design is a professional activity and it cannot be done on the cheap. Despite the inroads of desktop technology, while many people in your organisation may be able to work a computer, few have the necessary design skills. Nor do local printers for, while they employ in-house designers, their work is often dull and unexceptional. Remember, your visual image is something you will have to live with for many years.

2 Appreciate the value of a professional designer.

The use of a good designer is a long-term investment, and may be the best advertising investment you make. An experienced designer will bring both a lack of preconceptions and an entirely new perspective to the way you see your organisation. Indeed, she/he may force you to look at your business in a different way, encouraging you to clarify and strengthen previously unspoken attitudes, dreams and directions. Designers risk their reputation every time your logo, advertisement or brochure appears in public, so they have as much to lose, if their work is bad, as you do. But they will do a better job than you, so let them do it.

3 Know how to select a good designer.

There are the large advertising agencies who normally cater for large businesses, and there are hundreds of freelance designers and graphic artists in the suburbs who keep small businesses in business. Having checked the Yellow Pages or your professional contacts, you can set about selecting a designer best suited to your company. In making your choice, consider this advice:

- *Find one you can work with.* You're entering a partnership: if the designer can't help you make a profit, she/he will lose a permanent client. So it's important for both of you to be on the same wavelength.
- *Ask for testimonials* and the endorsements of the designer's other customers. Discuss the designer's successes, creativity and solutions.
- *Have a good look at examples of the*

designer's work. You can also judge a lot by visiting the designer's office.

- *Ensure the designer is committed to meeting deadlines.* Check this out with other customers or by commissioning a small project to begin with.
- *Consider cost last of all* because if the other points don't make the grade, price will not come into it. Remember, you are buying creativity, individual talent, artistic flair, advertising skills, and these don't always come cheap. Discuss the designer's approach to budget, cost estimates and total project charges. Some charge by the hour, some by the project, and some according to your set budget. If you're clear about the designer's policy on fees upfront, you'll avoid hassles later.

4 Always prepare a design brief.

Designers work from 'design briefs'. Your designer may want to know what you make or do, your business identity, long term plans, market strategy, your customers, your budget, and the way your mind works. The designer will need your ideas as a foundation to develop graphic concepts, an image, which will reflect your company's values and style. Many designers provide a creative brief form; if not, prepare a written statement of your own, the more detail, the better for all involved.

5 Be consistent with your visual imagery.

Consistency is important when it comes to visual imagery, which is one reason why you should try to use the same designer for all your work. A corporate identity is not developed from a rag-bag of diverse ideas and styles, the result of using a variety of designers for different items. If you remodel your company logo several times in a decade, change your letterhead design every two years, and dazzle your customers with ten different type styles in your latest product leaflet, how can you retain client confidence? Make the changes, make them well, and stick with them.

Management Memo

A designer must be really interested in understanding your situation and concerned about providing a thoroughly conceived image and message for your business. Your choice of designer can be measured in long-term results. A designer helps you visually communicate to clients, projecting the company's goals, values, purpose, style and direction. [196]

6 Remember also...

- Consider launching your company's new visual identity with a splash.
- Implement visual imagery changes quickly and thoroughly. When Coca-Cola released a new logo several years ago, every old Coke logo around the world was replaced *overnight!*
- Know where your old visual imagery will need to be replaced: stationery, signage, livery, publications, memorabilia, vehicles...
- While a letterhead or business cards may be your only project in the short-term, think long-term. Every visual item must eventually reflect your company's image – a professional image. People like to deal with businesses that look familiar and professional.

How to plan for a major public relations initiative

If you want to increase public awareness of your organisation and the programme or services it offers, or your company's stance on a vital community issue, you have to plan for it. It won't just happen. Writing a plan for such a special initiative or campaign is really nothing more than preparing a blueprint of what is to be done and how and when each task will be accomplished. Why not start with a simple PR project, using this approach...

1 Appreciate the value of a planned PR approach.

A planned approach can help your organisation in a number of ways. In addition to providing clear direction for a special public relations thrust, it can also, for example,

- inform the community and customers about your organisation's overall programmes and activities.
- build confidence in what your organisation and its staff are doing for the community.
- provide staff members with a common purpose which in turn will clarify their own concepts of the organisation's worth.
- raise awareness of common issues.
- rally support for the organisation's programme.
- improve the relationship between your organisation and community.

2 Establish a task force.

Large organisations often employ specialised public relations staff; others outsource this responsibility. However, if your company is not in a position to utilise such services, a self-help approach could be considered. In this instance, responsibility for developing and implementing a plan is best vested in a small task force or committee comprising capable staff, community representatives, and even customers.

3 Define the challenge and identify the objectives.

A one-off public relations initiative is usually designed to correct a negative situation for the organisation, to achieve a well-defined once-only objective, or to maintain or improve an existing positive situation. Whatever your motivation, your first step then is to define the message you wish to give the community. In 30 words or less, be able to answer the question: 'What precisely do we wish to accomplish?' A vague goal such as 'To get publicity for our company's environmental programme' is relatively meaningless. This aim might be better stated as: 'To make clients, customers and community aware of our company's concern for the environment and to induce community participation in our efforts to be concerned about our local environment.' Next, break this over-arching aim down into two sets of specific objectives, informational and motivational. Try to make them realistic, achievable and, hopefully, measurable.

4 Identify the target audiences and catalysts.

Specify as precisely as possible the groups of people who comprise the primary audiences for your message: clients, customers, local residents, other businesses and industries, local government agencies, community organisations, non-English speaking groups. Should a variation of your message be aimed at different groups? List also any community catalysts, such as schools, the local newspaper and radio, trade outlets, civic associations, or service organisations, who can help carry your message to the target audiences.

5 Develop a strategy and specify your tactics.

List as many ways as you can to take the message to your audience via a catalyst. Remember, to convey your message, it isn't always necessary to initiate grandiose new events. Rather, it might be possible to focus on existing activities presented in novel ways. Take each idea in turn and subject it to long hard critical review. Is it feasible? Have you the time, skills, finance? If not, where can help be found? A wide array of avenues is available: newsletters, displays, newspaper columns, videos, awards, ceremonies, community projects, public debates, news releases, stunts, T-shirts, speaking engagements... Target your strategies to specific audiences.

Management Memo

Issues management is the process by which a corporation can identify and evaluate those governmental and societal issues that may impact significantly on it. The issues can then be assigned priorities for appropriate response... Management, as a conscious part of its strategic planning process, should identify key issues that will affect the organisation in the future and take action in advance to overcome any problems these issues may create.[197]

6 Draw up a calendar of events and activities.

Conceptualise your ideas and events into a schedule of activity to form a consistent flow of stories or events over a period of, say, six months or a year. This timetable, usually in chart form, should show starting and completion dates for each component event in the overall initiative and will provide an essential checklist of progress.

7 Determine a budget.

Consider the financial aspects by outlining in sequence the costs of all activities. Balance aspirations and financial reality to arrive at a final list of usable proposals.

8 Specify evaluation procedures.

To provide essential feedback for the planning of future projects, determine in advance what criteria will be used to evaluate the success of each activity in your overall initiative. Short questionnaires, discussion and simple response slips might suffice. The effectiveness of the total initiative can be assessed by comparing the overall community response with your original objectives.

How to get the most out of the press

Just doing a good job isn't enough any more. It's a competitive environment these days and the local newspaper represents one important channel for communicating good news about your organisation. As a manager, you must know how to work effectively with representatives of the print media to build support for your organisation. Reporters appreciate cooperative, accurate and available sources for their stories, so here are some useful tips for getting the best deal from your local journalists...

1 Know your local newspaper contacts.

Is your organisation one that might be able to use the print media more effectively than others? If so, you'll need to get to know your local newspaper reporters as soon as possible. Meet with them personally over coffee or lunch, and ask how you can meet their informational needs. Act on the practical advice they give you.

2 Develop procedures for generating good news stories.

Set up an internal reporting system through which your staff can funnel news and feature story ideas to one person who has the responsibility for working with the newspaper. A good backlog of story possibilities may be just what the reporter needs on a slow news day.

Develop attractive news release formats for future use, and facts sheets and background materials for distribution to the press on a range of company themes and issues.

Become familiar with the skilful art of writing a news release.

3 Respond promptly to all inquiries from the press.

If a reporter calls and you are tied up, make sure you get back to the caller as soon as possible or you may miss the paper's deadline.

Always be aware of deadlines. Both weekly and daily newspapers have to work to fixed deadlines. Remember, old news is no news – so work to those deadlines.

4 Be professional in your dealings with the newspaper.

Be professional in all your business with the media. For example:

- Show no favouritism. Don't give one reporter a scoop and withhold details from others or you'll end up losing the trust of all of them.
- Be open and honest. Always tell the truth or you'll live to regret it. Your credibility will be destroyed as soon as a reporter finds out you haven't been honest.
- If you don't have the answer, don't try to make something up. If you can't answer specific questions, say so – and promise to get back to the reporter

with the answers before the deadline.
- Never ask a reporter to show you a story before it is published.

Because you are open and honest, things might not always go the way you'd like them to. But your candour puts your relationship on a firm footing and this can be a bonus in a time of crisis or when you request a favour.

Management Memo

Newspapers are the backbone of the media. Every time you do something in business try to get into the habit of asking yourself: Will this make a newspaper story? And if so, how? Instead of reading newspapers for information, look at them with a critical eye and ask yourself what makes them tick. What sort of material do they use most? What length and style are the news items? Treat them as an opportunity to tell their readers about yourself and your company.

Don't be afraid of them. They need you as much as you need them. [198]

5 Go out of your way to assist reporters in their task.

Newspapers usually respond positively to organisations which put themselves out to make the reporter's task easier. So:

- If the reporter can't make it to cover a story, offer to deliver some information to the newspaper.
- Keep reporters informed of upcoming events, projects or products suitable as stories or photographic features.
- A package of background material for reporters about your organisation, the project or the event will always help them present your story fairly and accurately.
- Remember to alert reporters when you have to cancel an event. Time is money in the news-gathering business.

6 Never try to be too smart with the reporter.

If you expect the media to provide a balanced, fair, accurate and interesting coverage of your organisation, make sure that you are always balanced, fair, accurate and interesting in your dealings with them.

Therefore, particularly in a time of crisis, be aware of the following:

- Never say 'no comment'. This tells the reporter that you're probably trying to hide something. The result could be 'bad press'. Say rather: 'I'm sorry, I can't answer that. The matter's under investigation and if I were to answer, I'd jeopardise my position.'
- Silence is never golden. Being unavailable for comment doesn't help much either. If a reporter is on to a story about one of your directors or an incident at the factory, your silence will only breed suspicion.
- Use 'off-the-record' statements judiciously – if at all. Certainly you should never go off-the-record if you do not know the reporter well. Remember also that if the reporter gets the same information on-the-record from another source and uses it, then your agreement has not been violated. And jumping erratically on- and off-the-record causes absolute confusion.

7 Tell reporters when they've done a good job.

A telephone call or a brief note of thanks is appropriate when a reporter has done a good job for your organisation. Occasionally, let the reporter's boss know it as well.

How to write a news release

The news media – newspapers, magazines, radio, television – can play a major role in your public relations programme. News releases are normally used to make initial contact. Often, however, they are poorly written, long-winded, and usually contain little that is newsworthy. If you want to get valuable and accurate media coverage of news about your organisation, then there are important guidelines to be followed...

1 Prepare the release for the appropriate medium.

Unless you package your news release for a particular medium, you may be wasting your time and theirs. For example, a television station will be interested if you highlight aspects of the event which are visual and involve movement and colour. The local newspaper will be more interested if the event features local identities and issues.

2 Make it timely.

Your news release must be sent before the event, not after it. The media want news as it happens, and are rarely interested in past history. Stale news is no news. However, if it is an old event or story, you might just be able to resurrect it as news if you give it a topical new angle.

3 Find an angle for your story.

Whatever the medium, your news must be something which is new, unusual, even sensational, up-to-the-minute, affects many people, and is in the public interest. So it's important to lead with something about your event to catch the attention of the news editor, something that will make interesting reading/viewing/listening. Look for an angle that is innovative, creative, beneficial, funny, or out-of-the-ordinary.

4 Follow the established rules of release writing.

Here are the important points to remember when drafting your release:

- It must be composed in journalistic style, which is quite different from essay writing.
- A short headline should encapsulate the story in a few simple words.
- The opening paragraph must summarise the whole story. Indeed, if no more was printed, this single paragraph would tell the whole story in a nutshell. This paragraph can make all the difference between acceptance and the wastepaper basket. It should include information based on the angle you have chosen: what is to happen, where it will take place, why, how, when and to whom.
- Write the remaining information in descending order of importance (known as the inverted pyramid

style), allowing the journalist to cut details from the bottom up while still retaining the sense of the story.

- Keep it simple, use familiar words and short sentences, and avoid jargon. Each sentence should form one paragraph.
- Include original, simple and strong quotes from an important company spokesperson or community identity.
- Avoid judgements, opinions or superlatives, unless they appear as a quotation.
- Accuracy in all aspects is essential.
- Have a secretary, janitor, or clerk check your draft news release for understanding.

5 Pay attention to how you present the release.

A release must have a professional look which is pleasing to the eye of the editor, to save him/her the trouble of having to make corrections or rewrite it. Adhere to these guidelines:

- Always type your releases, double-spaced, on one side of A4 paper, preferably your organisation's letterhead, boldly marked 'NEWS RELEASE'.
- To make your news releases more professional and more recognisable, always use the same headings, same paragraph indentations, same wide margins.
- Put the date of issue at the top of the page.
- Underline nothing, and do not hyphenate at the end of a line.
- Limit your release to one page if possible and type the word 'ENDS' at the end.

Management Memo

Editors assign more space to news when media releases conform to press standards. These take into consideration style of writing, quality of writing, and the mechanical makeup of the copy. Many editors confess that they use some stories that are not as good in content as some they reject. Why? Simply because those accepted were received in a style that enabled them to be used with a minimum of editing. [199]

- If a second sheet is necessary, write 'more…' at the end of the first page. Do not break a paragraph at the end of a page. Number the pages.
- Provide a contact name (or two) and telephone numbers (work and after hours) at the bottom of the page.

6 Follow it up.

You may write a number of quality news releases and never see any of them in print (or make the television or radio news) – unless you follow up each release with a phone call. Here's how:

1. Introduce yourself.
2. Ask if the release has been received.
3. Ask if it is of interest.
4. Ask if you can provide any points of clarification or elaboration.
5. Ask if any good photographs are required.
6. Invite the reporter to call or visit to follow up the item in detail.
7. Prepare the way for future contacts.

How to handle the media during a company crisis

As a manager, it may be critical for you to maintain a position of high visibility during a crisis situation. Your organisation may look to you as a symbol of strength and continuity at this time. A time of crisis is certainly not the occasion to 'play it by ear' with the media. A traumatic incident is news and the media will be quickly on the scene. Any lack of preparation by you could result in erroneous information, blatant distortion of fact, and publicly embarrassing gaffes. If disaster strikes at your organisation tomorrow, are you ready to handle a frenzied media? Here are some guidelines to prepare you for such a situation...

1 Be aware of the effects of being uncooperative.

Invariably in a company crisis a manager will be under immediate pressure from the media to make a practical response, so you'll need to weigh up the implications if you adopt a stance of being 'unavailable' or 'reluctant' to comment.

Silence breeds suspicion. If you are not prepared to give an interview, or you respond with 'no comment', then you must show that the company is not being deliberately obstructive or 'hiding' something. Offer good reasons for your silence. These might legitimately include insufficient information; legal proceedings, or the potential for such; a head office statement is pending; or a police inquiry is under way.

Remember also that the media have the ability to get the information they need – with or without you. As Diane Thomas says in *Crisis Communication*, 'almost without exception, your organisation will be more favourably presented *with* your input'.

2 Ensure that relevant parties are advised first.

Make no comments to the press until relevant authorities, company executives, legal representatives and next-of-kin affected by the incident have been notified.

3 Determine who takes responsibility as spokesperson.

You or a senior company executive usually assumes responsibility as sole spokesperson, immediately available to reporters who arrive on the scene or who telephone. This ensures consistency of comment throughout the crisis.

The spokesperson should take time to reflect on the facts of the incident and have them clear before interview. Two sets of information will need to be gathered: the actual information about what happened, how, when, where, to whom, why and the consequences; and collateral information that puts the incident into perspective, e.g. if an employee dies in a chemical spill, such details as the company's emergency action plan, safety record, staff competency and training, and investigation procedures.

4 Be judicious in your comments.

A tragic event is usually followed by a company, departmental, police or coronial inquiry. Media comments on public record may have a bearing on future proceedings, so any comments should be made judiciously and, if possible, free of emotional reactions.

Consider these points:

- Some companies require that head office approval be sought prior to granting media interviews. If necessary, make such contact promptly to avoid delaying your media response.
- Restrict answers to those facts which you know clearly to be true. Do not allow the media to elicit details of which you are unsure.
- A momentary lapse in concentration could give the media the opportunity to question in the area of negligence or blame. Avoid commenting in this area at all times, as there could be significant legal implications.
- When a matter is under police investigation, do not respond to any questions that fall rightly within the police department's purview. Discuss such parameters with police beforehand.
- Record the details of interviews as soon as they have been completed for possible future reference.

5 Protect employees against media intrusion.

Under stressful situations associated with a traumatic incident, it is appropriate for a manager to protect staff members from unwarranted

Management Memo

Whenever a major crisis strikes, you can be sure that representatives from the media will be some of the first to arrive on the scene. It's their job to report details of the incident as quickly as possible and the pressure is on to be first to report the story. Under such circumstances the correct handling of the media is essential. [200]

intrusive interviews by the media. At times this can be difficult. Be aware of these two points:

(a) Even if the media are denied access to staff on company premises, contact can still be made as they are entering or leaving the workplace.

(b) It is wise, therefore, to counsel staff on their rights and responsibilities. They have the right to speak to the media if they so wish, but they have a responsibility to speak truthfully and not spread rumours or speculate about matters where they may not know the facts.

6 Promote post-event services available.

As guidance and counselling staff could be needed to reduce stress after traumatic events, there is a need to promote these services to staff and community. It is highly likely that the community will be interested in knowing about the support available to employees and families. Consider involving a spokesperson for such services in any media interview.

7 Foster cordial relations with the media.

Cooperation from the company evokes a similar response from the media – so cultivate cordial relations with the media in good times to help ensure fair, balanced treatment in times of crisis.

How to get your message across through the printed word

As a manager you frequently need to communicate with your staff, clients, customers or general public through newsletters, brochures, leaflets and other published materials. Unfortunately, however, although you may have printed and distributed a newsletter, this doesn't always mean that you've actually succeeded in communicating with your audience. If you want to develop the ability to communicate effectively through the printed word, then consider these essential guidelines...

1 Know your audience.

Newsletters, brochures and similar material are effective and economical communicative vehicles – but only if they appeal to the people who are supposed to read them. If you are writing for a learned profession, then your style will be different than that required for a working class community. In a nutshell, write from the vantage point of the reader, rather than from that of the manager.

2 Determine what they want to know and give it to them.

Your readers usually want information about your organisation, its operation, programmes, activities, products, services and decisions that affect them. Often they need to be persuaded as well as informed.

3 Avoid jargon.

In some organisations, when you spend most of your day talking to colleagues, it's easy to forget that most of your shop talk can be basically incomprehensible to an outsider. Don't let jargon sneak into your writing – ever. Convert your specialised language into everyday language for the wider audience.

4 Keep it short, simple and lively.

Few people want to know as much about the subject as you think they should, so hit the highlights and go on to something else. Keep your writing punchy and use a journalistic style. And remember the three important rules of readability: simplicity, specificity and brevity.

5 Make your points quickly and clearly.

To capture the majority of readers, make your points quickly and clearly. Most of them are not waiting to devour every word. You must compete for their time. Remember the 30-3-30 rule... Many people skim – after 30 seconds, you've lost them; most will spend 3 minutes at best on your newsletter or brochure; your friends or the converted will probably be the only ones to spend up to 30 minutes on it. Keep the first two groups in mind when you write.

6 Make writing reflect your natural speech.

Newsletter writing must be as simple, direct and personal as speaking. Successful newsletters make readers feel they are hearing, not reading, information prepared just for them. Fancy or formal prose usually ends up in the wastepaper basket.

7 Write about people doing things.

Whenever you can, focus on people. Theorising, philosophising or detailing mundane matters makes dull reading for most people.

8 Work hard on your writing.

Few of us are blessed with this skill as a natural gift. It must be learned and requires constant practice. Most good writers write, rewrite and then rewrite again.

9 Ensure the layout emphasises the message.

Don't attempt to turn your newsletter or leaflet into a grotesque computer-generated masterpiece of decorative design. Concentrate on the words and clean visual simplicity.

10 Resist trying to cram in too much.

If your publication is formidable in both length and appearance, your readers will put it aside rather than tackle it. For this reason, a limited number of concise, well-written items, along with white space to make the page look less intimidating, will communicate a lot better.

Management Memo

Whenever I think of effective publications, I think immediately of the APES, those four essential components of any printed item: **A** – Appearance, **P** – Production Process, **E** – Editorial, **S** – Subject Matter.

For an effective publication, none of these components must be neglected. All four work together; they are interrelated; one is no more important than the others.

Let me clarify. You may produce an expensive, glossy, four-colour brochure – and score well in terms of Appearance. However, if the Subject Matter is boring or the content is riddled with typographical errors and grammatical mistakes due to poor Editorial supervision, then all the effectiveness is lost and, additionally, the organisation's image is damaged. Clearly, all these components are important. [201]

11 And remember: appearance counts.

Pay attention also to your publication's appearance:

- Limit your line of copy to no more than two alphabets wide.
- Try to use a very short line at the end of each paragraph to make more white space.
- Don't crowd your text. Use ample margins around your copy.
- Avoid large areas of italic type.
- Avoid putting headlines in capitals.
- Avoid putting screens over italic or thin type.
- Make sure each page of your publication has a visual focus.
- Don't use large areas of reverse type on large black backgrounds.
- Don't print over illustrations.
- Use action photographs in preference to portraits.
- Use copy-breaking devices (photos, headings, quotations, art, advertisements, and so on) when you have large blocks of type.

How to write a job advertisement that attracts the right applicants

If you decide to recruit your own staff, preparing an advertisement for display in the local and/or national press is an important consideration. Three groups will be attracted to your ad: recruitment agencies who will be interested in referring their clients, competitors who will be interested in your activities, and prospective employees who will be interested in what it is you have to offer. Your ad will certainly be spotted, so it's important to get it right – and here's how...

1 Identify specifically what you want.

If you don't know what (or whom) it is you're looking for, how will you know when you've found it? For this reason you'll need to spend as much time as it takes to construct the correct profile before proceeding with the ad. There are some simple, easy-to-use recruitment tools on the market that can help you construct that profile.

2 Grab the readers' attention.

When you're confident that you know the type of person you're seeking, find the up-front word or phrase that will attract that person. If it's simply an accountant, then say 'Accountant'. If you're looking for a person to fill a position that requires zest, initiative and independence, your header may read, 'Put Yourself In The Driver's Seat'. Or for a design studio, 'Are you creative enough for us?' The header should match closely the 'cultural mores' of the position being advertised.

3 Explain the job.

You can eliminate lots of hassles later on by letting the reader know what the job entails. If they are expected to walk on water, be up front about it. Interviews are not the place to introduce surprise information about jobs. If you're expectations are realistic, the right person will be out there waiting to reply to your ad.

4 Distinguish the job from others.

What is it about your job that helps to differentiate it from similar ones on offer? Why should the reader choose you and your organisation? Tell them. Often, it will be the little things that make the difference. That difference may be the human side of your business, the flexible hours, pleasant working conditions, great customers, good salary, overseas travel, and so on. Brainstorm for the attributes that make your organisation attractive. Current employees should be able to help you identify those qualities.

5 Explain your organisation's vision.

Attracting the right applicant can be as simple as saying something clear and honest about who you are, what you believe, and where you're heading – say, in the next five to ten years. You can't afford to have employees in your organisation who cannot share that vision. In addition, consider all of those other interested readers by using this opportunity to do a little public relations, by advertising your organisation's vision.

6 Tell them their next step.

Be specific about what you want applicants to do. If you want to screen applicants, you may request that they telephone you at a specific time to find out where to send their résumés. This will give you a chance to conduct a screening interview and to test their punctuality and voice presentation. If you want résumés only, make that clear in your ad, too. You should make a point of sticking to your request.

7 Disseminate copies of your ad.

Let others in your organisation who are likely to be affected by the ad know of its contents. The receptionist or any other person taking the initial calls will need to know so that they can be prepared for the resultant enquiries. Current employees who may be interested in applying for the position should also be afforded the courtesy of knowing about the position before it is made public.

> **Management Memo**
>
> It takes courage to identify and stay with a clearly defined target segment when advertising, but it pays off in the end. [202]

8 Make sure the ad is well-presented.

A well-presented, attractive advertisement reflects well on your organisation. A poorly presented ad can have the opposite effect.

9 Choose the right time and place.

Ensure your ad is placed in the most appropriate newspaper or trade journal, on the most appropriate day, in the most appropriate section, at the most appropriate time of year. After all, you want to ensure that it receives maximum readership by the right audience, don't you?

10 Track your ads.

Count the number of responses that your ad generates. Ideally, that number should reveal a high level of competition for the position, a situation which will allow you to settle on a shortlist of suitable applicants. If your ad does not encourage the desired response, review its contents before attempting a re-run.

References

1. Jeffrey Davidson, *Blow Your Own Horn*, Amacom, NY, 1987, p.29. **2.** W.N.Yoemans, *Seven Survival Skills for a Reorganised World*, Dutton Signet, 1996. **3.** Burdette Bostwick, *Résumé Writing*, John Wiley, NY, 1990. **4.** Cynthia Berryman-Fink, *The Manager's Desk Reference*, Amacom, NY, 1989. **5.** Beverly Davis & Genevieve Brown, 'Your Interview Image', *The Executive Educator*. **6.** Arthur Young (UK), *The Manager's Handbook*, Crown, New York, 1986. **7.** G. Morgan & A. Banks, *Going Up: How to get, keep and advance your career*, Collins Australia, Melbourne, 1988, p.182. **8.** Cheryl Reimold, *Being a Boss*, Dell, NY, 1984, p.120. **9.** Derek Rowntree, *The Manager's Book of Checklists*, Gower, Aldershot, 1989, p.129. **10.** Paul Stevens, *Career Management: Whose Responsibility?* **11.** Brian Tracy, *Maximum Achievement*, Fireside, 1995. **12.** Jimmy Calano & Jeff Salzman, *CareerTracking*, Gower, Aldershot, 1988, p.244. **13.** Edwin Feldman, *How to Use Your Time to Get Things Done*, Frederick Fell, NY, 1968, p.266. **14.** Mitchell Posner, *Executive Essentials*, Avon Books, NY, 1987, p.23. **15.** Stephanie Winston, *The Organised Executive*, Warner Books, NY, 1985, p.36. **16.** Helen Reynolds & Mary Tramel, *Executive Time Management*, Prentice Hall, NY, 1989, p.107. **17.** Calano & Salzman, *CareerTracking*, p.44. **18.** Roger Black, *Getting Things Done*, Michael Joseph, London, 1987, p.10. **19.** Peter Drucker, *The Effective Executive*, Butterworth, London, 1993. **20.** Jack Parker, *The Collier Quick and Easy Guide for Running a Meeting*, Collier Books, NY, 1963. **21.** Jack Gratus, *Give and Take*, BBC Books, London, 1990, p.20. **22.** John Lindelow & James Heynderickx, 'Leading Meetings', *School Leadership*, eds. Stuart Smith & P. Piele, ERIC, University of Oregon, Eugene, 1989, p.304. **23.** Clyde Burleson, *Effective Meetimgs: The Complete Guide*, John Wiley & Sons, NY, 1990, pp.95, 104. **24.** Michael Armstrong, *How to Be an Even Better Manager*, Kogan Page, London, 1988, p.270. **25.** Lou Hampton, quoted in Jeffrey Davidson, *Blow Your Own Horn*, p.156. **26.** Jim Sellars, 'If your yarn elicits yawns…', *American School Board Journal*, April 1987, p.40. **27.** Cynthia Berryman-Fink, *The Manager's Desk Reference*, p.242. **28.** David Peoples, *Presentations Plus*, Wiley, NY, 1988, p.147. **29.** *American Speaker: Your Guide to Successful Speaking*, Georgetown Publishing House, Washington, p.INT/3. **30.** *The Speaker's Sourcebook*, Zondervan, Grand rapids, 1960, p.229. **31.** Jarvis Finger, *Managing Your School: 3*, Fernfawn, Brisbane, p.132. **32.** Calano & Salzman, *CareerTracking*, p.140. **33.** Ted Pollock, *Managing Creatively: 1*, Cahners, Boston, 1971, p. 141. **34.** Mark McCormack, *Success Secrets*, Guild Publishing, London, 1989, p.179. **35.** Norman Cahners in IBM's *Think* magazine. **36.** Joseph Straub, 'Good first impressions on the telephone: There's never a second chance', *Supervisory Management*, March 1991, p.1. **37.** Reimold, *Being a Boss*, p.116. **38.** William Parkhurst, *The Eloquent Executive*, Times Books, NY, 1998, p.118. **39.** James Black, *How to Get Results from Interviewing*. **40.** Candy Tymson & Bill Sherman, *The Australian Public Relations Manual*, Millennium Books, Sydney, 1990, p.121. **41.** Denis Waitley, *The Psychology of Winning*, Brolga, Ringwood, 1994, p.101. **42.** Denis Waitley, *The Psychology of Winning*, p.62. **43.** Helen Keller. **44.** Arnold Brown, quoted in *Fortune*, 14 April 1997, p.95. **45.** John Mulligan, *The Personal Management Handbook*, Sphere Books, London, 1988, p.121. **46.** John Milne, *Management Minutes*, Vol. 4 No. 2, 1992. **47.** Calano & Salzman, *Career Tracking*, p.21. **48.** Posner, *Executive Essentials*, p.255. **49.** George Fuller, *Supervisor's Portable Answer Book*. **50.** Fred Orr, *How to Succeed at Work*, Unwin, Sydney, 1987, p.30. **51.** Jack Collis & Michael LeBoeuf, *Work Smarter Not Harder*, Goal Setting Seminars, Sydney, n.d., p.107. **52.** Greg Vance, *The Australian Manager's Guide to Success*, Hale & Iremonger, Sydney, 1994, p.125. **53.** Peter Drucker, *Innovation and Entrepreneurship*, Heinemann, 1985, p.23. **54.** Hester Cholmon - delay, *Judas*. **55.** Dwight D. Eisenhower, *Great Quotes from Great Leaders*, Peggy Anderson, ed., Great Quotations, Lombard, 1989. **56.** Armstrong, *How to be an Even Better Manager*, p.263. **57.** Sandra Wishner, 'Power: Wield it well, and watch it multiply', *The Executive Educator*, June 1985. **58.** Joseph Braysich, *The Complete Executive*, Joseph Braysich Australia, Sydney, 1986, p.1. **59.** Ted Pollock, *Managing Creatively: 1*, p.168. **60.** Brian Caldwell & Jim Spinks, *The Self-Managing School*, Falmer, London, 1998, p.185. **61.** Mary & Eric Allison, *Managing Up, Managing Down*, Simon & Schuster, NY, 1984, p.189. **62.** Peter Hanson, *Stress for Success*, Pan, London, 1989, p.19. **63.** M. Brown, 'Survival of the fittest', *Management Today*, July 1996, p.77. **64.** Laurence Morehouse & Leonard Gross, *Maximum Performance*, Granada, Suffolk, 1980. **65.** source unknown. **66.** James Kouzes & Barry Posner, *The Leadership Challenge*, Jossey Bass, San Francisco, 1995. **67.** Calano & Salzman, *CareerTracking*, p.228. **68.** P. Dixon & S.Tierstein, *Be Your Own Headhunter On-line*, Random House, Canada. **69.** R. Koonce, 'Ensuring your employability', *Training and Development*, July 1996, p.14. **70.** William Cohen, *How to Make it*

Big as a Consultant, Amacom, NY, 1985, p.2. **71.** Robert Ramsey, 'New year's resolutions for supervisors', *Supervision*, January 1996, p.8. **72.** Stephen Covey, 'How to hire people', *Executive Excellence*, December 1996, p.3. **73.** G.F.O'Shea, 'Induction and orientation', *HR & Development Handbook*, W.Treacy, ed., Amacom, NY, 1994, p.986. **74.** Ecclesiastes. **75.** Thomas Quick, *The Manager's Motivation Desk Book*, John Wiley, NY, 1985, p.310. **76.** *Person to Person Managing*. **77.** Andrew Szilagyi, *Management and Performance*, Goodyear, Santa Monica, Cal., 1981, p.41. **78.** R. Alex Mackenzie, *The Time Trap*, McGraw Hill, NY, 1972, p.154. **79.** Marion Haynes, *Stepping Up to Supervisor*, Executive Round Table Publications, Houston, 1987, p.92. **80.** John Bartunek, 'What to do when your employees plateau', *Supervisory Management*, July 1984, p.26. **81.** Glenn Van Ekeren, *The Speaker's Sourcebook*, Prentice Hall, Englewood Cliffs, NJ, 1988, p.48. **82.** Andrew Szilagyi, *Management and Performance*, p.561. **83.** Thomas Quick, *The Manager's Motivation Desk Book*, p.427. **84.** Stephen Covey, *The 7 Habits of Highly Effective People*, Australian Business Library, Melbourne, 1990. **85.** Jack Collis & Michael LeBoeuf, *Work Smarter Not Harder*, p.139. **86.** R.Kemp & M.Nathan, *Middle Management in Schools*, Blackwell Education, Oxford, 1989, p.165. **87.** Mary & Eric Allison, *Managing Up, Managing Down*, p.165. **88.** H.Taylor, *The Administrator's Guide to Personal Productivity*, Princeton Junction, NJ, 1993. **89.** Cheryl Reimold, *Being a Boss*, p.67. **90.** Michael Armstrong, *How to be an Even Better Manager*, p.118. **91.** Willard Parker et al, *Front-line Leadership*, McGraw Hill, NY, 1969, p.240. **92.** Ted Pollock, *Managing Creatively: 1*, p.38. **93.** Robyn Johnson in Mandy Tunica, ed., *Leading the Way*, Macmillan, Melbourne, 1995, p.151 **94.** Anne Evans, *Managing People*, Australian Business Library, Melbourne, 1990, p.118. **95.** Thomas Quick, *The Manager's Motivation Desk Book*, p.25. **96.** Robert Luke, 'Meaningful praise makes a difference', *Supervisory Management*, February 1991, p.3. **97.** M.J.Woodruff, 'Why companies should say thanks', *Supervision*, June 1992, p.9. **98.** Kenichi Ohmae, Head of McKinsey Tokyo. **99.** Greg Vance: *The Australian Manager's Guide to Success*, p.70. **100.** R.Kemp & M.Nathan, *Middle Management in Schools*, p.138. **101.**Norman Vincent Peale, *The Power of Positive Thinking*, The World's Work, Kingswood, Surrey, 1953, p.249. **102.** Tom Hopkins, *The Official Guide to Success*, Warner Books, NY, 1982, p.17. **103.** J.Allan, 'The power of persuasion', *Management Accounting*, December 1996, p.26. **104.** Anne Evans, *Managing People*, p.67. **105.** William Nothstini, *Influencing Others*, Crisp, California, 1989, p.3. **106.** Peter Hanson, *Stress for Success*, p.89. **107.** Gifford Pinchot III, *Intrapreneuring*, Harper & Row, NY, 1985, p.xiii. **108.** Marshall Loeb, 'Ten commandments for managing creative people', *Fortune*, 16 January, 1995, p.92. **109.** Anne Evans, *Managing People*, p.67. **110.** Robyn Johnston in *Leading the Way*, Mandy Tunica, ed., p.147. **111.** Cynthia Berryman-Fink, *The Manager's Desk Reference*, p.112. **112.** William Parkhurst, *The Eloquent Executive*, p.100. **113.** *Person to Person Managing*. **114.** Janet Carter, 'How to cope with angry employees or colleagues', *Supervisory Management*, April 1991, p.6. **115.** Robert Bramson, 'Blaming isn't changing', in Calano & Salzman, *CareerTracking*. **116.** Cynthia Berryman-Fink, *The Manager's Desk Reference*, p.48. **117.** Jack Gratus, *Give and Take*, BBC Books, London, 1990, p.112. **118.** William Pfeiffer and John Jones, *The 1980 Annual Handbook for Group Facilitators*, University Associates Inc, San Diego, Cal. 1980. **119.** Derek Rowntree, *The Manager's Book of Checklists*, p.116. **120.** V. Clayton Sherman, 'Eight steps to preventing problem employees', *Personnel*, May 1988, p.48. **121.** Sally Johnston, 'Dealing with grieving employees', *Management Solutions*, July 1987, p.26. **122.** James Van Fleet, *The 22 Big Mistakes Managers Make and How to Correct Them*, Parker, NY, 1973, p.190. **123.** source unknown. **124.** Peter Thomas, 'Calling in the consultants', *Certified Accountant*, January 1993. **125.** Beth Fowler, 'Working with consultants', *Supervision*, August 1996, p.15. **126.** Jeffrey Mayer, *If You Haven't Got the Time to Do It Right, When Will You Have the Time to Do It Over?*, Simon & Schuster, NY, 1990, p.107. **127.** B. E. Holm, *How to Manage Your Information*, Reinhold, NY, 1968, p.151. **128.** Patricia King, *Never Work for a Jerk!*, Dell, NY 1987, pp.19, 26. **129.** Mary and Eric Allison, *Managing Up, Managing Down*, p.17. **130.** Patricia King, *Never Work for a Jerk!*, p.19. **131.** Willard Parker et al, *Front-line Leadership*, McGraw-Hill, NY, 1969, p.318. **132.** Russell Bintliff, *Crimeproofing Your Business*, McGraw-Hill, NY, 1994, p.112. **133.** Louis Imundo, *The Effective Supervisor's Handbook*, Amacom, NY, 1980, p.148. **134.** George Odiorne, *How Managers Make Things Happen*, Prentice Hall, Englewood Cliffs, NJ, 1987, p.279. **135.** Paul Stevens, *Staff Problems Solved*, William Brooks, Sydney, 1984, p.123. **136.** Joe Catansariti & Mark Maragwanath, *The Workplace Relations Act: A User Friendly Guide*, Newsletter Information Services, Sydney, 1997, p.71. **137.** T.S.Eliot, *Four Quarters*. **138.** Romuald Stone, 'Mission statements revisited', *SAM Advanced Management Journal*, Winter 1996, p.37. **139.** Gary Hamel, 'Strategy as revolution', *Harvard Business Review*, July-August 1996, p.82. **140.** Michael Porter, 'What is strategy', *Harvard Business Review*, November-December 1996, p.62. **141.** W. Sahlman, 'How to write a great business plan', *Harvard Business Review*, July–August 1997, pp. 98–99. **142.** Andrew Szilagyi, *Management and Performance*, Goodyear, Santa Monica, 1981, p.132. **143.** Szilagyi, *Management and Performance*, p.161. **144.** Les Bell, *Managing Teams in Secondary Schools*, Routledge, London, 1992, p.151. **145.** Peter Ryan, 'Cleaning up a dirty word – policy', *The Practising Administrator*, Vol. 16 No. 2 1994, p.30. **146.** source unknown. **147.** Harold Kerzner, *Project Management*, 5th edn, Van Nostrand Reinhold, NY, 1995, p.18. **148.** George Odiorne, *How Managers Make Things Happen*, p.134. **149.** Quoted in *Why Teams Don't Work*, Harvey Robbins & Michael Finley, Petersons Books, 1995. **150.** Hedley Beare, Brian Caldwell & Ross Millikan, *Creating an Excellent School*, Routledge, London, 1989, p. 174. **151.** 'What is Facility Management?', The Facility Management Association of Australia 1997. **152.** Michael Porter, 'What is strategy?', *Harvard Business Review*, November–December 1996, p.61. **153.** Lucy Gaster, *Quality in Public Services: Managers' Choices*, Open University Press, Buckingham, 1995, p.74. **154.** W.H.Weiss, 'Benchmarking', *Supervision*, March 1996, p.14. **155.** Michael Hammer & James Champy, *Reengineering the Corporation*, Allen and Unwin, Sydney, 1983, p.2. **156.** 'Tubemakers SPD', *Australian Best Practice Demonstration Program*, 1995, p.11. **157.** Richard Hamlin, 'A practical guide to empowering your employees', *Supervisory Management*. **158.** Peter Senge, *The Fifth Discipline: The Art and Practice of the Learning Organisation*, Random House, Sydney, 1990. **159.** R.Doybe, 'The new bargaining order,' *The QANTAS Club*, December–January 1994–95, p.17. **160.** Employment Equity Branch, Public Sector Management Commission, Queensland, July 1991, p.17. **161.** Cynthia Berryman-Fink, *The Manager's Desk Reference*, p.286. **162.** *Cross-Cultural Communication*, National Centre for Vocational Educational Research, AGPS, Canberra, 1992, p.xxxiv. **163.** M.Burdeu & A. McLean, 'Integrated management systems', *Management*, 1994, p.17. **164.** Judith Howlings, 'Sober solutions to help tackle substance abuse', *People Management*, 5 December 1996, pp.43–44. **165.** John Ruskin, quoted in *The Speaker's Sourcebook*, Glenn Van Ekeren, Prentice Hall, Englewood Cliffs, 1987, p.375. **166.** Ted Pollock, *Managing Creatively: 2*, Cahners, Boston, 1971, p.99. **167.** J.T. Straub, 'Productive gripe sessions', *Getting Results for the Hands-on Manager*,' Vol. 41 No. 96, p.8. **168.** Mark McCormack, *Success Secrets*, p.119. **169.** Michael Armstrong, *How to be an Even Better Manager*, p.129. **170.** Larry Davis & Earl McCallon, *Planning, Conducting and Evaluating Workshops*, Learning Concepts, Austin, Texas, 1974, p.223. **171.** Derek Rowntree, *The Manager's Book of Checklists*, p.217. **172.** Tom Payne, *From the Inside Out: How to Create and Survive in a Culture of Change*. **173.** James Sydow & Clark Kirkpatrick, *The School Administrator*. **174.** Linda Moran et al, *Keeping Teams on Track*, Irwin, 1996. **175.** Theo Haimann & Ray Hilgert, *Supervision*. **176.** John Ramée, 'Managing in a crisis', *Management Solutions*, 1987, p.25 **177.** Stephanie Winston, *The Organised Executive*, pp.56,169. **178.** Bess May, 'How to cut your company's costs', *Supervision*, October 1994, p.14. **179.** Milo Frank, *How to Run a Successful Meeting in Half the Time*, Simon & Schuster, NY, 1989, p.31. **180.** Clyde Burleson, *Effective Meetings: The Complete Guide*. **181.** George Odiorne, *How Managers Make Things Happen*, p.194. **182.** Theo Haimann & Ray Hilgert, *Supervision: Concepts and Practices of Management*. **183.** Quoted by James Van Fleet in *The 22 Biggest Mistakes Managers Make*, Parker, NY, 1982, p.7. **184.** Robert Ramsey, '101 ways to crime-proof your workplace', *Supervision*, May 1996, p.10. **185.** Glen Walker, *Positive School Management*, Educational Consulting & Financial Services, Maleny, 1993, p.49 **186.** Neil Flanagan, *Creative Debt Collecting*, Plum Press, Brisbane, p.8. **187.** Anthony Cordato, *How to Collect Business Debts*, Australian Business Library, Melbourne, 1990. **188.** Theodore Levitt, *The Marketing Imagination*, The Free Press, NY, 1983. **189.** Neal Chalofsky, 'External evaluation', *HR Management and Development Handbook*, W.Treacy, ed., Amacom, NY, 1994, p.1341. **190.** Sun Tsu, *The Art of War*. **191.** A.S. Slywotsky, *Value Migration: How to Think Several Moves Ahead of the Competition*, Harvard Business School Press, Boston, 1996. **192.** Greg Vance, *The Australian Manager's Guide to Success*, p.107. **193.** Tom Peters and N. Austin, *A Passion for Excellence*, Fontana, Glasgow, 1985. **194.** J. Smith, *The Advertising Kit: A Complete Guide for Small Businesses*, Lexington Books, 1994. **195.** Linda Vining, *School Image by Design*, Spirit of Adventure, Randwick, 1994, p.4 **196.** D. Lanyon, 'Draw in more sales with a designer', *Australian Small Business Review*, July 1990, p.33. **197.** Tymson & Sherman, *The Australian Public Relations Manual*, p.210. **198.** Michael Bland, *Be Your Own PR Man*, Kogan Page, London, 1983, p.76. **199.** Leslie Kindred, *The School and Community Relations*, Prentice Hall, Englewood Cliffs, 1976, p.234. **200.** Tymson & Sherman, *The Australian Public Relations Manual*, p.218. **201.** Jarvis Finger, 'The school's image on paper', *The Practising Administrator*, Vol. 9 No. 3 1987, p.16. **202.** J.Smith, *The Advertising Kit*, p.26.

Index